Also by Alec MacGillis

The Cynic: The Political Education of Mitch McConnell

Fulfillment

Fulfillment

Winning and Losing
in One-Click America

Alec MacGillis

FARRAR, STRAUS AND GIROUX | NEW YORK

Farrar, Straus and Giroux
120 Broadway, New York 10271

Printed in the United States of America
First edition, 2021

Portions of chapters 3 and 7 were originally published,
in slightly different form, in *The New Yorker*.

Grateful acknowledgment is made to Rockathon Records
for permission to reprint the lyrics to "Dayton, Ohio—19
Something and 5," by Guided by Voices, and to Draze for
permission to reprint the lyrics to "The Hood Ain't the Same."

Library of Congress Cataloging-in-Publication Data
Names: MacGillis, Alec, author.
Title: Fulfillment : winning and losing in one-click
    America / Alec MacGillis.
Description: First edition. | New York : Farrar, Straus and
    Giroux, 2021. | Includes bibliographical references and index.
Identifiers: LCCN 2020046596 | ISBN 9780374159276 (hardcover)
Subjects: LCSH: Amazon (Firm) | United States—Economic
    conditions—1945– | United States—Economic conditions—
    Regional disparities. | Equality—Economic aspects—United
    States.
Classification: LCC HC106.84 .M334 2021 | DDC
    381/.14206573—dc23
LC record available at https://lccn.loc.gov/2020046596

Designed by Gretchen Achilles

Our books may be purchased in bulk for promotional,
educational, or business use. Please contact your local bookseller
or the Macmillan Corporate and Premium Sales Department
at 1-800-221-7945, extension 5442, or by e-mail at
MacmillanSpecialMarkets@macmillan.com.

www.fsgbooks.com
www.twitter.com/fsgbooks · www.facebook.com/fsgbooks

10 9 8 7 6 5 4 3 2 1

In memory of Donald MacGillis,
my first editor

I remain near the entrance, handling goods as they
are shoved in, listening and nodding. I have been slowly
dissolving into this cavity.

—*from* Nog, *by Rudolph Wurlitzer*

Contents

Fulfillment

The Basement

Hector Torrez was living in the basement because his wife told him to. He had done nothing wrong, committed no matrimonial transgression. He simply worked at the wrong place.

The irony of it was, he had taken the job at his wife's urging. He had spent eleven years unemployed, ever since losing his $170,000-per-year tech-industry job during the Great Recession. He had fallen into despondency and depression, the trough of the fifty-something person cast aside in an industry that privileged youth. The family had gotten by on the income of his wife, Laura, who sold training sessions for medical diagnostic equipment, but they eventually had to downsize to a smaller house in the Denver suburb where they had moved after fleeing their $5,500 monthly mortgage in the Bay Area in 2006.

Eventually, Laura had issued an ultimatum—if Hector didn't get a job, he couldn't stay. So he had left, moving back with his family, Central American immigrants who had settled in California decades earlier. He lived with his older sister's family in an exurb of San Francisco. If he left the house, he had to be home by eight-thirty every night so as not to disturb his brother-in-law, who woke at four-thirty every morning for his long drive to Silicon

Valley, making him one of the more than 120,000 Bay Area workers who commuted more than three hours every day.

After five months of this, Hector had accepted Laura's offer to return, on the condition that he get a job, which he finally did half a year later, in June 2019. He was driving by the warehouse one day and saw a sign that they were hiring and pulled over and asked about it, and they said he could start the next day.

He worked overnights, four nights a week, typically from 7:15 p.m. to 7:15 a.m. He worked all over the warehouse—stacking boxes in outbound trailers, loading packages onto pallets, and inducting envelopes and packages, which meant standing at the conveyor belts for the entire shift (there were no chairs on the warehouse floor) and transferring hundreds of items per hour from one carousel to another, while turning them right side up so that scanners could read their codes.

He lifted a lot of boxes, some as heavy as fifty pounds—the challenge wasn't so much the weight as that you couldn't really tell, based on size, whether a box was going to be heavy or not when you went to pick it up. Your body and your mind never knew what to expect. He wore a back brace for a while, but it would get so hot that he felt like he was being cooked. His elbow tendinitis flared up. He often walked more than a dozen miles per shift, according to his Fitbit—he thought the device must be wrong and got a new pedometer, but it said the same thing. He put on a topical numbing cream before he went to work, took ibuprofen pills while he was at work, and, when he got home, stood on ice packs, put ice on his elbow, and soaked his feet in Epsom salts. He switched shoes often to spread the impact across the sole. He made $15.60 per hour, a fifth of what he was making at the tech job, and infinitely more than what he was making unemployed.

The warehouse in Thornton, sixteen miles north of Denver, had opened just a year earlier, in 2018. Its general manager, Clint Autry, was a seven-year veteran of the company who had already helped open several other facilities around the country; he had even helped test the radio-wave-emitting vests that workers wore when they had to step near the path of the "drive unit" robots that carried around big tubs of merchandise, to warn off their fully automated coworkers. "The whole name of the game is getting the product to the customer in the quickest, most cost-effective way based on shipping costs," Autry declared on a grand-opening tour of the building.

The ramp-up at the warehouse started in mid-March of 2020, same as everywhere else around the country, as the coronavirus lockdowns took hold. Orders soared to holiday levels as millions of Americans decided that the only safe way to shop was from their home. It was just nine months into Hector's time at the company, yet he was the only one who remained from his orientation class of twenty—the others either hadn't been able to handle the pace, or had gotten injured, or had been terminated because they had run out of excused absences after getting injured. Now turnover had climbed even higher than usual as many decided they couldn't handle the stress of the surge and the risk of the close quarters in the warehouse. As the number of workers dwindled, the pressure on those that remained rose. The company demanded that Hector work overtime—five twelve-hour night shifts per week. With longer shifts and one less day of rest, the tendinitis got worse.

He found out about his coworker, with whom he worked closely every day, not from the company but from other workers. The coworker, a man in his forties, had stopped coming in, and Hector had assumed he had simply drifted away like so many others. But then came word that he had the virus and that he'd been very sick. Hector relayed this to Laura, and she got worried about the family, especially her elderly mother, who lived with them and suffered from chronic obstructive pulmonary disease. So Laura sent him to the basement. It was unfinished, but they set up a bed and got a little refrigerator and a microwave and a coffee maker. He snuck upstairs to use the bathroom.

What bothered Laura was that they were figuring it out all on their own. Hector had gotten no notice about the coworker. He had gotten no information about how to respond to the risk of contagion. There was no 1-800 number to call. When she had gone online looking for any tips the company offered about how to deal with situations like this, all she found was the company's page touting everything it was doing as a corporation to deal with the crisis. "They may be doing quite a bit," she said, but the company "is also profiting every step along the way on the backs of their employees, who are *not* being protected, and neither are their families being protected."

She couldn't help but feel some regret for having goaded Hector there in the first place. "They call themselves a technology company, but it's really a sweatshop," she said. "They have such a hold on our economy and our country."

Like all great crises, the global pandemic of 2020 revealed the weaknesses of nations it attacked. In the case of the United States, that weakness was the extraordinary inequality across different places and communities. When it reached the country, the coronavirus first struck its upper echelons, the highly prosperous precincts that had tighter connections with their global peers than with scruffier places in their own backyard: Seattle, Boston, San Francisco, Manhattan. But within weeks it had leached into less privileged redoubts, as if guided by an unerring homing instinct for the most vulnerable, among whom it would do the most damage: up in the Bronx, where confirmed cases were twice as likely to be fatal as elsewhere in the city; in central Queens, where it ravaged small houses packed with large families of Bangladeshi and Colombian cab drivers and restaurant workers, and where a hospital demanded that a boy come up with the money for his mother's cremation while his father lay in intensive care, unlikely to survive; in Detroit, where far more people would die than in Seattle, San Francisco, and Austin combined; and in the small city of Albany, Georgia, where a single funeral seeded a contagion that led to more than sixty deaths within a few weeks in a county of only 90,000 people. "It hit like a bomb," the county coroner said. "Every day after [the funeral], someone was dying."

No one should have been surprised by the disparity of the impact, because the divides had been there for anyone to see, getting more noticeable by the year, wherever your travels took you. Maybe you were driving into metropolitan Washington, D.C., from the mountains in West Virginia or western Virginia or western Maryland. One minute you were in small, underpopulated towns blasted by the opioid scourge and bereft of any retail except the omnipresent chain dollar store. Barely an hour later you were heading into the capital's great exurban maw on a ten-lane interstate, creeping past glass and concrete cubes with inscrutable corporate acronyms, in some of the very wealthiest counties in the country.

Or maybe you were taking the train out of Washington, getting off less than an hour later in Baltimore and experiencing a drop in atmospheric pressure extreme enough to cause dizziness. From a city teeming with money and young strivers to one that was full of emptiness. You emerged from the handsome Beaux Arts train station into a plaza that was too quiet, a major downtown thoroughfare that was too quiet. At a gas station two blocks away, two people—white woman, Black man—were sitting on the ground, in plain view outside the teller door, snorting something off the back of their fists.

The gaps were everywhere. Between booming Boston and declining industrial cities like Lawrence, Fall River, and Springfield. Between New York and the struggling upstate cousins of Syracuse, Rochester, and Buffalo. Between Columbus and the smaller Ohio cities it was pulling away from: Akron, Dayton, and Toledo on down to Chillicothe, Mansfield, and Zanesville. Between Nashville, the belle of the Upper South, and its poor relation, Memphis.

The country had always had richer and poorer places, but the gaps were growing wider than they had ever been. Through the final decades of the nineteenth century and for the first eight decades of the twentieth century, as the country grew into the richest and most powerful nation on earth, poorer parts of the country had been catching up with richer ones. But starting in 1980, this convergence reversed. In 1980, virtually every area of the country had mean incomes that were within 20 percent of the national average—only metro New York and Washington, D.C., fell above that band, and only parts of the rural South and Southwest fell below it. But by 2013, virtually the entire Northeast Corridor from Boston to Washington and the Northern California coast had incomes more than 20 percent above average. Most startlingly, a huge swath of the country's interior had incomes more than 20 percent below average—not only the rural South and Southwest but much of the Midwest and Great Plains as well. As for the places already wealthy in 1980, they were now off the charts. Income in the Washington area was a quarter higher than in the rest of the country in 1980. By the middle of 2015, that gap was more than twice as large.

Yet even as the regional divides grew, they got relatively little attention. The inequality debate focused on individual income—the top 1 percent and bottom 99 percent, and so on—rather than on the landscape of inequality across the country. To the extent the regional problem got notice, it was often described as an urban-rural divide, and it was true: rural America was in crisis. But the divide was also between cities—between a handful of winner-take-all metropolises and a much larger number of left-behind rivals. Job growth was almost twice as fast in the first six years after the Great Recession in large metro areas as in small ones, and income grew 50 percent faster. A few generations ago, urban prosperity spread across the country: in the 1960s, the twenty-five cities with the highest median income included Cleveland, Milwaukee, Des Moines, and Rockford, Illinois. Now, nearly all the richest cities were on the coasts. Wages in the very largest cities in the country had grown nearly twenty percentage points more since 1970 than wages in the rest of the country's cities. By 2019, more than 70 percent of all venture capital was flowing to just three states: California, New York, and Massachusetts. "A handful of metro areas have seen such concentrations of wealth almost unprecedented in human history, while a much larger set has seen their jobs evaporate and their economic bases contract," wrote the sociologist Robert Manduca.

As this regional inequality grew, so did its consequences. There was, above all, the political cost, a rising resentment in the left-behind places that made voters susceptible to racist and nativist appeals from opportunistic candidates and cynical TV networks. Economic decline did not excuse racism and xenophobia—rather, it weaponized it. Such resentment carried especially strong weight in the American political system, which apportions power by land, not just population, most obviously in the Senate. As regions declined and emptied out, those left behind retained outsized clout to express bitterness.

But the damage went beyond that. Regional inequality was making parts of the country incomprehensible to one another—one world wracked with painkillers, the other tainted by elite-college admission schemes. It was making it difficult to settle on nationwide programs that could apply across such wildly disparate contexts—in one set of places, the housing crisis was about blight and abandonment, while in the other, it was all about affordability and gentrification.

Inequality between regions was also worsening inequality within regions. The more prosperity concentrated in certain cities, the more it concentrated within certain segments of those cities, exacerbating long-standing imbalances or driving those of lesser means out altogether. Dystopian elements in cities such as San Francisco—the homeless defecating on sidewalks in a place with $24 lunch salads and one-bedroom apartments renting for $3,600 on average; high-paid tech workers boarding shuttles to suburban corporate campuses while lower-paid workers settled for 200-square-foot "micro-apartments" or dorm-style arrangements with shared bathrooms or predawn commutes from distant cities such as Stockton—were a feature of both local and national inequality.

The growing imbalance of wealth was making life harder in both sorts of places. It was throwing the whole country off-kilter.

Economists and sociologists who worried about this new reality began trying to identify its causes. To some degree, regional inequality was simply a corollary of income inequality, which itself, by 2018, had grown wider than it had been in the five decades since the census started tracking it—so wide that Moody's issued a warning that it could threaten the country's credit profile and "negatively affect economic growth and its sustainability." As the very rich got ever richer, so did the places where they had always tended to live.

But there were other factors, too. There was the nature of the tech economy, which encouraged agglomeration of talent. There was the changing nature of employment: the less you could expect to spend a career with one company, the more you wanted to be somewhere where there were many employers in your field. With the rise of the two-income couple, you wanted to be somewhere where both of you could find fulfilling work.

There were social dynamics. The country's most successful people were seeking each other out, taking mutual comfort in their comfortable lives, to a degree they never had before. Even within cities, the wealthy had become more likely to live with each other—from 1980 to 2010, the share of upper-income households living in wealthy neighborhoods, rather than more mixed ones, had doubled. Meanwhile, further down the ladder, fraying social bonds and the collapse of the traditional family—trends driven partly by the diminished prosperity in left-behind places—were making it less likely that you were going to move somewhere with greater opportunity. If you were a single mother, you couldn't leave behind the relative who provided childcare, even if you could hope to afford rent in a thriving city.

It was no accident that wealth was growing more concentrated in certain places at the same time as whole sectors of the economy—three-quarters of all U.S. industries, by one estimate—were growing more concentrated in certain companies. This trend had been underway for decades as the federal government had relaxed its opposition to corporate consolidation, and it caused regional imbalance in all sorts of ways. Airline mergers led to less service in smaller cities, which made it harder for them to attract businesses. Consolidation in agriculture meant that less of the money spent on food ended up with those who had actually produced it in rural areas and small towns. Mergers in sectors like banking and insurance meant that many small and midsize cities lost corporate headquarters and the economic and civic benefits that came along with them.

Put most simply, business activity that used to be dispersed across hundreds of companies large and small, whether in media or retail or finance, was increasingly dominated by a handful of giant firms. As a result, profits and growth opportunities once spread across the country were increasingly flowing to the places where those dominant companies were based. With a winner-take-all economy came winner-take-all places.

To the extent that regional inequality and economic concentration were being written about, it was often on their own terms, without relation to one another. In fact, they were intertwined. And as I began to think about this intertwining, it became clear that one of the most natural ways to tell this story was through Amazon, a company that was playing an outsized role in this zero-sum sorting. To take a closer look not so much at the company itself, exactly—that would be the terrain of other accounts—but rather, to take a closer look at the America that fell in the company's lengthening shadow.

The company was an ideal frame for understanding the country and what the country was becoming, given how many contemporary forces it represented and helped explain. There was the extreme wealth inequality encapsulated by its founder's outlandish personal fortune and the modest wages of the vast preponderance of its employees. There was the nature of the work most of them were engaged in: rudimentary and isolating, out on the edge of town, often with unreliable hours and schedules. There was the immense influence the company had amassed over the country's elected government, both in the states and in Washington, where it had insinuated itself into the power structure of the nation's capital. There was the unraveling of the civic fabric that the company contributed to, through its undermining of face-to-face commercial activity and the tax base of countless communities. In upending how we consumed—the ways that we fulfilled ourselves—it had recast daily life at its most elemental level.

Amazon was far from the only force driving regional divergence. Rival tech giants, Google and Facebook, had hoovered most of the country's digital advertising revenue into the Bay Area, in the process eviscerating local journalism; across a swath of other industries, private equity firms based in cities such as New York and Boston had profited greatly by extracting the value of companies scattered in small and midsize cities across the country before shrinking the companies' payrolls or shutting them down altogether.

But Amazon far more than any other served as the ultimate lens on the country's divides because it was present just about everywhere, in very different forms. Early on, it had promised to be an equalizing force, offering its initial products—books—to every corner of the country, like a Sears catalog for our time. Over time, in its astonishing proliferation, it had segmented the country into different sorts of places, each with their assigned rank, income, and purpose. It had not only altered the national landscape itself, but also the landscape of opportunity in America—the options that lay before people, what they could aspire to do with their lives.

And it was the company that was poised more than any of its fellow giants to emerge from the pandemic even more dominant than before. For tens of millions of Americans, the mode of consumption it had pioneered for a quarter century had transformed from a matter of convenience to one of necessity—it was now, by official decree, essential. As many of its smaller rivals were furloughing and laying off workers, or preparing to enter bankruptcy or cease operations forever, the company was hiring hundreds of thousands more people to fulfill its new role in American life. As the health risk of these people's work grew, so did the fraught implications of the easy clicks that directed their exertions. And as the company's pervasiveness spread, so did those fissures that it had been helping to create all along.

1.

Community

The hyper-prosperous city

California did not let veterans leaving the service qualify for in-state university tuition, and Washington state did. It was as simple as that. So Milo Duke, discharged from the U.S. Navy in the Bay Area in 1971 after spending a couple years under an alfalfa field eavesdropping with the Naval Security Group, made his way to Seattle, to pursue a degree in oceanography at the University of Washington. His pursuit lasted all of one quarter, until he ran into differential equations. He had flailed before them once already, while getting his bachelor's in history at the University of Nebraska. Milo thought he could handle them on a second try, but he was mistaken.

He made his way into a different line of work. Motivated by his own unpleasant experiences with the military bureaucracy, he started volunteering to help veterans who'd exited the service on poor terms achieve "discharge upgrades," and soon enough was working for an organization dedicated to this task as a de facto paralegal, funded by a federal program. He and his wife, whom he had met at college in Nebraska, rented a two-bedroom apartment in the Wallingford neighborhood for $150, then found a larger one nearby for $120. He decided he would be more effective at his work if he had a law degree, and in 1975 enrolled at the University of Washington law school. Alas, two years later, President Carter issued his amnesty for draft dodgers, which had the side effect of drying up funding for organizations like the one Milo Duke worked for. The group disbanded, but Duke finished law school anyway, in 1978, and, after a short stint with the public defender's office, got a job with a big criminal defense firm downtown.

By this point, he and his wife had two kids, and he had started making art. During law school, he and his wife had moved into a hippie commune in Madrona, along Lake Washington just east of the historically African American Central District. They lived in a home that one of the commune members had bought for $5,000. Milo and his wife bought their own house there in 1978, for $50,000. But Milo was growing rapidly disillusioned with his job at the firm, and more drawn to his art. When he would mention this inclination, the wife of one of the firm's partners would joke that if he was serious he should go sell his work at Pike Place Market like the guy who made the linoleum woodcut prints of flowers that the firm's attorneys all seemed to have in their bathrooms at home.

In 1980, Duke's firm took on some of the twenty-six defendants in a racketeering case against the Carbone family. It was a huge case, the first time, he was told, that the RICO (Racketeer Influenced and Corrupt Organizations) statute had been used in the Ninth Circuit. One day, Milo Duke joined dozens of other lawyers working on the case in a large conference room. It occurred to him that in a few months he'd gone from being a public defender for the indigent to representing mafiosi. He thought, *What the fuck am I doing here?* He quit the next day and joined the artists at Pike Place Market. His marriage dissolved six months later. He took $200 for himself, left the rest of his money and the house to his wife, and ensconced himself in his new community at the market.

As a newcomer, he had been assigned one of the least desirable spots: the "slabs" at the northern end of the market, essentially a segment of sidewalk for which you paid $3 on weekdays and $5 on weekends, and where you were exposed to the weather, which in Seattle often meant rain. But on his very first day there, Milo Duke fell in with the adjacent artists, who sensed in each other a common mission—"we shared the same notion that we were going to take the art to the people," he said later. Before long, they conspired to rig up a communal shelter over their half dozen slabs. This had the double benefit of keeping them dry and making their spot look like a sort of gallery, and thus making it more likely that the crowds of passersby might actually stop and look at their work. They even gave themselves a Kerouacian name: the Dharmic Engineers, from the Sanskrit *dharma*, meaning "that which holds up or supports." This was the purpose of their collaboration in the most practical terms: to hold each other up.

Looking back later, Milo Duke thought of the city in the years leading up to this moment as the first of three Seattles he would live in. This Seattle was a relatively small city—its population had dropped under 500,000, not much more than St. Louis's and Kansas City's. The city's economy was still dominated by Boeing and the shipyards and the port. It had evolved only so far since 1851, when it had started as a natural resource outpost. Dropped off by a coastal schooner, the original inhabitants built cabins and intended to develop farmland but eventually realized there was better business in harvesting logs for the docks in San Francisco. Soon enough, an entrepreneurial Ohioan named Henry Yesler arrived to build a sawmill on Puget Sound.

The boom came with the railroad. The Northern Pacific reached Tacoma in 1883, and the Great Northern Railway reached Seattle a decade later. Seattle's population grew more than tenfold during the 1880s, surpassing 40,000. The Yukon Gold Rush of the late 1890s further fueled the young city's fortunes—prospectors needed a supply post. In 1916, William Boeing co-built his first seaplane at Lake Union. Over the decades that followed, the city grew more or less on the course set by Yesler and Boeing. If Seattle of the 1970s was not exactly a factory town, it was hardly wealthier than cities that *were* factory towns: per capita income in the Seattle metro area in 1978 was barely higher than that in Cleveland, Pittsburgh, and Milwaukee. "It still bore the marks of a raw settlement in a new territory," said the British writer Jonathan Raban, describing his first impression of the city in that era.

Early in the '70s, Boeing had in fact laid off tens of thousands, prompting the mounting of an iconic billboard: WILL THE LAST PERSON LEAVING SEATTLE—TURN OUT THE LIGHTS. *The Economist* reported that the city had "become a vast pawnshop, with families selling anything they can do without to get money to buy food and pay the rent." The writer Charles D'Ambrosio, who grew up in Seattle in the '70s, evoked the city's lack of dynamism in that era, which was not without its melancholic charms. "There was Elliott Bay Book Company, which offered both a bookstore and a brick-walled garret in the basement. You could loiter without having to skulk. You could bring your empty cup to the register and ask for refills. And you could read," he wrote later. "The Seattle of that time had a distinctly coma-like aspect and at night seemed to contain in its great sleepy volume precisely one of everything—one dog a-barking, one car a-cranking, one door a-slamming, etc.—and then an extravagant unnecessary amount of nothing. Beaucoup nothing."

Elliott Bay Book Company was where the Dharmic Engineers would meet weekly to lounge and talk art. And then Milo Duke would return by ferry to Vashon Island in Puget Sound, where he lived on a bus. He had spent his first night after leaving home under the Alaskan Way Viaduct, but had soon found his way to the island, where a friend owned a farmhouse and welcomed others onto her land. Milo suggested another friend use the island to park an old school bus that was constantly being ticketed on the street. Milo lived for a while in the bus, one of the short ones, but after a year bought an old Continental Trailways coach and upgraded into that. "The cost of living was pretty reasonable," he joked later. "I was a pioneer of the tiny house movement."

For Patrinell Staten, Seattle began with a Continental Trailways bus, rather than led to it.

Her trip from Carthage, Texas, lasted three and a half days and she held it the whole way. She had to sit in the back of the bus, by the nasty bathroom, but she was not allowed to use said bathroom, nor was she allowed to use the bathrooms at the depots the bus stopped in as it made the endless traverse of Texas. For her, it had to be the outhouses down dark paths, and she, recently turned twenty, wasn't going to walk those paths alone. So she held it, and limited fluids to make it easier to hold it even after the bus finally emerged from Jim Crow Texas into the Ambiguous West. By the time she arrived in Seattle, her system was a mess. "You look sick," said her sister. She took her to a doctor, who was alarmed at how dehydrated Patrinell had become. "I don't know how you did this for four days," he said.

This was in 1964. In Carthage, Patrinell's father was a pastor and her mother was a schoolteacher, and they owned thirty-five acres outside town. But even for the African American select, East Texas offered little relief from the thick climate of prejudice. One sister, Anna Laura, had stayed in Seattle after her husband was stationed there in the military, and another, Ora Lee, had joined her. After a couple years at Prairie View A&M, a Black college near Houston, Pat decided to follow—she went up to care for Ora Lee's kids after Ora Lee divorced their father.

Their journey was typical of the Great Migration, which took a few decades to reach the farthest north and west big city of all—by the late 1930s, there were still fewer than 4,000 African Americans in Seattle. This small scale had allowed for a certain exceptionalism: from the start, Black men could vote without restrictions in Seattle, and after 1883, so could Black women—a tolerance that was not afforded to the Chinese or Native American minorities, who were already facing virulent discrimination in the city. "The small numbers of blacks in the city," notes the historian Quintard Taylor, "allowed white Seattle to indulge in a racial toleration toward African Americans which, when compared with the segregationist policies sweeping the nation, led both blacks and whites to conclude that their city was fundamentally liberal and egalitarian."

By 1950, the city's Black population had jumped to more than 15,000, surpassing its large Asian communities. The increase had come, at last, with the Second World War and the surge of production at Boeing and the shipyards. And the population kept growing in the three decades that followed—there were jobs and there was, in the midst of the civil rights struggle spreading across the South, the appeal of a city removed from it.

Though not as removed as Pat Staten expected. On arriving in town, she had moved in with Ora Lee in Renton, a working-class suburb southeast of the city. She noticed on visits into downtown Seattle how few Black people were visible. She approached one of the few that she did see, a janitor.

"Where are you?" she asked.

He knew what she meant by "you." "Oh, there's a place called the Central District," he said. "The Central Area."

Early on, the few Black people who lived in Seattle had gravitated to two places. There was waterfront Yesler-Jackson, with its bars and bordellos; it became home to the more transient, the porters and shipboard crews—two of the primary occupations available to African American men amid widespread discrimination in the shipbuilding and longshoremen's unions. And there was the wooded area out East Madison Street, where William Grose, the second African American to arrive in the city, had bought a twelve-acre farm, and where many of the more settled Black families had followed.

Over time, these two areas had fused into a reverse L. This was the Central District. And that fusing was not altogether natural. Racial covenants barring sales to Black people proliferated in other neighborhoods, and those seeking to rent apartments found that buildings tended to be full whenever they applied. So it would have to be the CD. By 1960, after a decade in which the city's Black population had surged by more than 70 percent, three-quarters of its 26,901 Black residents lived in just four census tracts in the Central District.

Pat Staten would come into the city for church, at True Vine Missionary Baptist, and it was there that her good looks—her broad, dimpled smile had a knowing allure—caught the eye of Benny Wright. His family had come north earlier, from Arkansas. Pat and Benny dated for six months before he asked her to marry him. They rented an apartment on East Denny Way, on the northern edge of the Central District, then started looking for a house to buy. The real estate agent showed them houses only in the CD, which confounded Pat. "I couldn't believe it," she said later. "I was living in a northern 'southern' place, that the only place I could buy a house was right *here*."

They ended up on the eastern edge of the neighborhood, in a tidy three-bedroom brick house they purchased for $17,000.

Benny Wright became a history teacher, eventually at majority-Black Garfield High School in the Central District. Pat got a job at a bank, working the night shift as a proof operator, processing checks. This led to a job as a teller at Liberty Bank, the first Black-owned bank west of the Mississippi, after it opened in 1968 in the heart of the Central District. By then, she knew everyone in the neighborhood, or so it seemed, and she loved how people would stand in the longer line just to get to see her.

Though there were other moments, too. There were the men who would come in and say something to the effect of, "Oh, we got a *nigger* working in here!"

To which Pat Wright would answer, her eyes wide, "What the . . . anybody seen a nigger? Are some *niggers* around here? What do they look like?"

Like Milo Duke, Pat Wright began drifting toward her art, which in her case was a voice so resonant that she had sung in her father's church from a very young age, led the teen choir, and later joined a high school trio called the Jivettes. Seattle, it turned out, was a mecca for Black music. The jazz clubs had sprouted in the '30s, up and down Jackson Street and in adjacent blocks of the red-light district: the Black and Tan, Basin Street, the Black Elks, Ubangi. Count Basie, Louis Armstrong, Cab Calloway, and Duke Ellington might stop by after playing at an establishment venue uptown; they might stay at the Black-owned Golden West, if the uptown hotels wouldn't take them. The after-hours clubs—Rocking Chair, Doc Hamilton's, Congo Club—drew white people, too: Washington banned serving hard liquor by the glass until 1949, but there was a "tolerance policy" toward Black clubs, greased with police kickbacks, allowing them to sell "setups"—glasses, ice, and mixers to accompany the liquor patrons brought in. The clubs grew even more happening in the '40s with the wartime influx into the factories and shipyards and military bases.

That influx included the family of Ernestine Anderson, who arrived from Texas in 1944, at age sixteen, and was soon performing on Jackson Street; and the family of Quincy Jones, who arrived in 1943, when he was ten and his father took a job at the Puget Sound Naval Shipyard; and Al Hendrix, who arrived in 1940 and bore with his new wife, Lucille Jeter, a son they named Johnny Allen Hendrix but several years later renamed James Marshall Hendrix.

In 1970, Pat Wright sang at Jimi's funeral. She had started her own gospel group, Patrinell Wright's Inspirational Seven. She had put out a single with Sepia Records—"I Let a Good Man Go"/"Little Love Affair." And she'd started singing in clubs—not only in Seattle, but down in Portland, Oregon, where the pay was higher.

Benny did not care for Pat's playing out-of-town clubs. Years later, she would insist she hadn't cared for it either. "I don't like not being able to see your face," she said. In 1970, she got word of a need at Franklin High, just south of the Central District. The Black student population had grown considerably and the music director invited Pat to start a gospel choir. The demand from students was overwhelming, and it didn't take long for the outsized success of the choir to grate. The same music director who had invited in Wright said the choir was blurring church-state lines. So in 1973, Wright took it out of the school and into church, to Mount Zion Baptist on Nineteenth Avenue, and dozens of students followed, often joined by younger siblings—whoever was willing to live up to Pat Wright's exacting standards. It would become a community fixture: the Total Experience Gospel Choir.

By this point, the old jazz clubs were fading. Drugs and street crime were growing scourges, as in other cities. And yet it seemed that the Central District community was becoming only stronger. There were constant block parties. If someone fell sick, it felt like the whole neighborhood would rush to help. "You should've seen all the food cooked for them," Pat said. If she came home late, she felt safe walking from her car, knowing her friends were looking out for her from inside their homes. And they were her friends. "We'd yell at each other across the fence," she said.

———

n the winter of 1978–1979, two young men set out north from Albuquerque, New Mexico. They went in separate cars, on different routes, one
month apart. The first, Paul Allen, drove a Monza, slipping through the icy
mountains of Utah and Idaho with chains on his tires and Earth, Wind &
Fire on the radio. The second, Bill Gates, drove his Porsche, speeding so
brazenly that he was ticketed twice by the same airplane flying overhead.

But they had the same destination: Seattle, where both had grown up
and attended the same elite private school, Lakeside, whose rudimentary computer system they had hacked into. They had both left for Boston
after high school—Gates for Harvard, then Allen for a job at Honey-
well, after dropping out of Washington State University. In 1975, they had
gravitated to Albuquerque, home of a small company called Micro Instru-
mentation & Telemetry Systems. This company, located in a shopping strip
bracketed by a massage parlor and laundromat, had come up with a simple
computer it called the Altair, using an Intel 8080 chip. Allen and Gates had
set out to prove the worth of their BASIC programing language on it. There,
in Albuquerque, they had founded a company called Micro-Soft.

Two years later, they were wearying of the high desert landscape and
fretting about drawing programming talent to New Mexico. Allen suggested they move the company—then a mere thirteen people—to Seattle.
He missed home—the pine trees and water, the cool weather. He argued that
the city's climate was actually ideal for the company: "The rainy days were a
plus," he wrote later. "They'd keep programmers from getting distracted."

Gates was less committed to Seattle. The other obvious option was Silicon Valley, already a hub for micro-computing thanks to Stanford University's leveraging of its considerable real estate holdings and Cold War defense
spending. Seattle, on the other hand, was hardly a tech magnet. So it would
take some persuading on Allen's part. Finally, he struck on a winning tactic: he prevailed on Gates's parents to work on their son, knowing how close
they were. Eventually, Gates sided with Allen. Seattle it would be.

Gates leased an office on the eighth floor of the Old National Bank building in Bellevue, across Lake Washington from Seattle. Unable to get a line

of credit, Gates and Allen cashed in some certificates of deposit to pay for a new computer system at the office. The company's phone number ended in 8080, same as the Intel chip they had proved their worth with a few years earlier, a happy coincidence that may've been made possible by the fact that Gates's mother was on the board of Pacific Northwest Bell.

Soon after arriving in Seattle, Microsoft (it had dropped the hyphen) scored its big coup: IBM tasked it to deliver the operating system for its entry into personal computers. Allen and Gates finagled a fledgling system from another programmer in Seattle and tweaked it to create MS-DOS. By 1981, the company had grown to more than one hundred employees, and it moved into a larger space near Lake Washington and a Burgermaster, a favorite fast-food spot. The company looked for young programmers fresh out of college, unsullied by other employers. "Above all, we were after the brightest lights," Allen recalled. As hoped, Seattle proved an easier sell than Albuquerque, even if some recruits were lost to Silicon Valley.

By the end of 1982, revenues had doubled to $34 million and the company had reached two hundred employees. But it retained some scrappiness. After work, there was foosball at the Nowhere pub. On weekends, there was volleyball and barbecue at the home of Bob O'Rear, Allen's deputy, with the company's first employee, Marc McDonald, making daiquiris.

Allen hosted a Halloween party at his house on Lake Sammamish, where, in Allen's telling, Gates "did chest slides on the balustrade from my upper floor down toward the kitchen. He'd run fast as he could, throw himself on the bannister, and glide to the parquet below."

The city that followed Microsoft's arrival was the second Seattle Milo Duke lived in. There was a little more tech, and things got a little more upscale. But you could still manage.

To get by, since his own surrealist work was selling only so much at Pike Place Market, he had started serving as an agent of sorts for other members of the Dharmic Engineers. And he started selling at science-fiction conventions, where people seemed to like his work. At one convention in 1982, he met Wendy Dees, a St. Louis native who was flourishing as a book illustrator as well as writing some poetry and fiction of her own. They would marry, but not for another decade. Milo kept living in the bus on Vashon Island until 1989, when he started spending nights at a studio that he and several of the Dharmic Engineers were using in Pioneer Square, the historic waterfront quarter and site of Yesler's original timber docks that would, over the next couple years, become a locus of the grunge scene. The studio, in one of two Washington Shoe Company buildings, had no windows, was kept cool by its proximity to a cold-storage building, and cost $80 a month. Milo became part-owner with two others of a nearby gallery. The summer of 1991 was nights on the fire escape, smoking weed, the music all around. "It felt like the center of the world," he said later.

The moment couldn't last. One of his friends, a partner in the gallery, died of a rare cancer at age thirty-eight. The gallery had to be sold. Milo moved out of the studio and joined some other artist friends in a rickety house owned by a notorious slumlord up on Sixty-Fifth Street, in the Roosevelt district. There was a huge empty lot full of dirt in back. When a fuse blew, the landlord would shove a quarter into the box to fix it.

After he'd spent two years there, Wendy rescued Milo. She had a regular job, at an expensive gallery of Japanese art. They moved into a communal house in Phinney Ridge and then, at last, a place of their own, in 1996: a rental bungalow in Tangletown, a neighborhood just south of Green Lake. There were 800 square feet on the main floor, plus 400 upstairs for Wendy's studio and 800 in the garden-level basement for Milo's. One of his sons would use the garage as a metalworking and motorcycle repair shop. The landlady charged $1,000, and she would leave it there for years. She was a school administrator married to a Boeing executive, and both she and her husband got some titillation from having artists at the place.

Their vicarious pleasure grew only greater when Milo started running an art school in his studio. He had gotten into teaching sideways—in 1998, he and Wendy had taken a class in oil painting at the Academy of Realist Art, a well-regarded, rigorously traditional art school in town, after seeing a course catalog left at a bar. After one semester, the academy asked Milo if he wanted to teach the class himself. Soon enough, he'd moved his instruction to the bungalow. He even started calling it by its proper French name: an atelier.

T he second Seattle was good for Pat Wright, too.

The revolution underway across Lake Washington had yet to reach the Central District, but the neighborhood was changing already. It was, at this point, mostly a change to be celebrated, driven as it was from within: bit by bit, Black Seattle was breaking out of its box.

The move had been years in the making. In 1957, the state legislature had passed a ban on housing discrimination, but two years later, a King County Superior Court judge struck it down, ruling that as lamentable as prejudice against potential tenants and buyers was, "the court rules for the right of the owner of private property to complete freedom of choice in selecting those with whom he will deal."

Reformers of all races pressed on through the early '60s, pushing for an "open housing" ordinance in Seattle itself. The city council—which did not get its first Black member until 1967—declined to pass any legislation, and instead put the ordinance up for referendum in 1964. A letter protesting the proposed ordinance in the weekly *Argus* newspaper was representative of the opposition: "Suddenly these homeowners are asked to surrender part of this gain . . . for something called open housing. For this surrender the voter gains nothing but the feeling that he may be helping the oppressed . . . negroes."

The ordinance was defeated on March 10, 1964, by more than a 2–1 margin: three months prior to the passage of the Civil Rights Act in Washington, D.C., more than 110,000 voters in one of the most purportedly progressive cities in the country voted to protect the right to discriminate on the basis of race. It was a sign of how far even Seattle still had to go.

Undeterred, reformers pressed to dismantle barriers through voluntary measures. They sought out people of good faith outside the Central District who pushed to make their own neighborhoods welcoming regardless of the law, and created the Fair Housing Listing Service for Black families looking to move. These efforts were not uncontroversial within the Central District itself—Quintard Taylor quotes Keve Bray, a CD businessman and an activist, who branded those seeking an exit as "social climbers who were trying to get away from their people." Nor did they escape resistance in the targeted areas either. In the suburb of Kent, two Black families had shotgun blasts fired into their new homes.

But the steady outward flow continued, regardless. In 1970, only 9 percent of the 42,000 African Americans in the metropolitan area lived outside the city. By 1980, that share had more than doubled—to 20 percent of 58,000. And by 1990, the share had grown to more than a third of 81,000.

The moves weren't only to the suburbs, but also to parts of the city that were gradually becoming more welcoming. By 1980, the Central District was no longer home to a majority of Black residents in the city.

As Pat Wright saw it, these years represented a sort of happy medium. No longer did residents feel constrained to reside in this one corner of the city. But enough of them were still living in that corner to sustain a critical mass of community identity.

Pat Wright was providing more than her share of that identity. She opened a record store on Fourteenth Avenue, Gospel Showplace, where you could find the music that the Total Experience choir sang on Sundays, as well as Christian books and paraphernalia. And the choir was on a tear. "A lot of kids that were born and raised here had a hard time catching on to the style that I was insisting that they learn, but once they learned it, they were unbeatable," Wright recalled later. In the mid-1970s, the choir had started performing in steadily more impressive contexts—at the Seattle Center Food Circus mall, at the opera house, at a campaign rally with Rosalynn Carter, the future First Lady. It hit the road for the first time, to Yakima and Spokane—worlds away for young people who had never left Seattle and preparation for what came in 1979, a bona fide nationwide tour, three weeks with stops in New York, Washington, Philadelphia, St. Louis, and Chicago.

That year, the choir had moved from Mount Zion to a church in South

Seattle amid a conflict over its unbridled enthusiasm, which had discomfited some church fathers. "If the music is too loud, that's too bad," Wright liked to say. The official letter of dismissal from Mount Zion stated that the choir had "outgrown" the church—dubious given that the church was one of the largest in the city. It was hard not to detect simple envy—Pat Wright had created something that had not so much outgrown the church as was outshining it.

The tours grew ever more ambitious. A swing through the Deep South, with kids squeezing two to a seat to fit the choir into two Greyhound buses . . . the Bahamas . . . Hawaii . . . Mexico, El Salvador, and Nicaragua. Pat's younger brother, Gregory, came along to play the drums; sometimes Benny came along, to take pictures and catch his wife in her element—Pat sashaying along a motel balcony in her bathrobe, Pat leading the choir in three-part harmony through "Going Up Yonder" and "Oh Happy Day" and "When the Battle Is Over." Not all was sweetness: arriving in Salt Lake City, some kids on one bus heard an onlooker remark, "The niggers are here!" Pat gathered the kids on that bus to settle them down: *We represent God. We're going to sing, we're not going to entertain all that. Let's pray. And let's K.A.* And then she went and told the same thing to the other bus.

In Seattle, the choir sang to raise money for Cambodian refugees, it performed at the International Brotherhood of Electrical Workers Hall in a "showcase of pro-worker entertainment," and it began an annual tradition of performing in a Christmas production of Langston Hughes's *Black Nativity*. It had grown into a cohesive unit, even family-like: when Pat dropped off one girl at her foster home and the family would not open the door, Pat invited her to stay as long as she wanted with her and Benny, and she did stay. She went on to get her doctorate in speech pathology at the University of Michigan.

By the early 1990s, choir members were aging into college and moving on, and it was getting harder to enroll kids to replace them—who knew if it was Pat's demanding reputation or the loosening grip of church and church music. To keep up its numbers, the choir started enrolling adults. It bought a 1960s touring bus and installed the Wrights' son, Patrick, as assistant director. It went all the way to Russia and Australia. But the pace and scale of the enterprise were wearing on Wright. She announced that the choir would cease to exist in its current form. It would be reduced from thirty-two members to a handpicked group half that size. The existing choir would perform its final concerts in late 1993.

Half a year later, in the spring of 1994, a thirty-year-old senior vice president at the New York investment banking firm D. E. Shaw arrived in Santa Cruz on a scouting trip for the company he was about to start with a $100,000 boost from his parents. Jeff Bezos's idea was fairly simple: to take advantage of rapidly accelerating activity on the World Wide Web, the new user-friendly internet interface, to sell consumer goods there. "Most successful entrepreneurs start a company because they're passionate about the business they want to enter," wrote Richard L. Brandt in his 2011 book on Bezos's company. "Bezos was simply interested in the fact that growth of the Internet meant somebody was going to make a fortune or two from the phenomenon, and he wanted one for himself." Bezos wasn't sure what type of goods to sell and made a list of twenty possibilities, among them office supplies, computer software, apparel, and music. He settled on books for one reason above all: there were so many different titles, a near infinitude, that an online marketplace could offer an advantage over stores in a way it couldn't with other goods.

He came to Santa Cruz, on the Pacific coast seventy miles south of San Francisco, to pitch two experienced computer programmers on his idea. He enticed one of them, Shel Kaphan. Together, they checked out office space in the city, which offered a pristine coastal location and proximity to Silicon Valley.

There was just one problem. In 1992, the Supreme Court had mostly upheld a 1967 ruling that merchants needed to collect sales tax only from buyers in states where the merchants had physical operations. If Bezos set up his company in California, he would have to assess sales tax on all his customers in the biggest state in the country. This would eliminate, in the huge

California market, a crucial advantage his company would hold against traditional retailers: they had to charge sales tax, thus raising the cost of their products, but Bezos, as an internet retailer, would not. Bezos did not want to cede that big edge. If he located in a relatively small state, the company would have to assess sales tax on only a thin slice of customers. He said half-jokingly years later that he even considered setting up on a California Indian reservation to avoid taxes entirely.

His gaze fell on Seattle. Unlike Bill Gates and Paul Allen, he had no connection to the place—he had grown up in Albuquerque, Houston, and Miami and gone to college at Princeton. But one of his initial investors in the new company, Nick Hanauer, lived in Seattle and made a strong case for it. There was, as Jonathan Raban had noted upon arriving a few years earlier, a "bracing smell of possibility" there: "Even now, this late in the game, a guy could make a living out of such a provisional and half-built landscape—could arrive out of nowhere, set up shop and become an *alrightnik* in the classic immigrant tradition."

The city was large enough to have a major airport, a prerequisite for shipping books around the country. It was only a six-hour drive from one of the largest book distribution warehouses in the country, in Roseburg, Oregon.

There was something else, too. Bezos knew that his company, if successful, would need to hire lots of programmers. The best place to poach such talent was in the Bay Area, but Seattle was a respectable fallback. The University of Washington's computer science department was churning out graduates. More importantly, there was Microsoft, which had attracted a smattering of smaller companies to the area as well. It was "the recruiting pool available from Microsoft," Bezos said in 2018, explaining his choice of Seattle.

It would emerge, years later, as a classic example of the defining rule for economic development in the high-tech era: winner takes all, rich get richer. The internet was supposed to let us live and work anywhere we wanted to, connecting us no matter how far-flung we might be. It would liberate us from cubicle and office park, disperse opportunity across the country.

Instead, the opposite happened. Tech entrepreneurs quickly found that location mattered more than ever. It helped to have your company clustered among similar companies because it made it easier to attract employees—not only those poached from the company across the street, but those who'd newly arrived because of the area's reputation as a hub. And for employees in an industry as volatile as tech, it made sense to be somewhere where you could count on getting another good job if the first one fell apart. So you wanted to be in the hub, which in turn drew more employers there, too.

Clustering mattered not only for human resources, but for innovation, the essence of technology. There was, in one sense, nothing new in this: history is the story of cities with the right confluence of people in close quarters to spin the world forward, whether in classical Athens or Renaissance Florence or industrial-age Glasgow. "Cities are effectively machines for stimulating and integrating the continuous positive feedback dynamics between the physical and the social, each multiplicatively enhancing the other," wrote theoretical physicist Geoffrey West in his treatise on the growth of cities and companies.

But there was something about the new digital economy that took this dynamic and trebled it. In the industrial age, a mechanical advance might be more likely to be discovered in an industrial hub, but that advance could then be dispersed to whichever place had the natural resources and manpower and transportation links to make use of it. Once Henry Bessemer made his discoveries in steelmaking, anyone with enough capital and access to coal and iron ore could build a mill. And they did—in Braddock, Pennsylvania, and Weirton, West Virginia, and Youngstown, Ohio, and Gary, Indiana.

The tech economy was different. Now the huge rewards lay in the innovation itself, which could produce outsized returns with very little additional capital. Once you came up with great new software, you could reproduce it at barely any cost—no coal and iron ore required. Everything lay in having the minds to produce that initial breakthrough. "Economic value depends on talent as never before," wrote Enrico Moretti, an economist at the University of California, Berkeley. "In the twentieth century, competition was about accumulating physical capital. Today it is about attracting the best human capital." Crucially, this held true even if the cluster became ever more expensive. Instead of a market rebalancing—a dispersal to more affordable locales—a feedback loop prevailed.

The implications of this for Seattle were not yet clear in 1994 when Bezos and his wife, MacKenzie, arrived in town. They rented a house in Bellevue for $890 per month, deliberately choosing one that had a garage, albeit converted into a rec room, so that Bezos could later adopt the customary "garage start-up" mythology. For a few months, Bezos ran the company out of the garage before finding an office and basement space in a building in the industrial district south of downtown Seattle.

By this point, the company had a name. After starting with Cadabra .com and mulling Awake.com, Browse.com, Bookmall.com, Aard.com, and Relentless.com, Bezos settled on Amazon.com. "This is not only the largest river in the world, it's many times larger than the next biggest river," he said, as reported by the journalist Brad Stone in his 2014 book on the company. "It blows all other rivers away."

Years later, Charles D'Ambrosio, the writer who had evoked the Seattle of the '70s, could scarcely recognize the city.

"For me the city is still inarticulate and dark and a place to call home because I'm in thrall to failure and to silence—I have a fidelity to it, an allegiance, which presents a strange dislocation now that Seattle's become the Valhalla of so many people's seeking," he wrote. "The idea of it as a locus of economic and scenic and cultural hope baffles me. It a little bit shocks me to realize my nephews and nieces are growing up in a place considered desirable."

"Failure" was indeed a concept now foreign to the city, which was winning constantly, winning to the point of excess. It was hard to find a modern precedent for a major American city so transformed in a matter of two decades. In the decade since the Great Recession, the city had added 220,000 jobs. More than twenty Fortune 500 companies had decided to open engineering or research and development branches in the city, among them the Silicon Valley giants Facebook, Google, and Apple.

By 2018, per capita income in metropolitan Seattle had grown to nearly $75,000—roughly 25 percent above its peers of a few decades earlier, cities like Milwaukee, Cleveland, and Pittsburgh. And this rising wealth was not being spread evenly: by 2016, a city once known for its strong middle class, its lack of extreme poverty and wealth, had matched San Francisco for high levels of income inequality. The average income for the top 20 percent of Seattle households shot up by more than $40,000 in 2016 alone, hitting $318,000; these households took home 53 percent of all the income in the city.

By 2018, the median cost of buying a home, across all home types, was higher in Seattle than anywhere in the country except the Bay Area: $754,000. The salary needed to afford this median home had risen from $88,000 to $134,000 in only three years. Rent, which had been on par with the national average before 2010, had increased by 57 percent in only five years to more than $2,000 on average, three times higher than in the rest of the country.

One result was that Seattle was now a city where it was increasingly difficult to afford raising a family: the city was also second only to San Francisco in the scarcity of children—less than a fifth of all households had them. Yet its population was swelling nonetheless: by 2015, it was the fastest-growing large city, and a disproportionate share of these new arrivals were young, highly educated, and highly paid. By 2018, there were an estimated fifty software developers moving to the city *every week*.

But such numbers alone could not really convey the extent of the change. They could not capture the dense thicket of cranes rising across downtown—by 2019, there were fifty-eight deployed in Seattle, more than in any other city in the country. Or the ostentation of new money in a city once stereotyped by flannel and grunge: the Teslas prowling Capitol Hill and Belltown; the Black Suburbans circling for ride-share fares; the Gucci store selling slippers for $650; the rooftop bar with a "millionaires menu" that included a $200 martini; the forty-one-story Nexus tower, a stack of twisting glass cubes topped with penthouses that spread across 3,000 square feet and cost up to $5 million; the Insignia towers, which offered a "sky retreat"—indoor lap pool, sauna, and screening room.

The numbers could not capture the cultural change wrought by the arrivals, who frequented the appointment-only wine tasting room at the base of a new luxury residential tower in Bellevue, or the "wizard pub" in the trendy Ballard neighborhood where patrons could get personal wands— "made to fit each individual, with date of birth determining species of wood, then infused with one of 12 magic essences by the wandmaker." The city had few children, but it had many adults with the disposable income needed to reenact childhood.

This hyper-prosperity had many corporate fathers, among them Starbucks, Nordstrom, and Microsoft, which was still thriving across Lake Washington. But one loomed far above them. There were now 45,000 people working at Amazon in Seattle, plus another 8,000 in the suburbs. They earned $150,000 in average compensation, plus valuable stock options that incentivized ardent corporate loyalty. The company accounted for 30 percent of all jobs added in Seattle over the second decade of the century. It occupied a fifth of all the office space in Seattle—the highest proportion of any company in any city in the country, and more than the next forty largest employers in the city combined; Delta and Alaska Airlines added a special check-in line for Amazon's employees at Sea-Tac International Airport.

In 2007, the company announced it would consolidate its offices in a single campus on a swath of land just north of downtown called South Lake Union. Early on, the area had been home to big sawmills. By the 1990s, it was a light-industrial zone of warehouses, car repair lots, and a strip club that advertised 100S OF BEAUTIFUL GIRLS AND 3 UGLY ONES. There were plans in the 1990s to redevelop it with homes and offices around a large park. Paul Allen, the Microsoft cofounder, had started buying up land toward that plan, eventually owning more than sixty acres, but it came to naught.

Instead, Amazon asked Allen to build it a 1.7-million-square-foot headquarters there. He built that, and more. The company grew to more than 8 million square feet in the city, most of it in more than thirty-five buildings in and around South Lake Union—the largest urban corporate campus in the country. It was a grid of mid-rise office cubes—*Tetris*-like blocks of glass, stainless steel, and aluminum panels painted rust-red to mimic industrial-era brick, what Keith Harris, a local engineer and critical theorist, called a "neo-modern high-tech ghetto." To help keep the buildings apart, since many of them looked quite similar, they bore names with insider connotations: Rufus (the Welsh corgi owned by two of the company's earliest employees), Dawson (the street that was home to one of the company's early warehouses), and Fiona (what the Kindle was almost named).

The company allowed employees to bring their dogs to work, and more than 6,000 were registered for that purpose, so the sidewalks were full of dogs being walked by people with Bluetooth earpieces and blue company badges and backpacks adorned with the company's smile logo. In one building, a seventeenth-story terrace with sweeping views had been designated as a dog park, complete with Astroturf and yellow fire hydrants. On the ground floor of another building was a café that cooked food only for dogs.

Inside one main passageway, employees handed out free bananas to anyone who passed by. There were twenty-four coffee shops throughout the campus. There was a store owned by the company where people could purchase things without paying—cameras kept track of selections and charged their credit card. A block from campus, there was a much larger store, part of a nationwide chain of nearly five hundred high-end grocery emporia that was now also owned by the company.

Bars and restaurants sprouted within the campus, catering almost exclusively to company employees. At Brave Horse Tavern, on weekday evenings men in blazers played shuffleboard. One Wednesday in June, a waitress with green hair poured champagne for a fortyish man in a fleece zip-up and his parents, who then all sat and looked silently at their phones for most of an hour. Outside, a dog was tied to a post, waiting.

And there were biospheres. Over five years, the company built three enormous interlocking orbs. They were made of 620 tons of steel and 2,643 panes of glass and stretched half a city block on the edge of the campus closest to downtown. Inside the orbs were several levels linked by open stairways rising to 90 feet. There was a café that sold doughnuts for $4.25 and meeting spaces called "treehouses" and even a human-size bird's nest made of cedar, for more secluded brainstorming, all tucked amid a sort of rain forest that contained some 40,000 plants of four hundred different species from around the world, among them bromeliads and anthuriums from Ecuador and philodendrons from Bolivia and spikemoss from Southeast Asia. There were more than forty trees, including a 50-foot-tall, 36,000-pound weeping fig (nickname Rubi) that had to be lowered in through the opening of a removed glass panel. The orbs could hold as many as 1,000 people at a time.

The company's senior manager of horticultural services told a reporter that the orbs would help employees "find their inner biophiliac that really responds to nature."

On the day that the orbs opened, in early 2018, employees gathered with high anticipation. The company's founder stood in front of a wall sheathed in greenery that was emblazoned with the smile logo. The time had come to turn on the lights and the misters.

"Alexa," he said. "Open the Spheres."

"Okay, Jeff," said Alexa.

This would be the third Seattle that Milo Duke had known, and, for both him and Pat Wright, the last.

2.

Cardboard

Downward mobility in Middle America

DAYTON, OHIO

What Todd and Sara told the kids was, they were at camp. It was a strange camp, to be sure. There was a security guard in the front vestibule whom they had to sign in with before one of the surly, seen-it-all ladies at the front desk waved them in. There were the women lying in the corridor off to the right, whose unruliness had gotten them kicked out of the cots in the dormitories and would've had gotten them kicked out altogether if it weren't fifteen degrees outside. The only thing that was even slightly camp-like was the medication room downstairs where guests' pills were kept. But no camp saw medication bags like this—large Ziplocs bulging with pill containers, the labels worn to illegibility, expiration dates long passed. And no camp counselors dispensed the goods as freely as these attendants did—handing out the bags with little regard to what pills were or were not ingested. There were bigger problems to deal with.

Such as preventing reoccurrences of tragedies like that of a fifteen-week-old baby, Jeremiah, who'd been found dead inside the shelter the year prior. Such as the pregnant woman, tall and blue-eyed Nicole, who was probably using again. Such as all the unfilled volunteer shifts in the kitchen, where a paid staff of six made 1,200 meals every day for this facility's 270 women and children and the 225 men in the former jail on Gettysburg Avenue.

No, the St. Vincent de Paul Gateway Shelter for Women and Families in Dayton, Ohio, was not camp, but Todd and Sara's two older kids, Izacc, age five, and Jazzlynn, age four, had not challenged the claim. Perhaps out of some preternatural sense of discretion, having recognized what a hard time their parents—their mother especially—were having with being where they were. Or perhaps because they had never actually been to a camp of any sort and so would not know the difference. Would not know, for example, that camps did not have day rooms where several dozen people—many of them mentally ill, some in wheelchairs—sat all day watching talk shows and game shows on television with vacant eyes and slack jaws. That camps did not require you to have your belongings searched and body wanded by the security guard every evening before you went up to the dormitory.

On the weekdays, other kids at the shelter lined up outside to get picked up by school buses that had long since made St. Vincent de Paul a part of their routes, but Sara hadn't enrolled Izacc anywhere since arriving a few weeks earlier in early January, an outward sign of her refusal to accept that she and her children would be at Gateway for any length of time. She'd simply marked him as "homeschooled," which meant that instead of school he spent hours with his mother, his sister, and their little brother, Nicholas, eighteen months old, in the family day room, which was free of the hunched-over TV watchers but far from idyllic. There was a TV up on the wall, and some rusted lockers painted fire-engine red on two sides, and a small room inside the day room that, in its scale and with its internal-wall window, could've been an interrogation room in a police station, but here was the "library"—a couple shelves of books and a couple chests of toys and a magnetic board with plastic letters. Izacc could build his name on the board, insisting to the skeptics that he required a *z* and not an *s*, which was in fact the case, just as Jazzlynn was most definitely spelled with two *z*'s: her father,

Todd, was a jazz-dance fanatic, an unlikely enthusiasm in southwestern Ohio and one that he had memorialized in his daughter's name.

Signs in the library forbade taking books or games out of that space. This was one reason why kids in the main room ran so rampant, contributing to an atmosphere of barely controlled chaos, as one might find anywhere people weren't expecting to stay long and so accepted a certain level of din. Except in this case, many were staying for quite some time.

This tolerance of din confounded Sara, who could barely handle it for an hour, much less a week. To try to keep things in check, and keep her own kids from becoming too wired from all the static energy, she ended up minding a lot of the other kids as well, who differed from her own both because their mothers seemed not to mind the disorder and because they were mostly Black. Sara, who was fair-skinned bordering on translucent, insisted that what most bothered her was the former fact—that she was babysitting others' kids, as if her three were not enough to deal with.

She wished she had Todd with her to help out, but Todd was around only occasionally. There were several reasons for this. One was that the shelter's definition of "women and families" was misleading. In fact, men were allowed to stay there only if they were single fathers. A family such as Todd and Sara's was not allowed to stay together at the shelter despite the children, precisely because it included both a mother and father. So Sara and the kids stayed at the family shelter, and Todd stayed at the men's shelter, in the former jail five miles away, where, shortly after he arrived, one guest would be arrested for stabbing another. This division struck Todd and Sara as a corollary of the unfairness they had encountered at social services offices, where they were told that they were getting fewer food stamps and were ineligible for housing and childcare subsidies because Todd was working.

This was also why Todd was rarely at the shelter to help Sara. He had a full-time job, as he'd had for most of his adult life. Which was what made it all the more surreal to him and Sara that they had ended up where they had. This job wasn't paying enough, which was one reason, though most definitely not the only reason, why they had landed at Gateway.

But Todd had a job. He'd had many jobs. At present, he was making cardboard boxes.

Like gentrification in coastal cities, postindustrial decline in the Midwest was too often cast in terms lacking scale and context. Seen from afar, it was a relentless and monolithic deterioration. Seen close up, there were gradations and plateaus. Fatalism fell away, and one could discern the responsibility of specific decisions and political and economic actors.

Life had never been easy for the Swallows family, but it fell totally to pieces late in the presidency of George W. Bush. This was true also for Dayton as a whole. Sure, the city had already slid a long way from the glory years at the previous turn of the century, when Orville and Wilbur Wright were building their Van Cleve and St. Clair bikes and dreaming of making their Flyers, and when their fellow inventors—*innovators*, you'd call them now—were putting out more patents per capita than those in any other city in the country. *The Silicon Valley of its time*, people would say now, leaving *Can you believe it?* unsaid. In the late 1870s, the saloonkeeper James Ritty came up with the mechanical cash register to stop his barkeeps from pilfering dough. John H. Patterson took the innovation national, building National Cash Register with an ingenious pitch: "A National Cash Register is not an expense, because it pays for itself out of the losses it prevents." Patterson was a true eccentric: he wore underwear made of pool-table felt, slept with his head hanging off the bed to spare the risk of breathing the same air he'd exhaled, and ordered his commissary to buy 4,000 pounds of paprika for his workers after noticing in Bulgaria that people there ate a lot of the spice and had good teeth. Yet Patterson all but invented the tools of modern American business: the trained salesman, the sales territory, sales quotas, and even the dread annual convention.

Above all there was engineer Charles Kettering, who turned the cash register electric and went on to contrive so much else: the electrical starting motor, leaded gasoline, Freon, colored paint for cars . . . So wedded to innovation was Kettering that he once took out a $1.6 million life insurance policy and made as its beneficiary "automotive research."

Not even the calamitous 1913 flood of the Great Miami River, which killed more than one hundred, set the city back. Three years later, the poet Paul Laurence Dunbar, son of formerly enslaved Kentuckians, wrote:

> *Love of home, sublimest passion*
> *That the human heart can know!*
> *Changeless still, though fate and fashion*
> *Rise and fall and ebb and flow,*
> *To the glory of our nation,*
> *To the welfare of our state,*
> *Let us all with veneration*
> *Every effort consecrate.*
> *And our city, shall we fail her?*
> *Or desert her gracious cause?*
> *Nay—with loyalty we hail her*
> *And revere her righteous laws.*
> *She shall ever claim our duty,*
> *For she shines—the brightest gem*
> *That has ever decked with beauty*
> *Dear Ohio's diadem.*

Scoff as you will, but there was undeniable grandeur in the place. It was there in the Third National Bank, where patrons did their business at bronze check desks in the lobby finished with imported marble and mahogany woodwork. It was in the Biltmore and Algonquin hotels, whose aspirations were writ in their names and not entirely unjustified. It was in the big department stores, like Elder & Johnston (later Elder-Beerman) and especially Rike's, which rose to nine floors and at one point sold Harleys in its sporting goods department, and which offered free alterations and home deliveries so that housewives could stop by the Maud Muller Tea Room unburdened by their loot.

The city's peak, in terms of numbers, came around 1960, after the surge from the South, which was biracial, comprising not only the Great Migration from Mississippi and Alabama, but the Hillbilly Highway from Kentucky and Tennessee. All from similarly humble backgrounds. All arriving for the same reason, to work for the companies making the things that the innovators had come up with decades earlier, at places like National Cash Register ("The Cash") and Kettering's co-creation, Delco (Dayton Engineering Laboratories Co.).

But of course not all were meeting with the same reaction. By the early 1960s, white flight was already doing its number on Dayton, draining thousands from two-story frame houses with porches built by handy Germans and Poles decades earlier out to modest bungalows whose primary advantage was their distance from West Dayton, where the Alabamians and Mississippians had clustered. They had not clustered there of their own free will, but because it was understood that they ought not settle east of the river, where downtown began, or north of Wolf Creek, home to Dayton's Jewish community. It was understood, too, that their offspring would attend only Dunbar High, which was named for the rapturous poet, long since dead of tuberculosis. For years, these invisible lines held. Once, in the '60s, some kids were scolded by the cops simply for crossing Wolf Creek from the West Side to check out a fire engine that had parked there, a spectacle too overwhelming to resist.

Like so many in other cities across the Midwest, Daytonians fled as the threat of such incursions spread—the working class to Huber Heights and West Carrollton and Miamisburg and Fairborn, the better-off to Centerville and Oakwood and Kettering and Beavercreek. By 1990, the city had lost more than a quarter of its population. Forty percent of those who remained—73,000 of 182,000—were Black. They could now range far from the West Side if they wanted: whole swaths of the city stood vacant for them.

Even as the population declined, a critical mass remained. Unlike long-dying steel towns and coal towns, Dayton was above all an auto town, the second biggest after Detroit, and in the 1990s America was still making cars: big cars, SUVs, and trucks that guzzled the cheap gas of the Clinton years.

There was the General Motors plant in Moraine and the GM-allied auto parts giant Delphi, descendant of Kettering's Delco, with a dozen plants still scattered around the area. There was NCR, by this point making ATMs and bar code scanners in addition to cash registers. There was the air force base on the edge of town, Wright-Patterson, where the Serbs grudgingly signed the Dayton Accords in 1995. There was the proudly local indie band Guided by Voices, riffing Dayton homer-ism to far-flung fans who could not have known what Robert Pollard was evoking when he sang in 1996:

> *Isn't it great to exist at this point in time?*
> *Where the produce is rotten but no one is forgotten*
> *On strawberry Philadelphia Drive*
> *Children in the sprinkler, junkies on the corner*
> *The smell of fried foods and pure hot tar*
> *Man, you needn't travel far to feel completely alive*
> *On strawberry Philadelphia Drive*
> *On a hazy day in 19 something and 5*

In that 19 something and 5, Todd Swallows was five, and his family was living at Lake Lakengren, thirty miles west of Dayton, near the Indiana border. As an adult, Todd would marvel that he had grown up in a "gated community," even if it didn't conform to the usual connotation. Lakengren, a planned development around a two-mile-long man-made lake, did in fact have a couple entry gates, but the Swallows' home was no McMansion. It was a simple 1977 yellow-brick rambler bought for less than $90,000. Still, a gated community was a gated community, and it was hard to begrudge Todd the claim: he was staking it not for bragging rights but to underscore the extent of his fall.

Life at Lakengren was far from perfect. Todd's mother had a temper and was not reluctant to resort to corporal punishment when it came to a son who was precociously bright, doing puzzles meant for much older kids, but also hyperactive. "My dad was gone on the road a lot and my mom had to deal with a lot. I was acting up," Todd said. "Some of the punishment was over the top. I don't hold it against her." But life was at least economically stable. Todd's father, Todd, Sr., had established himself as the owner of a small transport company with ten trucks, a cog in the great Dayton auto-industry machine: delivering all those parts from Delco and other suppliers up I-75 to Toledo and Detroit and Flint. Swallows Trucking LLC was an embodiment of supply-chain prosperity: manufacturers in smaller cities and towns would feed into, and depend on, the success of larger companies and cities, creating a dense network of symbiotic connections across entire regions.

Over the course of the aughts, that machine and network broke down, gradually but remorselessly. The natural inclination at the time was to blame it on NAFTA and the Mexicans, and there was no doubt that a lot of parts production and assembly was shifting the wrong way down I-75, to Monterrey, Celaya, and Aguascalientes. Eventually economists would finger a different primary culprit, the admission of China to the World Trade Organization in 2001, after which manufacturing job loss accelerated and hit especially hard in places like Dayton. The MIT economist David Autor concluded with his colleagues in a 2016 paper that competition from China eliminated nearly one million American manufacturing jobs from 1999 to 2011, and a total of 2.4 million jobs if you counted the suppliers and other related industries. "Trade adjustment is a slow-moving process, and . . . its costs fall heavily on trade-exposed local markets rather than being dispersed nationally," Autor and his colleagues wrote. In other words: if it felt in places like Dayton as if people in Washington and New York didn't care what was happening to them, there was a reason for that.

These academic assessments would come later. At the time, all anyone in Dayton knew was that the machine was shutting down. The Delphi auto parts plants were closing, one by one—over the decade, the company's local workforce would plunge from 10,000 to 800. On October 3, 2008, came the biggest blow of all, GM's announcement that it was closing its massive plant in Moraine, on the southern edge of Dayton, where, despite earlier shift reductions, some 2,400 people had still been making SUVs.

It wasn't just auto jobs either. NCR, the city's last Fortune 500 company, with roots reaching all the way back to James Ritty's saloon, was sending bad signals. The company's new CEO, Bill Nuti, would not deign to move to Dayton from New York, citing "family issues," which locals understood to be nothing more than his wife's revulsion at having to live in Dayton, Ohio. All told, from 2001 to 2008, the metro area spanning Dayton and Springfield, the smaller city to the northeast, had lost 32,000 jobs—7.5 percent of its labor force. And virtually all of those jobs—27,000 of them—were in manufacturing. Fully one of three local jobs in that sector vanished in less than a single presidency. Statewide, so many manufacturing plants would close over the decade that Ohio's industrial electricity consumption would fall by more than a quarter.

Like that, Swallows Trucking LLC lost its customers. The end came with efficient swiftness: on March 2, 2009, six weeks into the presidency of Barack Obama, a stretch in which the country was losing 700,000 jobs per month, Todd Swallows, Sr., filed for bankruptcy in federal court for the Southern District of Ohio. Todd's grandfather lost part of his GM pension, which would force his grandmother to work as a home health aide into her seventies.

Three months later, NCR announced it was moving its headquarters to suburban Atlanta, taking its remaining 1,200 jobs in Dayton with it. "We had a very difficult time recruiting people to live and work in Dayton," Nuti said, in case his own refusal to move to the city had left any doubt in the matter. Over the course of the decade, Dayton would lose 25,000 residents, bringing its population down to 141,000, barely half its peak. Over the same period, the city and the rest of Montgomery County would suffer the steepest drop in total payroll earnings of any large county in Ohio—about $3 billion lost.

Todd Swallows, Sr., had already been in court for another proceeding: to finalize his divorce from his wife. Todd, Jr., would later attribute their split to the collapse of Swallows Trucking LLC, though it was also true that the divorce had in turn accelerated that collapse, in that the settlement had cost Todd's father a considerable sum.

His father moved into a trailer park in Brookville, closer to Dayton. His mother, who by now was working as a computer repair technician, moved to Eaton, the town near Lakengren where Todd attended high school.

Todd was still a teenager. "For three years I was back and forth between my mother and my father and I couldn't stand living like that," he said. "Always, always being back and forth, seeing my dad struggle and then turn around and see my mom struggle because they were no longer a team." He headed out on his own, in a place that was hitting bottom.

Once, city boosters showcased Dayton as a hub of innovation. *Dayton: Birthplace of Aviation, Starting Place for the Electric Starter.* Now they talked about how close it was to other places that made things. The local airport had lost many of its flights in recent years, but the city was still at the juncture of two interstates, I-70 and I-75, and within a day's drive of more than a third of the country's population, a claim few other cities with more than 100,000 people could make. *Dayton: Least Far from the Places You Actually Want to Be!* The city that had been an earlier time's Silicon Valley would remake itself as a center of the "logistics industry": trucking, packaging, and sorting everything from Procter & Gamble household goods to Chewy mail-order dog food. The Dayton Area Chamber of Commerce created the Dayton Area Logistics Association. Dayton would eventually even start hosting an event called the Southwest Ohio Logistics Conference. And this makeover, from manufacturing hub to packaging and transportation hub, required cardboard.

The cardboard makers didn't like you calling it "cardboard." It was "corrugated." Cardboard was any damn thing made from heavy paper-pulp—technically, playing cards and greeting cards were cardboard. Corrugated, on the other hand, was serious stuff. Corrugated was made of three sheets of container board—two flat liners on the outside and the rippled one sandwiched in between, held together with a starchy glue. Corrugated was strong, which also meant that it could be printed on. This made it ideal for product displays and for shipping. And in post–Great Recession Dayton, there would be a lot of shipping.

It would take Todd Swallows, Jr., several years to figure this out, several years to make his way to cardboard.

He had started working in his early teens, detailing his father's trucks. At fifteen, he had gotten a job at Wendy's. He dropped out of high school at seventeen, after a fight in his junior year had landed the other kid in the hospital and landed Todd in front of a judge who was on the verge of trying him as an adult for felony assault. He avoided this fate by joining Job Corps, the federal program for wayward sixteen-to-twenty-four-year-olds. He was assigned to the Earle C. Clements Job Corps Center in Morganfield, Kentucky, a town of 3,000 across the Ohio River from Evansville, Indiana. "Jail without bars" was how he later described it: you were stuck there at the center with nowhere else to go. If you were on good behavior, you got bused to Walmart once a week and maybe the movies. He got his GED and tried to get into their computer programming cohort, but there was no room, so he signed up for "pre-military" instead and got a job working in facilities maintenance on-site.

The plan was to join the army after his one-year contract was up. Instead, he said later, filial concern for his father in his post-bankruptcy nadir drew him back to Ohio. "My dad's my hero, you know? I've always looked up to him. I'm his only son. Everything he'd done was for me and my sister," he said. "And I've seen the depression that it causes him and know it tears down motivation in him and then that turns and weighs on me, you know?"

He worked for a while making tube fittings at Parker, one of the few manufacturers left in Eaton, a convenient couple blocks from his mother's house, where he was staying. But then he and a friend started dabbling in the pain pills that pharmaceutical manufacturers had begun pushing earlier in the decade. Nothing too serious, the pills, but enough to get him ejected from his mom's house when she caught them with the stuff one day.

He made his way to Columbus, moving in with his sister and getting a job at Donatos Pizza. After six months, he was named crew leader, which put him in charge of eight people, most of them older than his own nineteen years, a status he still took pride in years later. "It was neat having people come to me and ask me for information," he said.

It was the first and far from the last time that Todd Swallows would find satisfaction in work that many others would find beneath them, work that didn't take advantage of his native intelligence. Somehow, through the collapse of the middle-class idyll at Lakengren, he had absorbed the ethic that work was the thing, that there was redemption in it. All around him, the rate of men of working age not gainfully employed was rising to unprecedented levels, but that would not be him. "I've never seen my father or mother go a day without work. I've never—growing up, my parents struggled and struggled so me and my sister didn't have to live that life," he said. "And then, when I became an adult everything was a hundred times worse than what it was for them growing up and working." It was an ethic he would hold to more closely as the years went on—as the need for redemption grew.

He found a job for the son of his father's new wife at a Subway, and they'd swap meals for the workers so that the Donatos people got a break from pizza and the Subway people got a break from subs. They moved in together. But the stepbrother lost his job and they ended up back with his father, at the trailer park.

Todd met a girl who lived in Middletown, between Dayton and Cincinnati, so he moved in with her and tried out college, at the Miami University of Ohio branch in town. He passed his prereqs, but he lost interest after the first semester—too into the girl, less into the classes. He got part-time jobs at Captain D's Seafood Kitchen and Domino's Pizza, opening up at the former and closing at the latter. He and the girl split up—"our lives were leading in different directions"—and he got his first apartment of his own, at the Williamsburg Place apartments in Middletown.

This was when he met Sara Landers. She was a pretty blonde, the same age as him, also living in Williamsburg Place, also the product of a broken family. In fact, Todd's path to this point looked smooth beside hers. Her family, too, had once been economically stable. Her father had worked in construction, her mother at the large AK Steel plant in Middletown. But her father had moved out when Sara was eight, moved all the way up to Canada and started a new family, which, years later, remained for Sara the formative event of her life, the event that would guide the decisions that so many others would second-guess. And when she was eleven, her mother had gotten hurt badly on the job—she had her arm in a machine, cleaning it, when someone else had started it up. She left the job and eventually went on disability.

Sara's mother got a new long-term boyfriend, who was addicted to heroin. She herself liked to party, and often left Sara and her younger sister with babysitters. When Sara was eleven or twelve, her mother left Sara with a neighbor, and the neighbor's husband raped her.

This brought Sara's father back for a visit, but then he was gone, back to Canada. It would be another decade until he would return to Ohio, and to her life. Sara fell into a depression after the assault, so much so that doctors prescribed her all sorts of medication. She did not like the medication. She preferred alcohol, which she used heavily through her teens.

Sara had three kids with another man, a Mexican immigrant whose status had been normalized partly through his relationship with her. He had a well-paying landscaping job, but in his treatment of her, he compared poorly to Todd, who was sweet, both toward her and the three small kids that were not his own. "He stepped in," Sara said.

Todd moved in with her. He got a job selling Kirby vacuum cleaners door-to-door, seeking out elderly customers who were susceptible to buying what he guessed was a $400 vacuum for $1,200 from a young man in a suit and tie offering a free carpet-shampoo demonstration as extra inducement. On rare occasions when someone bit, the distributor got his cut off the top, the guy who drove the van to drop off Todd and the other salesmen got his cut, and Todd would get the last $200, and that was his pay. "That was a tough one," he said.

Not long after they got together, Sara became pregnant. They broke up, thanks in part to Sara's mother's low opinion of the father of her expected grandchild—"I was devastated by what she had said," Todd said later—and also to Todd's doubt about whether he, and not the ex, *was* the father, based on Sara's calendar estimate from the clinic.

It was an ugly breakup, and he decided to get as far away as he could: to San Angelo, Texas, where a friend lived. He stayed there for sixteen months, starting in late 2011, working as a grocery cashier at a Lowes Market and then adding a second job, driving a forklift at a PAK frozen food warehouse. They were the best jobs he'd had to that point—"I really felt like I had finally found my thing," he said, once again finding meaning in his focused physical labor. But early in 2013, the DNA results came back showing that the clinic's calendar estimate had been off: Todd was indeed father of Izacc, who by that time was a year old.

Sara had by this point lost her three other kids to their father. The pregnancy had been brutal—she had developed hyperemesis gravidarum, a fancy term for constant vomiting during pregnancy, as well as gestational diabetes, and had been placed on bed rest—and as a result lost her jobs at a nursing home and McDonald's, her car, and her home. In such a state, she eventually acceded to the demands of her children's father that they would be better off with him and his family, though custody would remain theoretically shared.

She unblocked Todd on Facebook. He called her. The first thing she said was, "So, when are you coming home?"

Todd returned to Ohio, got back together with Sara, and met his son. His notion of himself as a diligent laborer now expanded into an even more traditionalist aspiration: he would be a breadwinner of the sort his father had been in that halcyon past at Lakengren. "My father raised me to always provide," he said. "I created a family; I provide for a family." But this family would not be centered around marriage—Todd and Sara would skirt that institution, as so many other members of the white working class had begun to do, as the rate of adults under age forty-four who had ever been married dropped 10 points in just a decade, to only half. And there was no more Lakengren in his life, nor Swallows Trucking LLC, at which Todd might by now have been a driver or dispatcher or manager. *Swallows & Son . . .*

Instead, Todd got a job at a welding shop in Dayton that made parts for Tesla. It was his closest brush with the Dayton glory days, even if he was merely a temp making $11.85 an hour. When that contract was up, he went to work part-time in the garden center at Home Depot, where his dad was also working while going back to school. This was not going to support Todd and Sara's family, which by this time included Jazzlynn, so Todd started thinking about going back to school himself.

In 2014, he enrolled at Sinclair Community College, in Dayton, in the EMT training program. He got a few courses under his belt, but not enough for certification. How was he supposed to go to class and still get enough hours of work to support the family when Sara herself couldn't work because she couldn't qualify for any subsidized childcare because she was living with a man who was working? College petered out halfway through 2015, by which point Todd was at a new job, making less than $10 per hour as a night shift manager at the Advance Auto Parts back in Eaton, west of Dayton, near Lake Lakengren.

It was the summer of 2015. Todd had, over the course of the Obama presidency, worked the following jobs:

Facilities maintenance at the Earle C. Clements Job Corps Center
Parker tube fittings in Eaton
Donatos Pizza in Columbus
Captain D's in Middletown
Domino's in Middletown
Kirby vacuum cleaners in Middletown
Lowes grocery in San Angelo
PAK frozen food warehouse in San Angelo
Select-Arc welding in Dayton
Home Depot in Middletown
Advance Auto Parts in Eaton

And Sara was about to have another baby—they weren't sure how that had happened, since she had gotten the birth control shot, but there it was.

Dayton had not even had a homeless shelter until the mid-1980s, when it opened one in a firehouse that held only twenty-five people. In 2005, St. Vincent de Paul opened Gateway, on Apple Street south of downtown.

Fulfillment

The large building it moved into had once served as storage for the Elder-Beerman department stores, housing all the dresses and suits until they went out on display at the flagship store on Courthouse Square. That location closed in 2002, a decisive blow for a downtown where empty sidewalks and vacant storefronts now made a mockery of the broad streets and terra-cotta facades.

By 2018, the former storehouse on Apple held 212 cots, the kitchen, and the day rooms. And still some clothes, too: in a garage space at ground level, volunteers sorted donations. The building's residents got first crack at them—whatever they wanted, they could have. Everything else went for sale in the thrift store appended to the building.

The men's shelter, way out on Gettysburg Avenue, had opened in 2007, in the building that had served as a jail and was still surrounded by correctional facilities, a state prison for women on one side and a jail for men nearing release on the other. This repurposing was cause for chagrin among the St. Vincent de Paul staff who administered both shelters. But they had to get by with a budget of $2.5 million to house around five hundred people per day, and the jail had been there for the taking. As inconvenient as the location was for homeless men downtown—it was a thirty-minute bus ride out—it could not have been more convenient for the men leaving the pre-release jail, who were sometimes known to walk down the driveway from the jail and into the ex-jail that was now a shelter bracketed by barbed wire.

Todd had never been part of this Gettysburg Avenue jail-to-shelter circuit. But there had been scrapes with the law, which, depending on how you looked at it, either came with the territory or suggested something more particular about his nature.

When he was eighteen, Todd was charged with theft for stealing a woman's wallet out of her purse—what he later described as a panicky, spontaneous attempt to help out his bankrupt dad. A year later, when Todd was smoking a lot of pot, he and some friends went into Walmart with a case of the munchies. He paid for his food but forgot to pay for the Nesquik he'd opened before he got to the register. They hit him with petty theft and a $190 fine.

Not long afterward, when he was living in Columbus, he was driving home in the passenger seat from a party for the Ohio State–Michigan game. The cops pulled the car over and booked the driver for DUI. As Todd was walking home, he was tackled from behind by one of the cops, who assumed the bag of powder they found under the passenger seat was his. It turned out the drugs—which he swore weren't his—were counterfeit. So that was on his record, too: a guilty plea for "possession of fake drugs," which came with a $150 fine.

And there was the disorderly conduct charge in May 2013, when, to hear Todd tell it, Sara had been pregnant with Jazzlynn and Todd, overcome with passion, had turned to her inside their Mercury at a Wendy's drive-thru and given her a head-gripped-hard kiss, which a witness had misinterpreted as something more like a chokehold. "Mr. Swallows explained that he and [Sara] are always playing around, and that he did place his hands around her neck, although his hands were never locked," the police report stated. "Ofc. Isaacs spoke with Ms. Landers who stated that she and Mr. Swallows were only playing around and that he would never hurt her." Todd was placed under arrest; Sara was provided a domestic violence information sheet.

Donald Trump came to Dayton—or, more precisely, to the airport north of town in Vandalia, where one of the shuttered Delphi plants was located—on March 12, 2016, the Saturday before the state's primary election. It was the day after his rally in Chicago had been canceled amid massive protests, and the friction from that standoff seemed to carry east to the flat, empty terrain around the airport. The access roads were jammed hours before his arrival and the protesters were out early, too. NO HATE IN MY STATE read one sign. TRUMP MAKE DAYTON GREAT AGAIN: PLEASE LEAVE. And WILL TRADE TRUMP FOR 100 REFUGEES.

Inside the airplane hangar, the mood was festive. The candidate's alpha-male soundtrack played on an endless loop (Stones, Billy Joel, Pavarotti). There were husbands in golf caps with well-manicured wives. There were frat boys. Most noticeable were the many fathers with their grown or near-grown sons.

One moment the plane wasn't there, then it was. The crowd surged forward, as on the first drumbeat in a rock show. Trump made his way to the podium at the edge of the hangar.

"Ohio," he said. "I love Ohio."

A few minutes later, he seemed to forget where he was—"NAFTA has destroyed New England," he said—but the crowd didn't seem to care. "You have fought for years and years and have never recovered completely from it, but you will if I get elected. NAFTA, in my opinion, anyone who puts his hand up for NAFTA—Clinton signed the bill—but NAFTA wiped out states. It wiped out entire states. It wiped out New England. It's taken years and years, you look at those factories, and they've made them into senior citizen housing. That's all wonderful, but we need jobs. We need jobs, folks. We don't have our jobs anymore. Our jobs are going to China, to Japan, to Mexico. Our jobs are going to Vietnam. We're losing our jobs, we're losing our base, we're losing our manufacturing, we're losing everything. We're losing at every single item, no matter what."

Dayton and its surroundings had once been a bulwark of Republican sobriety. Bill McCulloch, a country lawyer turned Republican congressman from a small town north of the city, had led the push for the Civil Rights Act in the House. Chuck Whalen, Dayton's congressman for a dozen years, was a Republican who had authored Ohio's fair-housing law in the state legislature, written a book on the passage of the Civil Rights Act, and vocally opposed the Vietnam War.

But McCulloch and Whalen were long gone. Suburban flight had created a new political terrain in greater Dayton. The exurbs were dominated by ideological conservatives, the offspring of Newt Gingrich, Jerry Falwell, and Grover Norquist. The shrunken city was dominated by Black people and white urban professionals who, removed as they were from each other, could find common cause in the liberalism ascendant in the national Democratic Party: pro–civil rights, pro-refugee, pro–safety net. In between, in the declining working-class inner suburbs and declining nearby towns like

Eaton and Middletown, were those left homeless by this sorting out, former Democrats and descendants of Democrats who felt as alienated from the liberal coalition in Dayton as from the McMansion conservatives on the periphery.

Now these voters had found their home. On March 15, Trump lost the Ohio primary to the state's governor, John Kasich. But he did better in Dayton's Montgomery County than in any of the state's other nine largest counties, racking up big numbers in the most depressed precincts and winning more votes in the county than Hillary Clinton had received in winning her own primary—remarkable given that the county had not gone Republican since 1988.

On September 13, 2016, Todd and Sara and the kids celebrated his twenty-sixth birthday. The next day, Todd and Sara got to arguing in the duplex they were renting on Main Street in Eaton, when Todd caught her texting with another man. "My boyfriend and I were arguing and he grabbed me by my hoody and choked me and then grabbed me by my ponytail and threw me down on the floor," she wrote in her statement to the police. She told the police that she had gotten in a few defensive punches. She had a small gash on her knee. She added: "He wanted us to leave. We argue over nothing."

The police found Todd at Walmart, placed him under arrest, and took him to the Preble County jail. On court forms, he listed his assets:

Checking, savings, money market accounts: 0
Stocks, bonds, CDs: 0
Other liquid assets or cash on hand: 0

He stated his income: $9.93 per hour at Advance Auto Parts. Also, he noted, he received Medicaid and food stamps. He listed his and Sara's expenses: $550 rent, $600 food, $70 phone, $180 transportation and fuel, $25 utilities.

Todd spent two weeks in jail. His charge was reduced from domestic violence to disorderly conduct. But the judge placed him under a temporary protection order, barring contact with Sara for ninety days. He also charged Todd $190 in court costs, payable by $25 per month. Complicating compliance was the fact that by the time Todd got out of jail, his job at Advance Auto Parts was gone.

It was a classic example of a conundrum around domestic violence. The data showed that domestic violence was far more prevalent in lower-income households. Abusers needed to be held to account, yet jail time, the primary recourse, often resulted in job loss and the heightening of the economic strains that had in some cases helped give rise to abusive behavior in the first place. "Relying primarily on arrest and prosecution exacerbates conditions associated with intimate partner violence, which strongly correlates with poverty," wrote Leigh Goodmark, a University of Maryland law professor. "Low-income women are more likely to be victims; under- and unemployed men are much more likely to be batterers. Having a conviction makes it much more difficult to find and keep employment." She noted another common feature of domestic abusers that also described Todd: a history of corporal punishment as a child. "Trauma also contributes," she wrote. "Childhood experiences like abuse, neglect or witnessing violence suggest whether a person will bring violence into his or her home." It was no surprise, she concluded, that jail time often did not have the desired effect. "Incarceration is traumatic," she wrote. "We punish people for violence by putting them in places where they are likely to witness or experience violence, and then send them back into their communities and relationships."

The job was gone, but Todd was out in time for something else: the 2016 election. He had voted twice for Barack Obama. But he was receptive to what he was hearing from Donald Trump. Spending a decade at a string of jobs that paid no more than $11 per hour made one susceptible to a promise of prosperity delivered by a man with a private jet. "He is a businessman," Todd said later. "This man can run his businesses and he's worth billions of dollars and runs hundreds of businesses, he runs them and owns them and I thought to myself, 'This man will change the country.'"

Todd voted for Trump, who won Ohio by eight percentage points four years after Barack Obama had won it by two. "I couldn't *wait* to vote for Trump," Todd said. He quoted his own thinking at the time as if it was that of another person: "He's gonna bring in jobs. He's gonna raise the economy back to the way it was when my parents were working."

D onald Trump became president, and Todd Swallows got his job in cardboard.

Lewisburg Container was in the small town of that name, half an hour west of Dayton, a dozen miles from Eaton. The company was a subsidiary of Pratt Industries, a global paper and packaging company owned by an Australian billionaire, with 4,000 workers in the United States. There was a Pratt plant right next to Lewisburg Container: corrugated sheets were made at Pratt, with pulp straight from the mill, and then converted into boxes at Lewisburg Container.

Todd liked working corrugated. He liked being alone with the task before him, proving his capability to himself, over and over, on his own. A pallet piled with corrugated sheets was set in front of the big machine. The sheets ranged from one foot to seven feet wide. You'd then program the machine for whatever task was needed for that particular sheet: printing, creasing, folding, gluing. After you fed the sheet into the hopper, it would be held down by air suction, bolts would fold it, rollers would crease it, and the squeeze press would glue it. Then you'd off-load it from the machine and stack it up with others nice and neat and send them through a bander and make sure they were banded right. Then the new order would come and you'd reset the machine and adjust the belts to make sure the folds were made correctly. If you didn't set the machine right, the product didn't come out right, and there were a lot of ways it could come out wrong.

It was hard labor, harder than what Todd had seen in shops like the one he'd worked at making parts for Tesla. "If you walked in, it might overwhelm an average person," he said, with not a little bravado. They averaged between

6,000 and 10,000 boxes per hour. Once, they worked a 100,000-piece Duracell order that took them a couple days.

Todd started out as the float: he worked six machines, moving from one to another to relieve others who were taking breaks. He started out at $12 per hour, the most he'd ever made. And his life was falling apart, more than ever.

He and Sara were still together, sort of, as the ninety-day temporary protection order ran its course. But in late January, a few weeks into the job, he discovered that she had removed him as a family member from her benefits with Job & Family Services. He got off of an overnight shift before daybreak and drank some beers after he got back to Eaton.

Sara described what happened next in her written statement to the police: "This morning around 7:30 AM, Todd came in the house drunk screaming and yelling waking me up out of my sleep. The argument escalated to where he choked me and punched me twice in the jaw with Nicholas in my arms."

The police couldn't find Todd. Three days later, the court issued a new protection order barring any contact between Todd and his family. That evening, Sara came home to find the apartment ransacked—some pillows and her bras were cut. Soon afterward, Todd came to the police station and told them he had entered the house before learning of the new protection order. He was placed under arrest anyway for having violated it.

A week later, he filled out the same form as he had four months earlier. His assets were still zero. His take-home pay at Lewisburg Container was $1,800 per month. As before, he listed the members of his family: Sara, Izacc, Jazzlynn, Nicholas—laying claim to the exact four people he was now barred from seeing.

He pleaded not guilty and resumed work at Lewisburg Container. He was looking forward to his four-month mark there, when he would be hired on as a permanent employee rather than just a contractor from the temp firm. He would be a full-fledged operator's assistant, doing more of the machine setup than the manual labor. He would get a raise to $14 per hour. He would have more money to give to Sara for her and the kids, to build the case with both her and the court for their eventual reunification.

He had already received the paperwork for this transition when, once again, he screwed up. One Monday, he got so fed up with a younger guy who was slacking off, whining about everything, that he lashed out at him: "So stop being such a bitch," he said to him. Pronounced *be-atch*. The younger man promptly reported Todd to the HR director, who called him in and told him he would be suspended. But that took a couple days to be resolved, given that he was in limbo between the temp firm and the company.

While in that limbo, at daybreak later that week, he was driving to Eaton after a twelve-hour overnight—the regular ten plus two he volunteered for—when a deer jumped out of a ditch. He thought of what his dad had always told him: speed up to reduce the odds of the deer crashing through. He pushed down on the pedal. The impact killed the deer. It broke Todd's foot, weakened by a previous injury, in three places. And it totaled his car, an uninsured black 1993 Crown Victoria.

The first half of 2017 was also nightmarish for Dayton. Montgomery County had for several years been at the forefront of the opioid epidemic, a status the experts attributed to some unhappy confluence of the county's location at a major highway juncture (being a logistics hub also meant being a trafficking hub) and the depth of the economic collapse in the area (laid-off manufacturing workers not only were depressed but had legitimate injuries that had helped gain them the painkiller prescriptions that pharmaceutical manufacturers had marketed very heavily across southern Ohio).

But in the winter and spring of 2017, as the share of fentanyl and even more potent carfentanil in the local supply vaulted upward, Dayton was spiraling as never before. From January through May, 365 people died of drug overdoses in the county, nearly as many as had died of such causes for all of 2016. The coroner, whose staff performed autopsies for other counties as well, was so worried about running out of room for corpses that he made contingency plans: asking funeral homes if they could take extra bodies, bringing in the refrigerated trucks held in reserve for "mass casualty events."

Without his car, Todd had no way of getting to Lewisburg Container, where he was already in a precarious state with the imminent suspension. He lost his cardboard job. And he was prescribed Percocet for the pain in his foot.

Since his early dabbling in pills, he had generally resisted the siren call of opiates that was growing ever louder in southwestern Ohio—weed and beer had mostly done the trick for him. But as weeks went on, he found that he needed a couple more pills than the two or three he was supposed to be taking daily. "I noticed the longer I was on it, the more I needed it," he said later. "I kept feeling the need to be high and relieve some ghost pain that was no longer there." And when the ninety-day prescription was up, the withdrawal was brutal. He was beleaguered, couldn't eat, had night sweats. He compensated with pot and with pills he'd get from others. "I was in a dark place," he said later. "I gave up on myself for a while."

He kept requesting delays of his court hearing on the charges from January and the protection order. He had found another apartment in Eaton for Sara and the kids after they'd been ejected from the other one for missing rent after he'd lost the cardboard job. In early August, he and Sara were back together briefly there when they got in another fight. She bit him, hard. He didn't call the cops, but when he was walking down the street to his mom's place, where he was staying, cops saw the blood on his arm, asked him about it, and, as their later write-up of the incident reflected, went to the house to arrest Sara, who spent a night in jail for misdemeanor assault.

She left Eaton with the kids and moved in with her mom and her mom's boyfriend, in Middletown. Todd moved into the apartment they'd vacated but was promptly rousted from it by a cop who said his being there violated the protection order, even if Sara wasn't there anymore. Shortly afterward, the police charged Todd with violating the order by having placed two calls and a text to Sara. After this arrest, Todd again listed his assets as zero. With the Lewisburg Container job gone, his income was now also zero. And, in the line for his address, he wrote, "No home address due to CPO [civil protection order]."

After he got out of jail this time, as if to guarantee that he'd honor the order, Todd started spending time with another woman. He split his time between her place and his dad's mobile home. He worked at a pizza place in Brookville.

By the second half of 2017, things started to brighten somewhat in Dayton. Loft apartments and brewpubs were sprouting downtown—for all the city's struggles, its former grandeur still offered a draw that the state's many smaller postindustrial cities lacked. The death rate was receding, a little. Rumor was, the dealers were easing up on the fentanyl ratio, realizing they were killing off their customers. There was hiring going on again at the former GM plant in Moraine, south of the city, which had been taken over by Fuyao, a Chinese auto-glass manufacturer. Hourly wages started at $13, a fraction of what GM had been paying, and federal inspectors reported rampant safety violations, and the owners fiercely resisted unionization efforts, but it was at least something.

And there were rumblings of another big new employer coming into southwest Ohio. It was inevitable, given how dominant the logistics industry had gotten in the Dayton area, all that packing and sorting and transporting, that the company that depended on those tasks more than any other would make its way there, too. When Amazon had debuted its Prime service in 2005—free two-day shipping for $79 per year—it had fewer than ten warehouses scattered around the country. By 2017, it was up to more than a hundred warehouses nationwide. It needed more capacity because it was now handling about 40 percent of all e-commerce sales in the country, which was double its next nine rivals *combined*. And it needed to disperse its centers across the country to honor its promise of two-day delivery to the more than 80 million Americans who paid for Prime membership, a figure that nearly equaled the number of Americans who voted in the 2014 midterm elections.

For years, Amazon had steered clear of Ohio, refraining from building any warehouses there to avoid having to assess sales tax on the considerable volume of purchases generated by the seventh most populous state in the union. Eventually, the calculus changed, as it did in other states that it had stayed away from. It had built its enormous customer base in those states due in part to the competitive advantage it held over traditional merchants that had to assess sales tax. Now that customer base had grown so large that it made sense to enter the states and build warehouses there, in order to fulfill the promise of two-day delivery. This would mean having to assess sales tax, but only on some of its sales—in all but a couple states, the company was still not bothering to assess sales tax on the half of its sales that came from third-party sellers, costing states hundreds of millions in revenue.

Making the move into Ohio even more appealing was the prospect of being offered a significant inducement. It took some audacity for a company to request tax credits from a state after having depleted its treasury with an e-commerce business that was designed to skirt the sales tax, but audacity was not in short supply at Amazon. In 2015, the company made its pitch for its first two warehouses in the state, near the I-270 beltway around Columbus, to the Ohio Development Services Agency and JobsOhio, the private nonprofit created by Governor John Kasich in 2011 to offer job creation incentives, which, by one tally, was soon handing out $3 billion per year in subsidies. Amazon had the right man to make the pitch: Tony Boetto, who had worked for the state as a "senior tax incentives specialist" a decade earlier.

The Ohio Development Services Agency was the successor to a larger state agency that had for years overseen economic development, but it now consisted of only a few people. The real action was in the office tower next door, which was home to JobsOhio, where several dozen people negotiated tax incentive deals without the inconvenient transparency that came with being an actual government agency. Every month, a board called the Ohio Tax Credit Authority approved the incentives negotiated by JobsOhio. The meetings, held two floors up from the agency office, were theoretically public but functionally secret. Agendas were released on Friday afternoons before the Monday meetings. Visitors had to pass through two security checks to get upstairs. On one occasion, the attendant at the agency's desk didn't even know where the meetings were held when asked by a first-time visitor.

Not that there was any reason why a citizen would have felt inclined to attend the meetings, which were as scripted and inscrutable as the gatherings of an obscure fraternal organization. The five board members, who were appointed by the governor and legislature, sat at a table in the front of the room. Staff members of JobsOhio and representatives of companies seeking tax credits sat in chairs facing the board. A collegial buzz filled the room—it seemed as if everyone knew everyone, which most everyone did. When the board chair called the meeting to order, company representatives and JobsOhio staffers took turns offering summaries of each incentive being sought. Each pitch followed the same formula: the promise of x number of jobs to be created or retained by the business, followed by the threat that the company was also considering states y and z, and needed the tax credits to commit to Ohio. This was followed by a few perfunctory questions from the board, and a vote. The vote was almost always unanimously in favor—over one four-year stretch, the board had approved more than seven hundred subsidies without a single "no" vote by any one of its members. The meetings were often done within a half hour.

And so it had gone for Amazon on July 27, 2015. The company promised to create 2,000 full-time jobs with a payroll of $60 million at the new warehouses. A JobsOhio employee told the board that Ohio was "competing with multiple Midwest states for both fulfillment centers." If the state wanted Amazon to commit to the state it had avoided for years, it would need to offer a fifteen-year tax credit worth $17 million. This would be in addition to a $1.5 million cash grant from the state liquor-monopoly profits controlled by JobsOhio.

The board approved the credit 4–0. Abstaining was Emmett Kelly, who worked for a doubly conflicted law firm, Frost Brown Todd. One of its attorneys served as law director or assistant law director for several towns seeking Amazon investment; other Frost Brown lawyers represented Amazon on employment law—that is, fending off unions.

The disingenuousness of the company's alleged uncertainty about the site of the warehouses was underscored by the speed with which things moved along once the board approved the credit. In early December of 2015, Amazon's Boetto sent agency and JobsOhio staffers an email seeking confirmation on the details of the agreement for the warehouses. It was all but finalized by year's end.

"Enjoy the holidays!" wrote Eric Lindner, a counsel with the Ohio Development Services Agency.

"Hope you all have a wonderful holiday season," responded Boetto, "and we look forward to working with you in 2016 and beyond."

In late 2016, one of the young JobsOhio staffers who had handled the Amazon application, Ryan Wilson, went to work for Amazon, on the exact opposite side of the table: seeking state tax credits from state agencies like the one he had just left.

The next year, the company trained its sights on the Dayton area. It was official: the city that had led the way in innovation would now lead the way in distribution for the innovator based two thousand miles away.

The company picked a site half an hour south of the city, just off Interstate 75 on the way to Cincinnati, a swath of farmland near an outlet mall, casino, and county jail that had been turned into a sprawling logistics park. By 2017, it was home to warehouses for Home Depot, Hayneedle, and Serta, among others. It was exactly what Amazon needed, and where it needed it: between two of the state's six biggest cities, on one of the country's biggest freight highways. I-75, where Swallows Trucking had once carried auto parts made locally, would now carry yet more goods made on the other side of the world to be packaged and sorted locally.

Yet the company would again manage to play the reluctant target rather than the suitor. This time, it sought incentives from both the state and the local community, Monroe. It insisted on total secrecy, to keep the negotiations from attracting public scrutiny until after the deal was done—local officials referred to the plans only as Project Lux, until they found out that name had already been used for another Amazon project elsewhere, at which point they went with Project Big Daddy.

Monroe officials were so scared of riling Amazon that they withheld its identity even from the Columbus law firm, Bricker & Eckler, that the town had hired for the negotiations. "Bricker does not know who your client is," Monroe's lead official on the project, Jennifer Patterson, assured Amazon's lawyer in August 2017. "The City is being super careful on this." A few months later, Patterson told a Bricker attorney that, when a county official had requested information on the project for a meeting, "I purposefully didn't create a public document with all of the numbers he needs, but the elements are in the email below if he wants to figure out numbers in more detail [smiley face emoji]."

The lack of transparency continued right through the announcement of the deal, when Patterson sent an email to two Amazon executives assuring them that an innocuous quote on the project she'd given a local TV reporter, Jay Warren, had not been from an interview. "We are continuing to not return calls/emails," she wrote them. "Jay literally just caught me in the parking lot of the City Building and I said no comment, but then he dug up this from today's meeting. It's still no comment. Tomorrow I'll be wearing a public works T-shirt and jeans so no one can find me."

The agreement called for a ten-year state tax credit worth about $3.8 million to Amazon, in addition to a 100 percent exemption from local property taxes for fifteen years. Monroe was not alone in its magnanimity—in 2017 alone, Amazon would collect well over $100 million in subsidies to open fulfillment centers around the country, for a total of more than $1 billion over the previous decade. The company had a whole department tasked with securing subsidies—it called this its office of "economic development."

As 2017 neared its end and the darkness ebbed slightly in Dayton, Todd Swallows started bouncing back, too. In early October, he finally had his day in court. He pleaded guilty to a count of domestic violence for the January incident, but prosecutors dismissed charges for child endangerment and violating the protection order. He was given an additional year of probation and assessed a total of $270 in court costs.

He had kicked the pill habit. He left the other woman. And he and Sara started talking about getting back together.

Sara's friends and relatives were incredulous. She tried to explain. Todd was finally going to anger counseling, a condition of his new probation. She had worn out her welcome at her mother's apartment, where it would've been impossible for her and the kids to fit into the small space—just a bedroom, a bathroom, a small living room—even if she hadn't dared to challenge her mother's new husband during his arguments with her mother. "She didn't like me stepping in and getting in between them," she said.

Above all, though, there was the legacy of her father's departure almost twenty years earlier, and all that it had led to. She desperately wanted for her children—at least these three, the second three—to grow up in a whole family, with a father present. She believed that she could yet place hope in that father, who had, despite everything, despite his own ugly impulses, tried to provide for the family as best as a man with his lot could today. "You know, I love him. I didn't want my kids to go through what I went through," she said. "You can't help who you love, who your heart wants. And you never lose sight of your dream. Everyone has a chance to change. I already had one broken family. I didn't want another."

There were only two problems: the protection order, and the fact that they couldn't afford rent on their own.

So Todd came up with a solution. Somewhere, he'd heard that homeless shelters, like churches, were considered "safe havens." He interpreted this to mean that he couldn't be arrested for being with his family at a shelter. And, of course, a shelter was free. He took a sort of pride in having conceived of this plan, as humiliating as he knew it was. "I don't want my family to live like this," he said. "I didn't grow up having to worry, 'cause my parents could both work and they did both work. And we lived in a nice community and I went to nice schools. It's—I'm afraid for my children more than I am myself." But he had at least managed to bring the family back together. He bore much of the blame for their nadir, he knew, but he was placing great hope in his new anger counseling, which he spoke of with the intensity of a convert to a new cause. "I go to counseling once every week," he said. "I *need* to be able to go to my counseling."

Sara was dubious about the shelter plan. Asked one week into Gateway how she was faring, she began weeping. It was so cold in the dorm, where she had not been able to sleep for the first three nights. "We've never been in this position," she said, effectively declaring that a short life that already included a child sexual assault, the loss of custody of three children, and living with an accused domestic abuser had now officially found its bottom. Nationwide, the percentage of families living in deep poverty, less than half the poverty threshold, had doubled since 1975. They were now among them.

There was also the matter of the gender segregation between the shelters. But Todd could, under his expansive interpretation of the safe-haven theory—and thanks to withholding the restraining order from shelter staff—spend some time at the family shelter during the day. That is, when he wasn't working. Because he was about to start another new job.

Between 2011 and 2016, e-commerce business had doubled to $350 billion. It had shot from 1 percent of all retail sales at the turn of the millennium to 17 percent, excluding cars and gas. This meant that there was a need for a great deal more cardboard boxes—online and mail-order outlets used about seven times as many boxes per dollar spent as brick-and-mortar stores did, consuming about half of all corrugated box shipments for the retail sector, some 40 billion square feet of material. Annual containerboard production in the United States had surged past 35 million tons in 2014, and was still growing steadily in late 2017: it was up 3.6 percent in December 2017 over December of the year prior. Soaring rail shipments of "brown paper" for making cardboard were, among other things, providing new purpose for the humble boxcar amid the falloff in other freight mainstays, such as newsprint.

So it was not so surprising that the job Todd managed to find in January of 2018, despite a criminal record that was even lengthier now than it had been just a few years earlier, was back in cardboard. Not at Lewisburg Container, but at a smaller place called Miami Valley Packaging Solutions, in Dayton. He looked forward to a return to work at which he'd considered himself able. There was a downside: the temp firm that got him the job told him he was going to have to start back at $10 per hour, not far above the state's minimum wage of $8.30, meaning he would be making pretty much the same, at age twenty-seven, as he had nearly a decade earlier at the pizza shop. In this, he was not alone: nationwide, the poorest 10 percent were earning only 4 percent more per hour, adjusted for inflation, than they had earned forty years earlier. A third of all U.S. jobs paid less than $15 per hour; the bottom half of the income ladder had less wealth, adjusting for inflation, than it had thirty years earlier. And men without a college degree were making far less, adjusted for inflation, than they had fifty years ago.

He started the job on a Friday. He couldn't tell yet who their customers were. At Lewisburg, they'd done orders for Bath & Body Works, Smirnoff, and Captain Morgan. But their biggest customer by far had been the new arrival in Ohio: Amazon.

Amazon bought 140,000 tons of cardboard annually from Pratt Industries, Lewisburg Container's parent company, just one of Amazon's many suppliers, and the growth in its demand showed no sign of slowing. "We live in an exciting time for the humble corrugated box," said Anthony Pratt, the Australian billionaire who owned the company of his name. Amazon was driving such strong growth for cardboard that Pratt Industries was building a huge paper mill to make containerboard fifty miles north of Dayton—as Pratt would later boast in a full-page ad in *The Washington Post*, it was "the largest factory pledged and built since President Trump's election," a boast that would draw a visit to the new plant by Trump himself.

Todd spent a lot of time with Sara and the kids at the family shelter the weekend before his first full week at Miami Valley. As usual, he was the only father who came over from the men's shelter. He even managed to stay for Sunday dinner—pasta with canned peaches on the side. He presided over the table as if it were his own, in his own home, with his own food. He prodded Jazzlynn, who had come to dinner with her sleeping bag pulled around her, to eat what was on her plate. "Are you not hungry, or are you cold?" he asked.

But then it was time to get back to the men's shelter. The next day, he would take two buses to get to the cardboard job, a forty-five-minute trip to cover six miles. He wasn't sure how he'd pay for the bus before his first paycheck came in.

His ride dropped him in front of the shelter that used to be a jail. Inside the door, the security guard waited with his wand.

3.

Security

The wealth of a nation's capital

WASHINGTON, D.C.

The Hilton ballroom was still empty except for the servers at the periphery who tossed the salad in large bowls, which others then carried out to the large tables to distribute on nearly 1,500 plates. The sound of the tossing spoons on the big bowls, metal on metal, was rhythmic and almost musical.

Shortly after 6:00 p.m., the servers' boss—a heavyset, pale young man not much past thirty—strode onto the mezzanine of the ballroom and shouted down: "Guys, salad done! Back in the kitchen for your briefing, please!" The servers, most of whom were not guys, hustled to complete the task at hand.

The dinners held by the Economic Club of Washington, D.C., were usually in smaller venues than this, the same ballroom that played host every year to the White House Correspondents' Dinner. But the club's meetings had never had such a guest. They'd had Bill Gates, Warren Buffett, the Speaker of the House—but this was on another level. This guest required tighter security—lots of men with wires in their ears. This guest was being honored with a full presentation by an air force color guard. This guest was going to draw a lot more attendees than the club was used to. Landing him was a tremendous coup for the club president David Rubenstein.

Rubenstein had been leading the club for a decade, and had rejuvenated it. He had doubled the number of events each year, had expanded the membership, and had changed the whole way the dinners were conducted. The way it used to be, the guest of honor would come up, after the meal and some minimal club business, and give a speech. But speeches could be boring. So Rubenstein decided instead to interview the guest onstage, something he proved surprisingly adept at, considering that he was once so painfully shy that he would barely speak up at meetings. His lack of polish, it turned out, was ideal for a straight-man routine. It allowed him to ask direct and personal questions that might've seemed prying coming from a smoother interlocutor.

Truth be told, Rubenstein's idiosyncratic personal touch was not the only reason that the Economic Club had become a hotter ticket around town. The club had been founded in 1986 as a meeting place for the city's business elite, its movers and shakers, and in the decade since Rubenstein had taken over, the ranks of movers and shakers in Washington had grown considerably. This might seem counterintuitive given that the date of his takeover, in 2008, coincided with the global financial crash, an event that had not been kind to chamber-of-commerce types in many other parts of the country.

But Washington was like no other part of the country. It had sailed right through the Great Recession. If anything, the crisis had been a boon for the city—not a few of the billions that the federal government spent on economic stimulus had stayed right in the area, both in the federal bureaucracy and with the countless contractors who had in recent years sprouted around the Beltway, whom the government increasingly entrusted to oversee its own programs, in exchange for a healthy cut off the top. In several inner suburbs of Northern Virginia, home prices continued to rise right through the housing crash: the name of a new apartment complex in Fairfax County was Prosperity Flats. By 2010, the area was home to seventeen Fortune 500 companies, up from four in 1975. By 2012, seven of the ten richest counties in the country, ranked by household median income, were in the Washington area.

The prosperity was most conspicuous in the District proper. In 2011, developers started building CityCenterDC, a ten-acre, $700 million, Qatari-backed housing and shopping complex downtown that would open a few years later with the full luxury gamut: Hermès, Bulgari, Louis Vuitton, Dior. In once dowdy Washington, you could now buy a Gucci crocodile tote for $41,000. At the city's top private schools, where tuition climbed toward $40,000, students drove Range Rovers, Lexuses, and Mercedes-Benzes; girls sought favor with star athletes in their class by giving them Gucci flip-flops and Air Jordans.

Embodying the glamour vibe was one new arrival in particular. Barack Obama had been elected president, and the mere fact of his being installed at 1600 Pennsylvania Avenue injected an aura of cool across the city. His campaign staffers flocked to the city for jobs in his administration, filling apartments in Shaw and Bloomingdale and the U Street corridor, a swath of the city once home to the Black working class. Terrain captured in the fiction of Edward P. Jones was remade as the playground of mostly white strivers, its past a marketing gimmick: you could dine at Marvin, named for Gaye but leaning more Belgian in fare; you could buy a $500,000 condo in the Langston Hughes building or rent a one-bedroom apartment for $2,000 in the Ellington.

It was an awkward transformation, for sure. Also awkward was how Washington's metastasizing prosperity looked from elsewhere in the country. The capital city of the United States had been designed to be a thing apart, an administrative district for a federal government that the Founders had intended to be modest in its reach. Now this district was a thing apart in an entirely different respect: in its sheer wealth and its insulation from the shocks experienced in the rest of the country. This exceptionalism became most conspicuous after the financial crisis. But it had been building quietly for years.

Fulfillment

The era of outsized wealth in Washington started with congressional hearings on hunger.

Gerry Cassidy was the first member of his impoverished Irish American family in Brooklyn and Queens to go to college. After graduating from Villanova and Cornell Law School, he went to work as a legal aid lawyer representing migrant workers in South Florida, which he envisioned as a brief prelude to more remunerative work as a lawyer and the financial security that his family so lacked when he was growing up. "He wanted to be rich," Cassidy's college friend and best man told the author Robert Kaiser for *So Damn Much Money*, Kaiser's 2009 history of Washington lobbying.

It was in South Florida that Cassidy met George McGovern, the liberal South Dakota senator, who had come there as part of a new nationwide crusade against hunger. The issue had risen to the forefront thanks to a confluence of events: a high-profile 1967 trip by Robert F. Kennedy and a fellow senator to see emaciated kids in Cleveland, Mississippi; and, a year later, the broadcast of the CBS News special *Hunger in America*; and the publication of the report *Hunger USA*, which revealed that obscure hunger-related diseases thought limited to the Third World were present in the United States.

In 1968, Congress convened the Select Committee on Nutrition and Human Needs, often referred to simply as the McGovern Committee, after its chairman. The committee, which was stacked with a bipartisan array of heavyweight senators, traveled to bastions of deprivation, and in March 1969 it arrived in Immokalee, Florida, home to several migrant-worker camps. It did not take long after meeting McGovern there for young Gerry Cassidy to talk his way into a job with the committee's staff in Washington. In 1975, he decided, along with a more senior colleague on the committee staff, Kenneth Schlossberg, to start a business using their connections in Washington.

Lobbying was as old as the republic—New York merchants had descended on the very first Congress in 1789 to stave off a tariff bill. The right to "petition the government for a redress of grievances" was written right into the First Amendment, alongside the right to freedom of speech, religion, and assembly. The aggressiveness of such petitions rose and fell over time—the "agents," as they were called in the nineteenth century, were especially active in the years during and after the Civil War, often to the point of simply buying off senators on behalf of the railroad companies. They were active again during the New Deal, deployed on behalf of big business threatened by new regulation.

But by the early 1970s, the lobbying industry still occupied niche status in the capital. There were no lobbying firms—there were law firms that lobbied for their clients under guise of legal representation. Cassidy's McGovern Committee colleague, Schlossberg, who grew up in a family of funeral-home owners in Massachusetts, shared the general squeamishness about lobbying and preferred that he and Cassidy bill themselves as "consultants." As envisioned by Schlossberg, he could use his expertise on food issues to advise institutions such as the Department of Agriculture or Agency for International Development. Articles of incorporation for Schlossberg-Cassidy & Associates—with the former's Capitol Hill townhouse listed as the office—omitted the *l*-word.

The problem was, there was no demand for Schlossberg's consulting services. And there was demand for lobbying. The firm's first business came from clients eager to sell their products to federal food assistance programs, which had greatly expanded under President Nixon. A California food company needed help in getting payment for $200,000 in ingredients for the federal school lunch program, and paid a $10,000 retainer in return; Kellogg Company wanted to get its cereals into school cafeterias and paid $5,000 for assistance; the National Livestock and Meat Board paid $25,000 for a report on how congressional nutrition policy might affect the cattle industry; Mead Johnson paid $10,000 for insights into the new food program for women and infant children, which bought a lot of its baby formula. Soon, Pillsbury, Nabisco, and General Mills came knocking as well. Like that, Schlossberg and Cassidy were making enough money lobbying for businesses around War on Poverty programs to be able to afford a proper, albeit small, office at L'Enfant Plaza.

The pair's real breakthrough came in a different realm: higher education. The new president of Tufts University, nutritionist Jean Mayer, was eager to raise the profile of a college in the shadow of bigger Boston-area institutions. In 1976, he reached out to Schlossberg and Cassidy for help getting funding for a new "national nutrition center." Over the next two years, they worked their connections, on a $10,000 monthly retainer, to snare for Tufts a $20 million congressional appropriation to build the center, plus $7 million for its operations.

It was highly unusual for Congress to appropriate funds to a single university for a specific purpose. Even more unusual was for the appropriation to be arranged by lobbyists. One can debate whether Cassidy and Schlossberg invented the modern earmark—the appropriation of funds for a specific recipient, tucked deep in legislation. Harder to dispute is that they created a highly lucrative new business: securing those earmarks for clients. "We perfected a technique of line items for people who otherwise would never have thought they could have gotten it," said Schlossberg. In short order, they had scored another $10 million for Tufts's new veterinary school and $19 million in building funds for its school of diplomacy to split with Georgetown. They added a third member to the firm, who specialized in getting research grants for universities. "Ken Schlossberg and Gerry Cassidy," writes Robert Kaiser, "had stumbled onto a new kind of business, making money by extracting money from the federal Treasury for their fee-paying clients."

As they were pushing across this frontier, the Washington influence industry was expanding on another front. By the early 1970s, the rise of the Great Society and the proliferation of federal agencies and regulations—which continued under President Nixon with the creation of the Environmental Protection Agency and the Occupational Safety and Health Administration—was causing alarm in the business world. Its fear of being overmatched by the likes of Ralph Nader, made famous by his auto-safety assault on carmakers, was crystallized in a 1971 memo by Lewis Powell, a corporate lawyer in Virginia who would later be appointed to the Supreme Court. "The American economic system is under broad attack," Powell wrote. "Business must learn the lesson . . . that political power is necessary; that such power must be assiduously cultivated; and that when necessary, it must be used aggressively and with determination—without embarrassment and without the reluctance which has been so characteristic of American business."

The threat grew with the activist-minded Democrats brought in by the 1974 election, in reaction to Watergate. "The danger had suddenly escalated," Bryce Harlow, Procter & Gamble's man in Washington, said later. "We had to prevent business from being rolled up and put in the trash can by that Congress."

Big business heeded the call. Deep-pocketed donors funded new conservative influence shops such as the Heritage Foundation. Businesses flocked to join lobby groups—the U.S. Chamber of Commerce doubled its membership between 1974 and 1980, while the staunchly conservative National Federation of Independent Business doubled in size over the 1970s. In 1968, only 100 corporations had "public affairs" offices in Washington—a decade later, more than 500 did. The number of firms with registered lobbyists in Washington grew from 175 in 1971 to 2,500 in 1982. In explaining the National Association of Manufacturers' 1972 move from New York to Washington, its head said: "The interrelationship of business with business is no longer so important as the interrelationship of business with government."

This new push for influence inevitably made its way into political campaigns. The number of corporate political action committees more than quadrupled between 1976 and 1980. (Ironically, the growth of PACs was spurred by post-Watergate reforms, which had limited the amount that individuals could donate, giving rise to coordinated giving by multiple donors.) In the early 1970s, organized labor PACs still gave more to congressional races than business PACs did, but by the end of the decade they'd fallen far behind, with unions providing less than a quarter of all PAC giving.

The surge of new corporate PAC money played a big role in the stunning 1978 defeat of legislation that would have made it easier to organize workers, a bill that unions had been confident would pass with Democrats controlling the White House and Congress. And, along with the boom in television advertising, the PAC money fueled the extraordinary inflation in the cost of running for office in Washington. In the post-Watergate election of 1974, the combined campaign spending for House and Senate races had been $77 million. By 1982, less than a decade later, the combined cost had more than quadrupled to $343 million.

The wave of corporate PAC money had been launched from the political right, but that did not stop former McGovern Committee staffers from partaking. One of Schlossberg-Cassidy's big clients was the Massachusetts-based Ocean Spray, which had been fighting to get cranberry juice included in the school lunch program despite its high sugar content. Gerry Cassidy helped Ocean Spray set up its own PAC and advised it on which congressmen it should support.

His partner, Schlossberg, was finding this sort of thing increasingly distasteful, though his ambivalence had not kept him from enjoying the fruits for several years longer. By 1984, the two men were each taking home about $500,000 annually—well over ten times what they had been making a decade earlier as Hill staffers. Both had homes in McLean, the exclusive Northern Virginia suburb along the Potomac River. Cassidy drove a Mercedes; Schlossberg built a tennis court and drove a Jaguar. "Ever since I was a kid, I had a dream of having my own tennis court," Schlossberg said. "So I went for it."

In late 1984, Schlossberg decided to leave the firm that had been started in his basement nine years earlier. "It was a lot of fun for the most part—and then it wasn't," he said. The firm that had shown a whole new way to make money in Washington, and in doing so injected a whole new level of wealth into the city, would henceforth be known as Cassidy & Associates. The firm had inspired countless imitators, as earmarks and five-digit monthly retainers paid in search of them mushroomed in Washington. But it would nonetheless stand apart: for years to come, it would hold the crown as the largest lobbying firm in the lobbying capital of the world.

If Cassidy and Schlossberg pioneered the influence industry in Washington, David Rubenstein showed how to take it to an entirely different scale by harnessing it to another industry, high finance.

Rubenstein would have seemed an unlikely person to enter the lucrative Washington fray, much less dominate it. He grew up in a two-bedroom rowhouse in northwest Baltimore. His father sorted mail at the post office; his mother was a homemaker and dreamed that her son would become a dentist. At age eleven, Rubenstein was stirred by John F. Kennedy's inaugural call to "ask what you can do for your country." In high school, "he was very, very quiet," recalled Kurt Schmoke, later the city's first elected Black mayor. "He liked to talk about government and politics—not so much about business."

Rubenstein got a scholarship to Duke, followed that with law school at the University of Chicago, and put in two years at a law firm in New York before gravitating to the obvious home for the government geek: Capitol Hill. He got a job as counsel to Senator Birch Bayh, an Indiana Democrat, on the Subcommittee on Constitutional Amendments, about as unglamorous a slot as one could ask for on the Hill. A year later, he was one of the young idealists who jumped on board the campaign of Jimmy Carter.

Carter won, and Rubenstein got a plum job: deputy to Stuart Eizenstat, Carter's domestic policy adviser. Rubenstein helped write memos for Carter, prepare him for press conferences, and draft State of the Union addresses. He stayed late and subsisted on snacks from the vending machine. Instead of speaking up in meetings, he'd get his points across by leaving his memos at the top of the stack when he'd finally leave after everyone else had already gone home. "David certainly didn't have charisma," Eizenstat said later. "What he had was a sort of intensity of intellect and dedication and devotion to public service."

But then Carter lost his bid for reelection, to Ronald Reagan. And David Rubenstein, thirty-one, took this not only as a sign of a nationwide political shift, but as a rebuke of his own public-service idealism. "I tried to help my country, and it didn't work," he said years later. He would try something else: breaking into the other Washington growing up around him.

Rubenstein noticed that many of his White House friends were prospering in business. "I thought I had a pretty good I.Q. myself," he said later, "and people were making a lot more money than me who I thought maybe weren't so smart."

He started to entertain one notion in particular. New York and Boston were seeing the proliferation of "leveraged-buyout firms," such as Bain Capital, which bought companies with borrowed money, improved their bottom line with layoffs and efficiencies, and then sold them at a profit—what would later come to be called "private equity." Washington, meanwhile, was seeing a surge in lobbying, at firms like Cassidy's.

But nobody had yet yoked those two lucrative enterprises together. What if you had a leveraged-buyout firm built around partners chosen on the basis of their relationships with government officials and their knowledge of regulated industries? Gary Shapiro, then a lobbyist for the consumer electronics industry, recalled hearing Rubenstein's pitch when they traveled together to Japan, in the early eighties: "His vision was to combine capital with politically connected people whose phone calls are accepted around the world. We laughed at him, like, Yeah, right."

In late 1987, Rubenstein founded the Carlyle Group, with two men from Marriott, which was based in Washington, and another from MCI, the telecommunications company. They named the firm after the New York hotel, to evoke old-money grandeur and the capital of finance. Yet the firm quickly came to be all about Washington, exactly as Rubenstein had conceived it, with the help of a fortuitous twist. Fred Malek, a longtime Republican fixer, was forced to resign as manager for George H. W. Bush's 1988 presidential campaign over the discovery that he had, in 1972, produced a list of Jews in the Bureau of Labor Statistics for President Nixon. Malek took a gig at Carlyle and brought with him Frank Carlucci, Reagan's final secretary of defense. With Carlucci's help, Carlyle was able to buy BDM, Ford Aerospace's defense consultancy, the first of many military-industrial complex investments. Seven years later, having expanded BDM's operations into Saudi Arabia, Carlyle sold BDM, netting a 650 percent profit.

Following in Carlucci's footsteps, two other top members of the Bush administration joined Carlyle: budget director Richard Darman and Secretary of State James Baker III. And in the late 1990s, Bush himself signed on and helped the firm win a bidding war for a big South Korea bank. Rubenstein was, by this point, a close acquaintance of the former president: in 2000, he and his family accompanied Barbara Bush and her grandchildren on a safari. That same year, he and his wife attended Barbara Bush's seventy-fifth birthday party, in Kennebunkport.

As Rubenstein later described it, he had moved beyond politics. "I don't really try to get involved politically by giving money to politicians or by saying I'm a Democrat or Republican," he said. "Right now, I just view myself as an American."

At 9:37 a.m. on September 11, 2001, American Airlines Flight 77 bound from Dulles International Airport to Los Angeles flew into the western side of the Pentagon. The crash killed 125 people, in addition to the 64 on the plane. This would have been the deadliest terrorist attack on American soil, with an even greater toll than the Oklahoma City bombing of 1995, but it was overshadowed by the much deadlier and more visually arresting attacks that same morning in New York. Further cloaking the deaths at the Pentagon was the discretion inherent to the military—seven of the victims were from the Defense Intelligence Agency, while others were contractors with varying levels of classified status. Where Ground Zero in New York would be memorialized by a museum and two large reflecting pools, the Pentagon would feature only a minimalist memorial consisting of a series of benches on the building's western side.

The local legacy of the Pentagon attack was complicated by something else, too. After 9/11, a metropolitan area already made prosperous by the influence industry would be lifted to a whole new level of wealth by the national security industry. The government reacted to the humiliation of having failed to detect warning signs of the attacks by allocating billions to detect another one. And much of that spending was absorbed by Washington.

Thirty-three federal building complexes designed for top-secret intelligence were built in the area in the decade after the attacks—the square-footage equivalent of almost three Pentagons. By 2009, the U.S. intelligence budget had grown to $75 billion, two and a half times what it had been at the time of the attacks. Much of that spending went to the government giants based in Washington. The Pentagon's Defense Intelligence Agency grew from 7,500 employees in 2002 to 16,500 in 2011. The National Security Agency, the eavesdropper on the world based at Fort Meade in the Maryland suburbs, doubled its budget over the same period. The Department of Homeland Security was created from scratch, twenty-two agencies thrown together under their new Orwellian name, with a planned $3.4 billion headquarters at the former St. Elizabeths mental hospital overlooking Washington.

But much of the spending would be dispersed to the archipelago of private sector contractors that saw a business opportunity and leapt toward it. Of the 854,000 people granted top-secret clearances by 2011, 265,000 were contractors, not government employees, according to *The Washington Post.* The CIA's head count included roughly 10,000 contract employees from more than a hundred firms—more than a third of the agency's workforce. At the Department of Homeland Security, there were as many contractors as federal employees. Robert Gates, Obama's first secretary of defense, admitted to *The Post* that he didn't even know how many contractors were employed in his own office. The ranks of contractors had grown even though they cost the agencies who employed them considerably more than regular federal employees did.

Many of the contract employees worked for giants like Lockheed Martin, General Dynamics, and Raytheon, which vied for applicants with coveted security clearances by dangling $15,000 signing bonuses and BMWs. General Dynamics, which set up and managed Homeland Security's offices, saw its revenue more than triple between 2000 and 2009, to almost $32 billion, while its workforce doubled to more than 90,000.

But countless other private employees worked at the smaller, anonymous companies that had proliferated across the region—the homeland security entrepreneurs. They had opaque names like SGIS and Abraxas and Carahsoft. They were often launched in the bedroom or den of their opportunistic founder. They grew as fast as they could to absorb the gusher of taxpayer dollars—by 2010, the government's spending on contractors had doubled to $80 billion. And with the contracting pot growing so fast, so did the demand for connections to help land contracts: from 2000 to 2011, money spent on Washington lobbyists more than doubled, to $3.3 billion. Far from supplanting the city's influence industry, the new homeland security complex was only fueling its growth.

The new industry was changing the face of the local landscape. At Liberty Crossing, a gargantuan complex in McLean, armed guards and hydraulic steel barriers guarded the headquarters of the Office of the Director of National Intelligence and National Counterterrorism Center. Buildings made to look like warehouses actually held eavesdrop-proof rooms available for rent. Windowless behemoths suddenly appeared in exurban farmland with no identifying signs, unrecognized by Google Maps. Vans raced down secondary highways and through shopping plaza lots in training runs for tracking counterintelligence targets. Denizens of this new landscape spoke their own language—they compared the size of their SCIFs (sensitive compartmented information facility) or whispered about SAPs (Special Access Program); when asked at happy hours at Applebee's or Chili's where they worked, they mumbled, "With the military."

Above all, the new industry transformed the region through the outsized growth it ushered in. Real estate prices in metro Washington increased more than prices in any other city over the first decade of the century—more than New York, San Francisco, and Los Angeles. The industry drew a new class to Washington—more interested in technology than government, more driven by profits than power. One research group estimated that the area's number of high-net-worth households, with investable assets of more than $1 million, had risen by 30 percent, to 166,000, between 2008 and 2012— that is, the period when much of the country was still struggling to recover from the Great Recession.

There was an Aston Martin dealership in Tysons Corner—more than five hundred people in the area drove the bespoke James Bond car, which cost around $280,000. The city's restaurants won their first Michelin stars; at one establishment, Plume, waiters arrived with a drink cart of sparkling juices to suggest pairings for the kids. (The Cuvee No. 25, a mix of sloe plums, Aronia berries, pears, and currants was served in a miniature champagne glass and went for $12.) In Great Falls, on the Virginia side of the Potomac, a family built a 25,424-square-foot mansion modeled on Versailles.

One might have expected that the boom in the new homeland security industry would have benefited the local firm that had done so well by the old defense industry, the Carlyle Group. But David Rubenstein and his partners had taken the September 11 attacks as a sign to diversify out of the Washington influence realm, because the attacks had unhelpfully highlighted how good the firm had gotten at that game. It happened that Carlyle's investor conference was taking place the day of the attacks, and that Shafiq bin Laden, a member of the sprawling bin Laden family, had been a guest, a reflection of the family's $2 million investment in a Carlyle fund. Sensing political risk, Carlyle shifted into a broader range of companies—Dunkin' Donuts, Hertz, the nursing home chain HCR ManorCare.

The diversification hardly hurt the firm's bottom line. In 2012, when Carlyle made its first public stock offering, it disclosed that Rubenstein and cofounders Daniel D'Aniello and William Conway, Jr., had been paid a combined $140 million the previous year, and had also received large returns on their own investments in Carlyle funds: Rubenstein alone had collected $57 million.

A s the wealth flowed into Washington, so did the media. Newspapers were in rapid decline in cities large and small across the country, their business model devastated by the triple whammy of first a company (Craigslist) that offered for free one of their main products (classified ads), and later a company that eviscerated the department stores that bought many of the print ads that sustained newspapers (Amazon), and then a couple companies that siphoned off the digital ad revenue that would replace lost print ads (Google and Facebook). From 2005 to 2015, one out of every four reporting jobs vanished across the country: 12,000 of them. City councils, school boards, and major trials went barely covered or not at all; candidates for state and local office went un-vetted.

But in Washington, over that same period, the number of reporters doubled. It was easier to make digital journalism work at national rather than regional scale—you could be guaranteed a lot more clicks from all over the country for a story about some Washington drama than for reporting in some midsize metro city or state capital; and if something truly eye-catching did happen Out There, you could simply rewrite the story— "aggregate" it, in the new media lingo—to collect the traffic on your own website. Meanwhile, the industry interests that were willing to pay more to influence Washington through lobbyists and trade associations were also willing to pay more to learn about the fruits of their lobbying, which explained the vast expansion of trade publications in Washington, some of which were able to charge subscription rates as high as $8,000 for their insider dope.

The expanding Washington media market came with at least one benefit: at least some of those reporters who'd lost their jobs elsewhere were able to find work in the capital, though not all of them were thrilled to be leaving behind the towns and cities they'd covered for years to sit at a Washington desk with two computer screens (better for aggregating) or to join the horde of reporters trailing after members of Congress on Capitol Hill. The concentration came at a real cost, too, when the collapse and recession hit in 2008 and 2009: having so many reporters in booming Washington instead of St. Louis and Buffalo and Tampa meant that more of the national media was living and working in the place where things were going better than anywhere, and could easily be mistaken about the country's condition by missing what was happening Out There.

Jay Carney had not himself taken part in the movement away from local coverage—he had had the professional fortune to make it to the national beat years before, almost from the start. He grew up in Northern Virginia, attended the Lawrenceville School in New Jersey, one of the oldest private schools in the country, and then went to college at Yale. After graduating in 1987, he got a job at *The Miami Herald*, then one of the best metro papers in the country; within two years, he'd jumped to *Time* magazine, becoming its Miami bureau chief before age twenty-five, and then he was off to cover the collapse of the Soviet Union, putting his collegiate Russian studies to good use. In Moscow, he first met his future wife, ABC's Claire Shipman, and on returning was rewarded with the White House beat. In 2005, he was promoted to *Time*'s Washington bureau chief. Michael Bloomberg, then the mayor of New York, insisted on giving a toast at the party to mark the promotion.

By 2009, Carney was wearying of his media gig, rarefied as it was. He'd found the press swoon over the Obama campaign a bit much. This made his next move all the more unexpected: he joined the administration, as a spokesman for Joe Biden. In January 2011, he was promoted to the front of the room, taking over as the White House press secretary.

Although he had been on the other side of the line for more than twenty years, *The New York Times* noted that he brought one key trait to the position: Carney "always seemed comfortable around people in power." It didn't take long at all for him to master the job—the corny stabs at humor, the endless demurrals. By 2013, one website had tallied the nearly 10,000 times in which Carney had declined to answer a reporter's question, with parries such as "I would refer you to someone else" (1,383 times), "I'm not going to tell you" (939 times), and "I won't speculate" (525 times).

He started getting ironic celebrity treatment, with articles on his beard and glasses, and even an un-ironic celebrity profile, in *Washington Mom* magazine. There they were, Claire and he posing in their five-bedroom, $2 million home with their two kids—conducting a mock press briefing, building a Jenga tower, flipping a fried egg in pajamas, complete with fashion captions.

In May 2014, Carney announced he was leaving the White House "to devote more time to his family." A new path was emerging for former members of the Obama administration—or rather, a new version of a very old path.

The revolving door had been turning in Washington from the start, but it had usually spun people back and forth from Wall Street. Alexander Hamilton founded the Bank of New York after serving in the Continental Congress and before becoming treasury secretary. The Washington-finance nexus was long identified with Republicans, the party of business, but it absorbed Democrats, too, around the time of the Second World War, when businessmen of both parties were brought into government. Herbert Lehman, a liberal Democrat and a partner in Lehman Brothers, his family's investment firm, succeeded Franklin Roosevelt as governor of New York before directing the State Department's foreign-relief effort, and then served in the Senate. Robert Lovett, a Republican, was an executive with the investment bank Brown Brothers Harriman, then served as a deputy to General George Marshall and as Harry Truman's secretary of defense, and helped create NATO and the CIA. Lovett was one of the coterie of foreign-policy mandarins who came to be known as the Wise Men, a term that captured how benignly Wall Street–Washington traffic was viewed in that era.

The movement accelerated after the war, amid the economic boom and the growth of the regulatory state created during the New Deal. John F. Kennedy appointed C. Douglas Dillon, a former investment banker, to be secretary of the treasury. Lyndon Johnson's treasury secretary, Henry Fowler, was recruited to join Goldman Sachs. For the Republican Party, the transfers became so predictable that few objected when the Merrill Lynch CEO Donald Regan became Ronald Reagan's treasury secretary, or when Senator Phil Gramm of Texas was named vice-chairman of the investment bank division of UBS, or when George W. Bush appointed the Goldman Sachs CEO Henry Paulson to be treasury secretary.

But the movement became more radioactive on the Democratic side in the 1990s, as NAFTA, welfare reform, and capital gains tax cuts, all passed under President Clinton, made Democratic leaders sensitive to the charge that they were abandoning their underdog roots. The tenure of Robert Rubin, the former Goldman Sachs executive whom President Clinton named treasury secretary in 1995, and who went on to earn $126 million at Citigroup, was so controversial that "Rubinite" became a term of opprobrium in liberal circles. Rubin and his successor, Lawrence Summers, thwarted an attempt to regulate financial derivatives and pushed to repeal the Glass-Steagall Act, which separated commercial and investment banking.

These moves, which boosted Wall Street, were later implicated in the financial collapse. Making matters worse for the reputation of the Wall Street Democrats was the Obama administration's failure to hold accountable the bankers most responsible for that collapse. The movement continued—a Morgan Stanley executive, Tom Nides, became Hillary Clinton's top aide in the State Department; Obama's budget director, Peter Orszag, went to Citigroup, which in turn sent Jack Lew to take Orszag's job and later become treasury secretary; Obama's first treasury secretary, Tim Geithner, headed to private equity firm Warburg Pincus. But this traffic now had a furtive quality to it.

What a blessing it was, then, that there was another realm that top administration officials could depart to, and still prosper in, without the stigma of Wall Street. The tech industry had for years kept its distance from Washington, viewing it as a bland redoubt of plodding bureaucrats and politicians who couldn't tell a server from a router, who described the internet as a "series of tubes." This condescension was a bit much, considering to what extent the industry had been boosted by federal investment in years past. But as the industry grew, the need to engage with fusty Washington became an unavoidable fact for even the proudest libertarians in Silicon Valley. You needed to head off an antitrust prosecution such as the one the Department of Justice brought against Microsoft in the 1998. You needed to deter nettlesome regulations over how you used the bounty of personal data that your online platforms were collecting. And you needed to stave off efforts to clamp down on the offshore tax havens in which you stashed your gargantuan profits.

So it was that a whole new set of clients came knocking at the doors of Cassidy & Associates and their rivals. In 2002, Google had spent less than $50,000 on lobbyists; by 2015, it was spending $5 million in a single quarter, making it the third-biggest corporate lobbyist. And as the companies expanded their own influence operations, they naturally reached toward the revolving door. Facebook hired Joel Kaplan, George W. Bush's former deputy chief of staff. Google hired Susan Molinari, a former Republican congresswoman. (She was one of more than four hundred former members of Congress who were now employed as lobbyists, earning as much as tenfold their $174,000 congressional salary. In 1970, only 3 percent of members of Congress became lobbyists on leaving office; three decades later, more than 40 percent did.)

But it was easiest to recruit top-grade former officials on the Democratic side. The tech industry had leaned liberal since at least the early 1990s, after all, when Democrats such as Bill Clinton and the technophile Al Gore had recognized where the future lay and helped draw Silicon Valley away from its libertarian, pro-business moorings in the Republican Party (David Packard, cofounder of Hewlett-Packard, had been deputy secretary of defense under President Nixon). The industry was still wary of Democrats' regulatory and tax inclinations, but social issues such as same-sex marriage and immigration had put it squarely in the party's camp. Obama himself had heaped praise on Amazon during a 2013 visit to a warehouse in Chattanooga: "Amazon is a great example of what's possible," he said. "I look at this amazing facility and you guys, you don't miss a beat. You've got these packages coming out. You've got dog food and Kindles and beard trimmers. There's all kinds of stuff around here. But once it's packed up, it's got to get to the customer."

An Obama administration official could cast his or her jump to Silicon Valley as a step into the future, toward hip enlightenment, in contrast to a colleague's blatant cashing in on Wall Street.

Thus the steady stream began. David Plouffe, whose tactical brilliance had helped Obama win in 2008, headed to Uber. Lisa Jackson, Obama's EPA director, headed to Apple.

And in February 2015, less than a year after leaving the White House, Jay Carney joined Amazon.

The house was purchased on October 21, 2016, for $23 million in cash, the highest recorded sale price in Washington. It actually consisted of two adjacent houses, designed in the early 1900s by separate architects, one of them John Russell Pope, who also designed the Jefferson Memorial. Most recently, 2320-2330 S Street Northwest had been home to the Textile Museum. Now it would become the fourth second home for Jeff Bezos, though not the last—a few years later, he would also buy David Geffen's Beverly Hills estate for $165 million, a record high for a California property.

Bezos had been spending more time in Washington—flying in on his $66 million Gulfstream G650 jet as often as ten times a year, staying at the Jefferson or the St. Regis or the Four Seasons. He had become a sort of man about town, which amused people in Seattle, a town in which he was barely seen. In Washington, he'd convene gatherings at buzzy restaurants—Cafe Milano, Le Diplomate, Minibar, Fiola Mare. These soirees impressed even the legendary D.C. hostess Sally Quinn, the wife of the former *Washington Post* editor Ben Bradlee. "Nobody wanted to go home," she said of one four-hour convening. "It was a blast."

And he had bought the local newspaper. In 2013, the Graham family, overwhelmed by upheaval in the news business, was looking to offload *The Washington Post*, which had been in its hands for eighty years. Don Graham met with Bezos to discuss the matter at the annual Sun Valley, Idaho, conference held by investment bank Allen & Co. Four weeks later, they announced the sale of the paper for $250 million, which at the time was less than 1 percent of Bezos's estimated net worth.

The purchase was followed by considerable spending by the new owner—expanding the newsroom staff, upgrading the website, renovating gleaming new offices overlooking Franklin Square. This investment came as a relief to the hundreds of *Post* employees who had endured reductions in years prior, and gave a boost to the cause of good journalism.

But it also greatly enhanced the Washington profile of a person whose company had rapidly growing interests in the capital. Between 2012 and 2017, Amazon's spending on lobbying quintupled; by 2018, it had the largest lobbying office of any tech firm in Washington, with twenty-eight people, in addition to more than one hundred lobbyists on contract at a dozen firms around the city. Among its team were four former members of Congress. It added to its board of directors Jamie Gorelick, a consummate Beltway insider who had served as U.S. deputy attorney general, received more than $25 million in four years at the mortgage lender Fannie Mae, and represented BP following the Gulf oil spill.

The company lobbied more federal agencies than any other tech company did. It lobbied on the sales tax, which it still didn't assess on most of the third-party sales that now made up more than half of its U.S. retail business. It lobbied against regulations for drones, which it hoped to use to deliver packages. It lobbied to maintain the discounted delivery rates it enjoyed with the postal service. It lobbied on government procurement, seeking to become the one-stop shop for all federal purchasing. It lobbied against any effort to bring antitrust scrutiny to the company.

Now Bezos owned the newspaper that was the primary organ for covering the nexus of corporate influence and politics in Washington. And he'd succeed the Grahams not only in bankrolling the paper, but in bringing official Washington under his roof, as Katharine Graham had done in her famous salons.

This was the purpose of the house. Bezos hired a star architect, Ankie Barnes, to oversee a $13 million renovation of its 27,000 square feet. *Washingtonian* obtained the plans via the Freedom of Information Act, revealing what the magazine called an "undertaking of pharaonic proportions."

The plans showed 191 doors (some custom mahogany or bronze), twenty-five bathrooms, eleven bedrooms, five living rooms or lounges, five staircases, three kitchens, two library/studies, two exercise rooms, two elevators, 287 fire-suppression sprinklers, and 1,006 light fixtures. The building designed by Pope would be the family quarters, with a wine room, a whiskey cellar, a lounge with decoratively painted plaster ceilings, two dressing rooms (each with a fireplace), and bedrooms distinguished with names such as "Ottoman," "Garden," and "Bunk."

The second building would entertain the guests, with a vestibule opening onto a staircase of slab marble, bracketed by a 36-foot-long gallery. The ballroom spread nearly 1,500 square feet and boasted floor-to-ceiling Ionic fluted columns and a limestone fireplace, with a balconied promenade above lined with iron rails. Guests would be able to wander outside on paths of crushed stone amid newly planted trees and around two fountains, a pergola, and a gaslit garden pavilion made of stucco and copper. "It's a very big house," said the *Post* editor Marty Baron. "I hope he has a party for us in the house."

The house—houses—were in Kalorama, one of the stateliest sections of the city. On one side was the Woodrow Wilson House, on the other was the embassy of Myanmar, and across the way was the residence of the Pakistani ambassador. The neighborhood was moving to a whole new level of exclusivity with the arrival of Bezos and several others. Barack and Michelle Obama decided to rent a home there after leaving the White House. And around the corner from Bezos were another famous couple, Jared Kushner and Ivanka Trump, who had moved to the city with the election of Donald Trump.

The election had cast gloom over a city that had voted almost entirely for Trump's opponent. But it had put barely any damper on its burgeoning prosperity. The new president vowed to augment spending on the military, which meant more spending on all those contractors lining the Beltway. And the new administration opened a whole new line in the influence business, for those who could claim a connection to Trump. By 2017, spending on federal lobbying was above $3.3 billion, more than double what it had been in 2000.

Among the new entrants was Brian Ballard. For years, he had been building a lobbying empire at the state level, in Florida. In 1986, the twenty-five-year-old had been a travel aide to the Republican gubernatorial candidate Bob Martinez, carrying his briefcase and fetching his Diet Cokes, but junior status did not translate into reserve. When Martinez flew around the state prior to the election with one of his Republican primary rivals, the rival, Tom Gallagher, kept talking about how his campaign had done certain things better. "I have a question, Tom," said Ballard. "If you're so smart and your campaign was so great, why is it that we kicked your ass?" After the election, Martinez made Ballard his director of day-to-day operations, with a $68,000 salary that Ballard used to buy himself a silver BMW.

Ballard was promoted to chief of staff before he was thirty. He wore suspenders with toy soldiers on them. He married the daughter of the state's former secretary of state and attorney general. He read *The Art of the Deal* and wrote to Donald Trump to tell him how much he liked it. Trump responded on fancy stationery. "I reached back out to him and said, 'If you ever have any issues in Florida, please don't hesitate to call,'" Ballard said.

After Martinez lost reelection in 1990, Ballard set up practice in "the private sector." When Republicans won control of the Florida House of Representatives for the first time in 122 years in 1996, lobbyists with Republican ties were in high demand, and in even higher demand two years later, when Jeb Bush was elected governor. Clients flocked to his door: AT&T, Prudential, the New York Yankees, hospitals, high-tech firms, racetracks. Ballard owned two properties in the Tallahassee area, each worth more than $1.3 million.

He worked hard for it: he got in at six in the morning and often worked until nine at night. "If you're good at this, you put the pressure on yourself," he said. "People pay you a good wage to advocate their issues and ultimately be successful." He was only thirty-seven.

By 2016, Ballard had offices in seven Florida cities. He had finessed the election just right. He initially supported Jeb Bush, whose governorship had been so central to his own rise as a lobbyist in Tallahassee. But as Bush's campaign had languished, Ballard had inched closer to the other Florida Republican in the field, Marco Rubio. And when Rubio had also fallen away, Ballard moved seamlessly to supporting Donald Trump. After all, Trump had sent him that handwritten note back in the 1980s, and the Trump Organization had paid him $460,000 for lobbying services in the past few years, mostly related to Trump's Mar-a-Lago resort. He raised $16 million for Trump's campaign; even before signing on with him, he had done him a great favor by sending his way one of his firm's top lobbyists, Susie Wiles, who went on to manage Trump's victory over Hillary Clinton in Florida.

Ballard's affinity for Trump was not ideological—the lobbyist had retained elements of moderation over the years, including on environmental issues. Rather, it was based in Ballard's willingness to look past the ugliness that had turned some establishment Republicans off of Trump. "A lot of people didn't want to wear the Trump jersey," he said. "Well, he was our nominee and frankly, I find him to be an incredibly fine human being."

With Trump in the White House, Ballard spied his main chance. He had built out his Florida influence empire about as far as it could go. The time had now come to go national.

In early February 2017, two weeks after Trump's inauguration, Ballard Partners opened an office in the opulent Homer Building, three blocks from the White House. The office included Wiles, fresh off running Trump's Florida campaign; a staff member to Trump's transition team; and Otto Reich, the former U.S. ambassador to Venezuela, who had been found by the General Accounting Office to have engaged in "prohibited covert propaganda" in support of Nicaraguan contras. The office's front lobby had the firm's name in silver against the customary steel-gray wall, and issues of *The Economist* and *The Atlantic* arrayed next to a jar of Antica Farmacista ambiance-diffusing reeds (orange blossom, lilac, and jasmine).

It was a small office, by Washington standards, with six lobbyists. But clients rushed it, desperate for access to a president that so many of the city's other firms had failed to take seriously. By May of 2018, after barely more than a year in operation, the firm had pulled in more than $13 million in fees, making it the eleventh-largest lobbying operation by revenue.

There were several conspicuous clients on the firm's new list. The GEO Group, one of the country's largest for-profit prison operators, signed a $600,000 annual contract with Ballard three months before landing a $110 million contract to operate an immigration detention facility in Texas.

The Republic of Turkey signed a $1.5 million-per-year contract with Ballard Partners mere days before the Turkish president Recep Tayyip

Erdoğan's security guards beat up peaceful protesters in a mini-riot outside Turkey's embassy in Washington.

And Amazon signed up Ballard for $280,000 per year.

The Washington Hilton ballroom was finally ready, but there was still business underway in the lobby area that had been set aside for VIPs, screened by dividers from the view of reporters or others lacking proper credentials. Among the select of the select were Tom Daschle, the former Democratic Senate leader turned lobbyist; Mike Allen, the insider Washington scribe; Katharine Weymouth, the former publisher of the newspaper her family had sold to tonight's guest of honor; and Muriel Bowser, mayor of the city in which he now owned the largest home. Also in attendance this evening: seventeen ambassadors from around the world; the U.S. postmaster general, who oversaw the discounted shipping that the guest of honor's company depended heavily on; and the head of the General Services Administration, who oversaw the federal procurement that the company was gaining an increasing share of.

David Rubenstein took the microphone to formally welcome the evening's guest before the assemblage of the VIPs. The moment had been building for a long time—a newspaper bought, a mansion renovated, an influence operation vastly expanded—but here it was, at last: the official coming-out in Washington.

"As you know, this event has attracted an enormous amount of attention all over this area, and the country as well—a lot of media and cameras and so forth," Rubenstein said. "And I think it's solely because we're honored to have Jeff Bezos as our special guest."

The VIPs applauded and made their way into the ballroom. The military guard awaited.

Break: Drop Zone 9

Jody Rhoads spent the evening of May 31, 2014, a Saturday, watching television with one of her two sons, according to the account the son later provided to the state police. She went to bed at 9:30 p.m., and got up at 5:20 a.m. to make it to the warehouse on Allen Road in time for her 7:30 a.m. to 6 p.m. shift, which she worked Sunday through Wednesday.

Rhoads, who was fifty-two and had survived breast cancer, had worked at the 833,000-square-foot warehouse for about three years—a relative veteran, given the high turnover there. Like many of the company's 690 employees at this location, she had started out as one of the 260 temps who also worked on the premises under the charge of a large manpower contractor, Staff Management | SMX. If you put in 280 hours at the warehouse with SMX and had good attendance and no written warnings, you had a shot at going on the payroll with the company itself—"converting"—as Rhoads had succeeded in doing. SMX workers wore a white ID badge. When they upgraded to regular employees, they got a blue one.

Rhoads now worked as a pallet mover, one of the six or seven people on each shift who transported inbound pallets of goods on a powered industrial truck, or PIT. The PIT was a forklift designed for warehouse duty—you drove it with forks trailing, like a pickup. On the version operated by Rhoads, a Crown PC 4500, an operator stood on a 34-inch-wide platform and controlled the PIT with a tiller handle that had thumb controls for forward and reverse. There was no foot or hand brake, which meant that to slow or stop the PIT, an operator had to pull the thumb control backward. A PIT could drift quite a ways without the operator giving throttle—up to thirty feet. A 53.5-inch-tall back support separated the operator's space from the forks, which extended eight feet to the rear. At this warehouse, PITs were set at "turtle" speed, with the "rabbit" setting disabled.

In July 2009, the Occupational Safety and Health Administration, or OSHA, had put out a bulletin regarding "under-ride hazards" involving standup forklifts. "One of the potential hazards faced by standup forklift operators is the crushing hazard that can arise when traveling, with the forks trailing, in a warehouse near a storage rack or similar obstruction," the guidance warned. "The risk is that a horizontal rack beam (crossbar) or similar obstruction might enter the operator's compartment in a situation referred to as 'under-ride.'" Over the previous fifteen years, at least nine workers nationwide had been killed and three had sustained severe injuries when operating such a forklift in reverse, the bulletin stated.

Despite her early bedtime, Jody Rhoads was visibly tired that morning. This may have been related to the depression and poor sleep she'd been experiencing, which her son later mentioned to the state police. Her husband, John, had died less than a year earlier, and she was worrying about a brother of hers who was in prison. Brian Hippensteel, fifty years old, had been convicted two months earlier for attempted murder after firing his bolt-action rifle from his pickup truck at the boyfriend of his estranged wife as he sat in his own truck at the corner of North West and C Streets in Carlisle.

Whatever the cause of Rhoads's state that morning, several people working near her noticed how exhausted she seemed. At 11:30, one co-worker asked if she was OK. "Yes, I'm fine," she said. Soon afterward, she was asked if she wanted some water. She demurred. "She looked tired, but who doesn't," another coworker said later. Rhoads called her son during her 12:30 lunch break and mentioned that people kept telling her to wake up.

It did not take long for Rhoads's lack of energy to attract the attention of her superiors. The average delivery rate for PIT drivers was thirteen pallets per hour. But Jody Rhoads was averaging only eleven pallets per hour several hours into her shift. A manager ordered a supervisor—a "process assistant"—to bring this shortfall up with Rhoads herself. The process assistant did so after Rhoads returned from her lunch break. Rhoads, the process assistant later said, attributed her rate to outbound workers who were taking too long at their task, slowing her down. The process assistant later told the state police that Rhoads "seemed normal" when they spoke.

Shortly after 2:30, Rhoads had completed a drop-off of inbound goods in Aisle 630 in Drop Zone 9, near where the pallets of dog food were stored, and was returning with her forks empty. As she reached bin location P1E630A240, she suddenly drifted off course and veered right, into the shelving.

The contact was hard enough that it shoved the goods stored on the floor—two Makita power cutters and eight boxes—into the aisle on the other side of the shelves. And it was hard enough that it pinned Jody Rhoads's neck between the PIT's back support and the lowest steel rack, forty-nine inches off the ground.

Others quickly noticed their trapped coworker. Someone called her name, and she didn't answer. Shouts went up for assistance. The first ones on the scene found Jody Rhoads's head bent to the side, her eyes open, and her hands gripping the tiller handle of the PIT. A hand scanner and a clear plastic baggie with animal crackers sat near the PIT's controls. Coworkers tried to put the PIT in reverse but were unable to.

Finally, they managed to shove it back six inches after pushing the emergency brake, enough to dislodge Jody Rhoads. She fell sideways, into the arms of a coworker who prevented her five-foot-six-inch, 140-pound frame, clad in jeans, a gray sweater, and a yellow safety vest, from toppling to the ground.

Her skin had a bluish tint. There were animal-cracker crumbs on her lips. She had a slight pulse, but was not breathing. Several coworkers noticed a bruise on her chin, where her head crashed against the steel shelving; one coworker assumed she had broken her back.

A coworker with a radio put out a summons for the company's in-house medic squad. But the squad was off duty on Sunday afternoons. So the call went out for an ambulance, at 2:42 p.m. A coworker in a Steelers jersey attempted to perform CPR, without success. Someone arrived with an AED defibrillator and used it on her. This also produced no results. A crowd of concerned workers had gathered round, but a manager ordered them to get back to work. Someone stretched red tape across Aisle 630 and adjacent Aisle 625, barring entry.

The EMTs from Cumberland Goodwill Emergency Medical Services arrived and also tried to revive Rhoads with defibrillator paddles. At about 3:20, they sped her one mile to the Carlisle Regional Medical Center. She was pronounced dead there at 3:55 p.m.

More than six hours later, shortly after 10:00 p.m., a regional safety manager for the company, Greg Williams, left a voice mail at a 1-800 number for the Occupational Health and Safety Administration, reporting a fatality at 675 Allen Road in Carlisle, Pennsylvania.

"The brief description of the incident is as follows," Williams said. "The associate was found unresponsive in a powered industrial truck. The associate was removed from the equipment by co-workers and checked for vital signs. CPR was initiated and 911 was called. EMS responded and left the site at 3:20 with the associate." He did not mention Rhoads crashing into the shelving, or her neck being pinned against the steel rack, or the bruise on her chin. "At this time," Williams said, "we do not believe that the incident was work related."

The next morning, the director of OSHA's Harrisburg office, Kevin Kilp, assigned one of his employees to contact the warehouse's site safety manager, Diana Williams (no relation to Greg), to gather more information about what was assumed, based on the message left the previous night, to be a non-work-related death. The OSHA worker asked again if the company was sure that Jody Rhoads had died from natural causes. Diana Williams said that, yes, the company was sure of this because "there wasn't any blood or anything."

The day after that, the OSHA Harrisburg office contacted the Cumberland County Coroner and learned that the autopsy revealed that the cause of death was in fact "multiple traumatic injuries due to a pallet truck accident," including "intestinal bleeding," "lacerated liver," and "bruised heart."

OSHA's Harrisburg office launched an investigation that same day. One of the agency's reports on the matter began by describing in general terms the nature of the business where the death had occurred.

"The company operates warehouses and fulfillment centers nationwide and sells and distributes retail merchandise throughout the country and overseas," the report stated. "The corporate offices are in Seattle, Washington. The establishment is engaged in interstate commerce."

4.

Dignity

The transformation of work

William Kenneth Bodani, Jr., needed to use the bathroom. He was sixty-nine years old and he needed to use the bathroom more often than younger men did, and it took him a little longer when he did. But he was allowed only twenty minutes of "time off task" over a ten-hour shift, in addition to his meal break, and the walk across the twenty-two-acre warehouse could take you half that. If you took longer than your allotted twenty minutes, you collected demerit points and risked being docked pay or being terminated. So he tried his best to hold it.

He was a forklift driver. His job was to unload pallets from the trucks and bring them inside the warehouse. Your supervisors kept close track of how long it took you to unload a truck. You were supposed to get through a truck in only fifteen or twenty minutes. For a typical 52-foot-long trailer, that was at least twenty pallets. You drove right up into the truck and grabbed up the pallets, one or two at a time. Sometimes the goods were loose and someone would need to palletize them before you could move them. Sometimes the pallets were loaded too high, all the way to the top of the trailer, and you needed someone to steady them as you drove to keep them from toppling over.

The way it usually worked, you'd bring the stuff in and it would get broken down by the "water spiders," employees who would distribute it to the workstations where the stowers would store the items in "pods," which were tall stacks of yellow shelving racks. Orange robots would eventually bring the pods to the human pickers, who would send them on to packing and shipping. Recently, at especially busy times like the holidays, the company had started moving high-demand goods straight onto the conveyor belts that led to the packing area—an instantaneous in-and-out to sate consumer demand. Knives. Dishes. Echos. Transformers. Laptops. iPads. "You've got to be on your toes," Bodani said. "You're feeding the lines. As you're unloading the trailer, they need the stuff you're unloading and you've got to get the things to the line."

He'd been doing the work for three years. He had retired from his previous job a dozen years earlier and hadn't planned on working anymore other than side jobs at his friend's motorcycle repair business. He had asthma, asbestosis, emphysema, chronic obstructive pulmonary disease, and PTSD. But the bankruptcy of his former employer had resulted in his monthly pension getting whacked from $3,000 to $1,600, and the expenses related to his medical conditions and his wife's diabetes were rising, and their bungalow needed repairs, so he'd applied for a job at the warehouse after it opened in 2015.

At first, they hadn't hired him—he figured it was because of his age and threatened to take them to court over it, and they'd hired him. The joke of it was, it turned out that he so excelled at the work that they were now having him train drivers. It was an odd spectacle, this old man, overweight and almost seventy, instructing all these young men and women, most in their twenties and thirties. But Bill Bodani—Bo, he'd always been called at the old job—knew his way around a forklift, in fact knew his way around all manner of equipment and machinery far more complex than a forklift. He'd spent three decades doing work even more demanding and dangerous than what he was doing now—but also more rewarding.

That work seemed of a whole other world, even though he had done it on the exact same piece of land where he was now. That piece of land had seen as radical a transformation as any worksite in the country. A story of American labor in the past century lived in this one place: Sparrows Point.

The Point was not named for the bird, nice as it might be to imagine so. It was named for Thomas Sparrow, the English colonist to whom Lord Baltimore granted much of the land in 1652. It was a peninsula of squarish proportions about a mile and a half wide and long, a claw jutting from the Patapsco Neck peninsula into the Patapsco River, the inlet that led from the Chesapeake Bay to Baltimore's Inner Harbor. The Point lay west of Fort Howard, near where 4,500 British soldiers had landed in the War of 1812, and within view of Fort McHenry, where American cannons had held off the British naval attack under Francis Scott Key's enraptured witness. But the Point itself had remained an expanse of marsh and farmland until 1887, when it was discovered by Frederick Wood.

Wood was an engineer for the Pennsylvania Steel Company, which was looking for a tidewater port within easy reach of its plant in Steelton, Pennsylvania, ninety miles to the north. Steel manufacturing was booming from Pennsylvania westward to Chicago, spurred by the technological advances of Henry Bessemer, the British inventor, and the voracious demand for steel rail from the giant companies racing each other to lay tracks across the country. To make steel you needed coal, limestone, and iron ore. Coal was plentiful up and down the Appalachian chain, and Pennsylvania was full of limestone. Iron ore was another matter. The biggest known U.S. deposits were in the Upper Peninsula of Michigan; the ore could be shipped through the Great Lakes to steel plants in the Midwest, but getting it to eastern Pennsylvania was arduous.

Fortunately for the eastern United States, Wood had found deep iron ore deposits on a scouting trip to Cuba in 1882, when he was only twenty-five. Pennsylvania Steel president Luther Bent and a steamship owner had persuaded the island's Spanish overlords to allow them to mine the iron for twenty years free of any royalties. All that was needed now was a port to which to deliver it. In 1887, Wood, not yet thirty, settled on Sparrows Point, and Pennsylvania Steel bought most of the peninsula from five landowners for a mere $57,900.

Within weeks, workers had put up a brickyard that was quickly producing 30,000 bricks per day to build the facilities as well as a 900-foot-long wharf, and had laid tracks on the pier. The Point would be more than a port—it would convert the imported ore into pig iron that would be brought north by rail to Steelton. The first locomotive arrived in mid-July, the company store opened in August, and ground was broken for the blast furnaces by October. The marshy ground was drained, with oyster shells used as fill. Over the next two years, fifteen tons of material per day were brought to the Point by rail and barge to build the immense new works. Wood's brother Rufus took charge of laying out the town that would house the army of workers needed for the plant. And in Annapolis, the company lobbied for the right to remain lord of its new domain, free of nettlesome incorporation or the reach of the elected government in suburban Baltimore County, to which it putatively belonged. Sparrows Point would be the ultimate company town.

On May 30, 1890, the works were ready for their grand opening. Dignitaries from Washington, Baltimore, and Philadelphia arrived by rail. The company hoisted them up eighty-five feet on an elevator to the charging platform on top of one blast furnace, from which they watched transfixed as workers shot off a blast in another furnace two hundred feet away, sending bolts of fire across the sky.

They were rewarded for their awe with a luncheon of crab hors d'oeuvres, terrapin, and whole spring chicken, followed by cigars and toast-making. In his authoritative history of the Point, Mark Reutter quotes Cardinal James Gibbons, the archbishop of Baltimore, as he hailed Luther Bent's new works as the solution to the "great problem of labor." "I have always spoken kind words for the laborers," said Gibbons. "To-day I am in the presence of capitalists and I feel that if anyone has the power to solve this great problem it is our friend who presides here to-day. He will gratify the capitalist by erecting these great furnaces and by producing large dividends; he will bring joy to the laborer by building comfortable homes and paying them good wages. The best interests of each are the interests of both."

Baltimore mayor John Davidson saw only happy symbiosis as well. "Your prosperity is our prosperity," he told Bent. "Your interests are our interests."

The capitalist was indeed gratified by what flowed from the Point. It soon became apparent that the Point could hold a full steelworks, complete with the "Bessemer converters" that made steel out of iron. Frederick Wood managed to contrive a compact, bottleneck-free production line unlike anything else in the country.

Three years after the grand luncheon, a Bessemer crew at the Point could produce 300 tons of steel per day. By that point, the plant had its own shipyard. By 1900, 3,000 people were working on the Point and 3,500 were living there. By 1906, it was producing enough tonnage per year to lay double tracks from New York to Sacramento.

Less clear was whether the works were bringing joy to the laborer. Frederick Wood had his workers on a brutal schedule: ten or eleven hours per day for a week of daytime shift, followed by thirteen or fourteen hours per night for a week of night shift—and on the changeover day, Sunday, the night shift would work twenty-four hours straight. It wouldn't get a day off until the following Sunday, when the other crew worked straight through for twenty-four hours.

For this relentless toil, Pennsylvania Steel paid laborers $1.10 per day in 1895. The company granted only two holidays all year, Christmas and the Fourth of July—unpaid. Even if a laborer worked every day of the year but for those holidays, he'd make less than $400. As Reutter notes, that was well below the $500 to $600 that the U.S. Bureau of Labor judged the minimum for an "American standard of living" for a family of five at the time.

To any such carping, the company could argue that it was at least providing subsidized housing. The settlement designed by Rufus Wood was a tidy grid half a mile upwind from the furnaces, bisected by Humphrey Creek and explicitly arrayed by rank. Managers and foremen lived in big houses with steam heating and electric lights on B and C Streets—there was even electricity in those homes one day a week, "ironing day" for housewives.

Skilled tradesmen, mostly of English and German descent and many transplanted from steel towns in Pennsylvania and Ohio, lived in modest rowhouses and cottages on E and F Streets, where the streets were lit by kerosene. Recent immigrants from Eastern and Southern Europe were relegated to shacks along the creek if they had families and to a crude shantytown behind the furnaces if they did not. But Frederick Wood did not care much for these immigrants, seeing them as unreliable.

His vast preference for the unskilled labor that powered the works was Black men. Not Black men from Baltimore, which, by 1890, had a sizable African American population of 67,000. They were too headstrong. Far more desirable were strong, young Black men from down in Virginia, which is where the company sent its recruiters. "City blacks might say straight out, 'I'm not going to do this job,'" the son of a worker from South Carolina told Deborah Rudacille, the daughter of a steelworker, for her 2010 book on the Point. "But not if you from down south." If these men came north with families, they lived in humble pine-planked duplexes on two streets on the north side of Humphrey Creek, I and J, which were linked to the rest of the town by a footbridge. If they did not have families, they lived in the shantytown. *The Baltimore Sun* marveled at the neatness of the company's arrangement in a 1906 article. At Sparrows Point, the paper reported, "the race problem . . . has practically [been] solved by putting the blacks on a far side of broad waters of a creek apart from the whites."

The rest of Rufus Wood's vision would grow alongside this meticulously segregated grid. The company store expanded to a large complex with a Smokers Hall and men's and women's clothing stores and the main goods store, where you could buy flour and sugar, pots and pans, furniture, firewood, coal, and hardware, and fruit pies for a nickel. The company baked its own bread, grew its own vegetables, milked its own 150 cows, slaughtered its own steer (twenty per week), and even blended its own gasoline. There was daily milk delivery. Bakery, meat, and produce wagons made rounds a few times a week. There were houseboats in the creek selling sweets. There was a restaurant attached to an inn where engineering students stayed while getting training during summer breaks.

The Point boasted two schools (one white and one Black) and had the first kindergarten south of the Mason-Dixon Line, six churches (four for white people, two for Black people), a blacksmith and wagon shop, a ships' chandlery, a movie theater with duckpin bowling in the basement (the Lyceum), and a bathing beach along A Street. The town offered the state's first home-ec courses for girls, who were trained in a model home, so "that the young ladies may not be remiss in the details of housekeeping." Sparrows Point High School opened in 1910 and got its own building, with castle-like spires and turrets, in 1922.

All the town lacked, really, were bars: the sale of alcohol was prohibited within a mile and a half radius. In practice, this meant that workers took the train to any of many saloons that sprang up beyond the Point's borders.

And who would blame them? The work was not only taxing but unremittingly dangerous. Rudacille lays bare the extent of the peril in her book. In a single six-month period in 1910, there were 10 fatal accidents, and that wasn't all: there were also 3 accidents in which workers were partially disabled, 304 "severe" accidents, and 1,421 "minor accidents." The company wrote these off as a trifling cost of business: Reutter relays an "accident expense account" from the Sparrows Point hospital in 1902 in which the "total cost per accident" for the 2,336 accidents that year was a mere $3.91. That included $150 for "artificial limbs, eyes, etc." and $638.50 for funeral expenses. Fatalities were so common that the company had a trolley car dedicated to carrying the dead to cemeteries in the city. It was called Dolores.

Such conditions—treacherous labor with little rest for very low pay—could, Reutter notes, "only work in a union-free atmosphere." Realizing this, the company did all it could to keep the atmosphere clear. Wood required that workers sign a "Conditions of Employment" slip listing "agitation" and "insubordination" as grounds for firing. There was also the threat of losing one's home: workers needed their foreman's signature to apply for housing in town. When workers went on strike in Steelton to no avail, Wood trumpeted Sparrows Point as an "open shop" free of the union taint. "Abandon Hope All Ye Who Enter Here," the Baltimore labor newspaper declared in an 1891 headline about the Point.

Remarkably, the anti-union paternalism of the Wood brothers would look preferable to what followed it. In 1916, Pennsylvania Steel was bought by Bethlehem Steel, its longtime in-state rival based in the Lehigh Valley city after which it was named. Under the leadership of Charles Schwab (no relation to the stockbroker), Bethlehem had been expanding rapidly by supplying the war machine laying waste to Europe. Bethlehem skirted the limits that U.S. neutrality early in the war imposed on selling munitions to the Allies—the company was the second-largest recipient of Allied orders during this period, after DuPont. Over a four-month period of late 1916 when the French, British, and Germans lost more than a million men, Bethlehem sold more than $23 million in arms to the British and French.

Under Schwab's direction, Sparrows Point expanded rapidly to do its part for this lucrative new mission. The company bought the last 533 acres of the peninsula and expanded it outward by another 100 acres, with steel pilings and fill. In July 1917, three months after the United States entered the war, the plant got its first sheet and tinplate mills, making it the only fully integrated tin plant east of Pittsburgh. And business surged at its shipyard, besting East Coast rivals that lacked adjacent steel plant production. Thousands more workers were brought in—average daily employment tripled to 12,500.

The 1918 armistice was bad for business, but Bethlehem seized on new markets. Automakers needed steel for the more than two million cars they made in 1920. Food manufacturers needed tin for the booming business in canned goods: By the mid-1920s, Sparrows Point was turning out enough tinplate to produce about two *billion* cans per year. This new line of business brought hundreds of women into the plant: the so-called tin floppers, who stood at long tables checking sheets of metal for flaws. The Point was also providing the steel for the mega-projects of the decade: cast-iron segments for tubing of the Holland Tunnel under the Hudson River, plate and girders for the Benjamin Franklin Bridge linking Philadelphia and Camden, New Jersey, and, a few years later, plate and other superstructure for the Golden Gate Bridge. The ranks of workers grew so large that a whole new town sprang up to the north, Dundalk, along with the adjacent Black enclave of Turner Station.

By the 1920s, Bethlehem Steel was the third-largest company in the country, ranked by assets, after only U.S. Steel and Standard Oil of New Jersey. A paltry share of that growth, though, was making it to the laborer of Cardinal Gibbons's exhortation at the grand opening years earlier. Pay had increased from the Wood years, but only so much: the average worker was making $2,000 per year in 1925, below $30,000 in today's dollars. Seasonal layoffs were common. The federal government had pressured the company to treat workers better during the war or risk losing contracts, but Schwab had staved off reprisal by invoking the company's "employee representation plan," an in-house body under the thumb of management. "We make our own labor unions," he declared. "I will not permit myself to be in the position of having labor dictate to the management."

Schwab was pioneering the dominant model of the American CEO later in the century. He urged a monomaniacal drive to success. "If you must be a glutton, be a glutton for work," he wrote in a 1917 how-to booklet. "I have yet to hear an instance where misfortune hit a man because he worked overtime. I know lots of instances where it hit men who did not. . . . Much more serious than physical injury is the slow, relentless blight that brings standstill, lack of advancement, final failure." He scorned long meetings—decisions were made without dithering at luncheons in Bethlehem. He discouraged civic engagement—sitting on a local bank board, involvement in local politics, anything that would take away from the company. "Always More Production" was the slogan devised by his protégé, Eugene Grace.

And Schwab made sure that a disproportionate share of gains flowed to him and his fellow executives. He set aside millions in bonuses—Beth Steel executives were the highest paid in the country. Reutter estimates Schwab earned $21 million from his Bethlehem holdings over the war years alone—nearly $400 million today. This fortune made its way into his block-long mansion on Riverside Drive in New York City. At seventy-five rooms filled with Old Masters and a dining salon that could seat two hundred fifty, it was the largest private residence in the city. His thousand-acre, eighteen-building estate in Pennsylvania required a full-time staff of seventy and included a replica of a farming village he had seen in Normandy.

Francis Bodani lived in the town of Sparrows Point, which was, by the late 1920s, home to more than 4,000 people. He had come from Sicily earlier in the decade, started out in New York, and moved to Baltimore instead. He failed to make it as a cobbler, so headed to Beth Steel, as a laborer in the blast furnaces. He rented a house on the north side of the town, where some of the lowliest white workers were relegated to living not far from the Black families. The creek had been filled in near the end of the war and replaced with playing fields, but Black people were still clustered on I and J Streets, and still spoke of "going over the creek" to the white side of town. Many Black women made that trek daily, to work in the managers' homes.

This was in 1929, not a fortunate time to start. The crash devastated steelmaking more than just about any industry—by early 1932, 9 of 10 of the nation's 500,000 steelworkers would either be laid off or put on reduced time. Average steelworker wages nationally plunged from $32.60 per week to $13.20. The ranks of workers at Sparrows Point were down by a third, and those remaining were almost all working only part-time; by the end of 1932, there were only 3,500 daily jobs at the plant. Workers survived by foraging crops in nearby fields. Schwab's minions held off on evictions of families who couldn't make the rent and forgave debts at the company store.

Sparrows Point had previously leaned Republican. But in November 1932, it swung heavily Democratic, along with other working-class precincts across Baltimore, to elect Franklin D. Roosevelt. He and Secretary of Labor Frances Perkins, the first woman to serve in the cabinet, made saving the steel industry a first order of business, seeing stabilization of wages as essential to restoring consumer demand. Roosevelt's administration presided over an industry-wide council that, in an emergency breach of anti-cartel laws, set minimum wage levels. The new Public Works Administration put $51 million into buying rails and rail fastenings. Perkins visited Sparrows Point, where she insisted on meeting with workers.

All this attention from the administration had, within a few years, helped to stabilize the industry. But it also came with a downside for industry overlords: the administration was explicit in its encouragement of efforts to organize steelworkers. John L. Lewis, the heavy-browed leader of the United Mine Workers, made it his mission to bring steelworkers into the union fold. The industry "has never throughout the past 35 years paid a bare subsistence wage, not to mention a living wage, to the great mass of its workers," he said in 1936. The time had come to decide "whether the working population of this country shall have a voice in determining their destiny or whether they shall serve as indentured servants for a financial and economic dictatorship which would shamelessly exploit our natural resources and debase the soul and destroy the pride of a free people."

A year later, the new steelworkers union achieved its breakthrough, signing a contract with U.S. Steel. That giant was motivated less by Perkins's theories of employee purchasing power than by demands from England, which was building up its military to counter the Nazi threat, that the company be able to guarantee production—i.e., avoid labor unrest.

Beth Steel, the second-largest steelmaker, would prove a tougher target. The company was still holding up the figment of its in-house employee representation plan, claiming that no fewer than 97 percent of workers had recently voted in its favor. To deflect Lewis's organizers, it matched U.S. Steel's wages and unleashed a tide of anti-union propaganda. "Outsiders have not been necessary in the past," one manifesto warned. "Nothing has happened to make them necessary now." It armed company police with several boxcars' worth of machine guns, submachine guns, army rifles, shotguns, pistols, and revolvers, and purchased more tear gas supplies than any law enforcement agency in the country.

Organizers pressed on regardless. They held secret meetings at a tavern in the southeast Baltimore neighborhood of Highlandtown. They tapped into discontent over the company's inscrutable wage incentive system, under which some workers were paid much less than others for similar work, and over its callous handling of the transition to a new, more automated mill that needed fewer men. And they engaged the plant's Black workers. In other industries and other towns, union discrimination had so often left Black workers in the role of strikebreakers. Organizers knew this would be fatal to their effort in Baltimore, given how many workers were Black—nearly a third of the plant, the largest pocket of Black steelworkers outside of Birmingham, Alabama. Organizers went door-to-door in Black neighborhoods and spoke at Black churches; white and Black pro-union workers paraded together in Dundalk, the white working-class town north of the Point.

In the end, it was the coming war that did it. In 1939, the National Labor Relations Board ruled that the company had engaged in a long-term strategy of anti-union intimidation and ordered the dismantling of the bogus in-house plan. Exerting more pressure was the risk of losing out on the gargantuan contracts to build Roosevelt's "arsenal of democracy." On September 25, 1941—barely more than two months before Pearl Harbor—a union election was finally held. Nearly 11,000 workers voted in favor—68.7 percent of ballots cast. Some 6,000 of the plant's 6,500 Black workers voted, the vast majority in favor.

So it was a fully unionized plant that would reap the extraordinary benefits of this wartime expansion, at a scale that dwarfed the First World War's extravaganza. The open-hearth furnaces, which had replaced the Bessemer converters for making steel, now spread across one hundred acres. Over the next few years, the shipyard built more than one hundred ships while the emergency wartime shipyard the company opened on the other side of the harbor, called Fairfield, ramped up from zero to more than 45,000 workers and built more than five hundred ships, mostly the unlovely but hugely important Liberty cargo carriers.

For those on the Point, the war was giving new purpose to work that, for many, was already more rewarding than such arduous labor might seem.

Here's how Mike Howard described working in the open-hearth furnace to Mark Reutter: "I felt good. When you're in your prime, physical work is a challenge, and if you're working with other people, there is a certain pride in being on top of the job. The demands of the work bred a kind of man who was fiercely committed to this work." Howard distinguished between "brutalizing work" and "challenging work": "In the open hearth, you had to cope with problems that involved metallurgy, that involved blacksmithing, that involved judgment. These were not guys who were a bunch of punch-drunk wrestlers. They were bright. There were split-second decisions that had to be made. There were a lot of challenges that kept you on your toes."

There was, in other words, an "artistry" to steelmaking, writes the Bethlehem, Pennsylvania, journalist John Strohmeyer in his 1986 history of the company named for his town. "Anyone who has the muscle can swing a pick and mine coal, they will tell you. Robots can assemble automobiles. But it takes uncommon talent, a strong body, and a mind that knows no fear to be able to transform piles of red dirt and scrap into the molten metal that is poured, rolled and pounded into the various shapes that support the mainframes of civilization."

By early 1942, Bethlehem Steel was the largest war contractor in the country. Reutter offers some of the astonishing metrics: Between 1940 and 1945, the company produced one-third of the armor plate and gun forgings needed by the navy. The company's gross sales soared from less than $200 million in 1935 to more than $1.3 billion in 1945. "When Hitler challenged such industries, he invited the rain of metal which he finds is beyond endurance," declared a *Baltimore Sun* caption to portentous 1944 images of the Point by photographer Aubrey Bodine.

With its global rivals lying in ruins, the United States was now producing nearly two-thirds of the world's steel. The industry that had done more than any other to help the United States win the war was nearing its apex. So, too, was the place that had been transformed by that effort, both the company town and the nearby city to which its fate was yoked. On May 14, 1945, one week after the Nazi surrender, the Baltimore mayor Theodore McKeldin made Eugene Grace, who'd taken over the company at Schwab's death in 1939, an honorary citizen of the city. McKeldin wrote: "The Bethlehem Steel Plant at Sparrows Point, with its tremendous permanent facilities and its use of local labor and production, is our special pride."

The postwar boom brought Sparrows Point even more work than it had when making steel for Liberty ships and fighter planes. Some 85 percent of manufactured goods required steel, above all the resplendent new cars—Detroit's demand for flat-rolled steel surged by 55 percent in 1946. Among those placing orders from the Point was the General Motors plant a few miles away, on Broening Highway.

Bethlehem Steel heaped capital into the peninsula to add capacity. To feed its voracious appetite for iron ore, the company's ships were now going as far as Chile and Venezuela. By 1953, Beth Steel's production was larger than that of all of rapidly rebuilding Germany, while production across the United States was larger than the rest of the world combined. When Arthur Vogel arrived at the Point in 1949 to work as a scrap baler, he was overwhelmed. "Going into the mill, seeing something that big—it actually frightened me," he said later. "I looked around and thought: 'This is it.'"

And as a result of Sparrows Point's unionization, workers were getting a considerable share of the prosperity. In 1946, a nationwide strike by the steelworkers—now the largest industrial union—resulted in an 18.5 cent boost in hourly wages. Aghast at such gains, the business lobby a year later got Congress to pass, over President Truman's veto, the anti-union Taft-Hartley Act, a big impediment to future labor organizing.

Regular contract bargaining in 1955 brought steel wages up an average of 15 cents more. Steelworkers had also won the nation's first private-sector pension for blue-collar workers. A nationwide strike in 1959 that finally ended after 116 days with an executive order from President Eisenhower brought another 8 percent raise in pay and full coverage of health and welfare benefits.

But the union gains went beyond that. With more worker input in plant management, the Point had gotten less catastrophically dangerous than it had been in the early days. And there was something less tangible, too. "What the men themselves wanted the union for," one retiree told Reutter in the 1980s, "was to have everyone respect your seniority and your ability, and not have these here bosses' pets and brown-nosers get the best jobs. We got more money, that was important, sure, but we got respect more, that was number one."

A year after the 1955 wage hike, Beth Steel authorized a $300 million company-wide expansion that would boost Sparrows Point's production by nearly 30 percent, to more than 8 million tons of steel per year, or 16 tons per minute, and add 3,000 workers, bringing the total very close to 30,000. "We're bullish in respect to demand," said Grace, the company chairman. And Sparrows Point, he declared, was "the greatest show on earth."

That was debatable. But by 1958, this much was true: Sparrows Point had surpassed the U.S. Steel works in Gary, Indiana, to become the largest steel plant in the world.

How to convey the Point's scale at this moment in time? Seen from across the Patapsco, it presented a veritable skyline, with its row of smokestacks stretching to more than twenty stories high. Seen from above, it was a mass of roofs and chimneys as dense as a rain forest canopy—crammed onto the peninsula were 1,700 buildings, and 45 miles of paved roads, and more than 100 miles of track used by more than 60 locomotives and 3,400 railway cars. Every single day, to keep machinery cool, the Point was consuming 540 million gallons of salt water, 15 million gallons of fresh water, and 100 million gallons of industrial water, the nice term for repurposed wastewater that still carried the uric whiff of its origins. The Point was also consuming more than 11,000 tons of coal per day and 1/500th of the nation's electricity, via 10,000 miles' worth of electric power lines. It had a 110-man fire department and a 196-man police department, the state's second-largest force after Baltimore's, which practiced its marksmanship at the Point's pistol range, the largest in the country. It had its own jail. Despite availing itself of few county services, it paid $2 million per year, more than $17 million in today's dollars, in local taxes. The company was so eager to hire young men at good wages that it set up a table at high school commencements—graduates could walk straight from class into a job.

This was the Point in which William Bodani, Jr., was raised. His grandfather, Francis, had come through the upheaval of the Depression and war, and moved from the furnaces and into the foundry. Francis and his wife had six kids. Their third eldest, William, graduated from Sparrows Point High during the war and was later hired as a truck driver in the transportation department, hauling bulldozers and other big equipment across the three-thousand-acre expanse.

Bill, Jr., was born in 1949. Housing was so tight that his family lived in his grandfather's house for the first few years of his life before getting their own nearby. It was an idyllic place to grow up. By now, the streets were lined with trees. The highlight of the year was the Steel Bowl on Thanksgiving, the Sparrows Point High football team facing off against Dundalk High, with a parade the day before. The number 26 streetcar from Baltimore, the "Red Rocket," came into the middle of town. Close by, the Sparrows Point Country Club had a golf course, marina, pool, and clubhouse with a dance floor.

The North Side had its own commercial cluster—a grocery, a dance hall, and a Black-run pool hall, barbershop, lunch counter, and snack shop, where kids could get ice cream in exchange for washing some dishes. Black people were free to shop on the south side—they just couldn't sit in the restaurant or at the lunch counter (carryout only) or see movies at the Lyceum (they watched them at the Black Methodist church). The Black school on the Point went no higher than seventh grade. In 1939, Baltimore County agreed to start paying to send Black students to high school in the city, but only if they passed a test; in 1948, the county built a Black high school in nearby Turner Station. Racist taunts sometimes arose during touch football games between white and Black. "Then we would have to fight our way back to J Street," recalled Roy Winston Cragway, Sr. "However, when the next week would roll around, we'd go back on the white side and play touch football all over again."

Bitterness over Jim Crow shines through in Black residents' accounts of the Point. So does nostalgia for the togetherness of the North Side, where supervision for kids was a mutual affair, where it was almost assumed you would marry the girl across the street. Louis Diggs: "Everyone had a garden, and shared their bounty with each other." Florence Parks: "Life in Sparrows Point was absolutely beautiful." Annia Ruth Randolph: "You never had to lock your door, you could always depend on your neighbors for anything." Theodore Patterson: "We looked out for each other. It was a shared existence." Roy Cragway: "The community was so close knit that it was unbelievable." Charlotte Cager Harvey: "Everyone had plenty of food, nice clothes to wear, good morals, not a lot of drinking." On winter mornings, Charlotte would watch her father ice skating on the creek. "He was so graceful."

There was one thing everyone shared—everyone from managers on B Street to the women on J Street who worked for their wives. And that was the air. You had to take a bath at the end of every day because of all the red flakes showering down when the stacks blew. The sky might be blue elsewhere on the Chesapeake, but over the Point it would be "this ashen red pall, much like the Martian sky photographed by Mariner," as the *Baltimore News-American* reporter Mark Bowden later described it. When the windows were open at school, papers turned red with the dust. Locals called it "gold dust," the traces of prosperity.

Not surprisingly, a lot of kids developed asthma—Bill, Jr., among them. When he was twelve, his family moved into the city, partly so that his siblings might be spared that fate, and partly because the town was by this point shrinking to make room for the ever-expanding works.

With its move back into the city, the Bodani family was swimming against a flow. Baltimore had swelled mightily during the war, brushing against the million-resident mark during the war before registering a tally of 949,000 in 1950, its highest ever in the decennial census. It was the sixth-largest city—larger than Washington, Boston, San Francisco, or Houston. But even in this moment of crescendo, the decline was quietly underway, in the steady leakage of suburban flight. They were leaving for bigger homes and bigger lawns, but they were also moving to get away. By 1940, even before the flood of workers that arrived later in the war years, Baltimore would have the highest proportion of Black people of the country's ten biggest cities—a fifth of the city, 168,000 people. Initially constrained to slices of the city's east and west side, in homes packed to the point of squalor, they sought more humane conditions and in doing so caused great consternation. First came discriminatory ordinances to keep them from moving onto majority-white blocks, then came redlining by banks and regulators. By the late 1940s, though, the pressure from the burgeoning ghetto, swelled by the Great Migration, was too much even for discriminatory maps to bear. The more prosperous of Black families—those with union jobs at places like Beth Steel—boldly advanced into new neighborhoods.

It is hard to overstate the suddenness of the resulting flight. Edmondson Village, a German Catholic neighborhood of 30,000 in southwest Baltimore, flipped almost entirely from white to Black in the late 1950s and early 1960s. Gwynns Falls Elementary School, in a Jewish section of the west side, was all white before *Brown v. Board* ruled school segregation unconstitutional in 1954. Baltimore officials complied, and when the school opened that September, it was 44.5 percent Black. Two years after that, it was 93 percent Black—in three years, it had transformed almost completely.

The teenage Bill Bodani was mostly oblivious to all this as he settled into his new school, Patterson High, in southeast Baltimore, the part of town where the white working class would hold out in greater numbers than elsewhere. Despite his asthma, he played in almost every sport he could: football, baseball, lacrosse, swim team. During high school summers, he worked at the GM plant on Broening Highway, putting bumpers on Chevelles.

After he graduated, better-paying work beckoned on the Point. Beth Steel was hiring, and his status as a legacy, and as a member of the Sons of Italy, gave him a leg up. He was hired as a laborer in mechanical maintenance in 1967. His paycheck sometimes got mixed up with that of Bill Bodani, Sr., now working in locomotive maintenance. His dad was Bo, too. He was Little Bo.

Little Bo was on the verge of being drafted, so he enlisted instead, in the navy. He spent six years in the service—two with the Seabees, serving under a young lieutenant named John Kerry, and four with the SEALs, going places he still wouldn't reveal decades later. On furloughs, he'd come right back and put in a few weeks or months at the Point.

When he finally got out, in 1975, he had a pretty bad case of PTSD. The job was still waiting for him. But it was not the same Sparrows Point, or city.

When Bo had first started at the plant in 1967, he made the mistake of going into the wrong bathroom by mistake. "Whoa!" someone hollered. "You don't go in there. Read the sign."

The bathrooms were still segregated at the Point. So were the locker rooms, cafeterias, and water fountains. Work was segregated, too: most Black men were still employed as laborers, making little more than $2 per hour and tasked with some of the most treacherous work of all, the "hot bull work," such as manning the coke ovens, where you had to wear thermals in the summer to protect yourself from the heat and pop salt tablets against the copious sweat, or putting tags on the red-hot wire coming out of the wire mill. There was one breakthrough: many Black employees now worked as crane operators. But there was only one Black electrician in a unit of over three hundred.

The union had, here and there, challenged management over its blatant discrimination. In 1949, it had gone to arbitration over the company's refusal to promote Charlie Parrish, a skilled Black repairman, to become the plant's first millwright—it promoted a white man with nine fewer years' seniority instead. "Mr. Parrish had 22 years of service, and you have isolated Mr. Parrish and the rest of this [Black] group by itself and have not given them an opportunity to advance," said the union lawyer. A plant supervisor responded: "We have assigned him to jobs within his ability."

Finally, in 1966, two workers marched into the East Baltimore offices of the Congress of Racial Equality to register a complaint about rampant discrimination on the Point. CORE assigned two white volunteers to investigate, and later sent four busloads of workers to protest at company headquarters in Bethlehem, and then a delegation to the Department of Labor in Washington, where they noted that, under a 1964 executive order signed by

Lyndon Johnson, Beth Steel should be at risk of losing federal contracts—including those related to the new war in Vietnam—because of its discriminatory practices.

The pressure worked, to a degree. In 1967, the government ordered the company to comply with a list of reforms or risk losing contracts. Over the next few years, the number of Black foremen reached one hundred, and Black workers were added to craft apprenticeship programs. A wildcat strike in January 1974 led by Black workers—with support from younger white workers, many of them recently returned from Vietnam—won better working conditions in the coke ovens.

Finally, later in 1974, the U.S. Department of Justice settled discrimination suits against Beth Steel and other companies with an industry-wide consent decree under which companies agreed to new seniority rules so that someone transferring to a new unit could count years in the former unit toward seniority, making it easier for Black people to ascend ranks. The settlement also came with payouts to all minority workers for past discrimination, but they were so meager—about $600 each—that many declined to accept them.

There was still plenty of resistance. After the decree was announced, flyers appeared at the plant advertising a local KKK chapter. A white electrician who dared to train secretly the first Black apprentice in the department found human feces in his lunch box. But over time, the new reality took hold. And it gave an immense boost to Black Baltimore. Even as laborers, Black Beth Steel workers had enjoyed a stability that eluded many elsewhere. "Our people may not have had the highest level of jobs, but they worked steady," said one, Theodore Patterson. "There was no welfare on Sparrows Point." Now, as they were allowed into skilled trades and higher-paid ranks, they could achieve true upward mobility.

James Drayton was making $2.30 per hour when he started at eighteen in the labor gang in the primary mill in 1965. He was following in the footsteps of his father, a Second World War and Korean War veteran. The locker rooms were still segregated. But bit by bit, the reforms took hold. He watched as many of his white coworkers bridled, and then adapted. (It didn't hurt that the new seniority rules were helping some of the older white workers, too, who were being displaced out of their skilled trades by technological advances and moved into new units.) "They finally got the message," Drayton said. "I guess that they understood that that was the way it was going to be. They had to settle in with the idea."

Drayton became one of the first Black crane operators. And in all of his other later positions in the mill, his years as a laborer finally counted toward his seniority, so that he enjoyed an earned authority over younger guys coming in. His income climbed steadily, surpassing $40,000 before his retirement in the 1990s. He bought a house in a nice section of far West Baltimore. All five of his children went to college. One son would become the head of the National Bar Association, an organization for Black lawyers.

"I was middle class," Drayton says.

What timing, though. For it was exactly as James Drayton and thousands of other Black workers at the plant were getting a foothold that the world of the Point began to unravel.

The warning signs had been there much earlier, during the boom years, in the company's complacent disinclination to explore new ways of doing business or prepare for shifts in the marketplace. There had been precious few innovations, other than a wide-flange high-rise beam introduced in 1909 that was pivotal for skyscrapers. The company had spurned an offer in the 1920s from a smaller steelmaker, Armco, to share its breakthrough technique for rolling wide steel. It spent strikingly little on research and development and favored straight-arrow company men over freethinkers (in its 1940s heyday, the company stressed its preference for men with "good physique"). In its late-'50s expansion, it stuck with the same formula from decades prior, building the largest open-hearth furnace in the world, two football fields long, instead of trying the more efficient technologies being pioneered by the Europeans, such as the basic oxygen furnace, which could produce as much steel in forty-five minutes as the open hearth did in six to eight hours.

The corporate somnolence reached macabre extremes after Eugene Grace, the new chief executive, suffered a stroke in 1957: while he turned over operations to his chosen successor, he still presided over meetings, where he would sometimes nod off to sleep. The board would sit in silence for as long as an hour, waiting for him to wake so the meeting could resume.

The arrogance was industry-wide. Beth Steel, U.S. Steel, and the lesser giants skirted anti-cartel rules to push through price increases that in the fat years easily outpaced the wage increases they were awarding for union contracts. Where was the money going, if not to wages? At Beth Steel, it was going to brute plant expansion—and to executive pay and benefits. The company, whose board for decades lacked any outsiders, poured millions into its executive country club in Bethlehem—a clubhouse with chandeliers, a three-pool swimming complex linked to an indoor pool lounge by a magnolia terrace, and executive squash courts. In 1956, Eugene Grace claimed the title of the highest-paid chief executive in the country; three years later, seven of the ten highest-paid executives in the country were at Bethlehem. "Bethlehem at that time had the reputation that its hallways were lined with gold, and when you became employed there, they gave you a pick to mine it," a member of the company's legal staff told Strohmeyer, the Bethlehem journalist.

Such overweening pride made a tempting target for upstart rivals. Aluminum makers made a cheaper can for beer; plastics and concrete also horned in as an alternative material for all sorts of products. So-called minimills in the South and West used nonunion labor to make smaller steel products from scrap in electric furnaces at much lower cost. The Europeans and especially the Japanese began challenging the giants with competitive prices made possible thanks not only to lower labor costs but to the sort of innovative technology the giants scorned—steel bars from Japan were running 15 percent cheaper, while sheet and coil was $60 per ton lower.

U.S. imports of steel surged from 3.3 million tons in 1960 to 21.1 million in 1978, surpassing U.S. Steel's production by year's end. By the end of that year, production at the Point had dropped by 2 million tons from its peak, more than 20 percent. Faring no better was shipbuilding—the Arab oil embargo had devastated an over-capacity tanker business, and by 1978, employment at the shipyard had dropped below 4,000, half its peak, while the tally overall at the Point had fallen below 20,000. And the company was finally being forced to reckon with at least some of the costs of the pollution pumped through the smokestacks and the outfall sewers and artificial lagoons: a daily flow of 640 million gallons of water laced with corrosive pickling liquors, oils, coke-tar chemicals, and heavy metals such as lead, copper, and nickel that had turned the waters of the bay, where once Point residents had been able to scoop up bushels of crabs almost at will, into a murk where young Deborah Rudacille was forbidden even to dip her toe.

The town, meanwhile, was gone completely. The last vestiges had been cleared in 1973 to make room for the nearly 300-foot-tall "L" blast furnace.

The turn of fortune on the Point had its counterpart in the city next door. The flight from Baltimore that had started stealthily a few decades earlier was now a rush. If there had been something shameful in that earlier escape from the new neighbors, this new flight could be easily rationalized. There had been a riot, in the days after Martin Luther King, Jr.'s assassination, which claimed six lives and resulted in more than 5,000 arrests; there was crime and drugs, as heroin grew more entrenched; and there was now, to a degree there had not been before, deindustrialization. The city's population fell by 119,000 over the 1970s, still its largest drop in a decade in both absolute and proportional terms. Virtually the entire loss was from white residents. In 1970, the city was majority white. After a decade's flight, that share had fallen to well below half and was on its way to less than a third.

There was still work to be done on the Point, and it was not overstating matters to say that Bo loved it. This, despite the fact that for most of his three decades there, he worked at laborer rank. When he started in 1967, his gang was mostly Black. As the reforms kicked in, some of those workers climbed the ladder. Bo remained in the labor gangs, getting pulled from one job to another. It meant holding a permanent junior status, but it also meant getting to do it all, see it all. There was hardly a part of the works he hadn't touched.

From laborer in mechanical maintenance, he'd moved to mechanic in locomotive repair, fixing the narrow-gauge trains that hauled steel ingots to the various finishing mills.

From there, he moved into the 68-inch hot-strip mill, working as a bander. The steel coils would come down the line cherry-red and you had to lasso on a metal band and draw it tight, while making sure not to lift up your head, because if you did, the heat would get in under the plastic shield they gave you and you'd have third-degree burns on your neck before you knew it. You could go through a dozen masks in a shift.

From there, to the transportation department, where his dad still worked. He'd run into his dad, who would make fun of his long hair. "This is my daughter," he'd say to the other guys. Little Bo drove dump trucks, hauling "precipitator dust" that came out of the open-hearth furnaces, the red dust that had likely given him his asthma.

He cleaned slag out of the hot-strip mill. They'd shut the furnace down and you'd go in with wooden shoes that were an inch and a half thick, half over your own shoes to protect you from the heat of the slag, and use a jackhammer to bust up the slag, which other guys would then carry out in wheelbarrows. It was so hot that you'd take turns working—forty-five minutes on, forty-five minutes off. It was so hot that the wooden shoes would sometimes start to smoke.

He cleaned out the flues, little tunnels that were a hundred feet underground in the No. 3 and 4 open hearths. The tunnels were about six or seven feet by three feet and you'd go in with jackhammers and clean out the mud, and contractors riding little bulldozers, like toy bulldozers, would push the stuff up and others would load it on a cart and a guy would draw it up in a crane. If a cave-in happened in one of those tunnels, forget it.

He worked in the skin pass mill, dealing with what they called crashes, where everything would jam up and you had to get in there with tongs to pull the metal out to get the machine moving again. Walking down the safety walkway in the skin pass one day when he was thirty-two, a four-inch steam pipe broke, swung down, caught him across the mouth, and threw him high in the air, through the mill. It smashed his teeth and broke his jaw in eight places. He got more than $30,000 worth of dental work, eight surgeries all covered by the company, and began years of speech therapy to learn how to speak properly again.

He worked in the brick department, going into the blast furnace to bust out the damaged brick, knocking it down to a lower level for a bulldozer to remove, so the bricklayers could reline the furnace, and then spraying six inches of asbestos on top of the brick after it had been laid. You'd get these little pits in your fingers from handling the rough brick that would burn when you sweat. They'd send you in with the four-inch fire hose to spray the asbestos and a little dust mask and you'd be in there for eight hours straight.

The first time Bo came out from the shift, his clothes were covered in asbestos and he took off the mask and pointed at his clothes and asked another guy, "What do I do with this?"

And the guy took an air hose and sprayed it off him, so that he was breathing in all the stuff the little air mask was supposed to have blocked all day.

"A lot of good that mask done," Bo said.

"Aw, that's nothing," the guy said.

Bodani got his asbestosis diagnosis in the 1990s, and became one of some 9,000 plaintiffs who would get a settlement, in his case a total of about $25,000 over the years.

He was a welder's helper in the 68-inch hot-strip mill, working alongside his father-in-law. He worked on the stage in the No. 4 open hearth and the basic oxygen furnace (the company had finally installed two BOFs in 1965), throwing bags of chemicals into the ingot molds so that the molds didn't blow up. He worked in the soaking pits, cleaning out flue holes. He worked in the plate mill, loading tractor trailers. He worked as a crane operator.

He was a slag bowl carrier operator in the BOF, transporting giant containers of slag across the street, where they'd be dumped in a pit. He worked in the blast furnace as a trough tender—when the molten steel came down you had to keep it moving to the railroad cars, pulling up a gate to direct it into the slag bowls, which the railcars would take up the hill to another pit, and then lowering the gate when the hot metal came out to direct it into the sub cars, enormous carriers that looked kind of like a swelled-up hot dog.

Once, when he was working in the BOF, a crane operator tipped the vat of molten steel a little too far, it poured out, and the heat tender couldn't get out of the way. Bo came running at him with the fire hose and watched his body disintegrate from the impact.

Such horrors were becoming more common as business turned for the worse. In a single eighteen-month period in 1978 and 1979, there were twelve fatal accidents. It hearkened back to the early days, when workers had lacked the protective layer provided by the union. Now the company blamed the union for the rash of deaths, saying the seniority reforms had put too many men in positions they lacked experience for. Perhaps, but the likelier culprits were deteriorating equipment and corporate corner-cutting.

By the mid-1990s, the company had shrunk so much and outsourced so much work to nonunion contractors that membership at Local 2610, which represented all the "hot-side" workers—actual steelmaking, as opposed to finishing—had plunged to 2,286 in 1995 from 11,393 only fourteen years earlier. The cutbacks had started for real in the early 1980s, when the company shuttered the pipe mill, rod and wire mill, and nail mill and more than 3,000 workers were sitting on indefinite layoff. The union had agreed to major wage concessions in 1983 and 1986, but the competition kept gaining: by 1988, U.S. steel production had dropped to 15 percent of the global total.

Years later, autopsies would list all the ways in which the union and the workers had been complicit in their own demise. Their contract gains had become unaffordable for the company—not just on wages, but on benefits such as pensions and retiree health coverage, and extended vacations that, for more senior workers, included thirteen weeks off every five years. Their insistence on the "past practices" clause in their contract, which they gained in the 1950s to protect members against automation, kept the company from assigning workers in the most efficient ways. The union too often covered for lazy or unproductive workers, the ones who tucked into a truck cab for a nap.

There was truth in all of this. It was also true that any indulgence or fecklessness on the part of the union was more than matched by upper management in Bethlehem. Veteran executives were getting seven-week vacations by 1980; there were twelve paid holidays for white-collar employees, including UN Day and a floating holiday. There were company-paid security forces and chauffeurs. There was bureaucratic bloat and empire-building to rival that of any government agency: in the quarter century prior to 1980, the company doubled its ranks of vice presidents or higher, and, as John Strohmeyer wrote, "each of these vice presidents required his own assistants, assistants-to, managers, assistant managers, and secretaries." In 1980, the company celebrated a new chairman with a party in Boca Raton for all its managers and their wives, five hundred people in all—and then sent the outgoing and incoming chairman and their wives on a global tour in the corporate jet with stops in Singapore, Cairo, and London. When the new chairman left six years later, after presiding over $2 billion in losses, he rewarded himself with an 11 percent pay raise and approved $1 million severance packages for all thirteen vice presidents. One vice president used a company jet to fly his kids to college and go to a vacation retreat in upstate New York.

Rank-and-file workers were not blind to such excesses, and took them as a model. "It was a screwed-up culture," says Len Shindel, a former union representative. "And the culture started at the top."

The decline was having a material effect on worker morale. Drug and alcohol use had always lurked at the plant's margins—it was common for workers to roll off an overnight shift into Dundalk bars like Mickey's, and pot was prevalent. Now more and more workers were turning to harder stuff—in addition to heroin, there was crack, which some younger workers started dealing to older ones, right in the plant.

Bill Bodani was immune to such entropy. He was a team player—literally so; he'd played several years on the purchasing department's baseball team. He was active in the union—first as a shop steward, later on the workers' compensation committee.

His favorite job came toward the end, in 1998. To cope with declining numbers, the company created a new "multi-craft" team called Capital Workforce. It was a mark of leaner times, but for Bo, being picked for it was a sort of nirvana, an affirmation of his versatility. If they needed an electrician, he went. If they needed someone to replace the lines in the continuous caster, he could do it. He helped build the new $300 million cold mill, which was as large as eight Walmarts, that the company finally opened in 2000, many years after workers had been pushing the company to open a cold-rolling plant.

Not much more than a year after the cold mill opened, the company filed for Chapter 11 bankruptcy, on October 15, 2001.

About a year after that, Bo was replacing the runout rolls in the continuous caster when the crane's cable snapped and he couldn't get out of the way in time. His legs were crushed between two of the massive rolls. He screamed in pain. Workers came running from the other end of the mill. They medevaced him out and told him he would never walk again.

He did walk again, after two years of surgery and metal rods and physical therapy. But he was done on the Point, retired on disability.

You might think he'd have embraced the respite. He was in his mid-fifties. He had lost his teeth on the Point, developed asbestosis, and now nearly lost his legs. He was still getting speech therapy from having his mouth smashed in twenty years earlier—there were still words he had trouble saying properly. And the plant was not a happy place to be during the bankruptcy negotiations. Workers were bitter about payouts being given to executives—lump sums two and a half times their salaries, and for the CEO who'd served only sixteen months prior to the bankruptcy, a $2.5 million severance package.

But Bo still hated leaving. "I would've stayed there forever," he said years later. "I never dreamt of retiring, because I enjoyed that job. I don't care how dirty, how dangerous it was, how busted up I got. I loved it."

He was making $35 per hour at the end, plus bonuses as high as a couple hundred dollars per paycheck. For a few years, depending on the rotation, he got at least seven weeks of vacation. He had finally made it to all day shifts after twenty years of rotating weeks of day shifts followed by evenings followed by overnights. But that wasn't what held him. He liked the work itself, the whole world of the work. You might even say that he found it fulfilling.

"I enjoyed the people," he said. "They made it enjoyable. The Black, the white. It was a family thing. I don't care if you knew them for five minutes, they took you in. They looked out for one another. Everyone knew it was dangerous. No matter how bad I got hurt or how bad things got, there was always a bright side. You had those guys with you."

The death of Sparrows Point, like so many deaths, came not quickly or cleanly, but in a prolonged drama of false hopes that proved to be mere deferrals of the inevitable. In 2003, the Wall Street financier Wilbur Ross's International Steel Group bought the bankrupt company—as a result, retiree health benefits were eliminated and the pension fund, which was short more than $4 billion, was offloaded onto the Pension Benefit Guaranty Corporation, which led to the big cuts in monthly payments experienced by Bill Bodani and thousands of others.

Ross sold his company, Sparrows Point included, eighteen months later, making $300 million, to a company led by the Indian billionaire Lakshmi Mittal. ArcelorMittal sold Sparrows Point in 2008 to the Russian company Severstal, which in turn sold it in 2011 to the Renco Group, a New York City investment fund, which combined it with two other mills to form R.G. Steel.

A year later, in May 2012, R.G. Steel declared bankruptcy. Sparrows Point was sold to a liquidator. The last bar of steel came through the 68-inch hot-strip mill at 7:21 a.m. on June 15. The Point, now down to 2,000 workers, was officially closed, a century and a quarter after Frederick Wood had started building it.

As drawn out as it was, many were still unprepared for the end. Surely, those in power would intervene to prevent ultimate termination. Surely, someone would see the mill as an asset to be redeemed. "The ultimate shock was that no one would want that mill," said Shindel, the union rep. "The conventional wisdom was that the water would protect us forever. Because we were on the water." But in the end, the water was just another burden: precisely because its location had allowed the Point to ship to far-flung markets, the Point was especially vulnerable to international competition. Meanwhile, being on the water had meant having to bear the high costs of having soiled it for decades.

The fault-finding had thickened over the course of the decade-long death, curdling into a palpable resentment all across Patapsco Neck. The peninsula's politics had been shifting right since the 1960s, but the turn accelerated now. The list of targets was lengthy. The Japanese, the Chinese, the Germans. The Export-Import Bank, for having financed mills in developing countries with American tax dollars. All the presidents, from both parties, who'd failed to act against imports made cheap by foreign government subsidies. The environmentalists. The feckless, greedy company. "Today, I just want to hate," wrote one former worker, Chris MacLarion, in an elegy for the Point. "I want to hate those that took you from me, from us, and condemned you to die. I want to hate those that didn't stand up for you, that didn't throw their bodies into a frenzied self-sacrifice in order that you might survive."

As Sparrows Point was in its final spasms, much of the rest of the city's industrial legacy was shutting down, too. In 2005, GM closed the plant on Broening Highway where Bo had started out making Chevelles in the 1960s, and where, more recently, 2,500 workers had still been making GMC Safari and Chevy Astro minivans.

By 2012, Baltimore's population had fallen to 621,000, placing it twenty-sixth in the country, down from sixth a half century earlier. It still had economic assets—it had its harbor, which handled coal headed to Europe and cars arriving from Germany; it had the biomedical empire of Johns Hopkins; it had its location on the Northeast Corridor, which spared it the isolation of postindustrial cousins such as St. Louis, Buffalo, Cleveland, and Detroit.

But this location also brought with it some unflattering contrasts, particularly with the city to the south. As recently as 1980, Baltimore had still been home to 150,000 more people than Washington, which hadn't made it onto the list of the country's ten largest cities until 1950. In the early 1990s, the cities had grappled equally with horrific violence. By 2010, Washington's homicide rate had fallen to barely more than half of Baltimore's. Over the next few years, its population would soar past Baltimore's, soon surpassing 700,000.

In January 2015, a few months before Baltimore would erupt in protests and rioting over the death of a young Black man named Freddie Gray from injuries sustained while in police custody, demolition contractors inserted ninety-four explosive charges into the largest remaining structure on the Point: the thirty-two-story "L" furnace, which the company had built in 1978 at a cost of $200 million. They kept the details of the operation under wraps, lest it provoke a crowd of aggrieved locals, who instead learned of it only as the booms of the implosion carried across Patapsco Neck. "This was a city on the hill that has gone away," Bill Barry, a retired labor studies professor at the Community College of Baltimore County, told *The Sun*. "There's nothing close to replacing it."

That September, the top elected officials from metropolitan Baltimore gathered at the site of the former General Motors plant on Broening Highway. There, on the same ground where thousands of men and women had assembled Safaris and Astros, now stood an enormous warehouse. It sprawled over one million square feet—equivalent to eighteen football fields—a boxy, light gray building with blank walls, nearly a third of a mile long and surrounded by 1,900 parking spots. Large black letters on its side read:

AMAZON FULFILLMENT

It was an arresting sight, those two words. It was, on one level, simply a term of the trade. The company called its primary warehouses, the cavernous buildings where workers and robots selected goods from racks and workers packed them for shipment, "fulfillment centers." They were, after all, where customer orders were *fulfilled*. There were also the "sortation centers," which were both smaller and smaller in number, where packages already assembled and addressed were sorted for delivery in a given area.

But the word, plastered in large black letters alongside the company name, seemed meant to conjure something larger than the building's functional purpose. It advertised the company's promise to all who passed by, all who had a longing—for what, exactly, they might still be trying to decide—and now knew from whence it would be delivered to them.

The word's promise applied less obviously to those who would be working inside. The GM jobs at Broening Highway had paid an average of $27 per hour and had come with generous benefits. Now, a decade later, the jobs at the same site paid $12 or $13 per hour and came with much thinner benefits. This had not kept local and state leaders from showering the company with incentives to open the warehouse here—$43 million in all.

The Broening Highway center, the company's first in the Baltimore area, had opened earlier in the year and had already grown to 3,000 workers by the time the elected leaders gathered for this, the grand opening. The leaders rose one by one not only to praise the company for coming to Baltimore, but to talk about how much it had improved their lives.

"I don't have to take off my sweats to get deodorant anymore," said Dutch Ruppersberger, a Democratic congressman from Baltimore County.

"You're very trustworthy for making sure my moisturizer gets to me on time," said the Baltimore mayor Stephanie Rawlings-Blake.

Inside the one-million-square-foot hall, the squat orange robots, roughly the size and shape of ottomans, buzzed around within a large caged area to bring workers the stacks of shelving racks from which they assembled shoppers' orders: this warehouse was one of several dozen designed for robotic pickers, rather than for people roaming the corridors with scanners in hand. The robots were made by a Boston-area company called Kiva Systems, which Amazon had bought in 2012 for $775 million, thus preventing its rivals from using the technology.

Robots brought the racks; humans took items from them. *Weight-loss supplements, basketballs, Listerine, power drills, Spinning Ball Poppers . . .*

Before the Kivas, fulfillment pickers were expected to reach speeds of about 100 items per hour. With the Kivas bringing the pods to them, the pickers were expected to reach speeds of 300 to 400 items per hour. They were spared the endless walking the aisles, which had left "Amazombies" soaking their feet at night and popping the Advils that Amazon provided in vending machines, but now they had to confront the monotony of their stationary post. The screen in front of them flashed the next item to retrieve and from which compartment in the stack of bins; at some warehouses, the bin in question even lit up, denying the picker the satisfaction of that one small hunt. As the *New York Times* business reporter Noam Scheiber noted, the addition of robots wasn't so much replacing workers yet as it was making their own existence more robotic. Automation could free us to use our minds in more productive ways—or, in this case, it could remove thinking from our actions altogether.

Steam and spray mops, bakeware sets, Smarter Rest pillows, BabyBjörns, raw unfiltered honey, rodent repellent . . .

There were 14 million items in the warehouse; there were fourteen miles of conveyor belts that could run 600 feet per minute; there were 40,000 yellow plastic "totes" to carry items on belts to be packaged. One hundred packages per minute, 6,000 per hour. They'd go shooting down the conveyor belt and the little pusher knob—or foot, some called it—would kick from the side of the belt when the package reached the sorting area for the trucks that were headed to its destination. If the packages shooting down the belt were not aligned neatly enough to be read by the scanners that would direct them to the right truck, they would get kicked off and looped back around.

As seamless as it all looked, the company was still searching for ways to eliminate slack. For one thing, it had secured two patents for a wristband that could track workers' every move, and even alert them via a vibration if it detected that they were going off task.

Things moved much less efficiently outside the building at shift changes, as hundreds of cars tried to get in and out of the parking lot. Baltimore had been on the verge of building a new rail transit line that would have traversed the city all the way from West Baltimore to within a mile of the warehouse, a short gap to fill with shuttle buses, but the governor, Larry Hogan, had killed the project a few months after the protests over Freddie Gray's death, returning the $900 million in federal funds and shifting state funds for the project toward exurban highways. Instead, the company was running shuttle buses all the way to downtown—paid for by $100,000 from the publicly funded Baltimore Development Corporation.

Bill Bodani, Jr., arrived at the Broening Highway warehouse in 2016. He started off working in maintenance, but after a few months moved to driving forklifts. Five decades after he'd worked in that spot building Chevelles, he was now unloading trucks packed high with mostly foreign-made goods.

There were several other Beth Steel veterans there, but he was by far the oldest. The younger workers called him "Pops" and "Old Man."

For a while, he was on the overnight shift: 11:00 p.m. to 7:00 a.m. It was tough on his system, but it came with one advantage: "The night shifts, they're not on you as much as the day shift," he said. "You've got too many bosses around you during the day." You might even be able to get a bit of extra time in the bathroom.

Eventually, he was assigned to the day shift, because that's when the company needed him training drivers. You had to worry more about the supervisors, you had to worry about the cameras, and you had to worry about the algorithm. The company had an automated system to track performance—productivity, time off task—and the system would flag you for termination if you lagged. That is, you could be fired by an algorithm. About three hundred people were fired for inefficiency at the Broening Highway warehouse over a thirteen-month stretch in 2017 and 2018. "Amazon's system tracks the rates of each individual associate's productivity," an attorney representing the company wrote in a letter defending one particular firing, "and automatically generates any warnings or terminations regarding quality or productivity without input from supervisors."

Bill Bodani started out making $12-something per hour. There was growing agitation nationwide about the company's wages and working conditions. Most notorious had been the 2011 episode at a warehouse near Allentown, Pennsylvania, where the company had stationed medics outside to handle workers fainting from the heat instead of paying for air-conditioning. Median pay across the company was only about $13 per hour, $28,000 per year—so low that even as its workforce was surging in size, it was dragging down average wages for warehouse workers nationwide.

Economists suspected "monopsony," the effect of having just one buyer of a good, as opposed to just one seller, a monopoly. In this case, the good being labor: the bigger Amazon got and the more it dominated local labor markets, the less competition it faced for workers, and the less it needed to pay to hire them. As recently as 2012, the company had had only 88,000 employees worldwide. But over the rest of the decade, it would grow with astonishing speed, making it the second-largest private-sector employer in the country after Walmart, and making monopsony a real prospect. By late 2019, it had more than 750,000 employees worldwide and 400,000 employees in the United States, the overwhelming majority of them in the company's more than two hundred fulfillment centers, sortation centers, and other delivery facilities. In 2017 alone, the company grew by 130,000 worldwide; in the summer of 2019, it hired 97,000, nearly the entire workforce of Google. And this was *before* the hiring spree that would arrive with the global pandemic of the spring of 2020.

Warehousing and distribution used to be considered somewhat higher-skilled jobs: one could make over $20 per hour and stay years at a time. At Amazon, it was a more fleeting existence. Workers tended to be younger. Turnover was exceedingly high. And the seasonal workforce was often literally transient, in the form of the CamperForce of retirees traveling the country in RVs that Amazon deployed for its holiday rush.

So much impermanence came with a major benefit for the company: it made it much easier to stamp out union efforts to organize warehouse workers when workers left before developing ties. Also deterring solidarity was the atomization of the warehouses themselves, where, as Emily Guendelsberger noted after a stint working in one, the layout and algorithms seemed almost designed to isolate employees from one another. Where organizing efforts managed to gain traction anyway, the company deployed tried-and-true defenses—hiring law firms that specialized in blocking unions, fomenting fears about union greed and corruption, the sort of tactics that had helped drive union representation to only 6 percent of the private-sector workforce nationwide.

Within a couple years, it became plain that the Broening Highway warehouse couldn't handle all the demand for the region, which included not only the Baltimore area but also the bigger market around fast-growing Washington.

The company looked around for other sites, and in 2017, it found one: Sparrows Point.

The peninsula had been taken over in 2014 by a consortium of developers and real estate investors who were remaking it as a hub for logistics. They got more than 3,100 waterfront acres, along with a deep-water port and one hundred miles of railway, at auction for $72 million, less than a tenth of what Sparrows Point had last sold for, and a promise to spend another $48 million on cleaning up what was quite possibly the largest of the 47,000 Superfund cleanup sites in the country.

There was now a FedEx warehouse and an Under Armour one, and a vehicle-shipping operation and a Perdue grain storage facility. The developers would receive $78 million from Baltimore County to build roads and water and sewer lines—the largest assistance package in county history—plus $20 million in federal money to modernize the port.

As part of their overhaul, they rebranded the peninsula. It was no longer Sparrows Point. It was now Tradepoint Atlantic. Amazon itself got $19 million in state and local tax incentives for the new warehouse. It was nearly as large as the one at Broening Highway—855,000 square feet, with eleven miles of conveyor belts.

The company put out the word that it was hiring in August 2018. It held eight events around the area. Applicants first had to fill out an online application and take an online skills assessment.

"Because our customers count on us, Amazon Associates meet all of these challenges with fantastic work ethics and positive attitudes," the applicants were told. "In the words of our founder, Jeff Bezos, our approach is: 'Work hard. Have fun. Make history.'"

In the first module of the Amazon Associate Virtual Job Tryout, applicants had to stack boxes of different sizes in a truck. In the second, they had to fill orders by picking goods from shelves, racing the clock while trying not to mix up long label numbers. In the third, they had to store incoming goods on the shelves under rules dictating that certain types of goods had to go in certain spots.

Applicants were then instructed to attend one of the hiring events. On the last Friday in September 2018, more than a dozen applicants arrived at the Sollers Point Multi-Purpose Center in Dundalk, a couple miles past the vacant former headquarters of the steelworkers local. The applicants were received inside the building's small gymnasium by representatives of the county workforce development office, and by some young women in Amazon T-shirts. They did not work for Amazon, but for a temp staffing company called Integrity. They told applicants to take a seat on folding chairs.

Finally, one of the Integrity women stood up and walked over to the people in the chairs, a laptop in her hands. She told the applicants that they would soon go into a different room to take their drug test and that they would be taking the test together.

"You take your drug test as a family because we work together as a family," she said.

She told them not to have anything in their mouth from this point on—no gum, no nothing.

And then, by way of a belated introduction, she said, "Congratulations. You guys are doing the first part to become Amazonians."

The job would require lifting as much as forty-nine pounds, she said.

The job involved picking and packing everything you could imagine, from candy to kayaks.

The job did not come with a dress code—you could wear anything you wanted. But you could not wear shirts with slogans that were PG rated or beyond.

If you didn't like being active, this might not be the job for you. But once you started doing it, your body would adjust to it.

These were physical jobs, so cute shoes were not going to work.

She played a video on her laptop, and walked up and down the row so that everyone could get snatches of it. The video showed the jobs they would be doing. There were pickers and packers and labelers and loaders. "That is how it gets to your homes," she said.

They would be paid $13.75 per hour. If they were on time for all of the first thirty days, they would get a 1 percent raise. If their team met performance goals, they would get another 1 percent raise. "That two percent comes in handy, especially if you have kids who take all your money," she said.

And that was it, the whole introduction. It was hard to imagine how the experience could have been any more anonymous and provisional. Once, young people headed to work at Sparrows Point had entered via a dense network of connections—the recruiting table at high school, the union hall, the introduction to new coworkers from their father or uncle. "Guys, you know Gary, right?" Now, on the hallway wall, there was a sheet of paper scrawled with AMAZON and an arrow pointing to folding chairs and Integrity contractors. One might have mistaken the event as part of some underfunded government initiative rather than the moment of entry into one of the most successful companies in the world.

The applicants waited to be called into the other room. One of them, a forty-five-year-old white man with a goatee, called up his twenty-eight-year-old girlfriend to FaceTime with her. He had been working security guard jobs, which paid barely more than $10 an hour. He needed to make more because he had recently bought a new car. He had met his girlfriend at a Dollar Tree, where she had been working. She was now down in Virginia

Beach working at a Dunkin' Donuts while dealing with some legal troubles there.

"I'm in orientation," he told her.

"Oh, you got it! You got it! That's so awesome," she said, audible to all.

Finally, the applicants headed into a former classroom where they waited their turn for head shots for their badge photos and then the drug test. For the test, they stood in groups of four along a table as another woman from Integrity handed them small plastic sticks with absorbent pads that she told them to put inside their mouths. They stood for five minutes with the little sticks protruding from their closed mouths, like kids with lollipops, dropped them in plastic baggies that were sealed and labeled, and then left.

A few days later, the ones who passed the test got an email: "Congratulations on your offer of employment with Amazon.com Services, Inc." Before they could click to accept, they had to e-sign an agreement not to disclose anything about the work at the warehouse, ever: "During employment and at all times thereafter, Employee will hold all Confidential Information in strictest confidence and will not acquire, use, publish, disclose or communicate any Confidential Information except as required in connection with Employer's work without the prior written approval of an authorized officer of Amazon."

The fulfillment centers were all named for airports. The first Baltimore warehouse, at Broening Highway, was named BWI2, after Baltimore's airport. The one at Sparrows Point was named DCA1, after Reagan National Airport in Washington, a name still available since Washington had no warehouse of its own. Washington was not a warehouse town.

Among those launching DCA1 was Bill Bodani, Jr. The company offered workers the chance to switch to Sparrows Point and he took it. You'd think he would have wanted to avoid the pain of seeing the place transformed, day after day. But that was exactly why he wanted to make the move, to experience that sensation amid the numbness of the job. "The feeling of being home," he said. "Just the feeling of being down there. I spent most of my life there. It's a feeling of being home. It was painful, but then it felt good, you know."

He teared up sometimes as he crossed the Key Bridge on his way there and looked down and saw it all gone—the vast industrial works and an entire town, the town in which both he and his father were raised, all wiped clean off the face of the tidewater expanse.

He would tell the younger guys he worked with about what had come before them. Right here was where the 68-inch hot-strip mill was, he said. Over here was the tin mill, over there was the pipe mill.

There was a downside to the move: the bosses at the new warehouse were driving him even harder than those at Broening Highway. Starting off at Sparrows Point, Bo was now making barely more than a third of what he had been making in his final years at that same spot, not even counting bonuses. He had no union representation, and in fact managers had warned him and his coworkers against seeking any or risk losing their job.

More than a century earlier, Frederick Wood had made workers sign that "Conditions of Employment" slip listing "agitation" as grounds for firing. Over the ensuing decades, workers had fought for the right to organize themselves for better pay and safer conditions, and had succeeded in doing so. For several decades, they had enjoyed the benefits of work that was better paying and safer than what had come before, and that had brought with it the dignity of being able to support one's family in a middle-class existence, and the dignity of being able to negotiate over one's labor as something approaching an equal.

And now things had circled back to where they had begun. Eugene Grace's slogan, "Always More Production," might just as easily have been applied to the giant warehouse now standing in the place of the hot-strip mill. In 1907, the journalist Herbert Casson had written after a tour of steel country, "There is little public opinion with regard to the perils of a steel mill, for the reason that few outside of the trade know anything personally of the conditions that exist." The perils of the warehouse were less, but the opacity was the same. The warehouse concealed all, abetting the consumer's incuriosity.

The trucks pulled in, one after another. Cameras and supervisors kept count.

The bladder pressed. Bo had already used his allotted breaks. He tried to hold it, he did.

But sometimes he couldn't, and he found a quiet corner, and parked the forklift as a hopeful shield.

5.

Service

The fight for local business

Teresa Gandara's father ran a small grocery in south El Paso. It was close to the border, and a natural first stop for many of those who'd come across illicitly. Edmundo Rojas installed two washers and two dryers in the grocery, and three showers. For a quarter, you could get a bar of soap and a towel. If this was an act of solidarity, it was solidarity at some remove: the Rojas family had come across the river ages ago, further back than anyone could recall. For Edmundo, it was simply the decent thing to do. "He believed everyone deserved a shower, to feel clean," said his daughter.

Gandara had seven siblings, and there wasn't much to go around, but there was little sense of deprivation among the kids—at least not until they got to high school and found out they weren't wearing the right kind of jeans. Among the goods the family rationed was higher education: Teresa's older sister Rosa was deemed college material, but not Teresa. Determined to prove her parents wrong, she started taking community college courses in Tacoma, Washington, where she went to live with Rosa and her army-captain husband for a while, and then kept taking classes on her return to

El Paso, even if it meant having to forge her parents' signature on the Pell Grant application. "My first federal offense," she joked later. She took as many classes at the University of Texas at El Paso as she could fit alongside her jobs: managing the UTEP pool, painting houses, cleaning houses. She finally got the degree years later, along with a master's, by which point she was working as a physical education teacher and married to Carlos Gandara, who worked in the office supply business, in a warehouse.

At school, Teresa insisted on teaching kids sports they might not be exposed to otherwise, like tennis and lacrosse. "I'll never teach you basketball," she told them. "You can play that on your own time." And she insisted on taking one day a week to give classroom instruction based on sports they were playing—measuring the area of playing fields, that sort of thing.

Eventually, she was promoted to assistant principal, but she didn't care for administration—she was chided once for spending too much time helping a group of at-risk students and shirking record-keeping duties. By 2000, Carlos had moved out of the office supply warehouse that he'd started cleaning as a teenager and held virtually every role at the company—inside sales, outside sales, management. The company had been sold and he'd been under a noncompete clause for a couple years. When it expired, he started looking around for a new place to work, but Teresa had another idea.

"Why do us Mexicans think we always have to work for somebody?" she said. "Nobody cares about customers like you do. I'd rather invest in us."

"We don't know about business," Carlos said.

"So we fail," she said. "There's only failure in not trying. We have an opportunity to try."

In 2001, they launched Pencil Cup Office Products. Teresa held on to her assistant principal job, funneling as much of her salary as possible into the business, and worked on weekends. Carlos ran things during the week. The owner of an industrial machinery shop let them use space in his warehouse. Their son, Carlos, Jr., thirteen at the time, helped out after school.

They had three customers at first: an accountant, an industrial supply company, and the YWCA. By 2006, they had reached the point where Teresa could quit her job. By 2010, they had grown to eighteen employees.

These included Carlos, Jr., who would become one of their top salesmen, and who for exercise liked to drag around the big chain in the storeroom that was attached to the crane that had been used to hoist engines out of the buses and trams stored there when it was a repair shop; and their daughter, Christina, who had gone to New Mexico State for her business degree, swore she wouldn't come back, but then changed her mind. "Dad, you paid for my degree," she said. "Let's put it to work."

A growing share of their business, at least a third, was with city government and with school districts, who gave preference to buying from vendors certified as local and woman- and minority-owned, which Pencil Cup was. But those certifications alone couldn't explain the success. Teresa and Carlos, Sr., chalked it up to their borderline dogmatic embrace of customer service. They always assembled any furniture for customers—you never received a chair or desk in a box from Pencil Cup. They made the rounds of their customers to pick up empty cardboard boxes and toner cartridges to take to recycling.

And they went out of their way to help customers in tight spots. One time, a school district forgot to include eight hundred highlighters in an order, and called at 8:00 a.m. to say it needed them that day. The Gandaras and their employees scoured the big-box office supply stores, their rivals, for as many highlighters as they could find, even if they cost more there than from their wholesaler. Another time, a Border Patrol manager called to say she had bought five thousand AA batteries instead of five thousand AAAs as she was supposed to. She was worried she might lose her job. And she had bought them from someone other than Pencil Cup. No matter. They bought five thousand AAAs from their supplier and swapped them out with hers, even if it came at a loss. "That's our customer," Carlos, Sr., said. "We're saving her job."

In 2017, Gandara got a call from Amazon, inviting Pencil Cup to sell through the website, which would give it a much larger marketplace—the whole world. She knew that her business was appealing to Amazon because it could be touted for its minority-owned status, which many buyers looked for.

But she couldn't help being flattered anyway. "At first we were so excited: 'Oh, Amazon!'" she said. "And then we started asking the questions."

S andy Grodin's path into office supply had started in jeans. Not just any jeans—stonewashed. It would not be going too far to call Sandy Grodin one of the fathers of the stonewashed Levi's 501. Or at least, he certainly wouldn't object to it.

He was born in Brooklyn, and his family moved to El Paso when he was one year old. His parents were both Jews, but their families had taken wildly different paths to the United States. His father's family had left Eastern Europe at the turn of the century for England and eventually Brooklyn, where his grandfather's work as a peddler was so unremunerative that his father was sent to live with another family, not uncommon during the Depression. The family of his mother, Dorothy Kaplan, had fled Poland in the 1930s, but their ship was turned away from Ellis Island. It headed for Havana instead, was turned away there, too, and landed in Veracruz, Mexico. The family made its way to Juarez before slipping across the Rio Grande to El Paso when Dorothy was seven. Her father opened a used-clothing store.

During the Second World War, Irwin Grodin was stationed at Fort Bliss, on the northeastern edge of El Paso. He met Dorothy before being deployed to the South Pacific. They married after the war and moved to Brooklyn, but decided to raise the family in El Paso instead. The whole Grodin family came with them—grandparents and even aunts. Irwin Grodin went to work in insurance; his father helped with the business.

Sandy, the second of five children, stayed home for college, getting a business degree at UTEP, but after graduating in 1975 took a job with Levi Strauss, which brought him to its headquarters in San Francisco. One day, he and others from the merchandising team were summoned to meet with the company's top U.S. jeans executive, Al Sanguinetti.

When Grodin walked into the conference room, he saw several pairs of jeans lying on the table. Not Levi's—competitors' jeans. Sasson and

Jordache. Their new stonewashed models were catching on and threatening Levi's hegemony.

"How is Levi Strauss going to respond to this?" Sanguinetti said.

One of Grodin's friends piped up: "Why don't you prewash your basic jean?"

"That's brilliant," deadpanned Sanguinetti. "Where are you going to do it?"

Grodin raised his hand. "I know two guys in El Paso with commercial laundromats," he said.

This was serendipitous, given that one of the company's main manufacturing plants was in El Paso. Sanguinetti told Grodin to get on a plane home.

Grodin looked up the first of the commercial laundromat owners he knew, Mr. Goldberg. No way was he going to let Sandy put stones in his machines, he said. So Sandy went to the other laundromat guy he knew, Mr. Goldman. He was all for it.

Now the question was what kind of stones to use. Grodin suggested that Levi's try soft stones, to avoid tearing the garment. And he had particular ones in mind: the lava stones used for landscaping. He even knew a guy, out on the New Mexico mesa, who ran a business grinding up stones from the lava fields. He ordered a truckload, dumped it outside Mr. Goldman's laundromat, and got some wheelbarrows and shovels. They tried mixing two shovel loads in with thirty pairs the first time, and different combinations from there, and sent them all back to San Francisco for the higher-ups to assess. It became quickly apparent that the jeans weren't going to withstand the stones. So the company started making a stronger jean. Mr. Goldman started washing more and more—thousands per week.

The breakthrough achieved, Levi Strauss decided to centralize manufacturing at its big factory in Knoxville, Tennessee, where it built its own washing operation and dispatched its in-house expert, Sandy Grodin. He was moving up the chain, so much so that he was now privy to the company's business plans. It was in the ten-year plan that he discovered the company's intention to shift all production out of the United States.

Fulfillment

Sandy Grodin wasn't going to wait around to see when his services would no longer be required. In 1986, he asked for a transfer back to El Paso and started looking around for something else to do. He drove around the industrial parks on the periphery of the El Paso sprawl and looked for businesses for sale. One day he was driving closer to downtown and saw a bunch of vans with Mexican plates lined up outside a business called Sturgis & Co., on Yandell Street. The name provoked nostalgia: he'd bought school supplies from Sturgis when he was a kid.

Sandy Grodin could tell, as he watched for several days in a row, that Sturgis was doing a snappy business, and he was intrigued. He called up and asked who the owner was. He was told it was Harvey Joseph. He called back a few moments later and asked for Harvey Joseph. A gruff voice came on the line.

"Harvey, my name is Sandy Grodin, and I want to know if you would like—"

Harvey Joseph hung up. Grodin called back. "Are you a sales rep?" asked Joseph.

"No, I'm not," Grodin said. "I want to know if you'd be interested in selling the business."

Joseph took this surprisingly well. "I really haven't thought about it," he said. "Let me think about it. Call me back tomorrow."

The next day, Joseph said he'd sell Sturgis for $1 million: $350,000 down, the rest later. He said it was doing at least $2 million per year in sales. There was virtually nothing in the way of record keeping to back that up, but Grodin had seen all that activity. He set out to raise $350,000. His father and brother each cosigned a $25,000 note, his grandfather cosigned a $50,000 one, and some friends lent him $5,000 each, with prime interest plus three points. When a Sturgis sales rep showed up one day at his Levi Strauss office, he joked with her. "I'm going to buy your business," he said. "Yeah, right," she said.

He stuck a FOR SALE sign on his car, a 1976 Oldsmobile Cutlass. He was stopped at a traffic light, about to get on I-10, when a guy pulled up next to him and asked how much he wanted for it. About $7,500, he told him. The guy told him to pull over, handed over $7,500 in cash, and told Grodin to mail him the title later. Grodin was left standing at a gas station without a car. He called his wife, Judy, and asked her to pick him up. She was confused about the sudden sale, not least because he had told her nothing about buying Sturgis.

Nine months after the conversation with Joseph, he called and told him he had the money. They met, and he put on the table a cashier's check for $200,000.

Joseph looked at it. "That's not enough," he said.

"Harvey, that's all I can get," Grodin said. And he made an offer. "Take that check. If I fuck it up, you keep the check and you can have your business back."

Joseph looked at the check, then at Grodin, back and forth for what seemed like an eternity. Finally, he said, "You better get a lawyer. We've got a deal."

Now Grodin had to tell Judy. He broke it to her at the college football Sun Bowl, which Levi Strauss always brought hundreds of employees to. "You what?" Judy said. "How much did this thing cost?"

"A million bucks," he said.

She reacted so unfavorably that he feared she might hyperventilate.

A few days later, he showed up at Sturgis. The sales rep was there. "Remember how I said I was going to buy this business?" he said. "Well, I did."

Mike Tucker started with slot machines. His father owned or ran a bunch of restaurants and barrooms in southern Maryland—the Chicken House, the Halfway House, the Modern, and the Black Steer, which was the biggest one. They drew weekenders from Washington and Baltimore, and guys from Naval Air Station Patuxent River, and from the tobacco farms, which were still flourishing. They had slot machines, and not infrequently coins would get stuck in them, and it was Mike's job to walk around with a big rubber hammer and whack the machines, which nine times out of ten would do the trick.

Fulfillment

Mike didn't go far for college—up the road to the University of Maryland, where he played on the baseball team. He was an indifferent student, and any discipline he'd developed at a local military boarding school melted away in the dissolute atmosphere of a large college campus circa 1970. He barely maintained the gentleman-C average required to stay on the team, but by the time his last semester arrived, he discovered he still needed twenty-three credits to graduate. The prospect of being drafted into the Vietnam War without even having obtained his degree was gloomy enough to spur him to quit the team his final season and bear down. He got his degree, in business, and, having drawn a low number in the draft, prepared to apply for navy flight school as an alternative to grunt service. While waiting for his fate to be decided, he made up for the lost baseball season by giving things a shot in a very minor league in the Shenandoah Valley. He lasted only about three weeks, which was about as long as he lasted at his next stop, playing in Florida for the lowest-level team in the Philadelphia Phillies organization. He wasn't going to cut it.

Mike Tucker never got the full story behind what happened next, why his draft classification suddenly flipped from 2S to 1H. Maybe it had to do with his grandmother being friends with the guy who ran the draft board in St. Mary's County. Maybe, more innocently, it had to do with the war starting to wind down. Regardless, it was hard not to discern in the success Tucker achieved in later years a resolve that had been absent in his college years and that reflected a desire to make the most of his turn of good fortune.

He got a job as a dairy salesman with Carnation, selling to grocery stores in the Baltimore and Washington area. On a sales call in Ocean City, Maryland, he met the woman he would marry. Not long afterward, the father of one of her friends asked him if he'd like to come work for Faber-Castell. He decided to make the move. Instead of selling milk, he would sell pencils.

And pens. In the 1980s, Faber-Castell became the national distributor for Uni-ball, the popular pen made by the Mitsubishi Pencil Company. Mike Tucker urged his bosses to capitalize on their new line of products by approaching a new line of buyer: the government. He got the company onto the supply schedule for the General Services Administration, which handles procurement for the federal bureaucracy. He got stock numbers for the products, which were housed in ten regional warehouse depots. He started traveling all around the country to military bases, and even to U.S. bases in Europe. "Hey, I got a federal contract," he'd say. "I got the numbers you need. You want to buy some pens?"

"You came all the way out here to sell some pens?" they'd say.

He sure did. A military base with five thousand people on it buys lots of pens. Faber-Castell's government sales revenue shot from zero to $7 million. After fifteen years at Faber-Castell, he switched to a company in Florida called All States, which distributed Paper Mate. He pulled the same trick there, expanding its sales to the government. But then All States was bought by Office Depot, which, along with Staples, was leading the big-box takeover of office supplies, and Mike Tucker discovered for the first time that he really did not like playing for the big guy. He wanted to be playing against the heavyweight, not with him.

He left Office Depot and decided it was time to try his hand running his own enterprise. In 1995, he managed to buy half of George W. Allen, a struggling office supply company in the Washington suburbs. He got the company on the federal supply schedules, and he arranged for it to be Faber-Castell's supplier to the government. Before long, George W. Allen's sales had swelled from $3.5 million to $26 million. He joined forces with another local office supply company with a base of commercial customers. The combined company had grown to $65 million in sales by 2016, when he and his partner decided to sell.

Mike Tucker was now sixty-six years old. He was a wealthy man, with a big home on three acres of land in the horse country of Howard County, Maryland, and a lot of grandchildren and a beach house in Ocean City. He could retire.

Instead, he decided to join a fight he had seen developing in his later years. The big-box companies had been surpassed by a much bigger rival that spurred his underdog affinities even more strongly. All the Davids around the country, the small office-supply companies, were trying to fight this

Goliath through an alliance called the Independent Office Products and Furniture Dealers Association. The association was looking for a director.

Office supply was one of those businesses that operated offstage, with little or no direct interaction with the ordinary consumer. It lived quietly in industrial parks or nondescript blocks free of the foot traffic it did not require. It was known to the public primarily through its having become the subject of a highly popular television show founded on the comedic conceit of the bland facelessness of the work being done by the characters.

Its counterpart, on the other side of the table, was the equally obscure realm of procurement: the people at other companies or public agencies who bought what the office supply dealers had on offer. In government, procurement was the bureaucracy within the bureaucracy. It was a funny word, *procure*—so illicit in its one meaning, so banal in its other context. Government buying the stuff needed to run the government. Pencils, pens, paper, computers, printers, software, desks, chairs, lamps, couches, tables, carpets, hand soap, paper towels, toilet paper, and on and on.

It was in this realm that Anne Rung had made her name, to the extent that renown was even achievable so far removed from public view.

Her father taught math at Penn State; her mother raised Anne and her five siblings. But much of her upbringing happened far from State College, Pennsylvania—her father took temporary teaching gigs in Hawaii, Canada, and Taiwan. Later, Anne Rung would cite this time abroad, along with her time studying at the London School of Economics after her undergraduate years at Penn State, as grounds for her desire to serve in Washington.

She had started out with the Democratic Leadership Council, the group that formed in the 1980s to steer the Democratic Party to the center and that gave rise to Bill Clinton, among others. She was its congressional director for five years, building contacts on Capitol Hill. But then she had gone back to Pennsylvania, to serve in the Department of General Services under Governor Ed Rendell. DGS was the part of the government that administered the rest of the government. It was as thankless as government work got. One made headlines only if things went wrong. Like the time when paper jams in a mail-inserting machine caused 2,845 welfare-benefit renewal packets to be sent to the wrong homes, nearly half of them with Social Security numbers included.

Such snafus did not slow Rung's rise on the inside track. In 2006, she moved from chief of staff in DGS to Rendell's deputy secretary for administration. And in August 2010, she made her move back to Washington, becoming the senior director of administration in the Commerce Department, an anonymous job within one of the most anonymous cabinet agencies. She set about building a profile within such gray confines. In November of that year, not long after the Obama administration suffered a devastating setback in the 2010 midterm elections, she appeared on a panel at the Center for American Progress, a major liberal think tank, to discuss reforming federal procurement. She had developed strong notions on the subject. She found it absurd to have one purchaser buying a wide array of items for an agency—vehicles one day, IT the next—instead of having a purchaser specialized in a product type buying for the government more broadly. She found it maddening whenever one agency paid much more for the same item than another. She still recalled one example years later: "We had a state hospital paying $23 per case of catsup, and we had another state prison paying $12 for the exact same case of catsup."

Such insights made Rung an exceptional procurer. She saved money for Pennsylvania, she saved money for Commerce. It was only a matter of time before she was called to the Death Star of purchasing, the General Services Administration. GSA was a 12,000-person agency that oversaw more than $60 billion in procurement and managed $500 billion worth of federal property. In 2013, Rung was named head of its Office of Government-wide Policy.

She threw herself into her new role, taking charge of initiatives to reform the way purchasing was done. Soon after she took over, she proudly reported that her office had saved the government $200 million in spending on office supplies.

A year later, the final move, beyond which one could rise no further: the

White House. President Obama nominated Rung as head of federal procurement policy within the Office of Management and Budget. She was now overseeing all federal purchasing: all $450 billion of it, carried out by some 100,000 federal employees in 3,000 acquisition offices around the world. Her official title said it all: U.S. chief acquisition officer.

This job required Senate approval. On July 24, 2014, Rung appeared before the Senate Committee on Homeland Security and Governmental Affairs. Her family came for the occasion: her father and his wife, a cousin, and her mother, now eighty-three, who, along with Anne's brother, his wife, and their two children, took an overnight, nine-hour bus from Tennessee for the occasion. "My large family, who are teachers, former military, career government, and small business owners, live their lives with integrity, a commitment to public service, and an understanding of the value of hard work," she told the senators. "I have always tried to do the same . . . I have had a singular focus on making the government work better for the people it serves."

The committee confirmed her, and she set to work. She released a memo calling for a "new paradigm" in procurement. She told reporters that she would create "SWAT teams" for purchasing, an elite corps of twenty specialists who, as one reporter described it, "have street cred with agency contracting officers and [she would assemble] them for six months of training before returning them to their agencies to help write simplified and more market-savvy requirements for federal purchasing solicitations."

She urged purchasing officers to innovate, to build relationships with vendors, to not be bound by old ways. "Don't break the rules," she said. "But take responsible risk."

Two years later, in September 2016, she declared victory. The government had saved $2 billion through her reforms, she wrote in a triumphant memo. Nearly half the government's $1 billion in annual spending on computers was now through three government-wide contracts. The first SWAT team had graduated, and IT acquisition specialists dispersed across the agencies. "I'm personally proud of this work, and we're not slowing down," she wrote.

The memo might have left the impression that Anne Rung would be continuing to lead those efforts. In fact, it had been reported two weeks earlier that she was leaving the government, and Washington.

She was moving to Seattle, to work for Amazon Business, a whole new division created by the company in 2015 to focus on selling goods to other businesses. She would lead a new unit: the "public sector" division, geared toward selling to government.

In other words, the person overseeing all $450 billion in federal procurement was now joining the large company most determined to get a bigger share of that business.

It didn't take long for Sandy Grodin to start wondering whether he'd been robbed. Since Harvey Joseph had kept barely any records, Grodin had taken him at his word that Sturgis's sales had been around $2 million, enough to justify a $1 million purchase. But once Grodin took over the business, he discovered that the volume had almost surely been less than he'd been led to believe. There was nothing to be done about that now but make the best of it. The first task was getting his hands around the dusty, disorganized inventory. Sturgis had a few guys assigned to the warehouse, and one day Sandy told them that they were going to spend the weekend with him, going through it.

They walked up and down the aisles together and Sandy asked of every item: Does it sell or does it not sell? Those that didn't sell got red dots and were cleared out. Those that sold got green dots, and he'd write down their parts numbers and manufacturers' numbers. There were a lot more red dots than green dots. And then he called up IBM and told them he needed a software package for tracking inventory, distribution, and finances.

Sturgis and Co. entered the digital age, and it flourished. By 1994, it had grown to forty employees and $12 million in annual sales. That drew the attention of a company called U.S. Office Products, which was in the process of snatching up small office-supply dealers. The age of the big-box consolidation was well underway, and Grodin figured he couldn't fight it. He not only sold Sturgis to U.S. Office Products, but he stayed on at the larger company, making the rounds to other smaller dealers to pitch them on selling, too.

After five years, he had enough. The sort of man who cold-called businesses asking to buy them was not well suited to the role of corporate emissary. In 1999, Sandy Grodin quit his job and decided to try the next frontier: online. The internet bubble was nearing its peak, and he figured if you could sell flowers and pets online, you could sell paper and printer cartridges, too. He hired two tech whizzes from Dallas to build a website, cool officesupplies.com, and software that allowed him, once he had done the hard work of cross-referencing his own item numbers with those of the big boxes, to then search their prices and create his own, a little bit lower. A customer could go on his website and see a list of hundreds of common items, with the prices charged by the big guys and next to that the Cool Office Supplies discount. The orders went right to Grodin's wholesale supplier, S.P. Richards.

And the orders came, from the oddest places. From the Far East, from Australia, from the American embassy in Moscow. Regular customers would be presented with the image of a handsome man or pretty woman—your choice—who would greet them by name. When customers would hit their five hundredth order, the system would place an order with 1-800-FLOWERS and send out a thank-you bouquet or plant. "It was a sophisticated site," said Grodin. The company grew to $1 million in sales in the first year—Grodin was making up for low-to-zero profit margins on discounted items with healthy margins on others. "The whole idea was to create the perception that I was the low-price office supply," he said.

The fun ended not with the bursting of the internet bubble—he hadn't gone public, after all—but with the rapid growth of Google after its founding in 1998. Within a couple years, it was taking over online search. To compete, Grodin would have to agree to its pay-per-click terms, sending Google a cut for every customer it sent his way. "They started to own that space, and I thought, there's no way," he said. "I do not have the financial resources to keep up with that."

He shuttered coolofficesupplies.com in 2001 and returned to brick-and-mortar. His noncompete agreement with U.S. Office Products had expired, so he could get back in the game. That fall, two weeks after the September 11 attacks, he opened El Paso Office Products in a nondescript building in the light-industrial zone on the eastern edge of town.

This time, he was starting from scratch. He reached out to old Sturgis customers and hired more than a dozen former employees. By 2017, he had grown to more than $4 million in sales, more than half of which was in the education sector: local school districts and his alma mater, the University of Texas at El Paso. He bought himself a canary-yellow 2008 Corvette. He was, again, what he had set out to be those many years ago when he went cruising through town looking for a business to buy: the successful local entrepreneur.

One day, he got a call from one of his largest customers, El Paso Independent School District, informing him that it might be shifting its purchasing to Amazon. Around the same time, Amazon itself reached out to him, to invite him to start selling through Amazon Marketplace, its platform for third-party sellers. That way, El Paso Independent and other large customers could still buy from him—they'd just do it through Amazon instead. And he could sell to any other customer on the site as well—a whole universe of new customers.

There was one catch: he'd have to pay a commission of about 15 percent on every sale, including sales to longtime customers like El Paso Independent, to Amazon.

Amazon scheduled a call with Sandy Grodin to iron out the terms. They could give him thirty minutes, they said. The people on the call sounded very young.

While they were making the pitch, Grodin had his purchasing director, Heidi Silva, look up what one of the most common products, Avery 5160 address labels, was selling for on Amazon. They were $15.25 per box, below the $18 Grodin got them for from the wholesaler. He was dumbfounded. He had Heidi call Avery to ask for a pallet of them at the Amazon price. The guy at Avery was confused, and came back a second later and told Heidi that the product on Amazon was counterfeit.

While this was going on, the Amazon pitchmen asked Grodin if he had any questions. Grodin asked if they could recommend another independent dealer who had joined the Marketplace so that he could get a reference.

They refused, saying the identity of Marketplace members was proprietary and confidential.

Grodin's next question was about counterfeiting on the site. They asked what he meant by that. He said, well, like this item he had come across on the site, which was selling well below the usual cost. He said he had checked with the manufacturer, who had confirmed that it was counterfeit.

Flustered, they asked Grodin what the item was. He demurred. "That's proprietary and confidential," he said.

And that was that. After the call, Grodin asked Silva to track the prices on Amazon, every hour for a week, for the top twenty office-supply items ordered by El Paso Independent and compile them in a spreadsheet. He was amazed by what she produced. The prices were fluctuating wildly, hour by hour.

He then asked the school district for an appointment. They gave him an hour and he stayed for more than four. He showed them the spreadsheet. He told them about the 15 percent cut. He showed them his 2016 profit and loss statement, which he rarely showed anyone. "Here are my sales," he said. "Here are my cost of sales, here are all the rebates I've earned that reduce my cost of sales. We're lucky to get two points. When you take fifteen percent out of that expense side . . ." He let it sink in. "Guys, I can't sustain my model."

He knew he'd made as strong a case as he could, but wasn't prepared for what came next. The district's purchasing director got up from behind his desk, came around and shook his hand, and thanked him for being so transparent.

"I get it now," he told Grodin. His recommendation to the superintendent would be that the district move cautiously with Amazon and only use it for items the district couldn't buy locally.

Grodin apologized for having taken so much of their time.

They shook their head. "We needed this," they said.

The push had started right after Anne Rung moved into her new role leading the public sector division at Amazon Business. In the fall of 2016, the Prince William County Public Schools, a 90,000-student district in Northern Virginia, the second largest in the state, put out a request for proposals for office supplies. But the RFP wasn't just for Prince William County. The system was serving as the lead agency for an enormous nationwide buying network of 55,000 school districts, police departments, and other local government entities operated by a for-profit company called U.S. Communities. For years the company had negotiated deals with vendors that provided the network's members bulk discounts and favorable terms.

The contract being put out for bid by Prince William County was estimated to be worth a total of $5.5 billion over its potential eleven-year term. Yet barely anyone bid for it—because it became apparent that the RFP had been written with one particular company in mind. This RFP was oddly different than the one that had been issued six years earlier, which had resulted in the contract being awarded to a cooperative of independent office-products dealers. This one was seeking bidders to provide not only office supplies, but a broader "online marketplace for the purchases of products and services," including not only office and classroom supplies, but also home, kitchen, and grocery ware, books, musical instruments, audiovisual and other electronic equipment, scientific equipment, clothing, and even animal supplies and food. Few office-supply dealers were in a position to provide such a broad array of goods—the cooperative that had held the prior contract didn't even bother to bid on it.

Most strikingly, the RFP didn't ask bidders to provide fixed cost estimates for the products being offered. Instead, under "Pricing Instructions," it asked bidders only to "provide pricing based on their marketplace model." In other words, bidders were not asked to offer any bulk discounts so that school districts and public agencies could use their vast purchasing power for the benefit of the network.

There was one company that had built its whole business model around fluctuating rather than fixed pricing, that offered every product imaginable— from pencils to pet food—and that even called its offerings a "marketplace."

One confused potential bidder asked Prince William County: "Are you looking for just the platform that can later add all of these commodity categories, or are you looking to award to a company . . . like Amazon?"

In the end, only five bidders submitted proposals deemed minimally responsive to the RFP. Four of them received scores ranging from 2.5 to 36.7 points, on a scale of 100.

Amazon's proposal received 91.3 points. The company won the contract in January 2017. And it managed to tweak it in key ways before signing it. The revised terms required school districts and public agencies to alert Amazon if anyone made a public-records request relating to the contract, giving the company the chance to block a release of information. It was an echo of the company's demand of secrecy from the local governments with which it was negotiating tax subsidies for its warehouses—an explicit insistence against transparency in the expenditure of public dollars.

Contract in hand, Amazon set about approaching school districts and local governments to encourage them to avail themselves of the contract to start making all their purchases from the company. The pitch was straightforward: since many employees were already using Amazon for purchases instead of whoever the contracted local supplier was, why not just make Amazon the official supplier? That way purchasing directors could stop fretting about having so much leakage of spending outside of the contract. If the contract was with Amazon, then it was all good.

If purchasing directors expressed reluctance about abandoning local suppliers, Amazon assured them they could keep buying from them—they'd just be doing so through Amazon.

Left unmentioned in this was the matter of the roughly 15 percent cut that Amazon would take from any sales that those local suppliers made on the Marketplace. "With this strategy," explained a report by the Institute for Local Self-Reliance, a research and advocacy organization that defends communities from corporate control, "Amazon is following an approach that it's already used with consumer goods: Positioning itself to be not just the retailer selling goods to public agencies, but the platform through which its competitors have to go to reach their buyers. This enables Amazon, through the fees that it charges sellers, to collect a private tax on their sales."

Amazon's persistent overtures to Teresa Gandara had set off a sharp debate within her family. Her daughter, Christina, the college graduate, was leery of joining the Marketplace, as soon as she learned of the 15 percent cut. "Twelve to eighteen percent? That's our profit!" she said. "We can't pay that. We'll be paying them to do business for them."

But Teresa's son, Carlos, Jr., argued for giving it a try. "Would you rather have one percent of something or zero percent of nothing?" he said. The fact was, Pencil Cup had been experiencing a steady decline in its sales to public sector clients, especially to the El Paso city government, a decline that had forced it to shrink to ten employees, and it was hard not to wonder if Amazon was behind that. If you couldn't beat them, was it time to join them?

The company kept emailing and calling. The gist: you've got to do this. When Gandara asked them about the 15 percent cut, they told her, well, yes, that's what people pay.

That's our margin, she told them.

If you don't want to do this, no one's pushing you, they said. No one's forcing your hand.

The family was still wrestling with it a year later when Teresa headed to San Antonio in 2018 for the annual trade show held by S.P. Richards, the office supply wholesaler. She saw an intriguing session on the agenda, titled "Amazon, the Invisible Competitor: Does Your Business Have a Plan?" She went to it. The session was standing room only.

The stage was empty when the session started. Suddenly, a man came out looking nothing like the typical trade-show presenter. His face was wrapped in Ace bandages. He had on sunglasses and was wearing a black fedora. He was H. G. Wells's Invisible Man. And he was running back and forth on the stage throwing counterfeit $100 bills at the crowd.

It was Mike Tucker, the onetime pen salesman.

He had come a very long way from his days as a button-down, ex-college-baseball salesman making calls to military bases with his Uni-balls. Leading the independent office-supply dealers association had been a radicalizing experience, given what his members were up against.

In late 2017, a year after Rung's arrival at Amazon, language was tucked within the House of Representatives' version of the National Defense Authorization Act that would shift the Department of Defense purchases of routine commercial products to "online marketplaces." The amendment also enabled government-wide use of such marketplaces—it would cover more than $50 billion in routine purchasing.

The amendment met with clamor from those who stood to lose from such a takeover: not only Tucker's dealers, but also organizations for the blind and disabled that had long been guaranteed a slice of federal purchasing. The proposal was put on hold. Later, it emerged that Rung had arranged a meeting in Seattle with a top GSA official in September 2017 to discuss the shift toward the new e-commerce portal. This was during the one-year "cooling off" period during which former government officials are not allowed to lobby former colleagues on projects they themselves had worked on in government.

All this had led Mike Tucker to conclude that it was time to sound the alarm in a way that would break through convention-hall tedium. He started with an editorial cartoon: a man is sitting in his armchair reading a newspaper article about Amazon buying Whole Foods when his wife comes home with their son, laden with shopping bags, and tells him, "Bobby got a shirt at Amazonbie and Fitch. I bought a nightie at Amazon's Secret. We had lunch at McAmazon's. Then I picked up your pills at Rite Aidazon . . ."

Tucker then showed the audience a graph of Amazon's revenues: a low, nearly horizontal line in the early years, and then the great upward swoosh over the past decade, from less than $20 billion in 2007 to $180 billion in 2017. He sketched the company's famous "flywheel" of success: use customer service and Prime's free delivery to capture online traffic, then use high traffic to compel other firms to join the Marketplace, which expands selection and lowers the site's cost structure and allows it to reduce prices, driving yet higher sales and attracting yet more sellers. Drawing heavily on arguments and data from the Institute for Local Self-Reliance, he showed how the company draws on those sellers' expertise and the stream of data their transactions generate to see which of their products sell well and then starts selling near-copies of those goods under Amazon's own brands: diapers, batteries, vitamin supplements, nicotine gum, mid-century modern chairs, trash bags, gel insoles . . .

Amazon, Tucker told the audience, operates as both a portal provider and a seller in its own right to maximize its market power. It picks off bestsellers for itself and promotes them over other products, leaving rivals to sell slower-movers, all while it collects a lucrative fee on others' sales. The copycat items it sells under its own brand could squeeze competitors even without big sales totals: Amazon prices them so aggressively that rivals have to price their own items at absurdly low prices, which drives sales—and thus fees—for Amazon, while leaving sellers with meager margins.

Sellers are blocked from building relationships with customers and strongly discouraged from selling items for a lower price on any other site; sellers' terms and fees on the Marketplace could change without warning. For many merchants, Amazon could collect more than 30 cents of every dollar spent, once you added up commissions, fulfillment fees, advertising on the site, and account management deals, some of which were optional for selling on the site, but hard to avoid for sellers hoping to succeed. (Amazon's advertising revenue jumped to $10 billion in 2018, making it a sudden rival to Facebook and Google, which dominated that realm.) It was making a 20 percent margin on its third-party sales, compared with only a 5 percent margin on its regular retail sales. In 2013, the number of third-party vendors selling via Amazon's warehouses jumped by two-thirds in a single year. By 2017, the company's cut of third-party sales was up to $32 billion, which by itself amounted to half of Target's total sales. By 2018, Amazon's cut of third-party sales was up to $42.7 billion, a fifth of the company's total revenue, and third-party sales now made up nearly 60 percent of all the merchandise sold on the site.

Amazon had eliminated about twice as many jobs at independent retailers as it had created, Tucker said—in 2014, it had sold $2 billion worth of goods in Illinois and $1 billion in Missouri without employing a single person in either state. (All told, only a quarter of all retail shopping now took place in independent stores, down from a half in the 1980s.) By driving out so many local businesses, it was devastating local and state property tax collection, and that was even before one factored in the hundreds of millions it had received in tax subsidies for warehouses. And then there were the intangible costs to the takeover: reduced street life, civic engagement, social capital. "We're not just consumers," Mike Tucker told his rapt audience. "We're neighbors, workers, producers, taxpayers and citizens with needs and wants that go beyond One-Click checkout."

The problem was, he said, these costs were not perceptible to the average American. "The damage Amazon is doing is nearly impossible for consumers to detect in real time," he said. "Amazon appears so consumer-friendly that it's hard to see them as a monopoly. Amazon's placelessness contributes to its invisibility and makes it harder to fight."

The association was doing its best to fight back at the national level, Tucker said. But it was up to the dealers in the room to resist in their own towns and cities, where it mattered most. They needed to reach out to the local media. They needed to urge local elected officials to reject the U.S. Communities contract, by showing them how the dynamic pricing model was costing them money, by reminding them how much the local tax base depended on prospering small businesses. They needed to make the invisible visible.

And then Tucker turned over the stage to one independent office-supply dealer to tell his story of successfully resisting: Sandy Grodin of El Paso, Texas.

Teresa Gandara of El Paso left the session on fire. All of her uncertainty about the Amazon overture had burned away. She recalled a favorite line of her father, the owner of the grocery with the laundry machines and showers. "Never let yourself be taken advantage of," he'd tell his children, "because if you do, you deserve it."

She came home ready to carry out Tucker's orders. Her first stop would be city hall. She didn't realize how much earlier others had already gotten there.

Every year, the El Paso city government hosted an expo at the convention center for vendors with whom it did business. It was a goodwill gesture and a tool for economic development—most of the vendors were local companies who could benefit from the networking and instructional sessions on how to find new customers and contracts.

In the fall of 2017, a year after Anne Rung left the government, there was another company interested in taking part in the expo. Bruce Collins, the city's purchasing director, sent an email to city hall colleagues with the news. "Amazon's Small Business Development Division has agreed to speak at our 2017 Expo," he wrote. "Amazon will provide information on how they work with and mentor small businesses regarding doing business with Amazon and its partners." The company would also take a booth in the exhibition hall.

"Thx for sharing," responded El Paso city manager Tommy Gonzalez. "Very good timing!" The city was in the process of making Amazon an approved source for city purchases, and having it take part in the expo would put a friendly gloss on this controversial step—it would simply be another one of the vendors in the mix.

The following year, 2018, Amazon decided to step it up a notch. It wanted to have an entire extended forum at the city's expo, in a space of its own, dedicated to pitching El Paso small businesses on joining the Marketplace. In June, Amazon's Daniel Lee, a "Government Marketplace Lead," emailed Collins and other city officials, asking for a list of business owners who might participate and proposing language they could use to pitch an Amazon forum:

The goal of this joint El Paso/Amazon event is to provide the opportunity for El Paso based commodity businesses to learn about selling on Amazon Business and for agencies to discover how they can direct their spend to these sellers. This initiative creates an opportunity to leverage the Amazon Business Marketplace to purchase locally, help our local business grow and gain access to more customers.

It was impressively brazen: Amazon, which was looking to supplant the link between local government and local businesses, was offering its event as a way to boost local business.

Two months later, in late August, Amazon sought to seal the deal with an approach by Mario Marin, the head of all U.S. government sales for Amazon Business. Marin had spent seven years in Los Angeles city government. He had run into Bruce Collins at the National Institute of Governmental Purchasing conference in Nashville, and was writing to tell him that he'd shortly be sending along the agenda for Amazon's forum in El Paso. "I appreciated our conversation and the ways we're going to work together," Marin wrote.

Later that day came the agenda—a three-page-long "run of show" laying out how Amazon wanted the event to go. Amazon wanted a "minimum of 100 businesses in attendance" to make its pitch to, and wanted Collins to provide a "target list." It wanted two and a half hours for its event. It wanted "multiple tables dedicated to Amazon Business," to prevent "a bottle neck at any one table." Collins, Marin wrote, would be allowed a ten-minute introduction and ten-minute closing. "You could use this time to reiterate your support of local businesses," Marin wrote. "Our goal," he added, "is to ensure every attendee knows the do's and don'ts of working with Amazon Business. We believe in transparency and want our customers (existing and future) to walk away with a positive experience."

Collins responded a few days later that the city accepted all the terms and would send Marin not only a list of local businesses to target but also businesses in El Paso's much larger sister city across the border in Mexico, Ciudad Juarez.

Collins also got an imprimatur from his boss, the city's deputy city manager, Cary Westin, a retired army colonel. Westin sent an email commanding an array of city officials to meet to work out the details of the event. "We have a great opportunity with this," he wrote.

As word of the event started getting around the El Paso business community, the expo took on a whole new name: it was now being called "Amazon Day."

Teresa Gandara caught wind of all this at exactly the moment of her return from her San Antonio awakening. She asked for an appointment with Collins, with whom she had always been on good terms. She went to city hall and showed him the information she had gotten in San Antonio, laying out Amazon's effect on local businesses and tax revenue.

He seemed taken aback, and said that he would look into it more closely.

That's fine, Gandara said, but meanwhile, he needed to cancel Amazon Day.

That wasn't his decision to make, he said. It was up to his boss, Westin, the retired colonel.

So Gandara made an appointment with Westin and repeated her case to him for canceling Amazon Day. Not long into her presentation, Westin cut her off and told her, sorry, but the city of El Paso was not interested in protectionism for small businesses, or, as he later recalled putting it, "We don't prohibit businesses from coming to our expo."

Teresa Gandara got the message. Mr. Westin, she told him, this is falling on deaf ears. You have more important things to do, and so do I.

And she got up and walked out.

On the evening before Amazon Day, the El Paso Convention and Performing Arts Center was ready. The event was a big enough deal that KVIA, the local ABC affiliate, did a segment previewing it on the ten o'clock news. Except the segment wasn't only about the expo.

"There's one session of the expo a local business owner takes issue with—the one focusing on Amazon," said anchor Erik Elken. "She says the retail giant is a threat to local businesses. ABC 7's Denise Olivas has the story."

And there, on-screen, was Teresa Gandara, in a floral-patterned silk blouse, walking across Pencil Cup's storeroom with Olivas. "One of the things we're very proud about is knowing that we have a strong, independent business base," she told Olivas. She recounted the initial overture from Amazon—her excitement over it, and then learning about the big cut they'd be taking from her sales.

Olivas followed up by noting that Amazon had recently increased its cut, and by noting a study, from the Harvard Business School, that described Amazon's penchant for seeing which products were selling most and then offering its own products to supplant them.

Gandara came back on-screen. "This is about our tax dollars that our city and anyone else who's ordering from Amazon using tax dollars are sending out of our economy," she said. "Every dollar you spend on a local entity stays and gets recirculated at least ten times in the economy."

The counter came from Bruce Collins, the city procurement director, standing in a suit inside ABC 7's studio. "I think it's a good partnership," he said. "Suppliers who are not moving their inventory, they have a choice to leave the inventory and not sell it. Now there's another vehicle that can be used."

Back to Teresa: "When our city decided to allow Amazon, in my humble opinion, to become part of their marketing platform, I considered it the worst procurement decision that could be made for the city of El Paso."

Collins: "From the city's perspective we're not telling people that you *have* to join the Amazon platform. We're just saying, here's another tool. My challenge would be, let's see if it can grow the businesses and help grow El Paso and afterward we can always revisit."

Gandara got the final word. Her voice was quavering. "I'm an El Pasoan through and through. And when I see that the tax dollars are leaving, and weakening us, and knowing that something could be done about it, and isn't being done, somebody has to do it."

Good morning, El Paso!"
With this greeting, Bruce Collins kicked off the 2018 Cooperative Purchasing Expo. Barely a seat was empty in the convention center ballroom. But the real action would come after lunch, when the event that had been

planned in all those emails and calls, that Teresa Gandara had gone far outside her comfort zone to publicly oppose, would commence in a windowless meeting room with a single door.

Not anyone could attend—only those who had registered in advance. Several dozen drifted in, and when the time came, the door was closed behind them. Amazon had not spared expense for this moment. It had four people in the room, among them Mario Marin, the former Los Angeles government official who was now the head of all U.S. government sales for Amazon Business; Daniel Lee, the younger salesman also on the email chains; and Danielle Hinz, the "global solutions lead for local government"—who until six months prior had been the procurement chief for King County, Washington, which includes Seattle.

To the front of the room moved Marin. He was tall and handsome and spoke so gently that one might have mistaken the session for a support group.

"You are here," he said, "to learn a little more about what Amazon Business is and, more importantly, how businesses are leveraging the Marketplace to both sell on Amazon's platform as well as to use it to support their business."

Marin knew that to sell, you needed to tell stories, and he started with the story of how Amazon Business had been born a few years earlier. "The reason why is, we saw a lot of consumers using their work email addresses," he said, "and they were buying no longer the toys they bought for Christmas or clothes for school, but reams of paper or toilet paper or office supplies and this was happening across the United States. And that's when we realized there might be something here, where businesses are leveraging the dot .com site. So why not overlay a solution that addresses their needs? Because we know that consumers buy different than government. We know that GE buys different than my sons." The session, he said, would be an "open, engaging conversation" to help the assembled businesspeople "have a better sense of what Amazon Marketplace can do for your business."

And then something odd happened. Marin introduced Bruce Collins, the city procurement director, as if Amazon had been hosting this event, when the expo was in fact Collins's big show, on city property. Collins came forward and issued what amounted to a preemptive warning to those in attendance. "As Mario indicated, this is a forum one hundred percent dedicated to understanding the Amazon platform," Collins said. "This meeting is *not* a meeting to discuss the history of Amazon or anything other than the Marketplace. We're going to be very respectful to the intent of this particular meeting."

The parameters thus established, Marin came back for another gentle word. "What we're trying to do is help federal, state, local, nonprofit institutions leverage Amazon Business to help them save time and money and focus on those things that matter to communities," he said. "That's truly what we're trying to accomplish here."

The details were left to Marin's junior colleague, Lee. He came armed with PowerPoint. He said that Amazon's "core competency" was that it was "the Earth's most customer-centric company." He said that the "three main pillars of that are price, selection, and convenience." He offered an aside: "Are you guys all Amazon shoppers? Yeah? How many times have you come to the Marketplace and thought, wow, I didn't expect to find that there?"

Knowing laughter filled the room. "Every time," said one woman.

"That's what we want," said Lee.

He told them about the "flywheel"—how convenience and low prices drew customers, which drove traffic, which drew more sellers and products, which drove yet more traffic and sales. He flashed the numbers on the screen: the year prior, 140,000 small and medium businesses had more than $100,000 in sales on the site. "Not too bad—that's a pretty good incremental sales channel, I would say," he observed with cool understatement.

In other words: only a fool would turn down the opportunity on offer. In just three years, Amazon Business had grown from zero to $10 billion in annualized sales. "It's kind of phenomenal being part of it and seeing it grow in front of you," Lee said. It now sold to nearly eighty of the largest universities and school districts in the country. It sold to fifty-five of the Fortune 100. It sold to more than half of the biggest hospital systems, and more than 40 percent of the most populous local governments. In other words: everyone was doing it.

A hand went up. It was Julian Grubbs, from Express Office Products. "City customers used to buy from my website, and then we transitioned to the city website. Are we transitioning to Amazon and it's going to replace the city website?"

The question cut through the fog of Lee's pitch. With Amazon now approved as a channel for city government purchasing, would city employees simply be buying straight from the site? Left unmentioned was the clear subtext: if they were doing so, what was to keep them from buying from the countless other suppliers on the site, not just El Paso businesses?

Bruce Collins jumped up to dismiss Grubbs's insinuation. Yes, he said, buyers could now go through Amazon directly. But, "as part of the synergy with the city, it'll be coded" that an El Paso supplier is local, and thus preferable to use.

Daniel Lee offered more consolation. Amazon Business gave sellers a window where they could describe themselves, where El Paso businesses could tout their roots. "You can tell your story," he said.

But Grubbs wasn't satisfied. A few moments later, he raised his hand again and cut even closer to the main point. "What's the tradeoff when they order from me directly and [from] me from Amazon?" he asked.

Lee acted as if he did not understand what Grubbs was getting at. "Tradeoff for you, sir?" he said.

"Tradeoff for me and the customers," said Grubbs.

Marin jumped in and started talking again about Amazon guiding El Paso buyers to El Paso sellers. Grubbs wasn't having it, and pushed even harder for candor. "My question is, I'm on the city's website for a ream of paper for ten dollars. They go through the city website to purchase from me. When they go through Amazon, they've added another tradeoff, whether price, service, or convenience. *What is the tradeoff?*" He was practically begging now.

But the avoidance continued, from each of the three men.

"Global distribution," said Bruce Collins. "When you go to Amazon Marketplace, you're now a global supplier."

"We're not trying to replace your current business," said Daniel Lee. "It's not El Paso. It's the Stanfords and GEs of the world that you get to sell to, in a pretty turnkey solution."

"We take on the responsibility of negotiations" when it comes to over-due payments and other hassles, said Mario Marin. "It's a phenomenal chan-nel to think about."

This was the Amazon vision in its essence, of commerce at its freest and most frictionless, a small business on the Mexican border able to sell its goods to any buyer in the world, without even having to worry about pack-ing and shipping: What was not to like about that?

Grubbs couldn't take it anymore. He had tried not to be too blunt. How could one be so crass as to inquire about price if the seller was acting as if there wasn't even a pitch going on, that this was all about helping El Paso businesses grow? They had left him no choice.

"That's great and sounds great to me," Grubbs said. "I haven't seen what it's going to cost me for this convenience."

And finally, with that, nearly forty minutes into the pitch, Lee told his audience that for the privilege of selling on Amazon, they would pay a $39.99 monthly fee. "And," he continued, "there's a referral fee that spans from six to fifteen percent depending on product category."

It was vague, and Grubbs called him on it. "Those categories go from six to fifteen percent. How do I, as a businessperson, identify my product category?"

"That's something we'll walk through with you," said Lee.

"That's something we'll come to terms with before we come to terms?"

"Kinda sorta," said Lee.

With the real terms of the deal finally on the table, there was little left to be said. A while later, Mario Marin wrapped things up, neatly as he could. "You heard two stories," he said. "One is, there's a play on suppliers on the sell side, onboarding, recruiting, helping you sell on this marketplace. And then you heard my story, on how we're teaching, showing, demonstrating how you can use this site, you can buy and mirror your procurement pro-cesses in such a way that you can help fulfill your socioeconomic goals."

"That's it," he said. "That's our story."

Back at Pencil Cup, that same day, Carlos Gandara, Jr., couldn't stop yawning. Maybe it was because he was doing so much. He was still working for the family company—he was now one of their two primary salesmen. But he was also preparing to launch a couple businesses with some friends. One was going to involve window-blinds sales. The other was in retail.

The truth was, he had been chafing under the constraints of Pencil Cup for some time now. He understood his obligation to the family business; he was grateful to have been employed by it all these years. But he was thirty-one now. It was time to try something on his own.

For a few years, in fact, he'd already had something going on the side, something small. He searched for liquidated goods on the internet, general merchandise of all sorts, and bought it for cheap and had it shipped to Pencil Cup. It was everything under the sun: for a while, it had been a lot of baby gear—cribs and those tabletop bouncer seats. He'd take pictures of the stuff, settle on a price for it, and then he'd sell it.

On Amazon.

He'd found out about it from a video he happened across online, when he was wondering how he might be able to make some extra cash. FBA. Fulfillment by Amazon. You shipped them the stuff, they stored it in the warehouse and took care of sending it to the buyer, of customer service, of returns. For a percentage, of course. FBA was so easy and frictionless that it helped explain the astonishing scale that the company was reaching: by 2019, it would have more than 600 million items for sale at any moment and more than 3 million vendors selling them. It also helped explain the problems that were starting to emerge: Amazon was allowing its third-party sellers (a third of whom were now based in China) to sell countless counterfeit goods, and clothes made in dangerous Bangladeshi factories that other retailers had stopped buying from, and toys, infant sleeping mats, and other products that had been declared unsafe by regulators.

Carlos, Jr., got grief from his family about his FBA sideline. But then, he had never been as bothered as they were by the threat they were facing.

Sometimes, sure, he'd go to a school district to pitch Pencil Cup and they told him they were buying from Amazon instead. "I'm not going to get my feelings hurt," he said. "Everybody buys from everybody."

The fact was, he won some, too, now and then. Not long ago, a district had called with the quote they got from Amazon for some audiovisual equipment and he had been able to beat it. He liked to think he still had a natural advantage. He was there, they weren't. He could go into the schools in person, present his young, charismatic, good-looking self. "Price is always a factor," he said. "But so is presence."

But it was more than that. He did not mind the threat so much because he couldn't help but be in awe of the company and person it was coming from. "The sad part about it is," he said, "I have an admiration for Jeff Bezos. I have somewhat of an idolization of him."

"Because," he said, "that's where I want to be."

6.

Power

<hr>

Under the cloud

NORTHERN VIRGINIA—COLUMBUS, OHIO—
WASHINGTON, D.C.

It grew on Nathan Grayson over many years, the fact of what he would eventually come to call his tan. "No matter what I do, I'll always have a nice tan," he would say, with a great rumbling laugh that was equal parts rue and mirth. "No matter what I do."

He might've noticed it first in the first grade, when his Northern Virginia elementary school, Antioch-McCrae, was shut down soon after he arrived there. The rumor spread that the owner of the land on which the school sat was displeased about the school's recent integration, and that this had led to the school's closure. Regardless, the school eventually became a bird sanctuary, and Nathan Grayson and his mostly Black classmates were moved to Gainesville Elementary.

He noticed it again when he tried to start his own business, years later, in hopes of following in the footsteps of his father, who had run a small trash-hauling business that had flourished for a time, with Nate in charge of sales, until it was edged out by the big guys, Waste Management and

Browning-Ferris Industries. Nate eventually ended up working maintenance at one of the high-end golf courses in Northern Virginia. He was proud of his work—irrigating the greens to verdant perfection, fixing anything in the clubhouse—and they treated him well enough. But he couldn't shake the yearning to be his own boss—to be like the man he had seen late one night cleaning a shopping center parking lot with a sweeper truck. The man had told him that he had brought in well over $100,000 the year prior from cleaning only three lots from Front Royal to Manassas, which took him only a few hours every night.

So Nate Grayson had gone to the bank, first for a $70,000 loan to buy large mowers and a dump trailer. He had good credit, and banks told him he'd qualify for a mortgage or for a car or motorcycle loan. The mowers and trailer, on the other hand, were intended for a business, and for some reason, Nate couldn't get a business loan: "I'm sorry, Mr. Grayson," the loan officer said, "but due to some complications we won't be able to do this for you." He tried again a few years later, this time seeking $40,000 for two sweeper trucks. Again, no. He stayed at the country club—setting sprinklers, fixing water fountains, cutting trees, replacing broken straps or rotted tires or steering knuckles on carts, repairing clubhouse doors that angry elbows punched holes in. "How do you keep the scale tilted?" he said later, posing one of the rhetorical questions he was given toward. He answered it himself. "If you don't open the door, I can't walk in."

But at least Nathan Grayson had Carver Road—Carver Road and all that came with it. So little was established about how this remarkable enclave had come to be, a fogginess in the historical record that was one of the legacies of centuries of forced illiteracy. All that was known for sure was that in the years after the Civil War, a patch of what used to be the Mount Pleasant plantation had been designated for possible purchase by the formerly enslaved people living there. They could buy land, but they had to buy it here. And among those to make a purchase was one Livinia Blackburn Johnson, who according to county land records paid $30 in 1899 to buy three acres from Jane C. Tyler, the daughter of the land's original owner, who had died in 1862.

Ms. Johnson, then in her thirties, would go on to buy additional land nearby, to the point where, decades later, she would come to be regarded as the progenitor of this community: some seventy people living amid tall pines on about fifty acres along Carver Road's mile-long stretch between Lee Highway and Old Carolina Road. The Johnsons, the Moores, the Graysons, all distantly related, all tracing their roots back to Livinia and the handful of other freed slaves who had also bought property from their former masters. The community was called, simply, the Settlement.

For decades, they had done farm labor or domestic work on nearby estates, riding by horse and buggy to some of the same plantations where their forebears had worked under the lash. Gradually, they had branched out: Charles Moore had started out in landscaping and yard work but had gone off to work at Sears, Roebuck in Washington, making the thirty-five-mile drive in his Dodge pickup, with a bag lunch beside him. Another neighbor, John Pye, had worked as a butler and chauffeur in Franklin D. Roosevelt's White House.

Life at the Settlement revolved around Mount Pleasant Baptist Church, founded in 1877. They held dances at Shady Inn Dance Hall. They shopped at Phil's Market and Gossen's Hardware, which, unlike Orndoff's truck stop, didn't make them use the back door.

Such indignities dissolved with time. So, too, did the Settlement's seclusion. The sprawl of Washington, D.C., marched westward, all but enveloping the Carver Road community. Developers built a nearby subdivision, called Hopewell's Landing. Lee Highway was widened to four lanes, and eastbound traffic was so heavy in the mornings that you could forget about turning left anytime after 8:00 a.m.

Yet the Settlement endured. In the 1990s, Nate Grayson inherited the two-bedroom, one-bath house in which he had been raised. It sat on more than four acres, on which he had as a boy hunted squirrels with his father using a 410 single shot from Sears & Roebuck. The land now accommodated his grown-up passion: training beagles, four or five at a time, which he brought to competitive field trials across the eastern United States.

Many of the older members of the community had made it into their seventies, eighties, even nineties. Their own children had moved away. Even in his early fifties, Nate was among the youngest remaining, as the family tree he had sketched out on a big board inside his house showed. He plowed their driveways, he fixed their gutters, he mowed their lawns. "I was raised by the neighborhood," he said. "They made me who I am today. They took care of me in the beginning. When I needed twenty dollars, Mr. Charles Moore would give it to me. They took care of me like I was one of their own."

Now it would be his turn to take care of them, as Carver Road fell at risk of being enveloped by the cloud.

The cloud. The term was so airy and ethereal. It conjured a fly ball arcing to left-center field, a lazy summer Sunday on the prairie.

In fact, the cloud was profoundly earthbound and material, the antithesis of lightness and luminescence. The cloud lived in data centers, the vast windowless structures that started proliferating in certain corners of the American landscape at the close of the twentieth century as communications and commercial life moved online. The millions of transactions and interactions and activities that had not so long ago made up daily life—a letter sent, a dollar bill extended, a newspaper read, a record played, a film screened—had gravitated from a quotidian and ubiquitous existence into a realm that was almost entirely hidden from view. Inside data centers were the giant servers through which everything moved: the business transactions, the government secrets, the lovers' emails. By 2018, we were creating 2.5 quintillion bytes of data every day, a sum that was increasing at such an exponential rate that 90 percent of the data in the world had been generated in only the two years prior. Every minute, on average, the world conducted 2.4 million searches on Google, watched 4.1 million YouTube videos, and posted 47,000 photos on Instagram.

The installations were virtually self-sufficient—a data center with more than 200,000 square feet and $400 million worth of servers and equipment required only twenty engineers and technicians to function. What they really demanded were power and water—the former to run the machines, the latter to cool them.

And they demanded security. The data centers were the nerve centers of the nation, and were protected as such. Their walls were twice as thick as those of most buildings, able to withstand winds of up to 150 miles per hour. Their concrete floor slabs could hold up to 350 pounds per square foot. The machines were locked in cages and set off by firewalls. Some had concrete ceilings to hold massive backup generators. The buildings could be mistaken for bomb shelters, large enough for an entire town of paranoiacs.

In theory, the data centers could be anywhere with proximity to fiber-optic cable, plentiful water, and cheap electricity. In reality, they clustered together, a near infinitude of human commerce and communication packed into a handful of buildings in a handful of locations. Even more so than other aspects of the digital landscape, the cloud could be dominated by a few places, and by a few companies, those with the most capacity and most connections.

And the biggest cluster, by far, was in Northern Virginia. From early on, the area had been home to an outsized share of commercial internet providers drawn by the concentration of military contractors and high-tech companies. The area also offered plentiful land—the gently rolling farms spreading west and south of the Potomac toward the Piedmont, with the Blue Ridge peaks in the distance—and cheap electricity fueled by Appalachian coal. In 1992, a group of internet providers met for lunch at the Tortilla Factory in Herndon, Virginia, to make a decision that would seal the area's advantage: they would physically bring their networks together in a new colocation point, greatly enhancing their reach and value to customers. The hub, dubbed Metropolitan Area Exchange-East, was housed in a cinder-block room within an underground parking garage in Tysons Corner, the edge city straddling the Beltway.

Providing additional gravitational pull were the tax breaks bestowed on the data centers by the state of Virginia and local governments, especially Loudoun and Prince William Counties. For these Washington exurbs, the data centers were ideal neighbors: they spun off tax revenue to pay for the deluxe schools demanded by residents moving into new McMansions, but they added few cars to the clogged roads. In that sense, the paltry number of jobs that came with them was, to use tech lingo, a feature and not a bug.

They cost between $50 million and $70 million apiece. They went up without identifying details—anyone passing by had no idea for whom, or for what, they were being run. "We don't comment on any project real or imagined," said Prince William's director of economic development in 2000, in response to a reporter.

The puncturing of the tech bubble that year left many of the centers vacant, raising the specter of a permanent blight of these huge husks, unfit for any other purpose. But the setback was temporary. The rise of the counterterrorism apparatus after the September 11 attacks created new demand for highly secure data storage—increasingly, the buildings came with "man traps," one-person entrances outfitted with biometric scanners capable of reading fingerprints, palms, or retinas; there were also fake entrances, bulletproof glass, and Kevlar-lined walls. Some of the data centers were even deliberately set behind hills, to obscure visibility and stop charging vehicles packed with explosives; those less topographically protected had perimeters of concrete posts.

And then came the cloud.

The term's functional origin—the idea of running applications off of servers that are not your own—came in the early 2000s, in Seattle. Amazon had been building a business called Merchant.com that provided technology for other companies' e-commerce websites, and it noticed how easy it was for outside users to access Amazon's technology with well-designed interfaces. Around the same time, the company discovered that many of its software development teams were spending months re-creating the same basic software infrastructure for their projects, over and over. Why not build an infrastructure platform that would make Amazon's own software development more efficient and also offer it to other companies? Those companies could design applications to run on the infrastructure—everything from computing to payments to messaging—and thus be spared the cost and hassle of building their own infrastructure and running their own servers and data centers.

The company created Amazon Web Services, its cloud-computing branch, in 2003, and began offering its first data storage service in 2006. By 2017, AWS was providing cloud services to, among others, GE, Capital One, News Corp, Verizon, Airbnb, Slack, Coca-Cola, and even direct rivals like Apple and Netflix, while bringing in more than $17 billion in revenue for the year—a tenth of Amazon's total. "AWS has built one of the most feature-full and disruptive technology platforms that's existed in my lifetime," declared AWS's global head for enterprise strategy, Stephen Orban.

Between its dominance of the cloud and its dominance of online sales, Amazon had positioned itself as a gatekeeper that extracted fees—what economists called "rent"—on two of the biggest realms of digital commercial activity, data storage and e-commerce. You could almost compare it to a tax, except this tax was being collected by a corporation, not by a duly elected government. Or you could compare it to a utility company—Amazon had, in essence, slapped a meter on the side of the nation's data centers, except without the regulatory limits that utilities faced.

Or you could compare it to the lucrative extraction play of the banks and hedge funds leading up to the 2008 financial crash, which amounted to "tails I win, heads you lose." No matter what, Amazon was collecting its fee. "I see parallels in Amazon's behavior to the lending practices of some financial groups before the 2008 crash," wrote the *Financial Times* columnist Rana Foroohar. "They used dynamic pricing, in the form of variable rate subprime mortgage loans, and exploited huge information asymmetries in their sale of mortgage-backed securities and complex debt deals to unwary investors including cities such as Detroit. Amazon, for its part, has vastly more market data than the suppliers and public sector purchasers it plans to link. Indeed, I see more and more parallels between online groups and large financial institutions. They each sit in the center of an hourglass of information and commerce, taking a cut of whatever passes through. Like a big investment bank, Amazon can both make a market and participate in it."

It was also reminiscent of the railroad giants in the late nineteenth century, which controlled both the tracks and much of the oil and coal that was being transported on the tracks, thus allowing them to squeeze smaller fuel producers.

As more and more companies moved to the cloud, and as more companies followed Amazon's lead in seeking to offer capacity, the data centers sprawled as never before. In Northern Virginia, they covered more than 9 million square feet. Dominion Virginia Power, the state's dominant utility, which relied heavily on coal as its energy source, was in 2013 projecting a 40 percent increase in data-center power demand over just the next four years. Each data center consumed about as much energy as 5,000 homes.

Land was filling up, especially in Loudoun County, where there were forty data centers by 2013, covering 5 million square feet, the equivalent of twenty-five Walmart supercenters, and the county was expecting to reach twice that over the next decade. In a single two-year span, 2011–2012, the county had added nearly 800,000 square feet in data center space, but not a single square foot of traditional office space. Land was going for more than $1 million per acre in the heart of the county's "Data Center Alley."

The county boasted that as much as 70 percent of all internet traffic flowed through its centers each day. Ashburn, an exurb beyond Dulles International Airport that was home to the county's original data-center cluster, was mentioned in the same breath as the world's other great internet hubs: Tokyo, London, Frankfurt. "I'm not overstating things by much to say that Data Center Alley has become essential to western culture's social fabric," said the Loudoun County economic development director Buddy Rizer. The county boasted, too, that more than $200 million in tax revenue flowed from the centers into its treasury each year, making it possible for the county, the wealthiest in the country, to provide services such as full-day kindergarten that needier communities were unable to offer.

Amazon already had several data centers in Northern Virginia, managed under the name of its data center subsidiary, Vadata. But it needed more capacity, a lot more, because it was angling for a new realm of business. In 2013, it won a $600 million cloud contract from the CIA, and branches of the military were starting to explore shifting to the cloud, too.

In 2014, an unidentified company applied to build a 500,000-square-foot data center near the town of Haymarket, in Prince William County. The site along John Marshall Highway was considerably farther west of the other data center clusters in the area, offering a higher level of secrecy. It was beyond Manassas National Battlefield Park, and abutted the Rural Crescent, a swath of land long protected from development.

But the unnamed company got county approval—Prince William had no zoning rules for data centers. It probably did not hurt that employees of the county's economic development team made two trips to Seattle in 2013 for meetings at the company's headquarters, one of the trips in the company of officials from Dominion, the Virginia utility.

All that remained to be done was hooking up the new center to power.

B y this point, Amazon was growing so rapidly that Northern Virginia would no longer suffice. It needed a second data-center hub in the eastern United States. It settled on the metropolitan area of Columbus, Ohio.

Columbus was not like the rest of Ohio. It lacked the industrial roots of Cleveland, Cincinnati, Akron, Toledo, Dayton, and Youngstown. Its economy had been built around state government, Ohio State University, transportation, and health care. In 1960, its population of 470,000 was still well behind Cincinnati and Cleveland. What growth it was achieving in these years was largely a function of annexation: in the mid-1950s, the city passed resolutions mandating that it would extend water and sewer lines only to outlying areas that agreed to be annexed, with the result that the city eventually sprawled over 223 square miles, nearly three times as much as Cleveland and Cincinnati.

Half a century later, Columbus was king. Its lack of an industrial base meant that it was far less affected by the decline of manufacturing than were Ohio's other large cities. (General Motors, once the top employer in the state, was on its way down to the seventy-second largest.) Its land annexation meant that as suburban flight accelerated from the urban core, it retained many more residents within its borders than did the state's other large cities—a family could move fifteen miles from downtown to a ranch house well outside I-270, the city's beltway, and still be in Columbus and be part of its tax base. And being home to the state's flagship public university meant that the city became the natural destination for so many of the bright young people from the state's struggling smaller cities and towns. They came to Columbus for college and never went back.

By 2014, the city had completely detached its fate from the rest of the state. Its population had grown by 14 percent since 2000, to more than 800,000, while Cleveland and Cincinnati had lost another 15 percent of their population over that period. It was the fastest-growing city in the country outside the South and West. Its median household income was roughly a third larger than that of the state's next seven largest cities; its median home values were more than 70 percent higher than those in midsize cities such as Dayton, Toledo, and Akron; it had nearly a third of the jobs created in the state since 2010, among them outposts of Apple and Tesla, and dominated start-up growth in the Midwest, while Youngstown, Akron, and Toledo were ranking among the bottom ten cities for job growth nationwide. Columbus was benefiting from the same winner-take-all, rich-get-richer effect that lifted the better-known prosperous bastions on the coasts, but at a regional rather than national level. Success bred success; even out here in the Midwest, the winnings would not be spread anywhere close to evenly.

It was hardly any surprise, then, that when Amazon chose Ohio for the second hub of what it called AWS US East, an expansion that would cost more than $1 billion, it homed in on metro Columbus, instead of parts of the state far more desperate for investment. Columbus's educated, young workforce was well suited to staff the centers. (AWS's Orban made plain its preference for fresh-out-of-college employees: "I love that they don't come with years of 'how they did it elsewhere' baggage.") And the area offered the right sort of exurban communities to target: wealthy enough to support good schools for employees' kids, but also sufficiently insecure in their civic infrastructure and identity to be easy marks.

The company zeroed in on three towns beyond the long reach of the Columbus city line along the northern, wealthier arc of the I-270 beltway: Hilliard ("Real People, Real Possibilities"), Dublin ("Where Yesterday

Meets Tomorrow"), and New Albany ("America's Best Suburb"), the last of which the billionaire Les Wexner had created out of the soybean fields with the help of his mysterious consigliere, the sexual predator Jeffrey Epstein.

Amazon laid down its terms, exactly as it was doing with the warehouses it was seeking to build in Ohio and elsewhere. It demanded large incentives: a fifteen-year exemption from property taxes, which, for a standard data center, would be worth about $5.4 million. "Vadata strives to operate its facilities as efficiently and cost-effectively as possible," the company stated in justifying its demands to New Albany. It insisted on special treatment at every step: accelerated building permit approvals, waivers of routine fees.

And it demanded total secrecy. The communities had to sign nondisclosure agreements before they could engage in negotiations with the company. They had to agree to refer to the company only by code names ("Project Granite" in Dublin; "Project Marble" in Hilliard). The company asked that elected officials discuss the project only in closed-door sessions, not at public meetings. And it demanded that the towns alert it to any public information requests about the data centers, and do their utmost to refrain from releasing information, even details as basic as the project's location.

The three suburbs rushed to comply. All three granted the fifteen-year property tax exemptions, as well as agreed to credit back to the company 10 percent of the payroll taxes it would be paying on its employees, which would number only twenty-five at each center. This was on top of a whole other tax break that the company negotiated with the Ohio Tax Credit Authority, a sales tax exemption for equipment that was worth $77 million.

Dublin went yet further: it gave the company sixty-nine acres of farmland appraised at $6.75 million on which to build the center. As long as Amazon proceeded to build at least 750,000 square feet of data center space there, Dublin pledged in writing, "the company will not have to pay for any portion of the land." The town tossed on another dollop: "Project Granite would not be required to contract with unionized labor for its construction as long as it takes ownership of the land before construction begins."

All three towns promised to speed the centers through their approval process, with Hilliard taking an extra step: "All City of Hilliard imposed fees pertaining to zoning, applications, permits and water and sewer tap/capacity fees are to be waived." And all three promised to do whatever possible to keep the projects out of public view and free from press scrutiny.

The towns noted, almost apologetically, that the official votes approving the tax incentives would need to be held in public session, and that the towns did need to abide by the Ohio Public Records Act. But they assured the company that they would do their utmost to release no more information about the data centers than the bare minimum required by law. Dublin and Hilliard both made the exact same pledge to the company: "The City will refuse to provide the information unless compelled by a court order to do so."

The job listings went up online in December 2014. Amazon was looking for an "energetic data center manager" in its Northern Virginia cluster, among other positions there. The manager would "be the primary first level troubleshooter for facility issues by being the eyes and ears recording and monitoring the general well being of the facility and the critical support equipment held within." Rare was the building that could be said to have well-being, but then such was the value placed on data centers. "Our data has become the mirror of our identities, the physical embodiment of our most personal facts and feeling," wrote the journalist Andrew Blum. "A data center is the storehouse of the digital soul."

The location for these job openings was given as Haymarket, Virginia, where the unidentified company had applied for permission to build. The detail made one local resident, Elena Schlossberg, all the more incredulous that Amazon and Dominion Virginia Power and confidentiality-agreement-bound county officials were, in late 2014 and well into 2015, refusing to admit who was behind the 500,000-square-foot data center proposed for the land along John Marshall Highway.

Schlossberg and other residents of Haymarket, a town of several thousand people residing in a small historic core and surrounding homes and subdivisions, had first gotten word of the center in the summer of 2014, when

Dominion had started seeking approval to run a new 230-kilovolt power line six miles from Gainesville to a new substation west of Haymarket. Schlossberg, an energetic mother of two (no relation to lobbyist Ken), was reluctant to get involved—she had multiple sclerosis and had been through a fight over another transmission line in 2005 and knew how taxing these battles were.

Then she got word that this new line was being built not for any company, but for one of the biggest there was. The thought of the 100-foot-tall line cutting through Haymarket on a 120-foot-wide right-of-way at a cost of $65 million all for the sake of serving Amazon alone irked her. It irked her even more when she learned that Dominion's planned route ran through the Rural Crescent and across her family's property. (Dominion had earlier proposed running the route along some freight railroad tracks; the plan was blocked by county officials for skirting too close to a 528-home development near town.)

She took on the fight. She cofounded the Coalition to Protect Prince William County at her kitchen table. She distributed thousands of flyers. She organized a meeting at Battlefield High School and filled it to capacity with 1,200 people. She pressed to take the fight not only to Dominion but to Amazon, over the protests of those who argued that it was a mistake to take on a company popular with so many consumers. "The fight was not about a transmission line and a data center, though it was," she said later. "What it was really about was, we were subsidizing as a community the wealth of monopoly utilities and corporations like Amazon. 'Oh, you don't want to . . . Everybody loves Amazon.' Everybody loves Amazon until they screw over your community."

At 4:55 a.m. one morning in January 2015, she fired off an email to Jeff Bezos.

Dear Mr. Bezos,

My name is Elena Schlossberg and I am a resident in Haymarket VA. I needed to share that your proposed 500,000 sq. ft data center is wreaking havoc on my community. Why? Because someone in your corporate office chose a site that has no infrastructure to support such an intensive industrial use. Your Data center will be built at the edge of the Rural Crescent, a much beloved conservation area in Prince William County.

The power your facility needs will require a substation be built on your property and a 230kv new transmission line installed. That power line, its massive towers, has the potential to destroy homes, our precious cultural and historical resources, and our rural landscape.

She urged Bezos instead to put the data center in the area that the county had set aside for the purpose, farther east, or at the very least to run the power lines along the Interstate 66 right-of-way, a route that would leave the lines partially buried and would be less disruptive but would cost Dominion more.

She added a personal touch, telling Bezos that she had chosen Montessori schools for her kids partly because Bezos had spoken often of how he himself had benefited from a Montessori education. "You and I both know that not only does Montessori instill a love of learning, but the goal is to foster love of community service, respect for each other, and to be caretakers of the environment we have been tasked with preserving," she wrote.

She concluded on a tougher note. "The fight for our community resonates, Mr. Bezos. We are the David against three Goliaths . . . Dominion Power, Amazon, and Amazon's 'customer,'" she wrote. "I have been saying this over and over Mr. Bezos, the community would be happy to welcome you, but what we won't do is sacrifice our homes and our unique resources for your gain alone."

She received no response to the email, nor to a hard copy of the same letter or to a subsequent letter. She and her fellow activists took the fight to the legislature in Richmond, pushing for a bill to encourage Dominion to take the mostly buried route. Several busloads of residents in red T-shirts descended on the capital to back the bill. But Dominion opposed it, and Dominion had enormous sway in Richmond—during 2013 and 2014, it had given $1.6 million to legislators and candidates for state office, this on top of $15 million in well-placed charitable donations every year. The bill went nowhere.

Schlossberg's group kept fighting in Prince William—rallying opponents to attend a Dominion open house on the project and write letters to the county's elected leaders, scrounging together enough money to get an experienced lawyer to represent them at a discount before the state utility commission.

Dominion started to get nervous about the opposition and removed the Rural Crescent route from consideration. In June 2017, the hearing examiner overseeing the case for the utility commission ruled that the line would instead go through the historic African American community on Carver Road.

In high school, Nate Grayson had invited fellow members of the Stonewall High Class of 1985 to his house for a graduation bash. More than four hundred turned out. His mom made heaps of macaroni and cheese and potato salad. He arranged for the homecoming queen to arrive in a late '60s blue Corvette Stingray.

More than thirty years later and in a place as transient as Northern Virginia, Nate Grayson was well known around the area and could still draw a crowd. Not that Dominion, state utility regulators, and AWS could have known this when they targeted the Carver Road community for the power line that would fuel the new data center.

The state hearing examiner overseeing the case had given Dominion the go-ahead to seize land by eminent domain from Carver Road residents. Grayson's property stood to be sliced right down the middle. It came as only the latest affirmation of that sense he'd developed over the years, that there was a pecking order and he and those who looked like him were at the bottom of it. "You've got a ninety-year-old person, where on earth is she going to go?" he said. "Mr. Charles Moore has no reason to go anywhere, Mr. Herbert Moore . . ."

Their ancestors had been told after emancipation that the only place they could buy land was in this one corner of the county, and now even that allowance was up, now that some higher use of the land had come along. "I don't understand as to how you can delegate and say, 'I want you and I need you here, this is the spot where you're staying. It's not very valuable, clear off the land, knock the trees down, get it to where it's habitable, and now you're not enough for this area.'"

It was hard not to think that it was precisely residents' longevity on Carver Road that made them an acceptable target, he said. "'Well, they're going to die anyway.' That's how it felt."

But they weren't dead, and it was his job to protect them. He put out the word, and the response was instantaneous: Carver Road and the broader diaspora of Carver Road were ready to enlist. "It was almost like a family event," Grayson said. "If you mention it to one person, it's like a Facebook chain that goes off."

Those who had opposed the earlier routes, led by Elena Schlossberg, could have sat back now that their own upscale homes and subdivisions had been spared. But they did not. They carried on to the Carver Road front, offering experience and resources. It was a multiracial assortment of seventy people that turned out to protest at Dominion's regional headquarters in Herndon, and that turned out again to protest at the entrance to the data center itself, where security guards stood watch and signs warned of attack dogs on the premises. Even the old folks from Carver Road had come out—Alwishias Johnson, in his late seventies and only a few years shy of deciding to take himself off dialysis, was there in his wheelchair.

Between this and the meetings Grayson and others were showing up at and the signs along Carver Road—UNPLUG AMAZON EXTENSION CORD— their cause gained notoriety: "Amazon Data Center Threatens a Century-Old Black Va. Neighborhood" read one news headline.

Meanwhile, Schlossberg and the Coalition's lawyer kept pressing on the inconsistencies in the official lines from Dominion and Amazon regarding the latter's ambitions for the site. She was preparing to challenge on grounds she knew the companies were vulnerable on—under state law, an extension intended for a single user needed to be paid for by said user.

The pressure grew so great that, in late 2017, county legislators announced that they were refusing to grant Dominion an easement needed to build the

Carver Road route. The state hearing examiner had no choice but to reopen the case, and Dominion announced that it would be willing to adopt the more expensive, less disruptive route that Schlossberg and her allies had been urging all along, along the interstate and partly buried belowground.

It was a victory for Carver Road. It was not, however, a defeat for Dominion and Amazon, who simply applied a show of power in a quieter, more consequential way. Only a couple months after the route reversal, the Virginia House of Delegates approved Dominion's proposal to pay for the line with a monthly fee on all ratepayers, not only Amazon.

Meanwhile, Amazon filed a seventy-eight-page application to state regulators seeking a special discounted rate for the power it would be using at its data centers. There was no way of knowing exactly what the terms of the discount were: one version of its application sat under seal with state regulators, while the public version was heavily redacted.

Knowing that they were paying more in their electric bills to cover Amazon's line took some of the glow from the Carver Road victors. So did simply seeing the gigantic humming box of the data center every time they drove past it. "It's like having a White House in the neighborhood. There's no penetration, no information, no nothing," said Nate Grayson. "You have a building there, you don't know who's coming, you don't know who's going. You don't know what's going on," he said. "You don't know if it's on, you don't know if it's off. You don't know nothing. You see no benefits of it. They've done nothing for my taxes, they've done nothing for the road infrastructure. They carved it out and they're making money."

Amazon was, in fact, making so much money, and growing so rapidly, that in September 2017, as the fight over the power lines in Northern Virginia was coming to a head, it announced that it would open a second headquarters somewhere in North America. It was on its way to occupying more than forty-five buildings in Seattle and it needed more room. The new headquarters would house 50,000 employees making an average salary of $150,000. It would be the beneficiary of a total investment of $5 billion. To select the lucky city, the company would throw open the selection process to all comers, a grand nationwide reality show, a *Bachelor* for cities to compete for the affection of a corporation.

No company had ever done such a thing for site selection before, but then, there was no company like Amazon. The company's sales had jumped by a third in 2017; it was expanding into the health-care industry; it had crossed the 500,000-employee count worldwide, a 66 percent increase in a single year; its market value had quintupled in four years to surpass Google's Alphabet to become the second-highest-valued company in the world, after Apple. Such vaulting growth was not only a sign of the company's success but essential for its very survival, in the eyes of its founder. "Bezos," wrote the journalist Charles Duhigg, "adamantly refuses to consider slowing the company's growth, fearing that its culture will break down if the pace slackens." It had other offices scattered around the country—San Francisco, Washington, New York, Boston, Los Angeles, and Austin all had at least 1,000 Amazonians—but its growth demanded a full second headquarters, not mere satellites.

It was hardly a surprise that Amazon would decide to make a spectacle of the process, given the success it had been having in the entertainment realm. Amazon would spend $4 billion on films and TV shows in 2018 and soon control a third of the market for streaming video; the year before, it had become the first streaming media service nominated for Best Picture at the Academy Awards.

To presume that there was enough interest in one's selection of a new headquarters to sustain a public sweepstakes also required having total confidence that one's company was held in sufficiently high esteem, that it could transcend the national divides in the manner of an Olympic champion or innocuous pop star. And Amazon had reason to believe that it did, in fact, inspire such general goodwill. A survey done in June and July of 2018 found that Amazon was the most trusted institution in the country among Democrats—ahead of government, universities, unions, and the press—and the third most respected among Republicans, ahead of only the military and police. It didn't hurt that the company was spending heavily to burnish its image: its spending on TV ads would swell to $679 million in 2018, almost double what it had spent three years prior.

The primary motivation for making the process a public competition became quickly apparent. For decades, cities had been trying to outdo each other by throwing tax incentives at companies—Amazon had perfected this game in siting warehouses and data centers. But that competition happened quietly, in euphemistically worded emails and city hall conference rooms. What better way to juice the bidding than to turn the auction into a mass-media production? Americans loved sports, they loved a winner, and their elected leaders would feel the pressure from below, a roar from the bleachers, to put their city in the running.

The roar came, almost instantly—*let it be us!*—and local officials responded with an alacrity that often edged into cringing desperation. Tucson hauled a twenty-one-foot saguaro cactus to Seattle by truck. The mayor of Kansas City gave five-star online reviews to a thousand Amazon products. Dallas, appealing to Amazon's dog fetish, offered to waive local pet adoption fees for company employees. Atlanta proposed adding an Amazon-only train car to the city's subway system, to help "distribute products around the city." Close by, the Atlanta suburb of Stonecrest offered to rename itself Amazon.

Amid this circus, there were those who recognized the gravity of the moment. In looking for a second home, Amazon had a golden chance to restore some balance to the national landscape, to share the spoils of the winner-take-all high-tech capitalism with some corner of the country that had been left behind. As Ross Douthat wrote in September 2017:

> What if Amazon treated their headquartering decision as an act of corporate citizenship, part public relations stunt and part genuinely patriotic gesture? . . . Instead of picking an obvious BosWash hub or creative-class boomtown, it could opt to plant itself in a medium-sized city in a conservative state—think Nashville or Indianapolis or Birmingham. Or it could look for a struggling East Coast alternative to the obvious Acelaland options—not Boston but Hartford, not D.C. but Baltimore, not New York but Bridgeport. Or it could pick

a big, battered, declining city and offer its presence as an engine of revitalization, building Amazon Cleveland or Amazon Detroit.

A particularly compelling pick, according to my extremely non-scientific "what's good for America" metric, might be St. Louis—a once-great metropolis fallen on hard times, the major urban center for a large spread of Trump country, the geographic center of the country and the historic bridge between East and West.

It was an appealing argument, and four months later, Amazon made clear that it was disinclined to heed it. In January 2018, it announced the twenty finalists for the headquarters, and they were skewed toward BosWash hubs and creative-class boomtowns, the sorts of places already overflowing with high-tech talent and likely to be most appealing to recruits from elsewhere. On the list: Boston, Washington, New York, and Austin. Not on the list: Detroit, Baltimore, Cleveland, and St. Louis. What few Middle American cities made the cut were those that had already established themselves as winner-take-all cities within their regions, such as Columbus and Nashville. Among the many bids not to make the cut was a joint one by Dayton and Cincinnati. "I'm starting to see a bifurcation of communities and separation around coastal cities and everyone else," said Dayton's mayor, Nan Whaley. "I'm worried that people don't understand midsize cities."

HQ2, as it quickly came to be called, was not going to be an uplift project or an effort to knit together the American fabric, but then again, the company and Jeff Bezos had never provided much reason for anyone to believe that it would be. It was right there in one of the company's "Leadership Principles":

"Leaders have conviction and are tenacious. They do not compromise for the sake of social cohesion."

As the company later put it bluntly to a reporter: "Nowhere did Amazon say HQ2 was a project designed to help communities in need."

Nick Hanauer, the early investor who had helped bring Bezos to Seattle, had since grown critical of the company and was unsurprised by Amazon signaling it was not going to use the HQ2 process to lift up a struggling city. "Right a social wrong? Are you fucking kidding me? Jeff Bezos is a straight-up libertarian," he said. "Those people believe that the only thing important in the world is how well Amazon does, at the exclusion of everything else. They're going to go where it's best for Amazon. How that impacts the place? Other than how the place impacts Amazon is not in consideration for them. It's not what they're going to be thinking about. Jeff's perspective is the canonical neoliberal perspective: that the only purpose of corporations, the only purpose of shareholders, is to enrich themselves to the exclusion of everything else. That is the highest sole responsibility. Maximize shareholder value and somehow magically that will create the common good. If the only fucking thing that matters is the stock price, why in the world would you do anything else?"

A lexa, would you please introduce our keynote speaker?"
"It would be my pleasure," said Alexa, her recently upgraded voice—redesigned to be more humanoid and less robotic, and unveiled in a Super Bowl commercial—booming through the hugely capacious hall of the Washington Convention Center. "Please welcome to the stage vice president of Worldwide Public Sector, Amazon Web Services: Teresa Carlson."

It was the ninth annual AWS Public Sector Summit, an event that had begun with a crowd of 50 in a Marriott across the river in Arlington, and now, in the spring of 2018, drew some 14,000 to the convention center in D.C. The summit's steroidal expansion was visual affirmation of Amazon's triumph in the cloud: by year's end, its cloud infrastructure would bring in $15.5 billion, nearly as much as all its industry rivals combined.

Its dominance carried over into the realm that was the subject of the convention: the government. Just as the company was moving to take control of government procurement in office supplies, it was also on its way to seizing the far more lucrative business of government information technology. It had won the $600 million contract to put the CIA in the cloud in 2013 and was one of the two top candidates for the biggest contract of them all, $10 billion to move the Pentagon into the cloud. It was no accident that the headquarters of AWS Worldwide Public Sector were in Ballston, an office cluster in Arlington, Virginia, that was a mere three miles, or six Metro stops, from the Pentagon.

Even before Amazon had decided where to put its second headquarters, its affinity for Washington was growing only more plain, and its role in contributing to Washington's new prosperity only more significant. Amazon now so dominated the universe of selling cloud services to governments that it was acting as the convener for all those other, smaller companies striving to get their piece. They filled the vendor hall, booths labeled with names like Fugue, Xacta, Alfresco, Okta, Snowflake, Enquizit, Veeam, Druva...

Carlson, speaking with a deep Kentucky twang, couldn't resist reminding her guests how far ahead of them all her company now stood. AWS now controlled nearly half of all spending on public cloud services; it employed some 20,000 people, up from 45 only five years earlier; and, with whopping 26 percent operating margins, the division accounted for more than half of Amazon's entire operating income. Essentially, the company's lucrative dominance of the cloud was allowing it to keep its prices so low in its original retail operation, selling items almost at a loss and thereby driving many competitors from the field altogether.

And the growth potential for the cloud was boundless—as Bezos himself had put it, AWS's "addressable market" was "trillions and trillions." Carlson touted the efficiencies produced by the company's astounding growth. "Thanks to our economies of scale, AWS has reduced our prices sixty-six times since we launched in 2006, under no pressure," she said. "When we get economies of scale, we give them back to our customers and our partners."

Gesturing to a world map covered in pinheads on the screen behind her, she described how insurmountable the company's edge had grown, like an eleven-year-old tallying the armies on his territories in a game of Risk. "We created industrial-scale regions, physical locations around the world where our clusters of data centers are," she said. "We have eighteen geographic regions, and we have fifty-five availability zones and one hundred eight edge locations and growing around the world."

"Believe me," she said, "we're not slowing down."

Later in the day, select attendees were invited to the VIP reception less than a mile away at Amazon's Washington office, in the new building near Capitol Hill.

Jay Demmler, a senior principal IT architect at Raytheon, the giant defense contractor, fixed his hair in the reflection of the glass doors before going in.

One Amazon lobbyist asked another as he walked up, "Have a good day on the Hill?"

And striding along came a man in full-dress military uniform, while two underlings in uniform scrutinized the parking meter at the SUV he had exited.

An Amazon employee waited at the door. "Yes, sir, I'm here for you," he told the commander: Admiral Karl L. Schultz, only three weeks into his tenure as the twenty-sixth commandant of the U.S. Coast Guard, which was in the midst of considering its own options for moving into the cloud.

There were a stream of executives from Amazon itself. One, Jon Petersen, from Partner Development, reminded some of his colleagues that all AWS employees had been instructed to wear white for the event, to aid other guests in identifying them. In fact, almost no one had worn white.

"I was Department of Labor in the Obama administration," said one man to another. "That was a big two and a half years ago."

Up walked John Hanly, from the Center for American Progress, the liberal think tank, and Manish Parikh, a chief technology officer for the defense contractor BAE, and James Armitage, a tax lawyer with Caplin & Drysdale, and Khuloud Odeh, CIO and vice president for technology and data science at the Urban Institute, another center-left think tank.

The line was growing at the elevator in the lobby. "Holy moly," said one woman as the line came into view.

Around the corner on F Street, a young, Black woman was sleeping on a sidewalk grate with a towel as a pillow. Someone had left a sandwich for her.

Odeh hugged Hanly goodbye as he headed back out on his way to another event. "There's a cyber thing in Reston," he told her.

The Midwestern frontier of AWS US East took less than two years to construct. By October 2016, all three of the new data centers were up and running along I-270 around Columbus. There was no more need for municipal officials to withhold their locations from prying local reporters, if any such reporters were around to pry anymore. The buildings were an incontestable fact, a great gray mass rising out of the fields. And they were only the first of many—Amazon announced plans to build a dozen more data centers in central Ohio. In 2018, total capital spending by Amazon, Microsoft, Google, and Facebook, mostly on data centers, had soared by 50 percent in a single year to $77 billion. The building boom had spawned a whole new line in data-center scrap recycling, since many of the machines lasted only a few years.

The center in Hilliard, at about ten o'clock on the dial of the Columbus beltway, was such a bleakly pale gray that it all but dissolved into an Ohio winter sky, as well camouflaged as a snowshoe hare. Behind the building spread a mass of a different gray, more intricate: the power substation that served the center.

The Dublin center, at about eleven o'clock on the dial, sat not far from a shopping plaza with a Costco and T.J. Maxx and PetSmart and Aldi and Wendy's and Tim Hortons. The young clerk at the Tim Hortons did not know what was in the giant building down the road; he had, in fact, never really given it any thought.

The New Albany center, at about one o'clock, sat not marooned on its own, but on the edge of a collection of warehouses and logistics buildings. Mast Global, Axium Plastics, Exhibitpro, Amcor, KDC/One. These sat in juxtaposition against the traces of semirural poverty that remained, a row of ramshackle homes and trailers spread out along Beech Road straight across from the Amazon center. I CARRY A GUN BECAUSE A COP IS TOO

HEAVY said the sign on one door. YOU GIVE PEACE A CHANCE. I'LL COVER YOU WITH MY GUN IN CASE THAT DOESN'T WORK OUT said another.

Not that there had been any risk of trespassing by the new corporate neighbors: one resident said there had been zero outreach as the center was being built. One year, there was nothing there. The next year, there it was.

A pizza delivery man pulled up to the security gate and was allowed in.

Just down the road, Dawn Dalton sat at the welcome desk at Faith Life Church. When the church was built a dozen years earlier, there had been nothing else around, only those homes and the corn and soybean fields. Then the warehouses and data centers came. The new $750 million Facebook data center over by the Bob Evans was even bigger than the Amazon one—970,000 square feet on 345 acres. Google was planning a $600 million one, too. To the extent that these companies had regional supply chains in smaller cities and towns, this was it—a few dozen jobs here and there to run the machines that held their data, nothing close to the dense fabric of suppliers that once connected big and small hubs. The cities that mattered to Amazon, Facebook, Google, and Apple as they sat in Seattle and the Bay Area were not Columbus or Cincinnati or Dayton, but the global cities they competed with for talent and capital, places like London and Tokyo, or the faraway places that provided whatever manufacturing they still required, such as Shenzhen, China.

Sometimes, if the wind was right, it would carry the scents across the fields from the new Bath & Body Works distribution center. "They're surrounding us," Dawn Dalton said.

Across the land, the bidding for the second headquarters grew only more intense, now that it was narrowed to twenty finalists. City governments strapped for time and money spent countless hours and dollars fine-tuning their proposals, hiring consultants, primping for the eventual visit by the suitor.

Above all, they piled ever-greater incentives on the table. Exactly how much was unknown in most cities, as the suitor had ordered contenders to keep negotiations confidential or be dropped from consideration, an insistence on secrecy all the more striking given the public nature of the overall spectacle. Even city council members who would eventually have to approve the packages being offered were barred from knowing the details for the time being. Indianapolis required four hundred employees to sign nondisclosure agreements. Montgomery County, Maryland, in the Washington suburbs, responded to a Freedom of Information Act request by turning over a ten-page document that was completely redacted, every line blacked out in prison stripes. Cleveland redacted its title page and table of contents. Of the 238 bids, 124 were completely secret. "We are not releasing documents related to Amazon HQ2. We are not subject to F.O.I.A.," said the head of the public-private partnership handling Miami's bid, echoing similar rejections in Austin, Atlanta, and Indianapolis.

Here and there, some numbers emerged, exposing the scale of the bidding underway. Columbus offered more than $2 billion. Chicago said it would return to Amazon the $1.32 billion in personal income taxes paid by its workers every year. Maryland approved a $6.5 billion package. Newark—which, it would be revealed a couple years later, was at that very moment failing to keep lead out of its drinking water—offered $7 billion.

Also cloaked were the company's visits to inspect the sites. Vague details slipped out—some cities had taken the visitors on boat tours, others on bikes. The key, it was agreed, was to be accommodating without appearing desperate, to avoid the sort of tacky baubles and over-the-top luxuries that so many of the failed first-round bidders had dangled. Things were serious now. The visitors wanted to know the SAT scores of local high school graduates, an echo of Jeff Bezos's famous obsession with knowing the scores of those interviewing for jobs at Amazon. They wanted to ride the buses and the trams.

With the process so hidden, bidders grasped at any clues they could find. Alaska Airlines had added a direct flight from Seattle to Columbus!

The dean of Carnegie Mellon University's School of Computer Science was resigning—perhaps to run a Pittsburgh HQ2?

And Jeff Bezos was spotted in Miami with a club promoter known as Purple. "It's not everyday you get to hang with the richest guy in the world," Purple gushed on Instagram. *The Miami Herald* seized on the sighting: "Could this be good news for Miami's HQ2 bid?"

Break: PHL6 Redux

Three days after the June 1, 2014, death of Jody Rhoads at the fulfillment center in Carlisle, Pennsylvania, the Harrisburg area director for the Occupational Safety and Health Administration, Kevin Kilp, sent a condolence letter to her sons. "We deeply regret the loss of your mother's life," he wrote. "We want you to know that OSHA is investigating the circumstances."

OSHA investigators delivered subpoenas to Amazon, conducted interviews at the warehouse, and watched the Crown PC 4500 powered industrial truck in action. They tried unsuccessfully to reach Rhoads's sons by phone. They visited the Crown dealership, where a branch manager referred them to corporate. They spoke with Diana Williams, the warehouse safety manager, and with the Princeton, New Jersey, attorney representing Amazon, John McGahren, who demanded that any questions be put in writing and requested a thirty-day extension.

On September 22, 2014, OSHA officials received a copy of the toxicology results from the blood lab work done on Rhoads. The results showed traces of a dozen medications and substances, among them nicotine; bupropion, which is marketed as both an antidepressant and a smoking deterrent; Delta-9-THC, the main active ingredient of marijuana; Benadryl; gabapentin, an antiepileptic drug also used to treat nerve pain; hydrocodone, which is found in opioids such as Vicodin and Zohydro; morphine, which commonly derives from codeine or heroin; oxazepam, a benzodiazepine prescribed for anxiety; and oxycodone, which is found in opioids such as OxyContin. She also had a low level of blood alcohol concentration, .02.

On November 14, Kevin Kilp sent a letter to Diana Williams saying that OSHA's inspections of the Carlisle warehouse had revealed "potential hazards" involving PIT operations, notably the under-ride risk associated with the vehicles. "Our investigation revealed that the lower horizontal shelf supports throughout a majority of this high rack storage were measured to be about 49 inches above the floor," he wrote. "This height presents a potential under ride hazard for the PC 4500 machines, in that the front of the machine can drive under this bottom shelf support and potentially pin the operator between this shelf support and the backrest of the machine."

Kilp suggested adjusting the bottom height of the shelving and replacing the PC 4500 with a different model. But, he wrote, "no specific OSHA standards apply to this hazard." As a result, "no citation will be issued at this time."

It was another two months before Kilp sent a letter to Rhoads's sons sharing the outcome. "Despite the inspection indicating that the employer did not violate safety and health standards, we know that no amount of money or compensation can measure the loss you and your family have suffered and your lives have been changed forever because of this tragedy," he wrote.

Less than three years later, on September 19, 2017, Carlisle EMTs were called once again to PHL6, as Amazon called the warehouse on Allen Road, which was conveniently situated near both Interstate 81 and the Pennsylvania Turnpike.

A driver with Revolution Transport, a local trucking company, was at the warehouse shortly after 5:00 p.m. trying to back his 2001 Volvo tractor up to a loaded trailer at Dock Door 129 in the outbound yard. He was having trouble getting the trailer's kingpin to connect to the tractor's pin plate, the "fifth wheel."

Devan Shoemaker came along and offered to help. He was a yard jockey—an Amazon employee tasked with moving trailers in and out of the loading docks after they had been brought in by drivers and before they were taken back out. He had been on the job since the warehouse opened in 2010, when he started out as a temp, two years after graduating from East Juniata High, where he belonged to Future Farmers of America.

Shoemaker stood with the driver at the back of the tractor and they discussed the problem. He went and got a yellow pole, a pipe handle from a trailer jack stand, to unjam the locking mechanism on the fifth wheel. The driver backed the tractor up again, but the fifth wheel still wouldn't engage with the kingpin.

The driver got back out and they discussed the problem further, speculating that there was too much grease on the plate of the fifth wheel. The driver got back in to pull the tractor forward to create space between it and the trailer, so they could work on the fifth wheel.

As the tractor drove forward, Devan Shoemaker was still standing between its rear dual wheels, next to the fifth plate. "Whoa!" he yelled.

But the driver kept going, catching him beneath tires that were 41.9 inches in diameter and 10.7 inches wide, and weighed 118 pounds each. Another worker saw what was happening and screamed. The driver heard the screaming and stopped.

Devan Shoemaker was lying facedown in a pool of blood. Someone called 911, and Amazon's on-site safety team arrived, along with an ambulance and the state police.

The Cumberland County Coroner's office pronounced Shoemaker dead at the scene, with crushing injuries to his head and torso. He was twenty-eight years old, married with a young son. He was a member of the Free and Accepted Masons, Lodge No. 619, in Middleburg. He loved spending time with his pets, Max and Daisy, riding four-wheelers, gardening, cooking, and doing craftsman projects.

Yet again, the Harrisburg OSHA office sent a condolence letter to the family of an Amazon PHL6 employee. "We want you to know that OSHA is investigating the circumstances surrounding Devan's death," wrote the new area director, David Olah. On October 2, Olah spoke with a family member and explained how the investigation would proceed. The family member said that no one from Amazon had visited or called on the night of the accident, and that the family had learned of what happened only after calling a coworker when Devan didn't come home from the warehouse as usual that night.

Olah wrote to Thomas Houtz, the new site safety manager at the warehouse, asking for documents, including photographs of the loading yard, witness statements, training records, work rules, and a list of other yard-jockey employees. Houtz responded with some documents and a cover letter topped with the word *fulfillment* in large bold letters over the corporate smile logo.

But Amazon did not make it easy to interview the employees. In February, Mark Fiore, a lawyer with the same Princeton firm that represented the company in Rhoads's death, wrote to OSHA saying that he would be present at interviews. One OSHA investigator objected, writing to a colleague, "I explained confidentiality rights and I would not interview employees if he was present. He stated there is case law that allows him to be present."

Olah, the area director, responded that it was a moot point, as the agency was already inclined toward "no proposed citations" in Devan Shoemaker's death.

Ten days later, the agency confirmed this finding of no violation in an email from Harold Rowland, in its Philadelphia office, to Olah, in Harrisburg.

"Dave," Rowland wrote, "we can put this one in the books."

7.

Shelter

Taxing and giving

In 2004, two young people set off on a Greyhound bus from Binghamton, New York, to find a new home. Katie Wilson and Scott Myers had met in high school while doing Food Not Bombs: participants would use donated food to cook a vegetarian meal once a week and serve it in a park to the homeless and anyone else who came along.

They had then proceeded to take wildly different paths. Katie, the daughter of biology professors at SUNY Binghamton, had attended the University of Oxford, drawn by its joint degree program in physics and philosophy—an unlikely pairing of her two favorite subjects—and by the English term system, which provided six-week breaks between each eight-week stretch of classes. She had been ambivalent about the conventional American college track and this seemed like a way around that. In the end, a more general ambivalence had won out, and she had dropped out six weeks before graduating. Her academic parents, recognizing this for the filial rebellion that it was, were not pleased.

Scott had rebelled from the start. He had quit school at fifteen, picked up his GED, volunteered on an Indian reservation in North Dakota, busked with his guitar in Bay Area subway stations, and lived in a Zen monastery there.

By 2004, they were on the bus. For two months, they crisscrossed the continent, looking for the right place for themselves, which they had decided was probably not Binghamton, "lovely a place as it was," Katie said later with characteristic drollness. The bus took them to Boston, Philadelphia, Toronto, Chicago, New Orleans, San Francisco, Seattle. Where Jeff and MacKenzie Bezos had set off in a Chevy Blazer with a business plan in search of a friendly start-up climate, Katie and Scott had nothing but a vague desire to become involved, to shake things up, wherever they might land.

And where Jeff had been drawn to Seattle for its tax advantages, Katie and Scott were drawn to it for its library card: while in town, they learned that, for a mere $100, they could become "friends" of the University of Washington library and enjoy full access to its holdings. This held outsized appeal for two young people whose aborted formal education had only amplified their determination to carry on studies in a more self-directed fashion. "We made our way through the Marxist canon," joked Katie.

They soon discovered that finding their city would be easier than finding their cause. Seattle had witnessed the raucous anti–World Trade Organization protests in 1999, but by the time of the couple's arrival, five years later, the local political scene was quiescent. While they looked for a fight to latch on to, they bounced from job to job. Katie worked as a lab assistant, a barista, a legal assistant, an apartment renovator, and a woodworker. Her favorite job was painting the bottom of boats at Lake Union.

Scott worked at a grocery deli and taught guitar. And together, they managed a brick apartment building in the Phinney Ridge neighborhood. They had been renting in the building, and the elderly lady who had been the manager, Verna, had warned them about the even more elderly landlady, who was 98 and would live to 104. "She squeezes the nickel until the buffalo roars," Verna said. After Verna moved into a retirement home, they took over her manager role for five years.

In 2011, the aftershocks of the Great Recession forced large cuts in service to the Seattle bus system, which Katie and Scott relied on to get around town. Katie began looking into public transit funding in Seattle and was startled by what she found. Seattle, one of the most progressive large cities in the country, had one of the most regressive tax systems anywhere. Washington State did not have an income tax. In 2010, a ballot measure to tax the state's wealthiest residents to raise $2 billion per year for education and social services went down in defeat despite initially having broad support, after an opposition campaign funded by some of the state's richest citizens.

The state's tech industry had fueled the opposition. "The absence of a state income tax gives Washington companies competitive advantage in their efforts to recruit and retain the best and brightest from across the country," said the Washington Technology Industry Association. The industry was admitting that Seattle was becoming a tech magnet not only because of Puget Sound and Mount Rainier and the University of Washington, but because engineers, programmers, and executives could pay less in taxes.

As a result of that 2010 referendum, metropolitan Seattle, despite being home to the two richest men on the planet, continued to rely on regressive sales and excise taxes to fund many basic services, including public transportation. The poorest households in the state paid as much as 17 percent of their income for state and local taxes, while the richest households paid less than 3 percent. And sales tax revenues were vulnerable to sharp declines in recessions.

Katie had found her cause. She and Scott founded the Transit Riders Union, which, with several hundred dues-paying members and support from some local labor unions, would advocate for the users of public transit. "It was a steep learning curve," she said. "Realizing that all your pie-in-the-sky ideas take some work to implement." As the years went on, though, it became clear that the overarching issue would not really be bus lines and light rail expansion. It would be taxes—taxes and their inextricable and rivalrous cousin, philanthropy. It would be about the civic infrastructure—who would pay for it, and whether it even really needed to be maintained in the first place.

———

The federal income tax came into being in 1913, with the passage of the Sixteenth Amendment. (There had been an income tax to help pay for the Civil War, but it lasted only a decade.) The tax was initially 1 percent on incomes above $3,000, with a 6 percent surtax above $500,000. Five years later, the top rate shot to 77 percent on income over $1 million to pay for the First World War. But the average rate for wealthy Americans was about 15 percent.

It took less than four years after the creation of the tax for Congress to offer a way to get around paying it: the charitable deduction. The argument for the deduction was that income taxes might deter wealthy Americans from philanthropic giving, a disconcerting notion in a country abounding with the hallmarks of robber-baron generosity: universities, museums, libraries, and so much more.

In theory, a government supplied with a predictable stream of tax revenue would be able to build and maintain universities, libraries, and museums on its own. But the titans of industry insisted that they knew best how to spend the millions that were the fruit of capitalist success, none more so than Andrew Carnegie, the Scottish-born industrialist and spiritual grandfather of American philanthropy. The "duty of the man of Wealth," he wrote in "The Gospel of Wealth" (1889), was to put his wealth toward whatever, "in his judgment, is best calculated to produce the most beneficial results for the community." Crucially, Carnegie believed that his own judgment in allocating "surplus revenues" was so superior that he did not see why such revenues should be spread more broadly in the form of, say, higher pay for workers. Making a large charitable gift was "a much more potent force for the elevation of our race" than dividing the money into "trifling amounts" for distribution as donations or higher wages, which would likely be "wasted in the indulgence of appetite." He was confident that "even the poorest can be made to see this."

Carnegie died in 1919, but his ethic would undergird philanthropy for decades to come: the wealthy knew best, and it was better for everyone if

———

they were the ones deciding how to spend money, rather than the public at large. It was, noted the writer Anand Giridharadas, "an extreme idea of the right to make money in any which way, and an extreme idea of the obligation to give back," one that rejected the notion that "the poor might not need so much help had they been better paid." As the top federal income tax rate dropped late in the twentieth century and in the first decade of the twenty-first, and as the nation's biggest fortunes ballooned in size, the cachet of philanthropy only grew. In 2010, Bill and Melinda Gates and Warren Buffett launched the Giving Pledge, urging the very wealthiest to agree to give away at least half their money. Much of the giving was going to far-from-needy institutions, such as Harvard and Stanford, which were each eventually receiving more than $1 billion over the course of a single year on an ongoing basis. As giving grew, so did its cost to the government: by 2013, taxpayers were writing off more than $40 billion annually, and the wealthiest were benefiting the most, since they were deducting income that would otherwise be taxed at the highest marginal rate.

Among the signatories of the Giving Pledge was David Rubenstein, the billionaire Carlyle Group cofounder. In recent years, he had outdone many other large-scale philanthropists with a series of high-profile gestures in Washington. He spent $21.3 million on a 710-year-old copy of the Magna Carta, which he loaned to the National Archives; later, he paid for a $13.5 million gallery to house the document. He bought two copies of the Emancipation Proclamation, signed by Abraham Lincoln, and loaned one to President Obama to display in the Oval Office. He made large gifts to Monticello, to James Madison's estate at Montpelier, to Robert E. Lee's mansion, to the Iwo Jima Memorial, and to the Lincoln Memorial.

And when the Washington Monument suffered fractures in a 2011 earthquake, Rubenstein announced that he would give $7.5 million toward fixing it. He liked to make a deadpan joke about the privilege this afforded him: on being taken to the top of the monument for a private tour, he said, "I took a pen out and I wrote my initials at the very top."

Rubenstein even had a special brand for his gifts to Washington institutions and other historic causes: he called it "patriotic philanthropy." In a

2015 *60 Minutes* segment on his giving, he said that he was simply helping fill voids left by a strapped Treasury. "The government doesn't have the resources it used to have," he said. "We have gigantic budget deficits and large debt. And I think private citizens now need to pitch in."

Left unmentioned in that profile, or in the many other glowing features on his philanthropy, was that Rubenstein had played a role in the depletion of those government resources. He and other private-equity investment managers had for years benefited from a loophole that allowed their compensation for managing other people's investments to be taxed at the capital gains rate for investment income, rather than at the much higher rate for ordinary income. The "carried interest" loophole saved the wealthiest private-equity executives close to $100 million annually, per person; by conservative estimates, it cost the Treasury $2 billion per year; one expert argued the sum was in fact many times that large. Rubenstein had not only profited enormously from the loophole, but at crucial moments over the years he had helped stave off congressional efforts to close it by working his ties on Capitol Hill.

Still, his reputation for public-spirited generosity spread. One day in 2015, Rubenstein arrived with several hundred other guests at the Stephen A. Schwarzman Building, the Beaux Arts main branch of the New York Public Library, rechristened in 2008 in exchange for a $100 million gift from Schwarzman, the head of the private equity firm Blackstone. Rubenstein and several others, including Paul Allen, the Microsoft cofounder, were there to receive the Carnegie Medal of Philanthropy. In his acceptance speech, Rubenstein said that as he was contemplating what to say, Andrew Carnegie had written him a letter from the beyond. "'Good philanthropists invariably live very long lives,'" the "letter" read, "'and when their time is up they are warmly welcomed into a special place in Heaven.'"

Seattle's housing crisis had been building for half a decade—ever since Amazon had started building that enormous headquarters in South Lake

Union—but the *Seattle Times* headline on April 6, 2017, still had the power to shock:

SEATTLE'S MEDIAN HOME PRICE HITS RECORD: $700,000, DOUBLE 5 YEARS AGO

In fact, the Seattle region had the fastest-rising home prices of any metro area in the country for the prior five months. Helping drive the increase was not only the city's hyper-prosperity and galloping growth, but a shortage of supply, exacerbated by the prevalence of single-family zoning across the city, even close to downtown. The housing market, one real estate executive said, was "straight-up crazy."

It kept getting crazier. The area northeast of downtown that included the hipster hub of Capitol Hill was about to cross the $1 million threshold for a median home sale, while southeast Seattle, the most affordable part of town, posted a 31 percent increase from a year earlier. Across Lake Washington, in Bellevue, the modest house where Bezos had started Amazon, worth $135,000 at the time, would be sold a quarter century later for $1.53 million—less than the neighborhood median.

This was the third Seattle that Milo Duke had known, and he knew that this city was no longer for him. He and Wendy were still in the bungalow in Tangletown, still, incredibly, paying the original $1,000 a month for it. But it was hard to miss the other signs. To try to reclaim some of the fellowship of the Dharmic Engineers, he and a few friends got together in 2010 to rent a studio in the seemingly affordable Georgetown area, well south of downtown, for $1,200. But within a year of their arrival, the rent started climbing fast. They were gone by 2013.

Then came the art-walk debacle. There were a couple of them around town—once a month, artists would show their work in a string of spaces in Pioneer Square and Georgetown. Milo and Wendy thought they'd arrange one for the northern end of town and found the ideal space, an Umpqua Bank branch in fashionable Ballard, northwest of Lake Union. The bank not only created a large gallery space specifically for the art walk, but would let them use its lobby, too. They started holding the Ballard Art Walk in 2014, and it was a complete flop. There was plenty of foot traffic—people streaming past to the ramen place, the poke place, the ice-cream place. But virtually no one was stopping for the art. They just walked right by. "That," Milo said later, "was when I realized the tech takeover was complete and a completely different kind of person was living in the city now."

Sales for both Milo's and Wendy's work were falling at the gallery that represented them in Bellevue, across Lake Washington. In 2016, Milo put great effort into an installation at a private library called Folio, which consisted of his art and a suite of furniture that he built together with one of his sons, a cabinetmaker. He had hopes that one of the city's billionaires might buy the furniture, but the installation received little notice.

That same year, he and Wendy got a call from their landlady, the wife of the Boeing executive. She had retired from school administration, was now focused more intently on managing her three properties in town, and had decided that renting a bungalow for $1,000, even to some nice artists, was unacceptable. "Did you look it up on Zillow?" Milo asked her. "Yes," she said. She would triple the rent, to $3,000. To ease the pain, she would raise it gradually, $200 every month, for ten months. For Milo and Wendy, it was a matter of deciding exactly which turn of the ratchet they could no longer endure.

The endless stories of record real-estate prices were followed by superlatives of a different sort. In early December 2017, *The Seattle Times* reported that King County now had the third-largest homeless population of any jurisdiction in the country, behind only the far larger cities of New York and Los Angeles: according to a new federal tally, there were 11,643 people without homes in Seattle and its immediate surroundings. Of these, 5,485, or nearly half, were "unsheltered"—living in the street or in tents—a 21 percent increase over the year before. The number of homeless kids in city schools hit an all-time high of 4,280. And more homeless people had died in the streets that year than ever—by September, King County's tally of fatalities had surpassed those the year prior, and by the end of November, it had far surpassed the highest tally on record, with 133.

Seattle had been home to the original skid row: Skid Road, down which greased logs would skid to Henry Yesler's sawmill. But what the city was experiencing now was on a new scale, an indictment both of its hyper-prosperity and of its liberal political ethos, whose claim to humanitarian concern and general decency was looking dubious. The dissonance was hard to miss. It was there at the southwest corner of Third Avenue and James Street downtown, where the crowd hoping for a table at Il Corvo restaurant overlapped with the crowd waiting for a spot in the nearby shelter that night. It was there in the encampments that popped up in open patches smack in the middle of stable neighborhoods of $800,000 Arts and Crafts bungalows. It was, it sometimes seemed, everywhere you turned. "I look out the bus and I see a guy taking his pants down and then I get off the bus and glance down an alley and see a guy shooting up," one downtown boutique employee told *The Seattle Times*. "Those aren't things I want to see."

Those who found this disjunction unacceptable included Katie Wilson. The Transit Riders Union built a coalition and soon had its first big win—the city council unanimously passed an income tax on the city's wealthiest households, part of a wave of progressive legislation that also included laws mandating a $15 minimum wage and paid leave. The tax would face a challenge but it was a start, the first income tax passed in the state in over eighty years.

Next, the coalition took on homelessness. In September 2017, it held a rally under the banner of Housing for All, with new coalition members— even a group of concerned tech workers calling themselves Tech 4 Housing— and a call for new revenue to tackle the problem. A few weeks later, the council's more liberal members responded with a proposal for an "employee hours tax"—a tax on businesses with gross revenue above $5 million, which would bring in $25 million for affordable housing, shelter, and homelessness services. "It's not punitive to ask those who've done the best to pay their fair share," one of the council members, Teresa Mosqueda, said later.

The employee hours tax had a history in Seattle. Back in 2006, the city had passed a very low-level one of $25 per employee, about a penny per hour, to boost the transportation budget. As small as it was, the local business lobby had objected to what it labeled a "head tax," conjuring the image of Seattle workers as so many heads of cattle to be milked for revenue, and in 2009, the city gave in and repealed it.

Faced with a larger employee-hours tax, the business lobby revived the old arguments against the "head tax"—that it would discourage hiring, that it was poorly designed. The council voted down the proposal by one vote. But the idea wasn't dead—the council appointed a task force to come up with a more carefully considered version. In early March, this task force, which included Katie Wilson, released a report recommending a tax on large businesses that would generate $75 million per year, three times as much revenue as what had been initially proposed.

Businesses decried the proposal, seizing on the fact that it assessed a small fee, a few hundred dollars, on even small businesses, as a way to share responsibility widely. On April 20, four council members introduced legislation for a $75-million-per-year "Progressive Tax on Business"—it would begin with an employee hours tax of $500 per full-time employee, before evolving into a payroll tax. It would exempt businesses with annual revenue under $20 million—only the highest-grossing 3 percent of businesses would pay, which amounted to fewer than six hundred companies. There would be no fee on smaller businesses.

Katie Wilson was amazed that her grassroots coalition had made it this far in the face of such strong opposition from the business lobby. An April poll showed majority support for the tax, and the coalition had a majority of five council members behind the proposal. Still, she couldn't help but feel anxious.

On April 23, after the first public hearing on the legislation, she texted one of its proponents on the council, Lisa Herbold: "Do you think the opposition has anything up their sleeve, beyond just continuing to make more of the same noise for another three weeks?"

"I feel it in my BONES," Herbold wrote back. "Just not sure what."

For years, Amazon had been strikingly unengaged in politics and civic affairs in Seattle, an absence that grew all the stranger the more it expanded. This was a reflection of the libertarian politics of its founder: government was not only a hindrance, it was irrelevant. Mike McGinn, the mayor from 2010 to 2013, had not met Bezos once while leading the city.

This lack of engagement stood in contrast with Microsoft, which had long been involved in local schools, even urging its engineers to teach computer science classes. Amazon's approach echoed the mentality of Bethlehem Steel in its early days, when managers were discouraged from civic engagement so as not to distract from their company duties.

The disassociation extended to philanthropy: Bezos had given away conspicuously little wealth, locally or otherwise. There were gifts to his alma mater, Princeton, and to the local cancer research center and museum of industry, but little beyond that. All told, he and his family had given away some $100 million—a tenth of a percent of his net worth. In April 2018, he would make headlines by saying that he viewed his space-exploration company, Blue Origin, as more worthwhile than anything else he could do with his money. "The only way that I can see to deploy this much financial resource is by converting my Amazon winnings into space travel. That is basically it," he said.

There had been only a few exceptions to his political remove. The previous year, as the efforts to fight homelessness had started to gear up, the company had given $350,000 to the successful mayoral campaign of Jenny Durkan, a centrist Democrat also heavily backed by the local chamber of commerce. In 2012, Bezos had given $2.5 million to support same-sex marriage in Washington. Two years earlier, he had given $100,000 to the side fighting the referendum on a new income tax on the state's wealthiest residents, which had put him in opposition to Bill Gates's father, who had helped lead the push for the tax.

It was the memory of the latter intervention that gave the proponents of the new big-business tax to pay for affordable housing and homelessness services such reason for unease. If there was one thread over the years through the company's intermittent political engagements, it was a strong, underlying aversion to paying taxes—an "overriding corporate obsession," as the author Franklin Foer put it.

Plenty of other big corporations sought to minimize their tax bills. What set Amazon apart was the sheer multiplicity of ways in which it sought to do it, the way the impulse pervaded its behavior and decisions at every level. The company's approach to tax avoidance was a veritable Swiss Army knife, with an implement to wield against every possible government tab. There was the initial decision to settle in Seattle to avoid assessing sales tax in big states such as California. There was the decision to hold off as long as possible on opening warehouses in many large states to avoid the sales taxes there. Amazon employees scattered around the country often carried misleading business cards, so that the company couldn't be accused of operating in a given state and thus forced to pay taxes there. In 2010, the company went so far as to close its only warehouse in Texas and drop plans for additional ones when state officials pushed Amazon to pay nearly $270 million in back sales taxes there, forcing the state to waive the back taxes. By 2017, the company had even created a secret internal goal of securing $1 billion per year in local tax subsidies.

There was the relentless hunt for tax exemptions and credits from states and cities in exchange for building warehouses and data centers—a total of $2.7 billion by 2019, according to the watchdog group Good Jobs First.

And there was the avoidance of corporate income taxes. For years, the company had managed to keep its tax bill down simply by claiming so few profits—the focus was on growing its customer base and driving rivals to the point of extinction by keeping its prices so low. But even now that it was finally racking up profits, it was sending precious little to the public commonweal. By funneling profits through an office in Luxembourg, Amazon avoided paying the U.S. government $1.5 billion, according to the IRS. In 2018, it would pay zero corporate income taxes for the second straight year, despite doubling its profits to more than $11 billion. In fact, it would so successfully game the tax code that it would receive a $129 million rebate. Overall, from 2009 to 2018, the company paid an effective tax rate of 3 percent on profits totaling $26.5 billion. (It noted in its defense that in 2019, it paid more than $1 billion in federal corporate income taxes, and that it was starting to assess more sales taxes on behalf of third-party sellers, after a 2018 U.S. Supreme Court ruling made it easier for states to collect taxes on online purchases.) Its success in avoiding taxes made it all the more remarkable, if that was the word, that the company was making so much money from government contracts—from federal agencies and the military on down to school districts.

For all that, the company had been content for the initial months of the Seattle tax fight in early 2018 to remain a face in the crowd of business interests. It joined a regional initiative created by Mayor Durkan—a transparent attempt to come up with a more limited set of solutions than whatever was going to come out of the council's task force, which Amazon and other businesses had refused to join. The company deferred to lobby groups—the chamber, the Downtown Seattle Association, the Washington Technology Industry Association.

It was the proponents of taxing big business to address homelessness, or one of them, who first singled Amazon out from the scrum. Kshama Sawant was a rara avis in American politics: an elected official who proudly claimed the socialist label. She had come to Seattle from India with her husband, a Microsoft engineer, gotten divorced, and remarried a fellow activist with Socialist Alternative, a Trotskyite organization. She had won election in 2013 to represent the city council's Third District, which included the Central District. She argued for a larger tax on big business than what the council's liberal wing was proposing—$150 million, at least. She believed in giving the target of the tax a clear face. And she was not hesitant about giving a face to the proponents: her own.

In late March, Sawant and other members of Socialist Alternative held a "Tax Amazon Town Hall." Soon afterward, she and supporters held a rally outside the big new Amazon spheres. TAX BEZOS, said their signs. "The tax we are demanding," Sawant said, "is pocket change for corporations like Amazon. . . . Pocket change for these billionaires."

The demands provided a jolt in a city that had fallen into a grudging apathy when it came to Amazon. As one software engineer watching the rally put it, "I don't agree with them not paying taxes, but they can kind of do whatever they want." And the explicit confrontation was cause for consternation for Katie Wilson and other advocates of the $75 million tax emerging from the council. The advocates, including the King County Labor Council, had been considering making Amazon a bigger part of their case—the rapid expansion of one of the world's largest companies had fueled an affordability crisis, and the company needed to help the city deal with that.

But it was another matter to have the confrontation framed starkly as Amazon on the one side and the notorious city council socialist on the other, a framing eagerly embraced by the local media. Wilson feared that it distracted from the real issues at hand—housing and fair taxation—and turned the fight into a tribal showdown. "There could've been a way to make it about Amazon that could have been productive," she said later. "But what happened with Kshama out front made that strategy not look so great. Because it made it look like showmanship, some symbolic thing. As opposed to, Amazon is having this great impact on our city and we need to mitigate the impact."

Amazon sensed the opening that Sawant's move had given it. On April 26, the company announced that it had topped $1 billion in profit for the second straight quarter. One week later, and nine days after Katie Wilson and Lisa Herbold were texting about their shared foreboding, the company finally tossed its thunderbolt. It announced that it was so opposed to the $75 million tax legislation that it was pausing construction on its next big tower, a seventeen-story building that was to accommodate an expansion of 7,000 to 8,000 jobs, and reconsidering its lease of 700,000 square feet in another tower, space for up to 5,000 jobs.

The implication was plain: the company was already well on its way to finding a second headquarters, and if Seattle kept up this sort of ingratitude, there was no guarantee that it would always have Amazon to kick around.

As Amazon surely knew it would, its threat to cancel its Seattle expansion helped draw out its favored opponent even further. A day later, Kshama Sawant, dressed in a long red scarf, returned to the Amazon spheres with supporters to protest the company's "extortionary" tactics. TAX AMAZON. FUND HOUSING & SERVICES read their bright-red signs.

This time, protesters had shown up on the other side. Dozens of iron-workers from Local 86 came to defend their livelihood. "No head tax! No head tax!" they chanted, drowning out Sawant's supporters, whom they out-numbered.

Never mind that there were still more cranes in the sky than in any other American city. Never mind that the building Amazon was threatening to cancel was still in the planning stages. The images from the standoff could not have been any more advantageous to Amazon. On the one side, a grab bag of political radicals led by a socialist whose accent reflected her origins in the western Indian state of Maharashtra. On the other side, hardwork-ing Americans in hard hats and safety vests who knew how to raise steel beams—a holdover of the blue-collar city that Seattle was no longer, but liked to imagine it retained some element of, nearly all evidence to the contrary.

The defection of the building trades unions represented more than a one-day public relations win for Amazon. The company's threat—so easily made, a one-sentence statement to a *Seattle Times* columnist—had frac-tured the labor movement, which had provided supporters of the new tax with what little institutional backing they could claim.

Still, the effort moved forward, carried by the sheer force of undeniable need. A week later, the public got view of a report that the chamber of com-merce had commissioned from McKinsey on the homelessness crisis but suppressed for months because its results were inconvenient. It was notable that even a consulting firm commissioned by a business lobby group that was helping lead opposition to the new tax had found that the crisis was of enormous proportions. It would take King County $400 million per year in additional revenue to properly tackle the problem, the report stated.

Over the following weekend, Mayor Durkan met with the bill's council supporters, Amazon officials, and others to produce a Mother's Day compromise: the tax would be shrunk by more than a third, to $275 per employee, collecting only $47 million per year. Amazon's share would be about $12 million, at a time when its revenue exceeded $230 billion. The company still made its displeasure plain: "We remain very apprehensive about the future created by the council's hostile approach and rhetoric toward larger businesses, which forces us to question our growth here," said Drew Herdener, a vice president. But one council member, Mosqueda, would later describe her relief at having reached consensus. "Not that we needed their buyoff," she said. "But it was important for us to have something that was at least a beginning, a starting point."

With the compromise in hand, the council voted unanimously on May 14 in favor of the new tax. Only eight months after kicking off their effort, Katie Wilson and her Housing for All allies had brought about a substantial if not fully adequate response to homelessness, carried out through democratic channels, paid for with a progressive tax on those whose outsized success had given rise to the problem. Herbold, the council member, again texted Wilson, this time without foreboding: "This was a VERY BIG THING & I'm finding it hard to have perspective in all of the compromise, but I think that this is the most structurally transformative thing the Council has done in 20 years."

The celebration lasted all of two days. The vote was on Monday. Durkan signed the bill into law on Wednesday. The next day, opponents announced that they were gathering signatures to put a referendum question on that fall's ballot to repeal it. The No Tax on Jobs referendum push would be heavily funded: by Vulcan (Paul Allen's development company), by Starbucks, by Amazon.

Teresa Mosqueda was stunned. "They said yes on Mother's Day. We voted on Monday. They funded the opposition on Tuesday. Within forty-eight hours you're going to change your word?" Months later, she would ask company officials about their move to torpedo a compromise law days after they had sat in a room and agreed to its terms. "Yes, we agreed with you that $275 was reasonable," they told her, as she recalled. "You didn't ask if we were going to fund the opposition." (Amazon disputed this account.) The brazenness was breathtaking. "When you're in the halls of a legislative building, if you give someone your word, it should be your currency," Mosqueda said.

Amazon might have devalued its moral currency, but it had gobs of the other sort. The defenders of the law were swamped by the opposition, which would spend nearly half a million dollars in less than a month, most of it on a $350,000 operation, run by a conservative firm that had worked for the Trump campaign, to gather the requisite 17,632 petition signatures. (Meanwhile, No Tax on Jobs hired as its campaign coordinator one of the main organizers of the Seattle Womxn's March.) Recordings caught signature gatherers peddling mistruths, such as claiming that the money would come straight out of workers' paychecks, or that it had already forced grocery stores to close. The dominant line of attack was simple: Why should the city be trusted to spend millions more when the large sums it was already spending on homelessness had left so many thousands in the streets? "The city does not have a revenue problem—it has a spending efficiency problem" was how Amazon's Herdener put it. "We are highly uncertain whether the city council's anti-business positions or its spending inefficiency will change for the better."

The law's defenders had next to no wherewithal to amplify their response. That much of the existing spending was going toward homeless families, with good results. That the additional funding was needed for the tougher population of chronically homeless adults, many of whom were mentally ill and addicted to drugs or alcohol, who required so-called supportive housing.

Such fine points stood no chance against blunt resentment over proliferating tent encampments. The opponents had revealed a strain of conservatism in the liberal Seattle electorate, a sense that government was broken and wasteful and worthy of contempt. The big-business lobby allied with a panoply of not-in-my-neighborhood groups—Speak Out Seattle, Safe Seattle, the Neighborhood Safety Alliance. NO NEW DEVELOPMENT! and

SHELTER YES! EASTSIDE NO! lawn signs proliferated right alongside ALL RACES ARE WELCOME HERE ones. "I feel like city government doesn't understand and respect taxpayer dollars, and doesn't take responsibility for them," said one resident at a raucous town-hall meeting in early May. "Your policies and what we're doing in this city has unleashed chaos and crime on law-abiding people," said another. The loudest cheers came in response to demands to clear encampments by force. The meeting left one city staff member stunned: "That did not feel like Seattle."

In early June, the Service Employees International Union, one of the few major backers of the tax, paid for a poll. The results were overwhelmingly negative. Harsh realism settled over the council: if a conservative tide kept rising, it risked washing away much else as well that fall, including a schools levy and Democratic state legislative candidates.

On June 12, less than a month after voting unanimously to pass the tax, the council held a hearing to vote on whether to repeal it. Pro-tax protesters jammed city hall, far too many for the council's hearing room to accommodate. Those shut out of the meeting milled and chanted in the large lobby; one of them added to the agitation by ringing a large gong.

Standing in the crowd, unable to get into the hearing room and unable to stop what was about to happen there regardless, was Katie Wilson.

She had been trying to make sense of the shift, how a city that had grown so ambivalent about the giant growing in its midst could suddenly become so protective of it; how a city suffering from the side effects of hyper-prosperity could at the same time be so insecure, so fretful about losing its golden goose; how a city that voted 92 percent against Donald Trump could turn against its neediest. "The last nine months of well-funded propaganda campaign was basically successful," she said. "The local news and consciousness has just taken this horrible turn."

Also trying to make sense of it all was Nick Hanauer, the early investor who had helped draw Amazon to Seattle. "It's the fastest-growing large city in the country and people are losing their minds," he said in the same week as the council hearing. "The head tax created just this crazy civil war in the city that all of us observed. Every one of us has friends who are otherwise good, rational, progressive people who just go off the rails about this. All of my friends are angry about something. They just are. All of the wealthy soccer moms I know who do nothing but drive their children around are angry about the traffic, are angry about the bike lanes. My friends who own and run these giant fast-growing companies are bitching about the apartment buildings going up in their neighborhood, and the massage therapists I know who have never been busier are bitching about the Amazon people. People cannot connect the dots. People's brains are not wired to process cognitive dissonance. People struggle to connect the benefits they're getting with the harm it is creating, and their heads explode. Everybody here has benefited mightily, but they just cannot connect the fact that the things they are doing are creating the problem they hate. The inability to process that exploded on the head tax. People got bullied. Everybody's been bitching about the traffic and nobody can afford a place to live, but then it's 'Amazon is going to leave, ohmigod what are we going to do?' People are easy to bully."

The hearing concluded with the council voting 7–2 to repeal the tax. The only two who opposed repeal were Kshama Sawant and Teresa Mosqueda. A month later, the city's median home price would hit $805,000. By the end of the year, Seattle would post the largest increase in homelessness of any city in the country. Amazon, meanwhile, would reach $2 billion in quarterly profit for the first time a couple weeks after the vote; that year's Prime Day, the annual summer shopping extravaganza, would surpass even Cyber Monday and Black Friday in sales. Its market capitalization would break the $1 trillion mark a few weeks after that, on September 4. It would announce that even after successfully blocking the tax, it wouldn't be moving into the leased space in the new tower—one of the towers it had previously threatened to abandon if it *didn't* get its way.

The day after the vote, Michael Schutzler, the head of the Washington Technology Industry Association, sat in his office reflecting on his side's victory. He had been out of town during the repeal vote, on a seventy-mile paddleboard race from Tacoma to Port Townsend. But he didn't need to be at the hearing. "Because of what we do, we're really well connected to the inside of this stuff and so we knew what was going down the day before," he said.

Schutzler could not suppress his delight over the spectacle of council members trying to decide whether to suffer the ignominy of reversing themselves less than a month after voting for the tax. "Do I pull a one-eighty and explain that?"—here he giggled—"or do I vote against the one-eighty and deal with whatever political repercussion from that?"

What was especially amusing, he said, was watching council members act as if their misgivings about the law were anything but political calculation. "All the posturing going on, it all sounds like it's trying to be principled," he said. "It's not principled. It was just a really stupid policy to begin with and now it's politically expedient to decide that this really great policy you believed in so strongly just a few weeks ago is suddenly bad. Come on."

Schutzler chortled again. "This city just doesn't know how to manage itself out of a paper bag and never has," he said. "It's always been a very provincial little town."

Three months later, the guests were starting to tuck into their salads in the Washington Hilton ballroom as the big Economic Club of Washington banquet for Jeff Bezos got underway. While they ate, the club president, David Rubenstein, ticked off the dinner's sponsors, among them Boeing, JPMorgan Chase, and Amazon Web Services. "Everyone in this room by definition is a distinguished person," said Rubenstein to appreciative laughter, but he would, he said, take the time to mention some of the most distinguished of all. He recognized all seventeen ambassadors in attendance: "Singapore . . . Indonesia . . . South Africa . . . United Kingdom . . . Australia . . . Ireland . . ." He recognized the postmaster general, and the head of the General Services Administration, and Maryland governor Larry Hogan, and Stephen Moret, who was overseeing Northern Virginia's bid for Amazon's second headquarters, and Washington mayor Muriel Bowser, and three former mayors also in attendance, and the chairman of the Washington Metro subway system.

"How many people here came on Metro?" Rubenstein asked. Barely anyone raised their hand. "This does not look like a Metro crowd," he deadpanned.

There were more welcoming remarks from the CEO of the evening's chief sponsor, the large local real estate company JBG Smith Properties. The formal introduction of the guest of honor was left to Warren Buffett, via video feed. Buffett compared Bezos to Babe Ruth. "Jeff Bezos is the slugger," he said. "This is the guy who has overturned, changed dramatically, two of the most important industries in the world: retail and information technology. He's changed the lives of hundreds of millions of people for the better. And on the weekends, he designs spaceships to go to the moon."

Buffett paused. "I imagine that the first passengers on that moon shot will probably be a bunch of retailers trying to get to a better environment."

The crowd loved it and finished its dinner, and then there was Bezos onstage with Rubenstein. Bezos wore a dark suit with a white pocket square and looked supremely at ease. His interlocutor did nothing to ruffle him. Rubenstein opened by noting that Amazon's stock was up by 70 percent from the year before, and that as a result of this, Bezos could claim a new title.

"You have become the wealthiest man in the world," Rubenstein said. "Is that a title you ever wanted?"

"I can assure you I have never sought that title," Bezos said. "It was fine being the second-wealthiest person in the world. That worked fine."

The ballroom erupted in laughter.

"I own sixteen percent of Amazon, which is now worth roughly a trillion dollars," Bezos continued. "We've built $840 billion of wealth for other people. From a financial point of view, that's what we've done. That's great. That's how it should be. I believe so powerfully in the power of entrepreneurial capitalism and free markets to solve many of the world's problems."

Rubenstein, himself an early investor in Amazon via Carlyle, remained fixated on the wealth ranking. "You live in Washington State, outside of Seattle," he said. "The man who was the richest man for about twenty years is named Bill Gates. What's the likelihood that the two richest men in the world live not only in the same country, not only in the same state, not only in the same city, but in the same neighborhood? Is there something in that neighborhood we should know about? Are there any more houses for sale there?"

The crowd loved this, too. But there was only so far one could take comedic repartee about extreme wealth between two billionaires, and a moment later Rubenstein made a pivot to the subject that he knew so well, that he had long deployed to mitigate disquiet about his own fortune. That very day—the timing was surely no accident—Bezos had announced that he was at long last diving into large-scale philanthropy. He was putting $2 billion toward providing shelter to homeless families and toward Montessori preschools. This would put his total charitable giving at less than 2 percent of his net worth.

Rubenstein now asked him how he had come around to deciding how to target the "most significant philanthropic gift you've made," a question that the audience followed with great applause. Bezos said that he had solicited ideas from the public, and gotten 47,000 suggestions. He had then followed his instincts. "All of my best decisions have been made with heart and intuition and guts, not analysis," he said.

There was no mention of the fight over the homelessness tax in Seattle three months earlier. There was no mention of the debate over the tax cuts signed into law by President Trump, which had slashed rates for corporations and the wealthiest while leaving the carried-interest loophole untouched. In fact, the word *tax* would not be uttered once by Bezos or Rubenstein in any context over the course of the seventy-minute interview.

Instead, Rubenstein turned toward the topic so many in the ballroom were most eager to hear about. "When you use your intuition to make decisions, where is the intuition leading you now on your second headquarters?" This met with wild applause, and even whistles.

"The answer is very simple," Bezos said. "We will announce the decision before the end of this year."

On this point, Rubenstein was willing to press further. "You already have something in one Washington," he said. "Why not another Washington area?"

The film, if one wanted to call it that, opened with a shot of a homeless encampment—tents, trash—east of Interstate 5, across from the stadiums. The camera pulled back and upward to reveal the city skyline beyond. Cut to a shot of a white man, a bandage on his neck, sitting in an opiate haze.

"What if Seattle is dying and we don't even know it?" began the voiceover. "This story is about a seething, simmering anger that is now boiling over into outrage. It is about people who have felt compassion, yes, but who no longer feel safe, no longer feel like they're heard, no longer feel protected. It is about lost souls who wander our streets untethered to home, or family, or reality, chasing a drug, which in turn chases them. It's about the damage they inflict on themselves, to be sure, but also on the fabric of this place where we live. This story is about a beautiful jewel that has been violated and a crisis of faith amongst a generation of Seattleites falling out of love with their home."

As the narrator spoke, the images unspooled: the homeless in heroin stoops, the homeless lying sprawled on the sidewalk, the homeless struggling to pull up their pants. This was the opening to *Seattle Is Dying*, an hour-long documentary on the city's homelessness crisis that aired in March 2019 on KOMO, the local ABC affiliate owned by Sinclair Broadcast Group, the nationwide chain with a strongly conservative bent.

From the opening montage, the video moved through a string of interviews with those "people who no longer feel protected": small-business owners losing goods to shoplifting or losing customers to the stink of urine, a neighbor appalled at homeless desecrating a cemetery, a veteran cop who quit in despair over being powerless to address the problem. "I couldn't do it anymore," he said.

There were numbers, too: numbers showing that Seattle was now second in property crimes only to even more dystopian San Francisco, where 5,000 homeless lived on the streets (and where, in June 2019, a man would make himself into a viral sensation by dumping a bucket of water onto a homeless woman), and numbers showing how few crimes were actually prosecuted (one homeless meth user who had been arrested thirty-four times since 2014 was highlighted and shown refusing to climb out of a trash can), and numbers showing how much the area was spending on homelessness: $1 billion per year. "They live in filth and despair, like animals, and we allow it," said the narrator.

But there was a solution! The narrator took the viewer to Rhode Island, which, he said, was having great success rehabilitating drug-addicted drifters—in prison. And then the scene shifted back to Washington State, to an overhead shot of a group of buildings on a lovely island in Puget Sound—it might have been a resort, but was in fact a state prison, sitting mostly vacant, just waiting for Seattle to do its homeless the favor of locking them up there.

"A city is a living thing—it has a rhythm and a heartbeat, a kind of soul. It is a collection of ideas that we protect and defend, old ideas and new ones," the narrator concluded. "But behind the beauty and the ideas . . . and the ballparks and the beautiful buildings, the dirty work is the fight. Great dreams and great cities don't survive without a fight. Seattle is dying. Maybe with all the wealth and growth, we became so pleased with ourselves or so busy that we forgot about the hard part. Maybe good people who go to work every day and raise families and pay taxes, the ones who built the city and dreamed the dream, forgot about the dirty work. Maybe we forgot about the fight."

One might have thought that a city that gave Donald Trump only 8 percent of its vote in 2016 would have recoiled against what was, essentially, a conservative propaganda film. Instead, the city was riveted. Less than half a year later, *Seattle Is Dying* had nearly five million views on YouTube.

Katie Wilson was not surprised by the response. Even before the documentary aired, she had detected a rising sourness in the atmosphere. Instead of simply pausing the debate over homelessness for the time being and clearing the air, the city council's repeal of the tax had fed the forces that had led to the repeal. It had made the council, already derided as misguided, appear feckless as well. Any notion that members might have had that voting for repeal would ensure their preservation was revealed as naive. Opponents of the tax, fueled with the same business backing that had funded the referendum push, were now gunning for a wholesale jettisoning of the council, not only those who had voted against repeal, but all those who had voted for the tax in the first place.

But the shift in the air was about more than the 2019 council elections. It was about an allegedly progressive city coming to terms with the fact that, if the pre-repeal polls were to be believed, a solid majority of residents had accepted the argument that their government was too broken to tackle a problem it had been elected to address. To an outsider, the anti-government sentiment was particularly odd given how well run the city seemed compared with so many others—its bus system was extensive and heavily used; city hall was spacious and gleaming; corruption was minimal. But somehow, one of the most liberal cities had lapsed into a local variant of Tea Partyism, a resentment of the grasping Other, and—this was key—it was not going to apologize for that.

Katie Wilson spent months trying to make sense of this, and composed a ten-page essay on the failure of her effort. The crucial passage was this:

The homelessness crisis is, after all, the convergence of trends any one of which reveals a social order on the rocks: soaring housing costs and stagnating wages; decades of cuts to safety net programs; an epidemic of depression, social isolation, and mental illness; self-medication and opioid overprescription; fraying community and family support networks; mass incarceration and systemic racism. The tent pitched in the greenway and the woman shooting up on the sidewalk are the tip of an iceberg of social catastrophe, intruding into public space in a manner impossible to ignore.

Millennials tend to feel at home with this reality, because it explains our lives. Growing up in the shadow of looming environmental disaster, entering adulthood with precarious job prospects, never having formed expectations of stability or security, the notion that a fundamental restructuring of society is in order doesn't feel all that radical. From this vantage point homelessness may be heartbreaking, but it's not confusing. . . .

But for many without this outlook, for people who have bought into the American Dream, the sense of social disintegration must be bewildering and terrifying. The city where they've built a life, or are struggling to build a life, is changing fast, turning into something unrecognizable, inhospitable—they feel beleaguered, unsafe. How to comprehend the seismic changes taking place in the world? Homelessness brings the question to their doorstep, prompting visceral feelings of frustration and rage. The belief that it all comes down to poor local governance, individual failures, and lax enforcement of the laws must be a comforting antidote to despair.

One of Katie's allies in the homelessness fight, the Seattle University law professor Sara Rankin, put it more bluntly: "Seattle has a lot of folks who fancy themselves to be progressive, but they're also immersed in this bubble of extraordinary wealth, so you can't help but start to develop a sense of entitlement," she said. In this, the city shared much with the other coastal cities and scattered thriving inland outposts that had increasingly become the base of the Democratic Party. The party that had long prided itself on being the party of the underdog was now, while still home to millions of working-class Black and Latino voters, dominated by highly educated professionals in the wealthiest cities in the country, which it could count on for its biggest donations and biggest margins of victory. In cities such as Seattle, this affluence had reshaped the politics of many proudly progressive Democrats. Countless people in town had seen their normal-seeming house soar in value in recent years, and had come to guard that asset fiercely against perceived threats, whether it was a tent encampment or simply an affordable housing development down the street.

Seattle had become proof that extreme regional inequality was unhealthy not only for places that were losing out in the winner-take-all economy, but also for those who were the runaway victors. Hyper-prosperity was not only creating the side effects of unaffordability, congestion, and homelessness, but injecting a political poison into the winner cities.

The cranes kept going up—there were fifty-nine in the air in April 2019, still the most in the nation. Work resumed on the tower that Amazon had threatened to cancel. Meanwhile, the company announced that it was taking steps to address the housing crisis it had helped create—philanthropically, that is. It would donate $5 million to an affordable housing developer and set aside eight floors in one of its new buildings for a 200-bed homeless shelter for families, complete with its own health clinic. It was far less than the $500 million that Microsoft had previously announced it was investing in local housing, but it was something.

Katie Wilson was unimpressed by Amazon's new philanthropy. She was putting more stock in a ruling by the state court of appeals that seemed to bode well for the city's income tax on wealthy residents, on hold since it was passed in 2017, possibly being upheld in the state supreme court. Who knew, Seattle might yet be able to tax the wealthiest among itself and decide how best to use that money to better the city. "In principle, there's a democratic process for deciding how we use that money," she said. "There's transparency and accountability. That's kind of what government is for. With philanthropy, there's none of that. We're just depending on our corporate overlords to decide what's good for us."

On a sunny midsummer weekday afternoon in 2019, around the corner from the Ferrari dealership on Twelfth Avenue, a young transgender woman was passed out cold on the sidewalk behind a sign advertising a nearby spa and in front of a bar with a large sign in the window: WE WELCOME ALL RACES, ALL RELIGIONS, ALL COUNTRIES OF ORIGINS, ALL SEXUAL ORIENTATIONS, ALL GENDERS. WE STAND WITH YOU. YOU ARE SAFE HERE. Down the street, around the corner from the tattoo emporium, a homeless man with a beard and blue blanket was peering into a new rum bar as a Porsche Carrera passed by. He knelt down, supplicant-style, before the window, though now, at midday, there was no one on the other side.

In South Lake Union, the big red signs outside the Whole Foods said, WE ♥ LOCAL.

At the Flatstick Pub, down the street from the dog-food restaurant and the Tesla dealership, a large group of South Asian Amazonians were playing indoor mini golf. Along Lake Union, amid the yacht dealerships, a Mercedes was nosing past a Jaguar in the parking lot outside a business called ADHD Solutions.

That Friday evening, with the city council primary election four days away, several dozen of Katie Wilson's allies gathered in a two-story condo with a sweeping view of the skyline and Elliott Bay for a fundraiser for a Democratic Socialist running for an open council seat. The disjunction between the message on offer and the setting—the condo had sold for $1.5 million five years earlier—would have been ripe for ridicule, but the candidate, Shaun Scott, did not let the opulence distract from his mission, to push back at the rising ugliness.

After the hostess offered opening remarks—including an acknowledgment that the condo building stood on "occupied land" that had once belonged to the Duwamish people—Scott took the floor. He was tall, young, and Black, one of the few nonwhite people in the room. And one of the first questions he got was on the harsh turn in the local political climate: "How do we improve the citywide narrative on homelessness?"

Scott responded vehemently. "We have to make it clear to people who are on the correct side of the issues of housing and homelessness that this really does boil down very explicitly to compassion and cruelty," he said. "What we have to understand is the language of moral indignation around having people sleeping on the streets in a city as rich as Seattle is, we can't let that be completely the purview of people to our right. They've done a very good job of mastering the language of 'Isn't it crazy we have a homeless-industrial complex in the city spending all this money for these people that are freeloaders.' They get really, really charged about this in ways that have influenced our political discussion and taken us in a more cruel direction. We have to be able to muster the same level of passion for our own ideas, which actually work."

Three months later, Shaun Scott would lose his race for the council by four percentage points to the candidate supported by the chamber of commerce and by an Amazon-backed political action committee. That PAC would spend $1.5 million in the council races—an intervention of unprecedented scale by Amazon when it came to local races. But of the seven council races, the Amazon-backed candidates won in only two—Shaun Scott's and one other. Among those to survive the onslaught was Lisa Herbold, who had texted her celebration after the housing tax initially passed, and Kshama Sawant, Amazon's socialist chief antagonist. Amazon had spent some $440,000 against her, more than against any other candidate, but she had survived narrowly.

Her opponent, Egan Orion, went so far as to blame Amazon's support for his loss. "It made the election not about my opponent's record and policies but about Amazon and their massive unneeded spending," he said.

Sawant was exultant. "It looks like our movement has won and defended our socialist City Council seat for working people against the richest man in the world," she said.

The Umoja Fest Black-heritage parade usually started at the corner of Twenty-Third Avenue and Union Street, one of the primary junctions of the Central District. But this year, 2019, the parade start had been moved a few blocks south, to Twenty-Third and Cherry Street. The chief organizer, Wyking Garrett, said the shift was necessitated by the construction underway at Twenty-Third and Union. In fact, there wasn't really much actual construction underway at that intersection for the time being. More plausible was that the parade had been moved away from the corner because its current state would be too disheartening a sight for many of those attending a parade to celebrate the Black community of the Central District.

However one defined the middle ground that Pat Wright's neighborhood had inhabited a few decades earlier—retaining an identity while no longer restricted within itself—it had been lost long ago. The extraordinary wave of money and new arrivals had swept up from downtown and South Lake

Union, and the Central District—the old Central District—had not stood a chance. It was a handsome, cohesive neighborhood of wood-frame houses and bungalows from the glory days of American residential architecture, located a short drive or bus trip or bike ride from downtown. It had always had those attributes, but it had been largely off-limits under the old strictures. Those strictures were gone, so it was there for the taking, its intrinsic appeal available to all. Or rather, all who could afford it. By 2018, median home prices in the CD and area immediately surrounding it had jumped from $370,000 to more than $830,000 in only six years.

When Wright had moved into the neighborhood, it was more than 70 percent Black. By 2016, that share had dropped to less than 20 percent, and demographers were predicting it would be below 10 percent in a decade. The city as a whole had dropped from nearly 10 percent Black in 1980 to 7 percent—the city that had been home to Quincy Jones and Jimi Hendrix now had barely a larger share of Black residents than Anchorage and Tucson. And this was being driven partly by the company at the core of the city's growth: Amazon's professional, salaried workforce in Seattle and its other office hubs was only 5 percent African American, a dramatically lower share than at its warehouses, where the workforce was more than one-quarter Black. By early 2020, not a single member of Bezos's "S-Team" of twenty-two inner-circle executives was African American. (To address the glaring diversity problem, the company had started funding computer-science instruction and college scholarships in hundreds of underserved communities around the country.)

The disparities were growing, too. As Seattle's wealth climbed ever higher—in 2019, its median household income would cross the $100,000 threshold, up nearly 10 percent in a single year—the economic standing of its Black families kept slipping. Despite being one of the richest cities, Seattle had the ninth-lowest median income for Black households among the fifty largest cities, about a third below the national median for Black households and below what the city's Black median income had been in 2000, not even accounting for inflation. Meanwhile, the rate of Black homeownership had fallen by nearly half since 2000—only one of five Black households in the city owned their home.

It was a reflection of the dynamic that two housing economists had identified a decade earlier, that in hyper-prosperous cities, a rising tide did not lift all boats: "In tight housing markets, the poor do worse when the rich get richer." It also reflected what two British researchers found in 2019, that high-tech job growth did spur additional employment—but almost entirely of the low-wage variety. And it was a stark manifestation of what Quintard Taylor, the chronicler of Black Seattle, had warned of when he published his history of the community in 1994: "Racial toleration is meaningless if people are excluded from the vital economic center and relegated to the margins of the urban economy."

Gentrification and displacement were hardly unique to Seattle—longtime residents were being pushed out of neighborhoods in winner-take-all cities across the country, in Austin and Boston and Brooklyn. But in the Central District, as perhaps only also in San Francisco, the transformation had become so complete that the term "gentrification" no longer really sufficed to capture what had happened. In gentrifying neighborhoods in other cities, one could see friction between old and new, between classes and races. The Central District was approaching wholesale erasure: to a newcomer, it was difficult to believe that this had ever been the locus of a Black community, so scarce were the traces.

"The Hood Ain't the Same" rapped the hip-hop artist Draze, born in the CD:

We didn't have much but were thankful for all we was given
It was our hood until weed and seed crept in . . .
Mark my words, it's gonna be white boys all on the team
I don't reminisce when I drive through this hood, I feel pain
I'm not proud of these new developments, I feel shame . . .
My man called me from the joint, I said this thing is changing
He said homey what you mean, I said I can't explain it, these folks
Moving us around just like an experiment . . .
Used to own our homes, now we're all renters
Got folks moving south like birds for the winter
They ask momma to sell her home, she said no, but

Then we had to shake when them property taxes rose . . .
Don't try to paint me as the Black man who's angry
When you gut my community, it's hard to build a legacy

Nowhere was the disappearance more jarring than at the corner of East Union Street and Twenty-Third Avenue, once the central juncture of Black Seattle.

The large low-slung commercial complex known as Midtown Center, which had once held Earl's Cuts & Styles and a liquor store and a coffee hut and a laundromat and much more, was completely gone, sold to developers for $23.3 million. All that remained on the 2.5-acre lot was a chain-link fence adorned with large signs depicting what would soon emerge. Over most of the lot, starting at the intersection, would stand a massive building with 429 units, mostly market-rate.

The intersection would now consist of boxy six-story new or nearly brand-new apartment and condo buildings, with one exception: Uncle Ike's, a large marijuana dispensary at the northeastern corner of the intersection, next door to the Mount Calvary Christian Center and across from the church's teen services program. Local critics had decried Uncle Ike's proximity to the church and teen center, but that was now moot: the church had put the teen center on the market for $2.8 million, followed by its own building for $4.5 million.

Liberty Bank, the Black-owned institution where Pat Wright had worked as a teller, had been demolished and replaced by a 115-unit apartment building. The building's facade had been decorated with strips of red, green, and black and the image of an upraised fist; at street level it was lined with plaques attesting to the site's historical significance:

Central District—Our "CD" Community
Pioneers and entrepreneurs since 1860
Here we migrated
North, South, East, West

Melding Faith, Family, Love, Spirit, Soul
Crisscrossing Union, Cherry, Jefferson,
Yesler, Jackson, Rainier,
Enfolding Martin Luther King, Jr. Way
Here we flourished in churches, professions, businesses
Looked out for each other; grew to 80 percent.

"Welcome to what we now call sacred ground," said Wyking Garrett at a neighborhood meeting held in one of its new commercial spaces in late May of 2019. Garrett, whose grandfather had been part of the founding team for the original Liberty Bank, had several years earlier founded an organization called Africatown, dedicated to preserving the CD's Black heritage. It organized the annual Umoja Fest, and had positioned itself as a collaborator in the development transforming the intersection, with equity stakes in two of the buildings, organizational space, and a city government grant of more than $1 million.

Garrett was doing his best to cast the corner's transformation in positive terms. The Liberty building would make room for Earl's barbershop and a Black-owned restaurant. It had, he said, leased nearly 90 percent of its apartments to those with "historic ties" to the Central District. The building in the former shopping-plaza space in which Africatown had a stake would also use so-called affirmative marketing to assure that many of its residents had local roots. "We basically filled a void in community-led development," he said. "Different entities are working to realize the vision of Africatown as a thriving community where African Americans can continue to grow and thrive in place."

It was hard not to hear in such assertions the promotional bent of someone who had become a key ally in the transformation—giving a stamp of approval to the big developers who were profiting from the overhaul, at the same time as he and his organization themselves benefited from it. One's own eyes suggested a much different future for the corner than that depicted in the banners on the fence. In reality, virtually everybody one saw—the family with the stroller, the patrons of the taco shop and the upscale burger joint with a brunch menu, the couples strolling to buy cookies at Lowrider Baking—was white, the stereotypical images of gentrification fever dreams.

"I don't go to Union and Twenty-Third anymore. It's hurtful," said Ronica Hairston, a Black woman who had brought her daughter to the parade and the festival that followed in Judkins Park, where bands played and vendors sold po'boys and deep-fried PB&J. "They put all the red and black and green color on, but it's like it's just a footprint."

The parade started down at Cherry, and moved south from there along Twenty-Third. There was a motorcycle crew, and the Buffalo Soldiers Black cowboys, and the Old Rides Car Club, and the Central District Panthers cheerleading squad, and several drill teams, and the Kappa Alpha Psi fraternity, and the Masons, and the Amalgamated Transit Union.

It moved past Fire Station No. 6, past the Douglass-Truth library branch, past Ezell's Famous Chicken (which was under new ownership and, people said, just didn't taste the same), past Garfield High School and Medgar Evers Pool, past the Quincy Jones Performing Arts Center, past Curry Temple CME Church, where they were selling hot dogs and water as usual from the front steps ("It seemed smaller this year"). It moved past a "beautifully remodeled Craftsman home" being sold for $845,000 ("commuter's dream, close to downtown, Amazon . . .") and another one being sold for $664,990 ("in one of the hottest neighborhoods in Seattle," said the listing, not naming said neighborhood).

And it moved past James Edward Jones, who was watching from his front porch. Jones had arrived in the neighborhood from Oklahoma at age twenty-seven in 1968, four years after Patrinell Staten. Like her, he had trailed after two siblings. "I didn't come to like it," he said. "I come to leave Oklahoma." And like Pat Wright, he had become part of the neighborhood and city through music. In his case, it was the Almighty Warriors, a gospel quartet that he'd joined soon after arriving in town. He had been top tenor, and had eventually learned to play the bass, which hadn't been easy, because his fingers were stiff from his work as a janitor at Sears and a laborer at Boeing. They had toured to Chicago in 1971 and Alabama two years later and performed at two World's Fair exhibitions—Expo 74 in Spokane and Expo 86 in Vancouver. Their theme song was "Doing All the Good I Can," from the Dixie Hummingbirds, and then they'd go into "I'm So Thankful" and "Jesus, Keep Me Near the Cross" and all the rest. Sometimes they took the ferry to gigs. Sometimes they got to perform alongside Pat Wright and the Total Experience Gospel Choir. "Music is my life," Jones said. "It has been my life."

Now he sat on his porch and smoked Marlboro 100s and listened to music he'd recorded off of the radio over the years and then hooked up to an amplifier. He was tired of fending off the agents coming to ask him to sell either or both of his houses. He had bought them for about $20,000 in 1975 and $50,000 in 1987. Now they were worth about $500,000 and $900,000. He could sell, but where would he and his wife go? Or his wife's aunt, who lived in the other house?

"I didn't buy it to sell—I bought it to live."

The parade neared Jackson Street, another major commercial junction in the old Central District. New buildings loomed on the northwest corner. Street-level facades were adorned with silhouettes of jazz musicians; white residents looked down on the parade from the balconies above.

At the southeastern corner of the block, another massive complex was rising in the place of Red Apple, the area's longtime grocery store, where you could find pigs' feet and chitterlings. On the chain-link fencing along the sidewalk, the developer had affixed banners designed by local schoolchildren: images of kids and houses and trees with stenciled words randomly floating around them:

PEACE. HOME. LEGACY. CULTURE. HOPE. GROWTH. WISDOM.

And again and again:

COMMUNITY. COMMUNITY. COMMUNITY.

———

On Pat Wright's block, there was only one African American neighbor remaining; on the next block, there were only two. One by one, people had been leaving. Some of them had died, and their heirs found it easier to sell off the property and divvy up the proceeds rather than to shoulder the property taxes. Others simply left, headed for the southern suburbs or even farther south, like the pastor at Mount Zion Baptist, where Total Experience had started out decades earlier. For years, he had been urging congregants not to sell, not to move. Then his wife had prevailed on him to leave for Lakeridge. "When he said he was going to move, I wanted to shoot him myself," said Pat Wright. Soon after the relocation the pastor's wife had slipped on her bathrobe and suffered a fatal fall.

The Realtors kept coming. "Are you interested in selling?" they'd ask Wright.

"I'm in my bathrobe," she'd say. "Do I look like I'm interested in selling?"

"Oh, sorry, ma'am," they'd say.

One day she was feeling especially salty and said she wasn't selling "unless you can make me an offer I can't refuse."

The Realtor asked eagerly: And what would that offer be?

"One point five million dollars," she said. She'd take that offer so fast, she said, "I'll leave my dirty drawers in the hamper."

She hadn't heard from him since.

She had had an amazing run. The choir had sung for Bill Clinton and Barack Obama, for Bishop Desmond Tutu and the Dalai Lama. She had started her own storefront church in the late 1990s, the Oneness Christian Center. The girl in the choir who was taken in by the Wrights was now a professor at Georgia State.

But in late 2018, Pat Wright would officially disband the choir, marking its end with a free concert, forty-five years after it had begun. She still went to church, but found fewer and fewer of her friends there. "Every one of those churches in the Central Area now, if you see twenty-five people, I'll buy you dinner," she said.

As for becoming acquainted with the new neighbors, some of whom worked at the big company in South Lake Union, that hadn't gone so well. She'd be out front when they walked by with their dog and a couple kids—it seemed they all had a dog and a couple kids—and she'd say, "Good morning!" and they'd turn and look at her and keep walking, or muster a perfunctory "Hi."

One time she said hello to a woman she didn't know and the woman looked up startled, as if she'd seen a ghost there on the stoop.

"Oh," the woman said. "You still live here."

M ilo Duke didn't still live there. In 2017, after a few months of seeing their rent climb toward $3,000, he and Wendy made their move: back to her hometown, St. Louis.

It was, seen one way, a most unlikely move. St. Louis had by this point become the ultimate example of a left-behind city. Its population had fallen from a peak of more than 850,000 in 1950 to barely more than 300,000, a decline as large, proportionally, as that of Detroit. Put another way: in 1970, St. Louis had nearly 100,000 more residents than Seattle. Half a century later, it now had much less than half of Seattle's population.

They arrived in what seemed a different country. From the constant congestion along the Puget Sound to a city that had nothing but embarrassing amounts of space—the breathtaking, heartbreaking expanses of all-but-abandoned North St. Louis, where ornately detailed brick homes sat for the taking, block after half-demolished block; the melancholy emptiness of the once monumental downtown, where a nascent comeback a decade earlier had stalled out first in the recession and then in the regression that followed the 2014 protests over a fatal police shooting in nearby Ferguson.

It was growing increasingly difficult to discern what, exactly, the city's path back to prosperity might look like. It was a textbook case of a once proud metropolis turning into a mere branch town, its banks and ad agencies and airplane manufacturer (McDonnell Douglas) subsumed into other, larger companies with headquarters elsewhere. The city's airport had lost so much traffic in recent years that one terminal sat completely unused.

But Milo and Wendy loved it. They had bought a loft in a Central West End building designed by Wendy's great-grandfather, an architect. It was 1,665 square feet with soaring ceilings and a soaking tub and a garden, pool, and pool house out back. They paid $269,000.

And they had, in short order, found the art scene they had lost in Seattle. They had fallen in with an arts entrepreneur who had turned his rehabbed 1892 house into a live-music venue and was presiding over a new arts district on Grand Boulevard in Midtown. They were getting meetings with the leaders of the city's contemporary art museum and Pulitzer Arts Foundation, the sort of thing that never happened in Seattle. And they had gotten gallery space in the new Grand Center Arts District, where, on the first Friday of every month, they would open the doors to passersby, just as they had at the Umpqua Bank in Seattle. Except that here, in this city with so much less money, people actually came in and bought art. In the first three months, artists in the gallery made forty-five sales. When Milo reported this to his friends back in Seattle, they couldn't believe it.

The gallery's rent was $100 per month. It was understood that if the owner found another tenant for the space, they'd have to go. But given the state of the city, that seemed remote.

8.

Isolation

The crisis of small-town America

They called the towns the "Little Cities of Black Diamonds," which was a wonderfully resonant phrase, but misleading on several levels. The black diamonds were almost entirely gone from this part of Southeast Ohio—the largest remaining coal mine, out past the town of Glouster, was expected to tap out soon—and most of the towns could hardly have been considered cities even in the best of times. Now several barely existed at all. If you visited, you'd find only a cluster of abandoned brick buildings with a historical marker or two, barely any less a ghost town than the iconic, tumbleweed-scattered silver-mining towns of Arizona or Nevada.

The only one of the dozen that still qualified as a city, at least by the standards of Ohio law, was Nelsonville. It had been founded way back in 1814 and flourished as a supplier of not only coal but also timber, both of which could be shipped out first via the Hocking Canal and later by rail. The coal boom ended in the 1920s, due partly to competition from larger, newly mechanized mines in West Virginia and Kentucky. The decline of the passenger railroads that had linked so many Ohio towns and cities to each other and beyond sped isolation.

But in the 1930s, in the heart of the Depression, Nelsonville had gotten a new industry: shoe manufacture, with the opening of the William Brooks Shoe Company. And the town, tucked picturesquely within the Appalachian foothills, had continued to serve as a regional market hub, famous for its handsome central square, with a grand hotel and opera house and rows of stores on three sides, and for the brick that lined the streets and sidewalks. In 1904, Nelsonville Block, the product of the area's rich clay deposits, had won first prize at the World's Fair in St. Louis with designs such as "flower with eight-point star," "snowflake and Celtic cross," and "bullseye with circle cube."

In recent decades, the town's worth as a small commercial magnet had fallen away. First came the Walmarts in Athens and Logan, the larger towns that lay a dozen miles in either direction on Route 33, and the Walmarts had done their famous number on smaller competitors. These were the years when Nelsonville lost mainstays like LS, a local discount retail and hardware store, leaving a smattering of gift shops on the square, a Kroger, and a family-owned pharmacy that tried to fill the void with some general-store offerings. Soon these were being threatened, too, by those new signposts of rural America, the chain dollar stores. Nelsonville had both Family Dollar and Dollar General, two blocks apart on Canal Street.

The town still had the shoe company, though. Bill Brooks had sold it in 1958 to another shoe company in Lancaster, a larger town thirty miles up Route 33. His nephew John had asked to buy it, but Bill, pessimistic about the company's prospects, had refused to inflict it on him. Seventeen years later, John Brooks got his chance, buying Brooks back. The business scuffled along, but John Brooks was in his element as the local owner of a local company: he managed the three-story brick factory down on Canal Street, negotiated contracts with Local 146 of the Union of Needletrades, Industrial and Textile Employees, served on the city council, drove an Oldsmobile, and lived a short walk from the factory.

John's son Mike had entered the shoe industry, too, but with a different perspective. He had attended the famous Ars Sutoria trade school in Milan, Italy, and gone to work for U.S. Shoe Corporation and two tanning companies. When his father bought back Brooks, he'd returned to Nelsonville to help him. And during the 1980s, father and son brought new life to the company. They carved out specialty markets: "occupational" shoes for letter carriers and police officers, whose employers appreciated or even required the Made in USA label; and boots for hikers and hunters made waterproof with Gore-Tex, whose maker was friends with Mike Brooks. To reflect its new market niche, the Brookses gave the company a rugged new name: Rocky Shoes & Boots.

Sales were growing so quickly that the small factory on Canal Street was having trouble keeping up. Rather than expand it, Mike Brooks decided in the late 1980s to add capacity elsewhere: in the Dominican Republic, and in Puerto Rico, which, crucially, still qualified for the Made in USA label. His father objected to the offshore expansion and decided to bow out of the company in 1991, at age seventy. Two years later, deciding the company needed more capital, Mike Brooks took it public, in a stock offering that raised almost $14 million.

John Hutchison arrived in the factory in the mid-1990s. He had grown up in the hills outside Nelsonville, with a single mom. His dad, who worked at the uranium enrichment plant in Piketon, seventy-five miles to the southwest, had moved out when he was a toddler; his mother was left in such a bind that she gave their third child, a newborn girl, up for adoption. She eventually remarried a trade-school teacher. Their home was across the line in Hocking County, so John had to go all the way to Logan for high school, an hour-long ride on the bus.

He kicked around a bit after high school. But then he got together with Bridget, whom he'd known from school. She already had two little kids, and then they had one of their own, a boy. John needed a steady job to support the family, and so he did what hundreds of others in town did: he made shoes. In his case, he became a toe laster.

By this point, the labor-intensive work of leather cutting and stitching had gone offshore. Among the tasks that remained in Nelsonville was working the toe-lasting machine. The boot—or rather, the leather "upper" that was on its way to becoming a boot—would come to him, and he would insert it into the big machine, which had a large pedal in the center. When you pushed down a little bit at first, the gripper would pull the toe fabric down in the front, and when you pushed down a little more, two more catchers would come up and bring the corners over, and when the pedal went all the way down, the machine would inject the glue and clamp the fabric, and then it would pop off the machine: the boot had a toe.

This all happened within a matter of seconds, and you had to be careful not to get your fingers caught in the machine; there were no safety guards of any sort, because there was no way to get the fabric into the machine but to have your hands right in there guiding it, and no way to get your hands in there with heavy gloves on. Some people lost fingers; John Hutchison only lost a chunk of his left thumb.

You did as many as five hundred or six hundred pairs of boots in an eight-hour shift. John worked the overnight shift; during the day, he was also working at the Advance Auto Parts in town. At Rocky, he made $13 an hour—which was more than he could hope to make just about anywhere in Nelsonville in the late-1990s. It was also double what Rocky's workers were making in Puerto Rico, and ten times what they were making in the Dominican Republic.

By the turn of the century, this yawning differential was no longer endurable for Mike Brooks and the shareholders to whom he answered. In March 2000, the company announced that it was cutting half of its 112 factory jobs and shifting the work to the Caribbean. A year and a half later, a week after the September 11 attacks, Brooks called a meeting and announced the factory was shutting down completely, laying off the remaining 67 people working there.

Rocky Shoes & Boots would stay in Nelsonville. But Rocky boots would no longer be made in Nelsonville. The company's products would be made in Puerto Rico and the Dominican Republic and eventually also in China, Jordan, and Vietnam. The announcement left a cloud of ambivalence that would linger over the town for years: sorrow over the loss of factory jobs leavened by the fact that the headquarters would remain, never mind if it seemed as if many of the people in those jobs didn't deign to live in Nelsonville but commuted from Athens or Lancaster or even farther away. There would also still be the factory outlet store and a warehouse up in Logan: about 160 jobs total.

John Hutchison felt no such ambivalence. "It's greed. Corporate greed. That's exactly what it is," he said years later. "They could still have manufacturing jobs in this town, but they wouldn't be as profitable as they are."

The last pair of boots went down the line at 2:00 p.m. on November 21. The day-shift workers lined up to clock out for the last time, while their managers, who were also losing their jobs, moved up and down the line for hugs and handshakes. Mike Brooks stayed in his office.

And with that, the last shoe factory in Ohio—a state that had once had more shoe jobs than any other state—was gone. In 1960, more than 95 percent of shoes sold in America were made in America; by 2002, it was the reverse: more than 95 percent of shoes sold in America were made elsewhere, mostly in China.

Three months after the closure, in late February 2002, Mike Brooks boasted of the company's improved bottom line in a quarterly earnings call with market analysts. "The significant reduction in our operating costs this past year allowed us to improve our financial results in a difficult retail environment," he said. "We anticipate the recent realignment of manufacturing operations will favorably influence our performance in the Year 2002 as we begin to realize the full benefits from that strategic decision."

John and Bridget had married in 1998. But by the time of the shutdown, they had split. John decided to leave town in search of decent work. And in Ohio in the first decade of the new century, that meant going to Columbus.

The country had always had its pockets of rural poverty, of course. But by the second decade of this century, rural and small-town America was in a broad decline. It was unlike anything it had experienced since the offspring of farm families had started fleeing to cities en masse a century earlier. From 2010 to 2018, as the country's population increased by 6 percent, some 1,653 counties lost population, a larger number than the 1,489 counties that experienced growth. Rural areas and towns with populations under 50,000 saw employment fall in the decade between 2008 and 2017, a period during which it grew by 9 percent in the country's largest cities. There was no shortage of explanations at the ready, including the demise of resource-based industries, such as Appalachian coal, or the offshoring of small-town manufacturing, like footwear.

Often overlooked, though, was the trend that cut across all sorts of industries, from agriculture to retail: consolidation. To grasp the role that market concentration was having in small towns and cities, it helped to understand how much growth in those places had been driven by the opposite dynamic years earlier: dispersal. For decades, commerce and prosperity had extended across the country through the initiative of countless businesspeople staking out a venture in their own town or territory. Even as the more successful of these concerns had grown into regional forces, they had maintained some of their local roots and investment. And one way to understand the power of that dispersal and regionalism was through the story of the Bon-Ton.

In late 1897, Max Grumbacher sent a letter from York, Pennsylvania, to his father, Samuel. "I think we will do a good business here," he wrote. "Everybody seems to think that there is opening for a live concern. . . . You can rest assured that I will hustle and get open as soon as possible."

Samuel Grumbacher was four years old when his family emigrated from Germany in 1847, at the leading edge of the great midcentury exodus from Central Europe prompted by crop failures and foiled revolutions. A half century later, established as a merchant in Trenton, New Jersey, he had sent his two sons and two sons-in-law to stake out territory, like the king in a fairy tale. The targets were the fast-growing small cities of eastern Pennsylvania. One was sent to Hazleton, one to Lebanon, one to Lancaster. Max was sent to York, between Harrisburg and Baltimore, which, with hundreds of manufacturing businesses—among them an ironworks and the York

Motor Car Company, the maker of the Pullman automobile—would more than double in population, to 34,000, between 1880 and 1900.

The family's business was dry goods. Ready-to-wear clothing was still scarce; the Grumbachers sold fabrics on the bolt, with clerks on hand to assist with cutting and measuring and a deliveryman ready to carry home large orders by horse and wagon. It was in hats, though, that Max Grumbacher would distinguish his shop. Each season he brought in two professional milliners from New York to produce designs representing the latest styles, which would then be adopted by the shop's own milliners. And, as he made sure to mention in all the store's advertisements, the shop trimmed hats free of charge.

The York shop, like the other three, was called the Bon-Ton. This was a not-uncommon name for dry-goods stores. Discount stores were often Bon Marché—good buy, affordable—while their more stylish cousins were often Bon Ton—good form, fashionable. York, awash in prosperity, responded well to this aspirational allure, and Max Grumbacher quickly outgrew his rented one-room shop on Market Street. In 1912, the store moved into a resplendent new building at the corner of Market and Beaver Streets, a four-story terra-cotta extravaganza with twenty-seven departments spread across 37,000 square feet (bedding and housewares, stationery, cloaks and suits, corsets...), and elevators operated by smartly clad women that had little seats that pulled out, and, in case anyone might confuse this Bon-Ton with some of the others, the name GRUMBACHER set in dark lettering below the roofline.

This was the golden era of the downtown department store: Lord & Taylor and Bloomingdale's in New York; Marshall Field in Chicago; Wanamaker's in Philadelphia; Hochschild, Kohn & Co. and Hutzler's in Baltimore; F&R Lazarus in Columbus, where a shopper once called Robert Lazarus at home to say that he and his wife had bought an elegant tea set at his store but weren't sure what the proper etiquette was for using it. These stores were a destination, emporiums of experience as well as consumption: the average visit in the late nineteenth century lasted two hours. The bold statement inherent in the Bon-Ton was that a small city like York deserved such delectation, too. PUBLIC CONVENIENCE—A STORE FOR THE PEOPLE, declared the billboard announcing the grand opening on March 20, 1912.

The claim to a "public" purpose was no ad-copy hyperbole—very quickly, the Bon-Ton assumed the role of a central meeting place, with businessmen and society women flocking to the tea room on the mezzanine overlooking the main selling floor; the most sought-after seats were at the railing. By 1923, when the company celebrated its twenty-fifth anniversary with a dinner for all its employees, the store was hiring a local orchestra to entertain guests on Friday and Saturday afternoons. Every Christmas season, elaborate window displays were bought secondhand from New York, and the store played host to a parade that culminated with Santa Claus being raised over the crowd on a hook-and-ladder fire truck.

Max Grumbacher moved with his new wife, Daisy Altshul of Baltimore, and their growing family to a forty-acre estate outside town, but stayed invested in town affairs—he cofounded a synagogue and the local chamber of commerce. Employees were welcomed to the estate for summer picnics; his and Daisy's kids worked alongside them at the store, starting in the candy department.

They were as prepared as they could be, then, when Max suffered a stroke. His son Tom skipped college to carry the Bon-Ton through the Depression, when sales plunged by more than half between 1929 and 1932 and the company yet managed to pay out $2,100 in bonuses in 1930, and then through the Second World War, when the store found customer-friendly ways to ration controlled goods like hosiery and hawked war bonds from its display window.

The Bon-Ton not only came through all this upheaval still standing—it came through it in a position to expand during the postwar boom. In 1946, it opened a store in Hanover, twenty miles to the southwest. Two years after that, it bought the Eyerly's department store in Hagerstown, Maryland.

Tom Grumbacher discerned the same opportunity his grandfather had half a century earlier: to serve the small outlying cities, to show that people in these places had an eye for the finer things, that urbanity existed beyond the metropolis.

Taylor Sappington was a few hours into his shift at the Texas Roadhouse in Athens, a dozen miles from Nelsonville, when he witnessed the Incident with the Fork. A man had come in with his wife and his son, who looked to be around thirteen. They seemed in a rush and had taken a booth in the bar area, maybe for faster service. But by the time the food came, father and mother were already gone, sailing away on their opiate high. Which was not unheard of in Southeast Ohio, even on a family outing at a family restaurant.

More unusual was what came next: the father slumped over his plate in such a way that his brow fell onto the fork clutched upright in his hand. The flat end of the fork propped up his head like a tentpole. It was funny, in an awful way.

What really stayed with Taylor Sappington was the kid. With both his parents passed out at the table, the boy took control of the situation, as if he'd been through this before. He spoke with the cop who arrived at the restaurant. He asked for a container to pack up his parents' uneaten dinners. And then he pulled his dad's wallet out of his dad's pocket to pay the bill.

For Taylor Sappington, who was barely more than a decade older than that kid, it was another of the small calamities he had witnessed in and around the place he had grown up in and had, against expectations, decided to return to. He had left Nelsonville for college in the nation's capital. Surely, a young man raised by a single mother in a manufactured home in an isolated clearing in the woods near his grandparents' house would not look back after finding so gilded an escape hatch as a scholarship to George Washington University, one of the country's most expensive institutions of higher learning.

But Taylor Sappington had come back, after two years, alienated by so much of what he found in Washington. The casual mentions of classmates' fathers' executive titles at multinational corporations. The blithe assumption that he could afford a $50 cover charge at a club. Above all, the dead-eyed look of all those Washington suits as they rushed down the crowded sidewalks, clutching smartphones or plastic clamshell salad containers from one of the ubiquitous fast-casual restaurant chains.

He tried to explain that look, how demoralizing it was, to people back home, but was unable to. "Everyone's unhappy here," he'd say. "Nobody talks to each other. What *is* this city?"

They would tell him he was being oversensitive. "No," he'd say. "You don't understand. You have to be there."

He came home after his sophomore year and finished up at Ohio University, in Athens. He moved back in with his mother, who was working as a substance abuse counselor. He worked for the Ohio campaign to reelect Barack Obama. He fell in love with a man, Jared, who had studied physics at OU and was so passionate about the subject that he filled notebooks with theories yet somehow hadn't been able to finish his degree. Taylor moved in with Jared and his own brother, Spencer, a correctional officer, in a rental house on Poplar Street in Nelsonville, where Jared spent his spare time teaching himself to make furniture and musical instruments.

And then Taylor decided to not only stay in that place, but to become of the place. In December 2014, one month after Democrats had suffered another brutal setback in the midterm elections, he announced his candidacy for the Nelsonville city council. Jared cut out the *Athens Messenger* article about the announcement and stuck it on the wall in the apartment with a cursive note added: "Good luck. You'll do great."

Taylor campaigned hard, trying the best he could to make it to every door in town. Sometimes, as he climbed onto the porch of one of the dilapidated Victorians with trash piled in the yard and listing front steps, he'd look down on his voter list and recognize the last name as that of a classmate at Nelsonville-York High School. It startled him to think that those kids, who had seemed part of the general middle-class mix of his middle-American town, should have relatives living in such squalor. He knew it shouldn't have startled him, because he'd known all along that those houses existed, and it only stood to reason that he'd know some of the families in them. Still, it came as a shock. "They were recognizable names," he said later, "but in unrecognizable homes."

But the door-to-door visits had also invigorated him, reminded him why he had embarked on this unusual first post-college job. Taylor Sappington still believed in government, in its power to make people's lives better. He wasn't sure how he had come by this conviction—most of his extended family growing up had liked to sit around ripping on liberals.

Maybe it was his mom who had set him on a different path. She'd voted for Reagan and even George W. Bush once, but had always had an independent, feisty streak, going all the way back to when she'd gotten a reputation as a firebrand as a young arbitrator in the state employees union. Back then, she'd made a habit of striding into union meetings late in her tall boots, as if to let the all-male assemblage know how little deference she felt toward it.

Or maybe what did it was the night of March 19, 2003, when he was eleven years old and his mom let him stay up to watch Shock and Awe, and instead of marveling at the display, he'd been appalled by it, one Baghdad neighborhood after another going up in smoke.

Or maybe it was the book he read on Bobby Kennedy when he was sixteen years old, the one about the 1968 campaign. *If we believe that we, as Americans, are bound together by a common concern for each other, then an urgent national priority is upon us. We must end the disgrace of this other America.* He devoured the book, wrote his junior-year essay on it, then read it all over again. *But even if we act to erase material poverty there is another great task. It is to confront the poverty of satisfaction—a lack of purpose and dignity—that inflicts us all. Too much and too long we seem to have surrendered community excellence and community values in the mere accumulation of material things.*

Whatever it was, by the time of his first run for office, Taylor had discovered his identity as a latter-day New Deal Democrat, a style that might've looked precious on someone else his age somewhere else, but seemed less out of place on a young man in Nelsonville, a place whose historical peak had come at a time not that far removed from the days when Franklin Roosevelt's Works Progress Administration laid the water pipes through town.

By the time Taylor returned to Nelsonville, more than a third of its population was living under the poverty line, one of the highest rates in all Ohio. The bricks were still there, a curiosity for any traveler who happened through town—a rarer occurrence after the Route 33 bypass opened in 2013. Taylor liked some bricks in particular, the ones scattered here and there that were imprinted with PROGRESS. He took a picture of himself standing over some of them, two feet in running shoes bracketing the word. If he had been able to afford campaign posters, this might have been the art for it.

The election was on November 3, 2015. The top three vote-getters of the five candidates running would win seats on the council. It was an off-off-year election—not only not a presidential year, but also not the midterm year. Yet somehow the council campaign had stirred enough interest that for the first time on record, turnout for the municipal election had been higher than the utterly abysmal turnout for the election the year before, when the governor, congressmen, and state legislators had been on the ballot.

Taylor organized an election-return-watching party at the Mine, a bar that had looked out onto the square since the 1840s. Though there weren't really returns to watch—to get the tallies, one had to go to the two polling locations: the library and the Wesleyan church. He had gone with Jared, and had come back to the Mine with a long face.

"Well?" asked his mother, Amy.

"I lost," he said.

He took in her dismay, but he couldn't hold it. "I'm just kidding."

"How many votes?" Amy asked.

"First place."

B it by bit, the Bon-Ton extended its reach across the small cities of Pennsylvania and surrounding states: Lewistown, Pennsylvania, in 1957; Martinsburg, West Virginia, in 1961; Chambersburg, Pennsylvania, that same year. The most consequential expansion of that period, though, came right in York. Tom Grumbacher was intrigued by discount retailing and decided to experiment by partnering with Stanley Mailman, a local seller of what were called "hardlines"—appliances, paint, TVs, tools. In 1962, the partnership opened the first Mailman's, offering both discount apparel and discount hardlines. They opened it not in downtown York but at the new Queensgate Shopping Center on the edge of town.

The store flourished, which persuaded Grumbacher not only to expand his discount offerings—he assigned his son Tim to Mailman's once he was out of the army in 1964—but also to focus growth in the suburbs. Sprawl and white flight were in full force by the mid-1960s, even in small cities such as York, and Grumbacher saw no way to fight the tide, regardless of how attached the company was to its terra-cotta flagship at Market and Beaver. In 1969, the company opened an anchor store in the new North Mall; in 1975, it added a branch in York Mall on the eastern edge of town; and in 1981, with traffic dwindling ever further on the downtown grid, it closed the flagship, tea room and all. "People weren't coming downtown anymore," Tim Grumbacher said years later. "That was really the rise of the mall: the downfall of the cities."

The company's concession to suburbanization did nothing to alter the fundamental mission of serving small American cities. "Small towns want the same thing everyone else does," said one of the company's non-Grumbacher executives. "The difference now is that they no longer have to travel an hour and a half to get them." The expansion continued steadily throughout the 1980s, about a store per year, for a total of twenty-five by 1987.

By this point, Tom had passed control of the company to Tim, who was less risk-averse than his Depression-imprinted father. Tim believed the only way to avoid being devoured by giants like the May Company was to get bigger. In 1987, the Bon-Ton bought the thirteen-unit Pomeroy's chain, based in Harrisburg, sending the company from $150 million in sales volume to $250 million. Tom was so aggrieved over the debt being assumed that he didn't speak to Tim for two years. In 1991, to fuel further expansion, Tim took the company public. The IPO's success mollified Tom. "Dad started talking to me again," said Tim.

Now came the real expansion. The Bon-Ton set its sights on Hess's, a thirty-store chain based in Allentown, Pennsylvania, as well as family-owned department stores in Buffalo (AM&A's), Rochester (McCurdy's), and Syracuse (Chappell's), larger cities than it had previously entered. This put the company in direct conflict with the May colossus, which was angling for the same stores, possibly with the intention of closing them so as to reduce competition for its nearby stores. May was raking in $11 billion in sales from its 302 department stores and 4,000 shoe stores, more than thirty times what the Bon-Ton was bringing in as one of the last independent department store chains in the country.

But the Bon-Ton was undaunted, going so far as to file an antitrust suit that won it an injunction against May. By the end of 1994, the Bon-Ton had won control of many of the stores it was seeking, doubling its count to sixty-nine. These were the years of what would come to be seen later as the great overbuilding in retail: malls and strip plazas and big-box centers metastasizing across the land, fueled by tax laws that rewarded sprawl development.

At this new scale, certain touches were lost. No longer could Tim review every employee's annual evaluation, as he'd done until 1988. No longer could the company close stores for employee picnics. But it did what it could to retain the earlier spirit—the customer service of those free hat trimmings, the kindly paternalism toward employees, the tending of local roots. It was notoriously lenient in its return policy. It offered free fashion seminars as part of its push toward a more polished vibe in the 1990s, as competition grew at the discount end. There were champagne receptions for new product lines. Clerks received intensive training; one in Ithaca, New York, became a company legend for outfitting a woman head to toe for a wedding she was to attend in two hours.

It was made clear to managers at the company's newly acquired stores that they were to treat employees with respect, to listen to what they had to say, or else. It was, Tim Grumbacher admitted later, a self-interested policy: clerks who were treated well treated customers better. And the company did what it could to replicate its civic engagement in York in the other cities it arrived in—every store opening was preceded by a "Charity Day" when local groups could sell tickets for a preview day, and the company foundation asked branch managers in each town for suggestions on nonprofits to support. "Yes, it's tough to donate your resources when your major competitors don't," Tim said in the late 1990s. "But if I had to be like those other companies to survive, I wouldn't want to stay in business."

Years later, Nick Hanauer, the early investor in Amazon, would point to exactly this corporate impulse by companies like the Bon-Ton as an underappreciated asset. "Regional department stores, you used to have regional *everything*, right?" he said. "Some of those people who owned those companies were greedy fucks, too. But at least the money was in Cincinnati, or, pick it, at least those people donated to the local schools. At least there was an anchor of prosperity in these places. But now everything is in Seattle or San Francisco or Los Angeles or Chicago, and all that stuff got sucked out."

In 1998, the Bon Ton's one hundredth anniversary, it filed a secondary stock offering to raise capital for further growth. Company leaders speculated they might soon reach $1 billion in sales. In 2003 came the biggest expansion yet: the Bon-Ton won a bidding war for Elder-Beerman, based in Dayton, Ohio.

Elder-Beerman had grown from its grand store in the 1896 tower at Main and Fourth Streets in Dayton to 6,100 employees and 68 stores, nearly as many as the Bon-Ton's 8,700 and 72. The stores were spread across Ohio, Michigan, Indiana, Illinois, Kentucky, Pennsylvania, West Virginia, and Wisconsin.

One of its Ohio stores was in Athens County, on the State Street strip, in the same shopping plaza where Taylor Sappington would go work at Texas Roadhouse a decade later.

In one sense, life barely changed for Taylor after winning election to city council. It was not a paying job—well, aside from the $100 monthly stipend—so he kept working five or six shifts per week at the Roadhouse. It was hard work, but it paid as well as anything else he could hope to get in the area, close to $200 on really good weekend nights, and the experience was not irrelevant to what he was starting to realize would be his vocation. Approaching a strange house while canvassing was not unlike approaching a table of five guys who were wrapping up a hunting weekend and visibly upset that they would not be served by one of the attractive young women who predominated on the Roadhouse staff. Taylor took pride in his ability to win them over to the point of guffaws and a fat tip, and knew that this ability had applicability to his new line of work.

But the tolerance for the difficult shift work wasn't merely a matter of expediency. He liked the camaraderie—his boss, Deedra, who called him Tay-Sap; Joan, who was in her sixties and had gone back to work after her husband died; the eager young women who'd come to the university from elsewhere in the state.

On Saturday nights, after closing up, many of them would gather down at the other end of the State Street commercial strip, at Applebee's, which didn't close until 1:00 a.m. Jared worked at Ruby Tuesday—no way was he going to join in the staff line dances or don a superhero costume for kids' night, as Roadhouse servers were expected to; he wouldn't even let Taylor watch him play his self-built violin. But he would sometimes come over to Applebee's, too.

Taylor's night off was Monday, because that's when the council meetings were, on the second and fourth week of the month. Committee meetings—he was chair of the streets committee—were scheduled ad hoc. And there was a lot of extra time spent on the role around the edges, too, because it was shaping up as an eventful first year in office. The council hired a new city manager and removed its police chief. There was a big hole in the budget, the result of deep cuts in municipal aid from the state government and the erosion of a tax base whose decline neatly tracked the decline of the city's population.

Taylor, the youngest member of the council by two decades, caused instant friction. At his very first meeting, with his mother and brother in attendance to watch his swearing in, he had demanded to know why he and his fellow new arrival, Ed Mash, were being asked to vote on a budget proposal they'd never seen before. He upset his more senior colleagues a few months later with his proposal that the city be required by ordinance to balance its budget, to prevent further raids on its dwindling reserves; one council member found the proposal so presumptuous that he lunged across the table at Taylor during a closed-door session, nearly striking him.

Even more controversial was Taylor's notion that the city consider returning from a city manager to an elected mayor, to make the government more accountable. This was seen as all the more subversive considering that the city manager, Gary Edwards, was a member of the second-most powerful family in town and allied with its most powerful, the Brooks family, owners of Rocky Shoes & Boots, now known as Rocky Brands. Even with most of its workforce now located in the Far East and Caribbean, Rocky remained the biggest employer in town, and Mike Brooks demanded the deference that he believed should come with that.

Overlaid on Taylor's fights on the council that first year in office was his disquiet over what was happening around him as the race for the president of the United States grew closer.

Southeastern Ohio had been Democratic territory since the days of FDR. Even as most of the rest of Appalachia had flipped to Republican over the past couple decades, this corner had lagged in the shift. In 2008, Athens County had given Barack Obama nearly two-thirds of its vote. In 2012, even as Obama's nationwide and statewide margin had narrowed, even as he had lost the rest of Appalachia by even more than he had the first time around, his share of the vote in Athens County was unchanged.

And his strength in the area was not only about the college-town liberals down in Athens proper. Obama had won Nelsonville itself by forty points in 2012. Voters in this virtually all-white town, filled with the sort of working-class white Americans with whom Democrats were supposedly losing touch, had seen in Barack Hussein Obama someone who was more on their side than Willard Mitt Romney. Taylor had seen a similar dynamic in his work for the Obama campaign that year, which had him up in the Canton area, in charge of organizing supporters in Alliance and Minerva.

But in 2016, something else was happening. Taylor saw a conspicuous lack of enthusiasm for Obama's anointed successor, Hillary Clinton. In the primaries, he noticed Democrats drifting to Bernie Sanders. And as time went on, he saw more and more people who had voted for Obama drifting in a more unfathomable direction, to Donald Trump.

Taylor Sappington was appalled by this drift, but also understood why it was happening. He saw the ugly veins that Trump was tapping into. But he also saw what else Trump was tapping into—the sense that this part of the country had been left far behind the rising islands of prosperity. Since the financial crisis, large cities like San Francisco, Boston, and New York with metro-area populations over 1 million had flourished, accounting for nearly three-quarters of the nation's employment growth over the period. From 2010 to 2014, just twenty counties accounted for half the new business formation in the entire country. More than 44 percent of all digital-services jobs were in just ten metro areas.

By one count, a mere 1 percent of the country's job and population growth since 2008 had occurred in counties lacking a city of at least 50,000 people, which described Taylor's county. Meanwhile, the share of the working-age population with a college degree was now 15 percentage points higher in cities than in rural areas, a gap more than a third as large as it had been in 2000. And there was no sign that these trends would slow or reverse anytime soon. A report by McKinsey Global Institute would soon predict that twenty-five cities and high-growth hubs would generate 60 percent of all job growth through 2030, while fifty-four trailing cities and rural areas, where one-fourth of Americans lived, would have zero growth.

There were different factors fueling wealth in New York and Washington, D.C., and the Bay Area, but one thing the cities had in common was that as they had become much more prosperous, they had also become more Democratic. The party had increasingly become the party of the thriving, urbane upper-middle class. This was why it seemed entirely natural when the 2016 Democratic National Convention celebrated the progress being made in cosmopolitan America, almost as if places like Nelsonville did not exist. And why it was not so surprising that people in places like Nelsonville who did not recognize themselves in that celebration would be drawn to someone whose message, by contrast, spoke directly to the darkness they saw around them.

On Election Day, Donald Trump won 46 percent of the vote in Nelsonville, one point more than the 45 percent received by Hillary Clinton. His win was more by default than acclamation—he had drawn 30 percent fewer votes than Obama had gotten in town four years earlier. Clinton's share of the vote represented a stunning twenty-two-percentage-point fall from the Democratic share in 2012—one of the larger collapses in the country. Nationwide, Trump won eighteen of the twenty poorest states in the country, ranked by median household income, while nine of the ten wealthiest went for Clinton. Trump won 61 percent of rural voters, and also a majority of voters in metro areas with populations under 250,000.

Taylor Sappington watched the returns come in with Jared and another friend. Taylor had seen enough around Nelsonville to figure out that Trump would likely win Ohio, but was still unprepared for that night. At some point in those hours of rising dread, somewhere between the loss of Florida and loss of Wisconsin, he had sent out a tweet from his handle, @IdealsWin. It read: "Nov 8. Don't forget to set your clocks back 60 years tonight."

He and Jared finally headed out around 3:00 a.m. It was not only a miserable drive back on Route 33 to Nelsonville, but a tense one. Jared was not nearly as politically minded as Taylor, and while he was upset, too, he could not conceive of the gloom into which Taylor had been cast, and was clearly irked by it.

Taylor might have given Jared's distance more thought, but in that moment and the days to come, he was lost to the ramifications of what had just happened. It was becoming clear that the shocked uproar in the nation's coastal hubs over Trump's election was producing in many quarters an instant revulsion toward the parts of the country that had made him president. Rather than reckon with the role that their distance from left-behind regions might have played in the election, and about ways to correct for that, many liberals in prosperous redoubts were moving sharply in the opposite direction.

It was time, they said, to pull the plug on these places, economically and politically. Time had passed them by, their original reason for being—whether it was a coal seam or a canal or a railroad—had long since vanished, and if people there could not recognize this fact and move to places of greater opportunity, then there was little to be done for them. And their predilections in the 2016 election suggested that any further effort by the Democratic Party—the party of enlightenment—to win their support was utter waste. "Maybe," wrote Frank Rich in *New York* magazine, "they'll keep voting against their own interests until the industrial poisons left unregulated by their favored politicians finish them off altogether. Either way, the best course for Democrats may be to respect their right to choose."

Taylor saw this movement and knew that it was his mission to stop it. He would do whatever he could to keep that other America—the one he had inhabited for those two years in Washington, D.C.—from giving up on his America. It would prove that there was still the potential for a certain sort of prosperity in his place, and for a certain sort of liberal decency. And along the way, he might be one of the people rebuilding his party the way it was now apparent it would need to be rebuilt: from the ground up.

As Taylor was working this over, the distance from Jared that he perceived on election night persisted. Two days after Trump's win, Jared didn't come home for the night. Or the night after that. When Taylor finally reached him, Jared said that he was hanging out with some friends. This went on for weeks.

It had taken Taylor a while to grasp that what was happening was not really about them, but about his boyfriend. Jared had struggled with bouts of depression during their three-and-a-half-year relationship—it was likely a reason he had never finished his degree at OU—but this was of a different level.

By December, Jared was trying to reunite. One week before Christmas, he texted after midnight, as Taylor was watching *The Office* reruns. He asked if he could come over; the exchange ended inconclusively at 2:23 a.m.

Taylor got up the next morning and called his mom to suggest that they invite Jared over for Christmas and prepare a room for him at her house. He then went looking for him—something in the exchange of the night prior had made it sound as if Jared was staying somewhere close by.

It was very cold out. Taylor had gotten about a block, to Walnut Street, when he saw the car that belonged to Deedra, his boss from the Roadhouse. It pulled over. Inside were Deedra and Joan, the nice older waitress. They rolled down their windows. Joan started to speak but couldn't. Deedra broke in.

"What are you doing?" she asked Taylor.

"I'm looking for Jared," he said.

"He killed himself last night," Deedra said.

They had found him behind the Ruby Tuesday at 6:00 a.m. He was twenty-five years old.

Taylor Sappington lost his balance and crumpled to the bricks.

Sometimes, people who had lost their livelihood in declining small towns did manage to get themselves to thriving cities. But it was never as easy a transition as the economists would have one believe.

In Columbus, John Hutchison got a job working on the loading dock at Roadway, and while he was doing that he started teaching himself how to drive a truck, to get himself off the dock. He passed the test and got his CDL, joining the ranks of the nation's 1.67 million commercial truck drivers. But then in 2003, Yellow Corporation bought Roadway, they dovetailed the seniority lists for the two companies, and anyone with less than twenty-five years was out. John got a part-time job driving a tractor trailer for UPS, but they weren't hiring full time.

While he was living in Columbus, John met a woman online. They married, and they had a daughter.

Finally, in 2011, John got hired at Holland, the freight company founded in the western Michigan town of that name, which had grown to 7,500 employees, 53 terminals, and 6,500 trailers, and had, in 2005, become part of the same giant holding company as Yellow Transportation and Roadway, YRC Worldwide.

A decade after the shutdown at Rocky Shoes & Boots, John was established at last. Holland didn't pay as well as other trucking companies in town, barely more than $20 per hour, but it was a union job—Teamsters—which came with some protections for seniority and scheduling.

The main problem now wasn't the job. It was that he didn't like Columbus. He didn't like the traffic and the anonymity; he missed the hills. Around the same time as he started at Holland, he split with his second wife and moved back to Nelsonville. A few years later, he reunited with Bridget. She had developed chronic obstructive pulmonary disease after years of smoking and wasn't able to work much anymore. They remarried on New Year's Eve of 2015.

In returning to Nelsonville, John Hutchison was contributing to a striking nationwide trend that was confounding economists: despite the growing income gaps between regions, fewer people were moving from struggling areas to wealthier ones. Mobility hit the lowest mark on record in 2018—fewer than 10 percent of Americans moved that year, half the rate recorded in the 1950s. There was the role of the decline of the traditional two-parent household: it was more rational for John Steinbeck's Joad family to flee the Dust Bowl for California than for a single mom who relied on her mother or sister for childcare to pull up stakes and move with her children to an expensive city where she might get a better job but lack outside help. And there was the fact that workers without college degrees were gaining much less of an edge than they used to from being in large, expensive cities; while highly educated professionals could expect to make two or three times as much in big urban hubs, lower-wage workers were making barely more there than they would in other parts of the country, while paying much more for housing.

For others, like John, it was just barely possible to live in the one world and work in the other. He would leave home after the morning rush of traffic heading up Route 33 from all the depressed towns of southeastern Ohio—it was one thing to sit in traffic when he was being paid for it, but no way was he going to do it on his own time. He drove the seventy miles in his car and started his shift at the Holland terminal, way over on the western edge of Columbus, beyond I-270, the beltway, at about 11:00 a.m. His truck, a 2005 International day-cab semi, was loaded at the Number 95 dock, and he would set off with whatever goods were headed for his territory, the exurbs and small towns south of Columbus. The deliveries were eclectic in the extreme. On a given afternoon, he might drop off equestrian supplies, heaters for drying out grain, and HVAC parts for car repair. To him, it made no difference—it was all cardboard boxes. Whereas truckers like Todd Swallows, Sr., had once carried locally manufactured goods up the Midwestern supply chain, with value added every step of the way, John and his fellow truckers were engaged mostly in the final distribution of goods made elsewhere.

Sometimes he delivered to the state prison in Chillicothe, the same one to which Taylor Sappington's brother, Spencer, drove an hour to work as a correctional officer. The first time, John stopped the truck and sat in the prison yard waiting for the inmates to clear out so he could proceed.

"Just blow your horn and move," the guard said.

"You serious?" John said.

"Yeah, they'll move."

When he reached the unloading dock, inmates lined up, unbidden, to carry the pallets inside.

If John was lucky, he'd come back after the Columbus rush hour, and then he'd set off with more deliveries, often to one of the big-box distribution points or e-commerce warehouses along I-270. His typical day was ten or twelve hours—he'd sign off as late as 11:00 p.m. and then get in his car and drive the seventy miles back to Nelsonville. He put more than 35,000 miles on his car in a single year. He'd often not get home until quarter to one or so. Then a beer to settle down, and in bed by 2:00 a.m., and up the next morning by nine, and off again.

The other drivers would give him grief for it, his crazy routine. But when they did so, he would sometimes pull his phone out of his pocket and pull up a picture—the view onto the hill rising behind his and Bridget's house. He'd show them the picture. "Here's my backyard," he'd say.

Early in 2015, John received a message on Facebook. "Excuse me, sir," it read. "May have I have an hour of your time." It was from a young man whose name John did not recognize. He ignored the message.

The young man was undeterred. On Father's Day, he sent a note to Bridget, as well. Bridget called John over. "What do you think of this?" she asked him.

"I know nothing about it," he said. But he called the young man, whose name was Braden. He had John's class ring, Braden said. The more questions John asked, the more Braden seemed to know. John didn't recognize the woman's name Braden gave him, though. "I don't know her," John said. "I got no idea who your mom is."

Then Braden sent him a photo.

"I know your mom," John said.

He pieced it together. It was when he was just out of high school, before Rocky Shoes & Boots, and she was in college, at Ohio University. She had never mentioned it.

Shortly afterward, he met Braden, before Braden moved to Alabama. They got along well. They wouldn't become close, but they would exchange notes on birthdays and at Christmas. Like friends.

A year later, in 2016, John's mother and stepfather got DNA testing kits for the whole family for Christmas. Shortly afterward, John got an alert from the test-kit company that he had a "predicted sibling."

It was the younger sister his mother had given up for adoption. She lived an hour away and worked at a gas station. They met, and it was wonderful. In the space of less than two years, he had found a son he didn't know he had, and a sister he knew he did.

When the first Amazon Fulfillment warehouses in Ohio opened late in the summer of 2016, Taylor Sappington couldn't help but notice something about their location. Like the data centers, they were in the Columbus area, but in a different part of it—not in the more upscale exurbs on the northern edge, but in the humbler outlying areas to the south and east. The sites, in Obetz and Etna, were close to I-270—the beltway—and also to I-70, providing easy access to the east and west of the city. But they offered another advantage as well: they were close enough to the struggling towns of southern and eastern Ohio to be in plausible reach of a long commute for those desperate enough to undertake it. The company had, in a sense, segmented its workforce into classes and spread them across the map: there were its engineering and software-developer towns, there were the data-center towns, and there were the warehouse towns.

The calls started coming right away to the nearby first responders. West Licking Fire Station 3, three miles from the Etna warehouse, which was dubbed CMH1, was getting about one emergency call a day at first, then several a day once the holiday season ramped up, when workers were pressed to work up to sixty hours per week to get deliveries out in time. The calls ran the gamut: shortness of breath, chest pains, motley cuts and fractures. Some were more serious. One worker missed three weeks after a heavy item fell onto their foot from a pallet; another fractured a leg after getting a foot jammed between a reach truck and a guardrail.

Then there was the April 7, 2017, crash involving a forklift at the Obetz warehouse, CMH2. There weren't serious injuries, but a worker alerted OSHA a few weeks later that the forklift was being driven by someone who was legally blind. As a result, the worker wrote, "a lot of the employees are very concerned for there [sic] safety." OSHA investigated, and indeed, Amazon had assigned forklift-driving to someone who had failed the vision test for an Ohio driver's license—and it had another forklift driver in training who was also legally blind.

It was nothing that the local EMS and fire departments couldn't handle. What rankled them was that they were providing their services for free. The deal negotiated by Amazon and the state had freed the company from paying local property taxes—the taxes that paid for the functions of local government, from the schools to the police and fire departments—for fifteen years. The warehouses were in Licking and Franklin Counties, but they were not really of them. They drew many hundreds of cars and trucks onto local roads every day, and they put out the emergency calls, but Amazon paid for neither snowplows nor ambulances. The basic social compact applied to others, but not to them: in 2017, voters in the area served by West Licking Fire Station 3 would be asked to approve a five-year, $6.5 million property tax levy to keep the fire department going. They would be making up what the company withheld.

The taxpayer would have to make up for what the company did not provide in other ways, too. In 2018, it emerged that one in ten Amazon employees in Ohio was making so little on the job that they were receiving food stamps. Nationwide, the company was one of the top employers of food-stamp recipients in at least five states.

Yet the deals kept coming. A year after the state approved the Etna and Obetz deal, it gave Amazon a $270,000 tax credit to turn a former Chrysler plant in Twinsburg in northeast Ohio into a sorting facility with only ten full-time jobs, though with many more part-time ones during the holiday season. Twinsburg added a seven-year, 50 percent property tax exemption that would cost it $600,000, most of which would have gone toward its schools.

And the 2017 announcement of the subsidies for the new warehouse in Monroe, near Dayton, was paired with the announcement of even larger subsidies for another fulfillment center, in North Randall, southeast of Cleveland. In that instance, Amazon would be getting some $7.8 million from the state.

The North Randall warehouse would be on the site of the North Randall Mall, which had closed in 2009 and where demolition had begun five years later. Three weeks after the announcement, Amazon revealed it was building another warehouse in the Cleveland area, also at the site of a former shopping center, the Euclid Square Mall, which had closed the year before. And two years later, it would announce a warehouse at yet another dead Ohio mall, in Akron. In addition to the usual state subsidies, the city would grant a thirty-year tax rebate, reimbursing Amazon the more than $17 million it paid to buy the land plus other acquisition and demolition costs.

These locations were more than coincidental. Brick-and-mortar retail was reeling by the end of 2017. Nearly seven thousand stores closed that year, more than double the year prior. Toys "R" Us declared bankruptcy, at the eventual cost of 33,000 jobs, brought low by both the e-commerce revolution and mismanagement by private-equity owners who managed to profit off its final years. By late 2018, mall vacancies would reach their highest level since the Great Recession. Macy's alone had laid off more than 50,000 workers since 2008. Wall Street was predicting worse to come: by early 2018, the market valuation of Amazon was greater than that of Walmart, Costco, T.J. Maxx,

Target, Ross, Best Buy, Ulta Beauty, Kohl's, Nordstrom, Macy's, Bed Bath & Beyond, Saks/Lord & Taylor, Dillard's, JCPenney, and Sears combined.

In areas that were already struggling, the rash of mall closures hit especially hard. Some upscale malls were still holding their own, in places such as suburban New Jersey and Virginia—out of around one thousand malls in the United States, nearly half of the total value in malls resided with just one hundred properties. By one industry tally, more major malls died in Ohio over the previous decade than in any other state in the country. "It's not stores that are dying," wrote the business professor Scott Galloway, "but the middle class—and, in turn, the businesses that serve that once-great cohort and its neighborhoods."

Not many were crying over the loss of oceanic parking lots and windowless food courts. But the extinction was not wiping out only malls and strip plazas—it was also reaching stores in coherent downtowns, even in tony precincts of big cities like New York. And the trend was self-reinforcing—the fewer opportunities one had to meet one's needs in a physical space, buying goods face-to-face from another person in one's own town or city, the more likely one was to turn to the other option: shopping, often alone, from the comfort of home. Even before a global pandemic forced Americans to shop from home, they had increasing reason to do so: online shopping was appealing because it was more convenient than the competition. And it became even more relatively convenient as the competition vanished, leaving one with no other options in close proximity.

Jared's death left Taylor stunned and engulfed in self-reproach. Why had he not recognized his partner's sudden drift away as the depressive break that it was, rather than the fallout of a particularly melodramatic lovers' quarrel?

His mind cast over those final weeks, especially the time, about ten days prior, when Jared had shown up at the Roadhouse. Taylor had seen his car as he was walking toward his own after work; Jared had gotten out and walked toward him, and Taylor had noticed instantly that Jared's gait was different, almost as if he had forgotten how to walk. The sight had chilled Taylor somehow, but he had been oblivious to its import: Jared had grown so troubled that he was, quite viscerally, not himself.

Jared had asked if they could get back together. Taylor had said he wasn't sure about that yet.

"Do you want to see *Beauty and the Beast* with me?" Jared asked. It was going to be coming out soon.

"Yeah," Taylor said. "We can see a movie. I'd like that."

Taylor still remembered the light pole they had spoken under. He would never park under it again.

Taylor was especially hard on himself, his failure to comprehend, because the fact was that Jared's plight was hardly foreign. Suicide stalked Taylor's universe—rates were up by 30 percent nationwide since 2000, and the increases were especially large among young people and rural white people. Suicide was a primary element of what two economists called "deaths of despair"—the astonishing rise in mortality among white people without college degrees caused by suicide, alcoholism, and drug addiction, a trend that was concentrated heavily in Ohio and neighboring Pennsylvania, Kentucky, and Indiana. In just five years, from 2012 to 2017, death rates for white people between twenty-five and forty-four years old jumped by a fifth.

Taylor hadn't needed social scientists to identify the trend. His friend from high school who had fallen into opioid addiction after returning from serving with the army in Afghanistan had been arrested for trying to pawn his grandfather's heirloom rifle to pay for pills. There were all the people his mother tried to help in her job, day in and day out—after spending more than ten years working at the largest drug treatment center in the area, she was now working for an insurance company as a telephone counselor for young people who had attempted suicide. The world in which Taylor moved was one where young adulthood was fraught with peril, where standard actuarial tables were a thing for other people in other places.

Perhaps, then, it was because such losses were such a feature of the landscape that Taylor was able to absorb the trauma as readily as he did. Or perhaps it was something more self-protective, an awareness that the only way not to be overtaken by it—not to let Jared's death throw *him* into despair—was to commit himself further to the task he had set for himself, to try to lift up the place in which all these threats to longevity were running rampant. One week after Jared's death, the day after Christmas, he was back at the city council, where he got up during the hearing to speak about Jared, and about the need for better mental health care in rural Southeast Ohio.

"This is truly an epidemic, which I've become familiar with in the past seven days," he said. "Last Monday was the hardest day of my life. It was a day that we have seen so often across the country and in our communities. While grieving the loss of Jared, I thought often of the powerlessness of the situation, and how it's like a nightmare with no way or how to make it better."

"It's no coincidence," he went on, "that towns like ours have huge rates of depression, suicide, addiction, and other problems, just when mental health treatment is at its lowest. For us, it will take a village."

As he recalled this moment in days following, something stuck out to him: how the newly elected state representative for the area, Jay Edwards, had gotten up in the middle of his remarks about Jared and mental health and left the room.

There was history here. Jay was a scion of the second-most powerful family in town, the nephew of Gary Edwards, the city manager whose position Taylor had been seeking to eliminate. Jay was a few years ahead of Taylor in high school, the star quarterback on the same football program in which Taylor had been a bench-warming JV lineman. Jay had gone on to play linebacker at Ohio University, and had in 2016 decided to run as a Republican for the local state House seat that had been held for eight years by a popular Democrat who was leaving due to term limits. Jay had won by sixteen points, swept along by the Trump wave.

To Taylor, the Democrats' loss of that seat had been a particularly tangible example of the political shift he had set out to reverse. And the thought had probably already crossed his mind that this example was one that he, himself, could seek to correct in a direct way. But it was his recollection of that moment at the council meeting that had made it personal and set a notion smoldering in his mind for the year to come.

Fulfillment

It would be a daunting undertaking. He would be overmatched financially by Jay, who had raised enormous sums for his first run from business interests and was already raising more for his next one. But Taylor presumed he could count on traditional Democratic allies in organized labor and national progressive groups eager to reclaim lost ground.

He would have only so much time to devote to the effort. He was still working long hours at the Roadhouse, and even that wasn't enough to pay his bills—the Roadhouse, like many other big restaurant chains, made servers engage in more hours of untipped labor (cleaning up, helping in the kitchen) than was allowed under law. And his hours at the restaurant were also highly unpredictable, as had become the case for many low-wage workers around the country. So Taylor had taken another job on the side: fixing broken smartphone screens in a venture with his brother, the correctional officer.

He would also still be mired in all the conflict and intrigue of the city council, which gave him visibility but won him enemies. Somehow, at Taylor's urging, the town would scrounge together $200,000 for repairs of more than a dozen badly rutted streets, and he would also assist in the design of a $2.1 million renovation of the historic square, to try to make it more appealing to shoppers and visitors.

One day in August, eight months after Jared's death, Taylor's grandfather returned to his house in the woods, adjacent to the clearing on which Taylor's mom's manufactured home had stood. It was the house onto which Taylor and his brother had, as teenagers, helped build an addition for themselves and their mom to move into for their high school years.

There, in the living room, Taylor's grandfather discovered one of his grandsons, Taylor's cousin, who had been living in the house. He, too, had taken his life. He was nineteen years old.

Taylor grieved again. One month later, he informed Democratic Party officials in Columbus that he would challenge Jay Edwards for the Ninety-Fourth District of Ohio.

———

For a while, the expansion had continued at the Bon-Ton. The biggest purchase of all came in 2006: a $1.1 billion deal to buy 142 stores owned by what was then Saks, an assortment of formerly family-owned stores with names such as Carson Pirie Scott, Younkers, and Herberger's that stretched across the Midwest and Great Plains. The deal took the company's footprint as far west as Idaho. The thinking was that only by extending its reach could the company stave off decline or absorption.

But the expansion brought debt and interest payments that left less room to maneuver when the Great Recession hit a year later. The company had been through downturns, but this one was particularly devastating to the Bon-Ton's base, the small and midsize cities of the Northeast and Midwest.

And when these places finally emerged into something resembling a recovery, the company was facing an even more existential dilemma. American retail was shifting inexorably into the ether, or rather, into the ether that was linked to those government-subsidized warehouses in Etna and Obetz. In 2016, a major annual survey of five thousand shoppers by UPS found them reporting, for the first time, that they had made more than half of their purchases online. Over the first two decades of the century, online sales would rise from $5 billion per quarter to almost $155 billion per quarter—more than thirtyfold.

The Bon-Ton was hardly blind to this trend and had tried to build its own e-commerce operation. But its interest payments had left it with less to invest on this front. To survive in this new world, the analysts said, a department store chain needed to get its online sales up to around a quarter of the total. The Bon-Ton could barely manage half that. For one thing, it struggled with matching its biggest e-commerce rival when it came to delivery costs—it was hard to compete with the bulk discounts Amazon was getting from the postal service and others. Eventually, the Bon-Ton had even tried selling via Amazon, despite all the constraints on what it could sell and at what price. The company was also getting involved in real estate at some locations, doing what it could to help the struggling malls it called home to find ways to adapt and survive.

Fulfillment

As the post-recession decade wore on, the Bon-Ton watched losses pile up among larger rivals: By the end of 2017, well over half of the 3,800 Sears and Kmarts that existed a decade earlier were gone. Some workers from closed Sears or JCPenney or Kohl's stores would take a job at the Bon-Ton, and would invariably remark that the company was more pleasant to work for than the much bigger chains from which they'd come.

Collegiality only counted for so much by this point, though. In early 2018, 120 years after Max Grumbacher opened his shop on Market Street, the Bon-Ton, unable to make its latest interest payment, filed for Chapter 11 bankruptcy.

That April, the Bon-Ton went into liquidation. Everything went—the clothes, the household wares, the cash registers. It happened so quickly. The stores—all 262 of them, which had been doing $3 billion in sales not so long ago—closed that August. Surprisingly many of the employees stayed until the end—the firm that had been brought in to handle the liquidation couldn't stop talking about how helpful everyone was, how much easier they were to work with than those at other companies they'd dealt with.

Eight months later, Tim Grumbacher, now seventy-nine years old, sat at a Panera in York with his second wife, Debbie Simon, who had started out in the small-appliance department at one of the company's stores years earlier, and succeeded him as chairman when he retired.

"The great thing about retail was face-to-face. Not only with customers, but managers, with the associates that worked there," he said. "We had people who walked on the floor for fifty years. It was a community."

"The stores themselves were communities," she said.

"All these people that had jobs, I guess they found other places," he said.

"A lot landed on their feet," she said. "We didn't hear the stories from those who didn't."

"We still get letters," he said.

"I'm on a Facebook thing," she said. "The Bon-Ton Family." In York, there was also a monthly employee lunch, at Old Country Buffet.

"It was a community," he said. "It was a whole community."

The store at the West Manchester Mall, which had years ago super-seded the nearby North Mall, had closed back in 2011. West Manchester had been "de-malled" and was now a combination strip plaza and "life center."

The former terra-cotta flagship in downtown York had long since become something completely different: a human-services building that housed, among other county offices, adult probation, the drug and alcohol commission, and mental-health case management. The Grumbacher name had been removed from the facade. Visitors had to pass through metal detectors manned by a deputy sheriff who still recalled, as a boy, ogling the women in the cosmetics department and being told, when he didn't know what size socks he needed, to ball up his fist for a proxy measurement. The second story, which once held the tea room that looked out over the space, now held the Office of Children, Youth and Families.

Then there was the store at the Galleria, the more upscale mall that had opened in 1989 on the eastern edge of the city. The only anchors left there were a Marshalls and a Boscov's, the small Reading, Pennsylvania–based chain that was, it seemed, the last of the Bon-Ton's former breed.

"And Penney's," Tim Grumbacher said.

"Penney's is gone," Debbie Simon said.

"Kohl's. Who's at the other end?" he said.

"It's empty," she said.

Taylor Sappington set out with high hopes on November 6, 2018: Election Day.

His challenge of Jay Edwards had proved even more daunting than he expected. Most of the big institutional allies he had been counting on to support him had chosen otherwise. Nearly all the unions had, to his disbelief, sided with Edwards—not only the construction trades, which often favored Republicans, but the teachers union and the public employees union, to which his mom had belonged. Here he was, a member of the low-wage working class, and the unions were instead backing a prince of the local elite. They had made the calculation that Republican dominance in the Ohio legislature was so extreme that they needed to cultivate some friends, or at least non-enemies, among Republican legislators, instead of trying to actually help Democrats win back control.

Meanwhile, the state Democratic Party focused its efforts in the Columbus suburbs, and most nationwide progressive groups decided to steer clear of his race, drawing exactly the conclusion that Sappington had set out to disprove, that places like Appalachian Ohio were a lost cause. One group had sent him a package of dried apricots for moral support.

But he had put together a creditable campaign nonetheless. With the help of Ohio University film students, he had produced a powerful video, with evocative drone footage of Nelsonville. "Why is it that so many will grow up without parents because of this drug crisis? Why is it that our graduates struggle to find good-paying jobs?" he said in the video. "So much of this seems invisible in Columbus." He and his corps of volunteers had visited 31,000 homes. He had raised $80,000—far less than Edwards's $430,000, but enough for a state legislative race. And in August had come an extraordinary boost: an endorsement from Barack Obama, who included Taylor as one of eighty-one candidates nationwide to get his imprimatur.

Not to mention that it was shaping up to be a good election for Democrats. As Taylor set out that morning with two student volunteers, Jordan Kelley and Zach Reizes, to check turnout levels at polling stations, it was hard not to see confirmation that he might have caught a wave. The numbers in heavily Democratic Athens—the liberal college town and largest population center in the district—were far above prior years'.

But the giddiness ebbed as the trio headed into the outlying areas of the district. Taylor had affection for these places—they resembled the fringes of Nelsonville, where he had grown up, and he had put a lot of time into campaigning in them. When the Ohio River flooded in Pomeroy, in Meigs County, he had come to help out, spending hours moving the historical society's collection to higher ground. But the society's director had given money to Jay Edwards anyway. "I love Meigs," Taylor said. "It stings me that they're going to vote against me so heavily."

Turnout was strong out here, too—not off the charts, but showing little sign of Republican demoralization. "We're gonna have to go back to Athens and find it far higher," said one of the student volunteers, Reizes.

That evening, Taylor and his family and a few friends gathered at a cabin he'd rented in the woods to watch the results come in. His mom made chili. Taylor checked his laptop and saw great numbers from Athens, and then the brutal numbers from most everywhere else. The final tally would be 58–42, almost identical to Jay Edwards's win two years earlier.

He stepped outside the cabin to call Edwards to concede.

"Hi, Jay," he said. The connection wasn't great, and it was noisy wherever Edwards was. "It's Taylor."

"Taylor who?" Edwards said.

In a way, the loss changed very little. Taylor had been working at the Roadhouse right through the campaign—the night before Election Day, when he should've been making get-out-the-vote calls, he was instead attending a mandatory employee meeting. Now he kept on working there, signing up for longer hours to pay off bills that had piled up during the campaign.

One night, he came to one of his tables and found that it had been taken by Jay Edwards, his father, and several other guests. They were cordial enough, but it was awkward nonetheless. It got even more awkward when the kitchen accidentally dropped Jay's steak. Taylor was aghast.

"Why are you so upset about this?" one of the cooks asked.

"Because I'm going to go to explain why this happened and they're not going to believe me," he said.

The Elder-Beerman behind the Roadhouse remained vacant after it closed along with the rest of the stores owned by the Bon-Ton. It had been the last department store in Athens. One evening, the Roadhouse used it for a combination holiday and five-year anniversary party. They used dividers to seal off part of the cavernous space and conjure a festive venue.

Beyond that, though, lay an eerie expanse that struck Taylor as almost postapocalyptic.

I n Columbus, in January 2019, the Ohio Tax Credit Authority met for its monthly meeting to approve a new round of incentives. On this day, one order of business was to discuss whether to "claw back" incentives for employers that had failed to create jobs they had promised. One such employer was the now bankrupt Bon-Ton, which had received some incentives for a distribution warehouse in Obetz—the same town as one of the Amazon warehouses.

A JobsOhio employee recited the details of the original incentive.

The authority's chairwoman, Lydia Mihalik, shrugged. "Everyone knows retail is tough," she said. The authority voted unanimously to claw back the money.

It was tough, indeed. Sears had finally filed for bankruptcy a few months earlier and started the new year by closing another 80 stores. A month later, Payless would announce that it was closing all 2,100 of its stores nationwide, laying off 13,000 people. Four months into 2019, retailers had closed 6,105 stores, surpassing the total for all of 2018. Since 2012, no other occupation had shrunk more in number than retail salesperson; Scott Galloway, the business professor, put the number of retail job losses attributed to Amazon at about 76,000 per year. The company noted in return that it was hiring heavily to replace at least some of those jobs—that it, unlike rival giants like Facebook and Google, was employing hundreds of thousands of Americans across the country, far from the gilded tech capitals. In Ohio alone, it was up to 8,500 employees at its fulfillment centers and data centers. Yes, the jobs tended to be more physically taxing and isolating than the retail work they replaced. But they were still jobs.

By August 2019, the brick-and-mortar world would reach a telling threshold: about half of all retail openings over the prior six months were dollar stores and discount grocers. It was a sort of reversal of Henry Ford's philosophy in paying workers enough so that they could afford Model Ts—now workers were making so little that they could afford only the cheapest goods.

Elsewhere in retail, things were humming more than ever. Amazon had ended 2018 with profits exceeding its own Wall Street projections by more than $3 billion. Not surprisingly, demand for new freight trucks had soared all that year prior—in some months, it was double what it had been the year before. An online freight delivery service that matched loads to available trucks was seeing more than 500,000 loads on many days, twice the norm. Freight carriers were struggling to find and hold on to drivers, with annual turnover approaching 100 percent—it didn't help that many applicants were failing drug tests, that trucker pay had fallen over the years, and that it remained one of the most dangerous positions in the country, with truck drivers eight times as likely to be killed on the job as a cop.

One afternoon that April, John Hutchison picked up a load for Amazon. That morning, he'd been down in his usual territory to deliver medical supplies to McKesson, the giant medical distributor, and paint-making supplies to Sherwin-Williams. The day before, he'd made a rare trip north of Columbus that included bringing three skids of trees to a nursery.

"What kind of trees are they?" the man at the nursery had asked when he pulled in.

"I don't know what kind of trees they are, if they're watermelon or pumpkin trees," said John. "I just deliver them."

Now he headed with his new load from the Holland depot to the fulfillment center in Obetz. The warehouse was like the others around it, except larger. The first time he had seen it, he'd been so bowled over that he had FaceTimed with his wife, back in Nelsonville, to try to convey the scale to her.

There were flagpoles with three flags: Stars and Stripes, Ohio, and Amazon. One section of the parking lot was full of dark blue Prime delivery vans, plus U-Hauls and Penske rental trucks. A steady stream of semis pulled into the delivery entrance: DHL, EFL, UPS, USF . . .

And then came John Hutchison. He pulled up to the security checkpoint and handed over his papers for inspection. He drove on into the delivery lot, into the spot the checkpoint had assigned him, and unhitched his trailer.

On this day, he was bringing to Amazon:

- two skids from Liberty Hardware in Winston-Salem, North Carolina
- two skids from River of Goods home decor in St. Paul, Minnesota
- nine skids of bicycle parts from Dj's Boardshop in St. Paul
- five skids of plastic utility carts from Montpelier, Ohio
- three skids of aquarium parts from Spectrum Brands in Noblesville, Indiana

He walked across the big lot to the door where drivers dropped off their paperwork. Inside was a small area enclosed by a wire cage, about ten by ten feet. You weren't allowed to have your phone out in the cage. If there was no one around, he would scribble his parking-spot number on his paperwork and stick it into the cage. On this day, there were a couple Amazon workers sitting on the other side of the cage, so he slid it through to them.

He headed back to his truck. If there was an empty trailer from a prior run by a Holland driver, he'd hitch it up and bring it back—it made things easier for the women in the dispatch office. On this day, there were no empties. He pulled his truck back out, past the checkpoint, and headed to his next pickup, a trailer of lawn mowers and other outdoor power equipment at a warehouse a few miles away. He was driving over there, past a trailer park and a forlorn-looking church, when he was startled to see signs for an Amazon warehouse under construction. He was disoriented—hadn't he just left Amazon? But this one, at 3538 Tradeport Court, was in fact an entirely different location. It would be CMH6.

"Amazon's Profit More Than Doubles" read the headline in *The Wall Street Journal* that day. The company had posted a record $3.56 billion quarterly profit. It was expanding its logistics operations to fulfill its new pledge of making Prime deliveries in a single day.

John Hutchison drove on. He had hours of driving still ahead of him before returning down Route 33, into the hills, to Nelsonville.

9.

Delivery

The great forty-mile divide

Max Pollock had never been to Nelsonville, Ohio, but he knew about its bricks, and had in fact once ordered a few of them online, to add to his growing collection.

He had grown up near Washington, in the Maryland suburb of Takoma Park. His father worked at the State Department and a think tank; his mother owned a graphic design firm. He went to the University of Michigan and took the next step on the meritocratic ladder: law school, at the University of Pennsylvania.

But he hated law school, dropped out after only a month and a half, and went to work at a small design-build firm in Philadelphia, doing renovations in older houses, often with salvaged materials. He did that for two years and then headed to the London School of Economics for a master's degree in city design and social science, then returned to the Philadelphia job before an opportunity emerged to head back home to Washington, to do housing policy research at the Urban Institute, a think tank.

Except he found that he didn't care for D.C. Amid its swell of wealth, the city felt sanitized and stuffy. When his girlfriend got a job in Baltimore, he followed her, joining the legions who made the hour-long train commute to D.C. He had already grown tired of that routine after six months when a friend alerted him to an article about the Baltimore bricks.

His brick fixation was practically genetic. His mother's maiden name was Kirpich, which meant brick in Russian. His father would collect loose bricks coming home from work, putting them in his briefcase. Somewhere along the way, Max joined him in the hobby, looking out for good finds. He started to notice that some bricks had the names of the company or place of origin stamped on them. He learned about the epicenters of brickmaking—places like Nelsonville, and Haverstraw in New York's Hudson Valley. He'd sometimes play hooky from the Urban Institute and go looking for bricks—at first around D.C., later driving all the way up to Philly or the Hudson Valley.

Then he saw the *Baltimore Sun* article, about the potential salvage market for the city's bricks. Baltimore was fortuitously situated over a bed of excellent clay and had as a result developed a reputation for the high quality of its bricks during the boom years of the late nineteenth and early twentieth century. Silica and iron oxide in the shale gave local bricks an orangish, almost sunset hue. Baltimore's brickmaking industry had been boosted by geography in addition to geology: the city could ship bricks to other coastal cities, but was also the farthest west of the big coastal ports and thus best positioned to send bricks inland, via rail. By the first decade of the twentieth century, the Baltimore Brick Company, created out of the consolidation of many smaller firms, was producing an astonishing 150 million bricks per year, enough for some 10,000 homes.

A century later, Baltimore's bricks bore a new distinction: they were there for the taking, on a grand scale. By 2014, the city was estimated to have 16,000 vacant homes, most of them brick rowhouses, and city officials were making fitful progress in demolishing the most blighted blocks. This was creating a salvage market not only for those high-quality bricks, but also for the sought-after heart-pine flooring that prevailed in Baltimore homes, the result of another geographic quirk: as the most southern northern industrial city, Baltimore was closer to the great pine forests of the southern U.S. and thus more likely than northern counterparts to have prized heart-pine floorboards.

Demolitions were generating hundreds of thousands of bricks and board feet of lumber every year. The city didn't know what to do with it all. The April 2014 article in *The Sun* described a new contract between the city and a local workforce-development nonprofit, Humanim, and its construction arm, Details, to deconstruct dozens of homes a year and sell the salvaged materials—a minimum of 3,000 bricks and 1,200 board feet per home. Max Pollock sensed a chance to help the city he now called home, and to liberate himself from Washington for good. "I thought, 'I'll do that,'" he said later. "It just made too much sense."

He reached out to Humanim, offering to help it figure out what to do with the materials. He left Urban and joined Details. The group started with thirty-five homes in the 2400 block of East Eager Street, right along the Amtrak line, north of Johns Hopkins Hospital. They started hiring staff, mostly men from the same neighborhoods where the demolition was happening.

It was tough going at first. Bureaucratic approvals for the demolitions slowed to a trickle. The city wasn't paying enough to cover careful deconstruction, which cost several thousand dollars more per house than a regular demo, making it all the more important to find buyers willing to pay a good price for materials. Pollock was on his own trying to market them, working out of a warehouse next to a long-abandoned East Baltimore brewery that Humanim now called home. The warehouse had no electricity and a leaky roof; when it rained, it would flood. Details couldn't even afford a forklift; men were loading pickups by hand.

Eventually, the operation found its footing, helped by an infusion of funds—six months after killing the new transit line for West Baltimore, Governor Hogan announced that he *would* be willing to pay for the demolition of more vacant homes. Pollock set up a separate entity under Humanim to help market the materials: Brick + Board. Details and Brick + Board grew to thirty employees between them. By 2018, they had demolished close to 300 homes and salvaged 300,000 board feet of lumber and 1 million bricks.

Fulfillment

Max was not unambivalent about the work. He considered himself a pres-
ervationist, and it was hard to see homes that had stood for over a century,
that had been home to generations of families, being simply erased. But he
knew that the economics of restoring the homes didn't work in these neighborhoods: you'd spend $100,000 and you'd be lucky to get back half of that.
He also knew that most who lived in these neighborhoods were happy to
see the homes come down—they attracted vermin and squatters, some of
whom would be living in them right up until the moment of demolition. The
buildings could even kill: in 2016, a sixty-nine-year-old man sitting in his
Cadillac listening to Otis Redding had been crushed by a vacant home that
collapsed in high winds.

"When people walk by and see us, one hundred percent of them say,
'Good, they should've knocked this shit down years ago. They should do
the other side of the street next,'" Pollock said. "The preservationists are
like, 'But that cornice bracket!' If you live across the street and your kids
have to look at this every day, you're like, *fuck* the cornice bracket. I have
a hard time saying I'm pro-demolition, but if you're going to knock these
down, at least we're giving jobs for people."

His ambivalence was stronger, in fact, when it came to the other end of
the process, the delivery of the bricks and boards. Some of the buyers were
local, and they ran the gamut from the new Exelon Building at the harbor
to the guy around the corner who wanted to patch his floorboards. The out-
of-town buyers stretched up the East Coast, and there were even some in
the Midwest.

But the biggest source of out-of-town clients was just down the road:
Washington, D.C.

Forty miles. That's all it was between the two cities—two cities so close
that they shared a parkway and an airport, that one baseball team had
long sufficed for the two of them, that seventy-seven commuter trains ran
every day from one to the other. They had from the start been very different
cities—one an industrial heavyweight and harbor town with all the salt

and swagger that came with that, the other a seat of government, created for that very purpose out of the tidewater swamps, with a more circumspect and rarefied air, a city of offices and agencies, a city more concrete than brick. But they shared a rowhouse architecture, the nearby Chesapeake, and a strong Black culture, and had for decades been of similar scale—counterweights and complements, two sides of the American coin.

Increasingly, it was hard to believe they inhabited the same universe, much less the same region. There was no parallel for a divergence this extreme, two major American cities in such proximity headed on such opposite trajectories.

In Baltimore, the April 2015 death of Freddie Gray and the subsequent civil unrest had been followed by an extraordinary upsurge in violence that showed no sign of abating five years later. The city's homicide rate, steadily falling in the years before Gray's death, shot up by more than half, to levels not seen since the early 1990s—for five years in row, more than three hundred people were killed in Baltimore, making it by far the most dangerous large city in the country. There were more people being killed in Baltimore than in New York, a city more than fourteen times as large.

The deaths rippled outward across the city, an ever-present traumatic hum, even out at the Amazon warehouses. In April 2016, one Amazon worker, twenty-seven-year-old Rondell Street, was shot to death outside a hookah bar in East Baltimore. In June 2018, another employee, twenty-year-old Jasmine Pierce-Morris, was stabbed and strangled to death by her ex-boyfriend on high school bleachers. Fear was spreading so much in the city that it became a business opportunity for Amazon: a coalition of religious leaders used $15,000 in casino revenue to build a network of surveillance cameras, linked to the police department, with Amazon's Ring doorbell cameras. So many Amazon boxes were being stolen off of porches and front steps that a woman started a business: Package Rescue.

The post-2015 regression went beyond the homicide rate. The city's population was falling again after several years of small gains, dropping below 600,000 for the first time in a century. It had the highest rate of fatal drug overdoses of any city in the country—more than eight hundred in

2018. Since 2012, not a single Fortune 500 company had been headquartered in the city. One of the few retail options in West Baltimore, the Target at Mondawmin Mall, closed in 2018. The police department was embroiled in a corruption scandal of eye-popping proportions. City government was adrift—the mayor at the time of Gray's death, who had praised Amazon for prompt delivery of her skin moisturizer, decided not to run for reelection, and her successor barely defeated her predecessor, who had been forced out for petty corruption, and then the successor ended up going to prison for corruption. Other institutions were weakening—the symphony orchestra was in financial crisis; *The Baltimore Sun* shrunk to a skeleton crew and left its downtown newsroom for the industrial building past Interstate 95 that held its printing press.

There were many reasons for the unraveling, above all a breakdown in trust between a dysfunctional police department and residents less inclined than ever to take the risk of calling in tips or testifying on the state's behalf. But it was hard not to detect in Baltimore's plight the role of the broader economic context, the slide into the status of a secondary city, locked out of the winner-take-all gains flowing to cities up and down the coast from it.

Baltimore had put in its own bid for Amazon's second headquarters, offering up a prime waterfront parcel. "HQ2 will transform the lives of the current generation of Baltimoreans, give hope to the next, and permanently tie Amazon to the renaissance of one of America's greatest cities," the bid declared. But Baltimore hadn't made the cut for the twenty finalists—it was the only major city between Boston and Washington *not* to make the cut.

In Washington, the surge of prosperity that had begun with the growth of the influence industry at the end of the last century and expanded with the homeland security apparatus in the first decade of this century was turning the city into something unrecognizable. In 2017, median incomes had risen by nearly 10 percent in a single year, to more than $82,000—76 percent higher than the median income in Baltimore. The metro area had been adding 34,000 jobs per year, on average. Its population was growing at one of the fastest rates in the country, reaching 700,000 for the first time in four decades, and the metro area was expected to add 1 million residents by 2045. A huge share of the new arrivals were educated young people from elsewhere: in 2005, one in seven D.C. residents was a 25-to-34-year-old college graduate. By 2017, the share was up to one in five. Across the Potomac in Arlington, Virginia, the rate was even higher: more than one in four residents, one of the highest rates in the country.

The relentless growth was having predictable effects on the local housing market. In late 2018, the median price of a house or condo in the District crossed the $600,000 mark—five times the median home price in Baltimore. Single-family homes had nearly quadrupled in value since the early 1990s. In 2016, a single real estate agent sold five homes in the District for more than $3.7 million each, far more than any home sold in Baltimore. (Another local real estate agent was doing so well that he had built a Hot Wheels collection worth $1.5 million.) The median sale price in the Chevy Chase section of D.C., home of the lounge where Brett Kavanaugh liked to hang out, crossed the $1 million mark.

Millennials buying homes in the District carried an average mortgage of $450,985, more than twice the national figure. Units in a former church on the fringes of Capitol Hill were going for $2.8 million; one inside a former helicopter factory near Howard University went for $2.3 million. The schools in Montgomery County, the well-off Maryland suburb, were so overcrowded that officials imposed a building moratorium in several school zones; in search of more affordable homes, 44 percent of the county government's employees lived in other counties. Families desperate for homes in the county were paying $1 million for condo units in former suburban office parks.

In the District, the growth was transforming areas like the blocks around the Washington Navy Yard, where a new Whole Foods offered self-serve wine and build-your-own avocado toast, and where Young Republicans hosted parties to watch Donald Trump's State of the Union speech at a Mexican restaurant. The Washington Post Magazine's annual luxury issue ran news items on $18,300 watches, $50,000 sables, and Rolls-Royces, and ads for plastic surgery and private-jet carriers. Restaurant prices crept ever upward—the tasting menu at Pineapple & Pearls jumped to $325; the glass of champagne suggested by the sommelier at Plume cost $75. The markers of extreme wealth abashed even Ken Schlossberg, who had shown the way in the lobbying industry years earlier. "It's just become New York South, where money talks instead of anything else," he said. "That's basically what it's become."

The growth was also increasingly bringing the city to a standstill. It had long had some of the worst traffic congestion in the country—the third worst after Los Angeles and the Bay Area, with commuters sitting in traffic more than one hundred hours per year, on average. "From the operational standpoint, there were no major road incidents this morning," said a Virginia Department of Transportation spokeswoman after one especially hellish morning. "This was simply volume." To address the crush, Virginia had started charging very high rush-hour tolls on some highways—as much as $50 to drive ten miles.

The explosive prosperity was also exacerbating the city's extreme inequality. By 2017, median income for the city's white households—including all those young residents barely out of college—had jumped to $120,000, three times that for Black households. The difference in average net worth was even more gaping: $284,000 versus $3,500, giving the city one of the worst levels of racial disparity in the country. Virtually all white residents in the city—92 percent—had a college degree, while only a quarter of Black people did. The unemployment rate was six times higher for Black residents than for white residents.

The contrasts were hard to miss: on Fourteenth Street NW, where a youth boxing club that had drawn Black teenagers for four decades finally ceded ground to developers; and a few miles northeast of there, where a fire killed one of the Ethiopian immigrants crowded into rented rooms barely large enough to hold a queen-size mattress; and in the tensions at Howard University, where newly arrived white neighbors blithely walked their dogs across the hallowed historically Black campus.

With such yawning divides in income and wealth, coupled with the pressure of population growth, came displacement on a large scale. A 2019 study that largely downplayed the effects of gentrification nationwide declared that

Washington was the city where it had been most devastating: it estimated that 20,000 Black residents had been displaced. Not that one needed a study to confirm what census statistics had noted a few years earlier: "Chocolate City," which had been more than 70 percent African American in 1970, was no longer majority Black.

Washington had become what the former New York City mayor Mike Bloomberg had once envisioned for his own domain: it was a "luxury city" where, assuming one could afford the price of admission, one could dine out far better than ever before, go for bike rides on new paths along the Potomac and the monuments, and give nary a thought to crime. What crime remained was concentrated in the dwindling Black precincts—like the stretches east of the Anacostia River where, in 2018, the since-shuttered Amazon Restaurants refused to deliver.

It was not hard, though, to spy the limits to such splendor. With the extinction of the city's working class, there would be no one left to drive the Ubers, change the bedding in the $400-a-night hotels, clean the $3 million homes, or bus the tables for the $1,000 dinners for two.

On October 18, 2018, a white delivery van was turning to enter a large housing complex in Essex, about a twenty-minute drive from both of Baltimore's Amazon warehouses, on the eastern side of the Back River inlet from the Chesapeake. The complex, Harbor Point Estates, was one of about a dozen in the Baltimore area owned by the family real estate company of Jared Kushner, the president's son-in-law. As the van was turning, a seven-year-old girl, NaTasha Newman, who had spent that day on a school trip to the zoo in Baltimore, darted across the small street to join her brothers on the other side. The van struck her, fatally injuring her. The driver stayed at the scene and was not charged in the accident.

The Baltimore Sun and local TV news stations reported simply that it was a "work van" or "delivery van." There was no way for a witness to know that the unmarked van was in fact delivering packages for Amazon.

Increasingly, this delivery—the last leg, Amazon called it—was being handled not by UPS or FedEx or the postal service, but by Amazon itself. The number of packages it needed to ship in the United States was ballooning to more than 6 billion in 2019, so it made sense to build its own network to handle it, or as much of it as possible. With more than 110 fulfillment centers around the country, the company now had warehouses within twenty-five miles of about half of the U.S. population, in virtually every state, and it was delivering about half its orders. It leased sixty planes, and contracted with freight airlines for use of many more—pilots complained of having to work eighteen-hour days, and one plane contracted by Amazon would crash near Houston in February 2019, killing all three onboard—and it was planning a one-hundred-plane hub at the Cincinnati airport. It was experimenting with drone delivery and lobbying federal regulators to allow that to happen. It had started handling some of the shipping from China itself—sending more than 4.7 million cartons of consumer goods in 5,300 containers in 2018 alone. It was setting up almost 200 delivery stations around the country, in addition to the fulfillment centers, to get packages closer to buyers' homes. It had bought a fleet of 20,000 diesel vans and 7,500 trailers, and was about to order 100,000 electric vans for its drivers.

Except they weren't Amazon's drivers, technically—they worked for contractors who, while they might deliver exclusively for Amazon, were separate entities. This meant drivers were denied whatever benefits Amazon provided employees. It also meant Amazon could avoid liability if the drivers got in accidents, as was happening with increasing frequency as time pressures mounted with the shift to one-day delivery—drivers were making as many as 150 stops on a shift and handling 1,000 packages per week. Whereas UPS trained its drivers in high-tech facilities with virtual-reality obstacle courses to teach them how to avoid hazards, many drivers for Amazon got nothing but instructional videos on their phones.

NaTasha's mother said later that she did not hold the company responsible. "It wasn't Amazon's fault," she said. "It was the man that did it." Asked whether the family received any compensation, she said, "I'm not allowed to talk about it."

Two weeks after the accident, on November 2, a tornado touched down in

Baltimore at 9:42 p.m. It blew over a tractor trailer on Interstate 95 north of the Fort McHenry Tunnel and knocked over a fence line on South Newkirk Street. It moved east along Holabird Avenue, and it was there that it did its greatest damage. One large structure proved particularly ill equipped to handle the 105-mile-per-hour winds: the Amazon sortation center at 5501 Holabird.

The 345,000-square-foot building sat north of the larger fulfillment center on Broening Highway, the site of the former GM plant and the place where Bill Bodani had started working for Amazon. The sortation centers received packages already packed and addressed—a clearinghouse before they were sent out for final delivery.

One of the drivers who delivered from Holabird Avenue was Israel Espana Argote. The Bolivian immigrant lived in Bristow, Virginia, eighty miles away, near the Amazon data center in Haymarket, with his wife, Fatima Parada Espana, and their three sons. They had recently moved into their new house. Despite all the driving across the Baltimore-Washington traffic morass, Israel found time to coach his youngest son's soccer team and played soccer once or twice a week himself. He sang karaoke, and he liked to grill in the Bolivian churrasco style. He had gone to work earlier than usual on November 2 so that he could be done with his overnight driving in time for his son's soccer game the next day.

Sortation centers employed far fewer people than fulfillment centers, and many of those who did work inside of them were not on Amazon's payroll. There were, for instance, the material-handling technicians employed by large commercial real estate service providers such as Jones Lang LaSalle (JLL). These were the warehouse maintenance men: they fixed broken conveyor belts and electrical systems and most anything else that made a logistics warehouse run: "photo eyes, motor starters, relays, limit switches, proximity sensors, timers, solenoids, Servo drivers, frequency inverters, linear drives, tachs, and encoders," as one JLL job posting for Baltimore put it. It could be strenuous work, too: material handling technicians needed to "lift and move items up to 49 pounds each," "pull and push wheeled dollies loaded with products up to 100 pounds," "climb ladders and gangways safely and without limitation," and "stand/walk for up to 10-12 hours."

Work at the sortation center was not only demanding, but came with some perils. In August 2018, two months before the tornado, an employee filed a complaint with state regulators listing a host of safety risks at the building: the company's practice of sending workers back into the loading lot much sooner after lightning strikes than policy dictated; the frequent violation of "NO GO ZONE" signs around motorized belts; the collection of flammable materials on belts; the stacking of pallets close to fire suppression nozzles, rendering them ineffective; the blocking of exits with pallets and equipment; the thick layers of flammable cardboard dust built up on the automated sorter; the cancellation of fire drills to avoid slowing production. "There is a culture of silence here among leadership," wrote the employee. "Great strides are taken to prevent any detrimental reports leaving the building."

When managers knew in advance that inspectors were coming, the employee wrote, they would put up a Potemkin front. "Our building is temporarily cleaned and brought up to code only to fall back into disarray almost as soon as the official steps out the door," the employee wrote. "On the day of an inspection things like, 'OK. So we're being inspected today, so if someone asks you blank be sure to respond with blank . . .' are often coached to associates." If inspectors arrive without prior notice, they "are turned away at the door unless they have a subpoena." "I no longer feel safe here and my confidence in our safety team to represent the best interests and safety of the staff has dissolved," the employee concluded. "Please help."

Among the material-handling technicians working at the building under contract with JLL was Andrew Lindsey. He had spent most of his life in the Oklahoma City area, including a two-year stint at a mobile home park in Choctaw. In 2017, he had gotten the JLL job and moved to the Baltimore area, where he rented an $800-per-month apartment with his dog in a modest complex on Four Seasons Court in Dundalk, across Bear Creek from Sparrows Point. When he met one neighbor, Lorraine, in the hallway, he told her he felt "blessed" to find an apartment near the warehouse.

Lindsey was working the overnight shift on November 2 as the tornado flew down Holabird Avenue. It blew past the plastics-packaging plant where

Lorraine worked. It blew in large garage doors on both sides of a FlexiVan leasing facility. When it reached the sortation center, it pulled the roof, including iron rafters, right off of the western end of the building, where the loading docks were. Without the roof, the concrete panels of the west wall collapsed into the building, leaving a fifty-foot-long swath exposed.

Lorraine and others at the plastic plant heard a huge crash—it sounded like when they slammed shut the doors at the nearby industrial-scale bakery, except louder. The wind pushed over a dozen truck trailers parked at the Amazon loading docks and blew over light stanchions and signs. Debris smashed car windows. The tornado lifted as it moved east, touched down again to take the roof off an apartment complex in Dundalk, and was gone.

They found Andrew Lindsey, age fifty-four, first. Lorraine learned about it from their landlord at Four Seasons Court. She was confused because news reports referred to Lindsey as an Amazon "contractor," not employee. "I didn't know he was a contractor," she said. "I thought he was *there*."

The rescue workers didn't know that someone else was under the debris until Fatima Parada Espana arrived to say that she did not know where her husband was. She had gotten a knock late at night from a friend who also delivered for Amazon, telling her about the tornado. She drove the eighty miles from Virginia, and saw the hole in the building, and saw her husband's truck.

She told the first responders and workers who were removing the debris that her husband was missing. They had been doing their work without realizing there might be someone else in there, and now they stopped and waited for different equipment to move a large chunk of wall. Fatima asked one of them what the odds were that her husband was still alive if he was under that wall. "Let's think he's not there," he told her. "Let's stay positive." They found Israel Espana Argote, age thirty-seven, a few hours later.

"I want people to know he was a great dad," Fatima told reporters.

"It still hasn't really sunk in that my brother is gone," Angel Lindsey told her friends back in Oklahoma.

"Due to the damage caused by Friday evening's severe weather, deliveries associated with this package sortation center are experiencing delays," an Amazon spokeswoman said a day later, on Sunday. "We apologize for the inconvenience to our customers and are working quickly to resolve."

Bill Bodani, Jr., still met up every month with the other guys from Retirees United Local 9477. They met at the Battle Grove Democratic Club in Dundalk, a setting rich in irony given the voting trends in eastern Baltimore County, which had gone heavily for Donald Trump. It was a proper organizational meeting, with officers sitting at a table up front and minutes from the prior meeting and old business and new business. There was a reading of the names of those lost in the last month. There was a plea for the men to pay their $30 annual dues—as numbers dwindled, it was getting harder to keep the operation going. The operation included the spartan lunch served afterward, which was what most of the men had come for—lunch and fellowship, getting off the couch, out of the house.

At the November 2018 meeting, Steve Kotula, after reading the October minutes, alerted members to the ceremony that would be held at Sparrows Point the following month to light the iconic Star of Bethlehem that had graced the 320-foot-tall "L" furnace after its construction in 1978. He also alerted them to job opportunities at the Point.

"Amazon is hiring," he said. "Four days a week with a twelve-hour shift. If you work overtime, you can get $20. If you have a heartbeat, you can get hired."

That Bill Bodani was still connected to the union in this way, still benefiting from the camaraderie long after leaving the job, helped explain the step he took at his new job at the Point, a few weeks after the warehouse wall collapse. One day, he stopped by the local District 8 office of the United Steelworkers and picked up some literature. Basic stuff on the right to organize, broadly worded enough that it applied to warehouses as to steel mills.

When he arrived for his next shift at DCA1, he brought the literature in with him and showed it to one of the young men he'd been training on the forklifts, who seemed particularly agitated by the way things worked at the warehouse: the constant pressure to ratchet goals upward, the sense of total surveillance, the workers' lack of a voice.

"You need a union in here," Bo told the young man.

Bo said that he himself wasn't the ideal person to be secretly distributing literature—he was already suspect as a union lifer. But he encouraged the young man to do with it as he saw fit. He, after all, had more years ahead of him at the warehouse and more at stake in improving conditions. The young man thanked him and took the literature.

To hear the company tell it, there was less need than ever for unions at the warehouses. In October, it had with fanfare announced a company-wide minimum wage of $15 for its 250,000 U.S. warehouse employees and 100,000 seasonal workers. It didn't apply to its many contractors, like the men who would perish a few weeks later in the warehouse collapse. It still left workers far short of the shared prosperity that their counterparts had enjoyed in an earlier era: as the former U.S. labor secretary Robert Reich noted, if Amazon employees owned the same proportion of their employer's stock as Sears workers did in the 1950s—a quarter of the company—each would, by 2020, own shares worth nearly $400,000. (The company countered that it offered workers the chance to buy stock, but that they had shown preference for higher wages rather than stock benefits.) And it was a pay level that the company was already approaching in many parts of the country as it struggled to find workers in a tight labor market. "Aren't you excited? Come on, clap!" an HR manager said after announcing the raise at one of Amazon's many warehouses in the San Bernardino Valley. In response, workers started a slow clap.

But the announcement undermined efforts by Bernie Sanders, among others, to force the company to raise wages through legislation, and it signaled to consumers that they could continue to buy goods cheaply online with a clean conscience. So did the announcement nine months later that the company, which already offered tuition assistance for employees seeking vocational or associate's degrees on the side, would now also retrain 100,000 employees by 2025 to help them advance to higher-level work at the company.

That move was a particularly brilliant political stroke—in a single gesture, it made the company appear genuinely interested in the development of its employees, almost like a newfangled community college, while at the same time implicitly rebutting two of the most potent claims made against it.

Was work at a fulfillment center dreary? Well, perhaps, but the company was offering you a path to higher levels.

And was the company considering ways to eliminate many jobs with robots, of which it now had 200,000 worldwide? Well, sure: consider the difference between the newer warehouses, where the orange Kivas brought goods to pickers, and the older ones, where pickers still roamed aisles. Already, the company had made it through the 2018 holiday season with 20,000 fewer temps than the year before. But with the retraining announcement, Amazon could preempt questions about that shift: don't worry—if a robot takes your job, you can become someone who fixes robots.

The PR push ramped up further. The company started offering tours of many of the warehouses, which had previously been strictly off-limits. Visitors, including hundreds of elected officials, were greeted by peppy "ambassadors" overflowing with enthusiasm for the company. The ambassadors led them past conveyor belts and stowers and pickers and packers, answering some but not all questions (among those deemed out of bounds: how many robots were at the warehouse and how the company went about packing boxes with multiple items in them, which was deemed a trade secret).

Meanwhile, a small army of employees began sending out tweets raving about the joys of work at the warehouses. "At the bldg I work at I dont feel mistreated," wrote Nicholas. "My safety/well being are a top priority for my managers." Hannah offered: "At one point I wanted to quit Amazon. But I realized it was my fault for the problems I was dealing with, and not Amazon's. I'm allowed to talk to people, but sometimes I don't want to. Now I have some great coworkers to pass the nights with." The company also touted the fact that it was enlivening employees' days by turning aspects of their work into video-game contests that could be monitored on small screens by their workstations. As they rushed to complete their tasks, they could compete in games with names like MissionRacer, PicksInSpace, and Dragon Duel. The winners got "Swag Bucks" with which to buy Amazon-logo stickers, apparel, or other gear.

Despite such uplift and gloss, discontent persisted inside the warehouses and still occasionally made it to public view. In Kentucky, an employee at an Amazon call center asked for a more flexible bathroom-break schedule to accommodate the unpredictable inflammatory bowel condition that came with his Crohn's disease but was instead accused of stealing time and fired, as he alleged in a lawsuit. ("Associates are allowed to use the toilet whenever needed," Amazon said later.) In Minnesota, a group of Somali American workers forced the company to negotiate over productivity pressures that were leading to exhaustion and dehydration. After failing to make progress, the workers announced they would strike during the next Prime Day period the following July. HUMANS, NOT ROBOTS read their signs those days, when scattered protests across the country would not prevent Amazon from breaking a record with 175 million items sold—on the first day, Baltimore's Broening Highway warehouse alone would send more than 1 million items.

And every so often, news of accidents made it to the outside. A Minneapolis warehouse worker started a GoFundMe fundraiser to pay for his surgery after he suffered fractured vertebrae and a torn labrum when a wall of dog and cat food collapsed on him and, he said, his Amazon health insurance denied the claim. A robot punctured a can of bear repellent spray at a New Jersey warehouse, sending two dozen workers to the hospital. All told, a study of twenty-three Amazon warehouses by the Center for Investigative Reporting found that serious injuries were reported at a rate more than double the national average for the warehousing industry, a finding echoed by another in-depth report released around the same time by an alliance of worker activist groups.

Amazon said in response that it was simply more responsible about reporting injuries than other companies. It pointed to its increased investments in safety—one million hours of training and $36 million in capital improvements in 2018, plus another $57 million in future improvements that it committed to in 2019, among them a $16 million upgrade for its powered industrial trucks, the vehicle involved in Jody Rhoads's death in Carlisle, Pennsylvania.

Still, due partly to the sheer scale of the company's warehouse employment, there were other deaths at warehouses, at least a half dozen of them since 2013. A fifty-seven-year-old man died of a heart attack in Joliet, Illinois, in 2017 after not receiving immediate medical attention. His wife later sued, saying that supervisors waited twenty-five minutes before calling 911 and made EMTs walk through the huge warehouse rather than letting them in through the nearby loading dock where he was lying. The boxes for AED defibrillators scattered around the warehouse were empty, the lawsuit stated. A sixty-one-year-old worker died of a heart attack at a warehouse a year and a half later in Murfreesboro, Tennessee, after two-way radios used to alert AmCare failed to work properly.

In 2017, another worker, Phillip Lee Terry, fifty-nine, was crushed to death by a forklift he was working beneath in the maintenance area, in Plainfield, Indiana. He lay in a pool of blood for two hours before anyone noticed him. The state initially fined Amazon $28,000 for four major safety violations, including failure to train Terry in how to elevate the forklift properly. But the state OSHA director offered advice to company officials in how to negotiate down the fines and shift blame to Terry, in a phone call recorded by the OSHA inspector on the case, John Stallone. After hanging up with Amazon, the OSHA director said to Stallone, "I hope you don't take it personally if we have to manipulate your citations."

In a whistleblower report, Stallone said the state's labor commissioner and governor, Eric Holcomb, then called him into a meeting to impress on him that the case risked harming the Indianapolis bid for HQ2, which they later denied. The day Stallone filed his report, Amazon sent Holcomb a $1,000 campaign contribution. And a year after Terry's death, the state signed an agreement with Amazon to delete the fines and citations.

Ten days after the fatal warehouse collapse in Baltimore, Amazon was still scrambling to close the gap in the delivery stream. The word went out at the local fulfillment centers that drivers without commercial driver's licenses were being hired to haul goods to a temporary location in Anne Arundel County, south of Baltimore, a notion the company denied, saying its drivers had "all of the necessary permits required."

In Washington, the company was engaged in a completely different endeavor. On November 13, 2018, it announced that the city—or to be precise, a Northern Virginia suburb across the Potomac—had won the competition to be its second headquarters.

At first, it looked as if the Washington area—specifically, the inner suburb of Arlington, Virginia—would share the prize of the second headquarters with another city. After all the drama about seeking one city for the 50,000 jobs and $5 billion investment, the company had decided to split the loot, concluding that it would be easier to find the requisite space and workers in two cities rather than one. This lent the whole sweepstakes a bait-and-switch aspect—the prize, it turned out, was not as grand as advertised. More upsetting to many of the contestants, though, was the identity of the two winners.

After all the hype about a nationwide search, about scouring every corner of the land for a second home and encouraging cities far and wide to spend countless hours assembling their bids, the company had chosen the two most obvious candidates: the two wealthiest and most influential cities on the East Coast. (Nashville would get the consolation prize of a new satellite campus with 5,000 jobs.) It was hard to avoid the conclusion that everyone else had fallen victim to a giant ruse. They had generated free publicity for the company, handed over reams of information about their city (useful for the company's future expansion calculations), and ramped up the bidding, all so that the company could extract a bigger price from the cities it was likely headed to all along: the seat of the federal government and the center of global finance.

In picking the East Coast's two ultimate winner-take-all cities, though, the company miscalculated. One of the cities, New York, had reached a point of such hyper-prosperity that it had given rise to a vocal minority that recognized that there could be too much of a good thing. There were aggressively tall and slender towers rising over Midtown, like the one along Central Park where hedge-fund manager Kenneth Griffin would pay $238 million for a 24,000-square-foot apartment. There were people with means to pool together $11 million to prevent a building from going up next to them and blocking their view. There were ostentatious new neighbors such as the ex–Uber CEO Travis Kalanick, who dropped $36 million for a SoHo penthouse with a private twenty-foot outdoor pool in a Renzo Piano–designed building.

There were streets so congested that bicyclist deaths were rising sharply, though this didn't keep representatives of Jeff Bezos's Central Park West building, where one unit was on the market for nearly $10 million, from suing to block a bike lane. (In 2019, Bezos would upgrade to a larger New York dwelling, a 17,000-square-foot, twelve-bedroom spread on Fifth Avenue, purchased for about $80 million.) Much of the congestion was due to the growing numbers of trucks and vans delivering boxes to building lobbies, where they arrived in such quantities that landlords installed lockers to hold them all; in some cases, boxes were being spread in heaps on blankets on the sidewalk. There were now nine Amazon fulfillment centers in New Jersey, up from zero in 2012, and they, along with the extra-large one in Staten Island, were sending so many boxes across New York City that the number of overall e-commerce deliveries to households there had tripled since 2009 to more than 1 million per day. Amazon had developed a cachet for the urban professional consumer in a way that many retail rivals, notably Walmart, simply never had. Now others were following Amazon's lead in promising frictionless service, such as the food-delivery app Seamless: "Over 8 million people in New York City, and we help you avoid them all" read one ad. "Nothing ruins a good meal like other New Yorkers" read another.

Those with means were increasingly choosing to avoid all that congestion by commuting by helicopter (a ride to JFK Airport cost $200). In Manhattan, the median price for an apartment had crossed the $1 million mark a few years earlier; in Brooklyn, the average rent was about to cross the $3,000 mark, and parents were spending the night in line on sidewalks in sleeping bags to secure a spot for preschool. Every sign suggested this was all going to intensify further: Google was headed to the city as well, building a $1 billion campus that would allow it to double its workforce to 14,000. The number of tech jobs overall in the city had surged by 80 percent over the past decade, to more than 140,000.

The city was becoming a parody of the plutocratic metropolis, the sort of place where a family could leave its five-story Upper East Side townhouse for the weekend and not realize until its return that its house cleaner had gotten stuck in the home's elevator for three days, as happened in early 2019. And so when word emerged of yet more towers to accommodate the company led by the greatest plutocrat of them all—subsidized by nearly $3 billion in taxpayer incentives!—a newly energized minority, led by tribunes like newly elected U.S. representative Alexandria Ocasio-Cortez, age twenty-nine, rose up and said no. SCAMAZON read the graffiti sprayed on an abandoned restaurant near the chosen site in Long Island City, where one penthouse apartment saw its price shoot up by $250,000 with news of Amazon's arrival.

The company was stunned by the ingratitude and effrontery, so much so that, like an aggrieved seventh grader, it began keeping a secret log of all the unpleasant things various New Yorkers were saying about it, in a Microsoft Word document called "NY Negative Statements." It pleaded its case at one city council hearing after another. But the vocal minority wasn't buying it. It didn't help that the city was getting warnings from Seattle—Teresa Mosqueda, the council member who thought she had a compromise agreement with Amazon, came to New York and told them to get everything in writing. "That type of bad behavior when it comes to public policy making should not be replicated in another city," she said later. "They need to know what we experienced."

A few weeks later, it was over. One day, the company was negotiating with the critics over the treatment of the 5,000 workers at its mammoth Staten Island warehouse—there was talk of allowing them to organize freely in exchange for approval of the subsidies for the new headquarters. This was a bridge too far for Amazon. A day later, Jay Carney, the journalist turned influencer-in-chief, called up Mayor Bill de Blasio and Governor Andrew Cuomo and told them the company was pulling out. Not entirely—there would still be several thousand white-collar Amazonians in the city, clustered mostly at Hudson Yards, the giant new development on the West Side of Manhattan. But there would be no HQ2 extravaganza. A group funded by Robert Mercer, the hedge-fund billionaire, paid for a billboard in Times Square blaming the loss on Ocasio-Cortez: THANKS FOR NOTHING, AOC!

So there would be a lone big winner after all. Washington and Northern Virginia had mustered nothing close to the resistance in New York. Maybe it was that the tax subsidies offered by Virginia had been less offensively gargantuan—about $750 million. Maybe it was that Washington, with its building height limits, lacked New York's steroidal protrusions of excessive wealth; maybe it was that D.C. lacked an Ocasio-Cortez. Maybe it was that the newspaper in metro Washington, owned by Jeff Bezos, had subjected the deal to less scrutiny than its counterpart in New York had. "Amazon's HQ2 could be a launching pad for a bright future for the D.C. region," declared the headline of a *Washington Post* editorial. It would be left to a local business journal, not *The Post*, to uncover the emails showing the lengths to which Arlington officials had gone to ease Amazon's path, even giving the company advance notice of the questions they planned to ask at a public hearing on the deal.

Or maybe it was simply that this was the perfect union. For Washington, which despite its new wealth still carried the insecurity that it was at heart a government town, Amazon offered the fullest possible affirmation that it had transcended its dowdy bureaucratic roots—with 25,000 employees, it would be the area's largest private-sector employer. For Amazon, the area offered the technical talent it was looking for—there would be easy recruiting amid all the homeland security IT contractors and rival cloud providers.

Other cities, such as Boston and Austin, could have offered that, too. What they couldn't offer was proximity to power. Increasingly, the company had less to fear from rivals than it did from a government that seemed to be growing concerned about its lack of rivals, which helped explain why the company would soon pass the $4 million mark in quarterly spending on lobbying, nearly five times what it had spent five years earlier and second only to Facebook among tech giants. All told, Amazon had spent $80 million over the course of the decade on seeking to influence the federal government, though Jay Carney insisted the spending had more benign goals. "We can be a resource, an information provider to policy makers and regulators," he told PBS's *Frontline*. "It's not lobbying in the traditional sense in terms of trying to persuade somebody to do something. It's just answering questions and providing data and information."

The team making Virginia's bid—led by Stephen Moret, who had attended the Washington Economic Club soiree for Bezos—had been as blunt as possible in underscoring this benefit: it had created a map for Amazon showing how close Arlington was to key agencies and departments such as the Federal Trade Commission and the Department of Justice, both of which were making rumblings about scrutinizing the dominance of Amazon and other tech giants. There was the more diffuse benefit of proximity, as well: countless regulators, antitrust lawyers, and journalists in Washington would now become neighbors and acquaintances with Amazonians—in Little League bleachers, at PTA meetings—and thus more likely to regard the company in a friendly light.

And the Washington area offered the ideal site for the new headquarters. It would be built on the northern edge of Crystal City, the clump of mostly office buildings built on a wasteland along Route 1 in the early 1960s that had slipped into somnolence since then as the military contractors that had predominated there moved elsewhere. For Amazon, the site was ideal. It was only two Metro stops from a major downtown transit hub or a short Uber drive across the river, it was walking distance to Reagan National Airport, and it was so close to the Pentagon—one Metro stop, a third of a mile—that one could negotiate future defense contracts via semaphore. Much of the property it would be building on was owned by the same real estate company: JBG Smith, whose CEO had made welcoming remarks to Bezos at the Economic Club dinner.

The site's utter lack of character was an asset, as well—Amazon could impose its corporate brand across the area as freely as it had in South Lake Union. In fact, Amazon would even rename it. Henceforth, the area between Crystal City and the Pentagon City Mall would, by Amazon's decree, be "National Landing." No one really knew what the name was supposed to mean, but no one really objected either. National Landing it was.

———

A t Sparrows Point, the day after Bill Bodani gave the younger man the leaflets to distribute, Bodani's supervisor, a man in his thirties, confronted Bo and told him that he wasn't allowed to pass out literature on the job, religious or political or otherwise. The young man had apparently been less-than-discreet in how he'd proceeded to distribute the flyers.

"What, do you think you're working in a union shop or something?" the supervisor said.

Bo did not respond. Instead, he said he was going to the bathroom.

When he came out of the bathroom, the supervisor was waiting, ten feet from the door.

"You just got docked fifteen minutes," the supervisor said.

"For what?" Bo asked.

"For going to the bathroom." Bo had over the course of the shift now exceeded his allotted twenty-minute "time off task," he said.

"You got to be kidding me," Bo said. "I don't keep track. What do you want me to do, punch out in the bathroom?"

And then Bo went ahead and did it.

"I'll tell you what," he said. "You want me to train these guys? Well, I just gave you my notice. Next Friday is my last day."

It was the middle of the holiday rush. They tried to get him to change his mind, though not with any bump in pay or other concrete inducement. He stuck by his decision. In the last week before he left, he noticed that the young man he'd given the literature to had vanished, along with another young man who'd started talking unions. Bo reached the first young man and learned that they'd been furloughed until after Christmas. As desperate as the company was for more holiday manpower, the need to discipline for agitation seemed to have trumped. (The company later denied that any such suspensions had occurred, saying, "Amazon respects its employees' right to choose to join or not join a labor union.")

Bo wasn't sure how he and his wife would manage without a regular income—he was hoping he'd be able to get enough work at his friend's motorcycle repair shop. But this was it: fifty years after he'd started at Sparrows Point, Bill Bodani punched out for the last time.

The boom arrived instantaneously. The area around National Landing was already comfortable, with an average household income of $138,000 among the 15,000 living in closest proximity, but it was now shooting to a whole new level. One condominium had been sitting on the edge of Crystal City for ninety days with so little interest that the agent was about to take it off the market. When news of the new headquarters first leaked in November 2018, the condo sold in a day, for $70,000 more than its asking price.

By April 2019, the average sales price in Arlington County, which encompassed the new headquarters, hit $742,000, up by more than 11 percent from the year before. There were entire zip codes in Arlington and Alexandria with no homes for sale at all. Some prospective buyers in Del Ray, a charming and formerly middle-class section of Alexandria, were being told that the second round of negotiations would be cash only. By August, the brokerage Redfin had declared the Arlington and Alexandria housing markets the most competitive in the country: well over half the homes for sale there were being sold in under two weeks. The area's housing inventory had dropped to its lowest level since 2006, at the peak of the housing frenzy before the financial collapse. One buyer purchased an old house on a cul-de-sac in North Arlington without laying eyes on it, spending $900,000 with the intention of tearing it down, figuring he'd still make a big profit. When one agent posted a "coming soon" alert for a condo in Rosslyn, an area north of the new headquarters, someone called her in five minutes begging to be allowed to see it immediately. Just to the south in Fairfax County, developers were hawking deluxe units in what used to be the Lorton Reformatory, the prison that for nine decades had housed inmates from Washington, D.C. New residents would stroll down Reformatory Way and Sallyport Street.

All these rumblings were only a hint of what was to come. Amazon was barely on the ground yet. In 2019, it was planning to hire only 400 for its temporary offices. Its new towers still had to go through permitting. It wasn't planning to reach 25,000 employees at the headquarters until 2030. Once the jobs arrived, they were expected to generate indirectly another 37,500 across the region, for a total $6.5 billion in annual income, and $650 million more in tax revenue for state and local governments.

As housing advocates started fretting about an already unaffordable region becoming even more so, Amazon announced a $3 million donation toward affordable housing in the Arlington area. But the company's Jay Carney told the newspaper owned by Jeff Bezos that it was primarily the responsibility of local government to address that problem, not the company. "We want to be part of the solution," he said. "We want to work really closely with officials and others. . . . But as a citizen, I don't want to turn over government functions to private entities." Left unmentioned was that government at all levels had become less able to carry out its functions as a result of the tax avoidances the company had perfected.

Across the bland streetscape of Crystal City, an eerie stillness prevailed, the low-pressure vacuum before the funnel cloud. The vanguard employees and various building contractors strolled the sidewalks and plazas, looking up at this building to be refurbished, that one to be demolished. In the time-worn underground shopping mall connected to the Crystal City subway station, workers at humble shops and fast-food outlets went through their motions at businesses that stood not a chance to remain.

The invention of an entirely new place had begun: in the atrium of the underground mall, which was visible from street level, was a large sign: THE LANDING. In the ground-level space of one of the temporary office buildings, catering staff were readying a cocktail reception with life-size illustrations meant to conjure the prosperous urbanity to come: a coffee shop called Claire's, a restaurant called Daniel's, a club called Studio Beloved. It looked like South Lake Union in Seattle, although the coffee-shop chain that dominated that area, with three outlets within three blocks, wasn't called Claire's. If there was any doubt who the area's new tenant would be, there was the announcement of an upcoming "yappy hour" when neighbors could come and mingle with their dogs.

One Tuesday in mid-September, the clock flashed forward to the near future. Five thousand people descended on National Landing for the company's first "career day" for those interested in working at the headquarters. A big white tent, wedding-style, went up in the green space across from one of the sites of the planned new towers, which was in turn across the street from a new apartment building with a Whole Foods and a barre exercise studio. To provide a veneer of hipness, fences and temporary walls along the sidewalks had been festooned with brightly painted ride-share bicycles and random words and phrases: BRIGHT and WHAT IF and LISTEN TO THE QUIET VOICE.

The open house was to last five hours, but half an hour in, the line was snaking all the way down the block, past the Lenox Club apartments, around the corner to the DoubleTree Hotel. The line was remarkably diverse—all colors and outfitted in all styles: headphones, headscarf, bow tie, baseball cap. Some stared ahead; most stared at their phones.

A loudspeaker crackled and soon the line was regaled with a conversation happening on a stage inside the tent between Linda Thomas, who ran the company's Owned Content and Channels Team, which "tells stories about our company for an audience," and Ardine Williams, the vice president for People Operations. They talked about the company and what it looked for in applicants.

"We came to Arlington because of the talent," said Williams.

"Failure is an interesting thing at Amazon because it is something that we actually encourage," said Thomas. "If you're not failing, you're not trying and doing enough big thinking."

"If you're not failing, you're not stretching far enough," said Williams.

"Amazon is a very customer-centric company, *obviously*," said Thomas.

"We're builders," said Williams. "We're curious. We have the ability to collaborate. . . . Learn and be curious. I'm insatiably curious."

They talked about the company's STAR method for decision-making:

situation, task, action, result. They talked about its Leadership Principles. They talked about its "day one" culture.

A woman from a real estate company moved down the line passing out glossy brochures for two new housing developments in the area: "4-LEVEL ROOFTOP TOWNHOMES FROM THE UPPER $700S," "URBAN ROOFTOP TERRACE 2-CAR GARAGE TOWNHOMES."

The line included a project manager who already had a job but was coming anyway. "It's Amazon," he said. "Nobody wants to close doors. A lot of these people have a job already, but it's Amazon. All I know is they're coming."

And it included Latasha Bryant, who was from Baltimore. She had been out of high school for eight years and was desperate to finally get settled in a career. She had started out as a bank teller, then gone through a twelve-week program for basic IT work, which she'd put to use in brief stints with contractors at Next Day Blinds and the Baltimore city government help desk. It would take her as long as an hour and a half to drive to National Landing from her home outside Baltimore. "I'm willing to make the sacrifice," she said.

She knew that Baltimore had been in the running for HQ2 and wished it had won it, but also wasn't surprised that it hadn't. "Baltimore has been so stagnant for so many years," she said. "People are scared to make any kind of investment."

When people finally got to the front of the line, at the tent opening, they were rewarded with a portable toilet and a banana and a bottle of water. But when they got inside the tent, there were more lines. There was a long line for people to have their résumés reviewed, and a long line for interview tips. There were shorter lines at stations for all the areas where people could aspire to work: Amazon Web Services, Amazon Stores, Alexa Shopping, Finance & FinTech, and so on. Prominently displayed on the interior of one tent wall was a quote from Jeff Bezos: "Build yourself a great story."

There was another conversation happening on the stage inside the tent, between two young employees in Amazon T-shirts, sitting in cream-white swivel chairs.

"How long should my résumé be?" asked the young woman, playing the role of a job seeker.

"Yeah, so . . . let's say you're listing fifteen or twenty years of experience. I would cap the length at three pages max, while trying to keep it at one to two," said the man, whose name was Ryan, and who was exposing bare ankles above his slip-on Vans.

He said that bullet points were a good idea for résumés.

"How do I help make my résumé stand out?" said the woman. "I've heard things about Leadership Principles. How do we make sure I'm a good fit for Amazon?"

"Learn about our Leadership Principles," said Ryan. "Think about your inventory of experience and projects or initiatives you've worked on that might indicate your level of expertise in one of those Leadership Principles."

People emerged from the tent, blinking in the sunlight and holding bottles of water, one of the free bags of chips or popcorn that were inside the tent, and an orange information card that said, "Come Build a Future with Us."

Latasha Bryant was disappointed. She had stood in lines for the AWS and Apprenticeship stations. "It should have been more personal," she said. "You should have been able to sit down with a person, give your thirty-second pitch. It was more, 'So, here's a flyer,' and that was it. They told us to apply online."

She walked back down along the line of the hundreds still waiting, to find her car and hopefully beat rush hour for the drive back to Baltimore.

Keith Taylor was also looking for bricks. Not amid the demolished row-houses of East Baltimore, but in a dumpster on Sparrows Point.

Some remnants of Bethlehem Steel had remained here and there on the outer reaches of the peninsula, even after the arrival of the new warehouses. Now the deconstruction, the removal of its last traces, had been picking up pace, which had spurred Taylor to redouble his efforts to recover as many of those traces as possible. He had grown up in nearby Edgemere, he had gone to Sparrows Point High School, his father-in-law had been a millwright in the tin mill, and he himself had arrived there at age thirty-two, in 1989, after serving as a radar technician in the army and working for a couple defense contractors. "I said, 'I'm not going down there,' and of course, I ended up there," he said. He was an electrical turn engineer, using his computer background to modernize the 68-inch hot-strip mill. He had treasured the fraternity, which had reminded him, as it had Bill Bodani, of the bonds he'd formed in the service. "To be a steelworker with Beth Steel was an honor," he said. "It was your family. We all looked after each other."

In the late 1990s, he had become alert to the signs of decline—the lack of toilet paper in the men's room, the growing number of guys getting high on the job—and he looked for an escape hatch. In 1999, he started taking classes toward a teaching license, and a year later, he left the plant to start teaching a computer repair course at nearby Patapsco High.

In 2006, he was riding his bike on North Point Boulevard, training for a Make-A-Wish Foundation triathlon, when a driver buzzed his elbow and then kept drifting right, as if not seeing him at all, and stopped short in front of him to make a right-hand turn. Keith crashed into the car, hard. The accident left him with herniated disks and nerve damage. He retired from teaching in 2008 and spent several years in a haze.

One day, he was walking his dog at Sparrows Point High and it hit him as never before how rapid and total the erasure of Beth Steel was. "I'm seeing all my history and heritage being taken away," he thought. He had found his next task in life: he would be the guardian of the memory of Bethlehem Steel in Baltimore. "One door shut, another opened," he said. "I had my head damaged and I woke up, and when I woke up I had all these ideas."

He founded the Sparrows Point/North Point Historical Society and set about collecting every vestige of a vanishing world that he could get his hands on. "Sparrows Point is history," he said. "If it weren't for Beth Steel, we'd be talking Japanese or German now. Sparrows Point saved America."

This was what led him to the dumpster. He knew that it held somewhere in its bowels the bricks from one of the most significant buildings on the Point: the main administration building constructed in the 1930s to replace the original one from the 1890s. He wanted to retrieve the bricks for the project he had dreamed up: they would serve as the base for a thread of lampposts, also salvaged from the Point, that would lead across the playing fields at Sparrows Point High, powered by solar energy and interspersed with text displays about the Point and Beth Steel. He would call it the Beacon of Hope.

Unfortunately, by the time he'd resolved to go get them, demolition contractors had dumped heaps of regular trash on top of the bricks. He gave it not a second thought. One cold December day, he drove onto the Point in his truck and across the blank expanse that used to be the town. Eerily, GPS still recognized the expanse as being home to a city grid: "D Street . . . C Street." He put on some gloves and clambered into the dumpster, from which he began heaving the trash into a second dumpster that was serendipitously only ten feet away. Over it went: big coils of plastic drainage tubing, a DirecTV dish, Fireball bottles, Hennessy bottles, an oil can, a hard hat. By day's end, he had reached the lower strata that he was after. There were a few thousand of the bricks, more than enough for his project.

"I just kept thinking, how can I give back to the school?" he said. "I am extremely happy. I've got a lot of work to do, but I'm really happy." He looked across at the giant warehouse, standing where the 68-inch hot-strip mill was. A big red freight container sat in the grass nearby: CHINA SHIPPING, it read.

Standing in the dumpster, Keith Taylor chuckled at the word on the side of the warehouse. "Fulfillment," he said. "Everybody longs for that. A lot of people have drifted souls. They don't know what they want in life."

He had found his new calling, but making it more difficult was the conspicuous lack of cooperation from the Point's new owners, who seemed in a rush to erase the peninsula's former identity as they turned it into an all-purpose logistics hub. Within the next year, the ownership group would announce the coming of a wind-turbine storage facility, an urban farming operation, and more warehouses, for Home Depot and Floor & Decor. It was not only that they had changed the name of Sparrows Point in 2016, to Tradepoint Atlantic. They were also showing scant interest in joining the list of local companies and organizations contributing to Keith's efforts.

"They've gotten rid of everything," he said. "They just want everything gone." As Keith saw it, this violated the maxim he'd read in a book by Daniel Boorstin, the historian and former librarian of Congress: "Trying to plan for the future without a sense of the past is like trying to plant cut flowers." He loved that line.

The new owners were willing to make one concession to nostalgia, the holiday-season ceremony to light the Star of Bethlehem. Initially, they had hung the metal star—twenty-eight feet wide and one and a half tons—on the wastewater treatment plant, which, as Taylor and others had noted, showed how much they valued the symbol: "They put it on the shithouse!" he said. Eventually, they moved it to a more dignified spot, the water tower.

The cars started arriving at sunset, directed into the railyard by a team of security contractors. Somewhat less than one hundred people gathered under an open white tent. Keith Taylor came. So did Bill Bodani, Jr. Christmas music played. A half dozen members of a local church, New Light Lutheran in Dundalk, which had been formed five years earlier from the merger of three different Lutheran churches with dwindling congregations, were on hand to serve home-baked cookies and coffee. Among them was Dawn Dieter, whose father had worked at the Point for forty-seven years, from age seventeen until retirement. "I never in my wildest dreams thought that Bethlehem Steel would not exist at any point in my life," she said. "It's not going to be the same. They're not going to replace the wage rate that the steelworkers made, but it's still employment."

Aaron Tomarchio, Tradepoint's senior vice president of corporate affairs, welcomed the guests. "2018 has certainly been a very busy year," he said. "We pushed forward with our vision to create a global center for logistics and commerce."

He acknowledged the new Baltimore County executive, Johnny Olszewski, Jr. "I would like to invite him over here, and he will lead you in the countdown to the star." *You*, not *us*. The word choice underscored that Tradepoint was holding this ceremony as a favor for others.

Olszewski came forward. "It might be cold, but our spirits are warm, and I just cannot be more excited for the future of Tradepoint," he said.

A few weeks later, Amazon would announce that Prime Now service would be restored in the Baltimore area on December 18 after the hiatus caused by the warehouse collapse, in time for Christmas. Amazon would see its profit in the holiday quarter of 2018 top $3 billion for the very first time and its share of all preholiday online sales increase by half, dominating its rivals more than ever before. By year's end, it would surpass 100 million Prime members in the United States, on the cusp of penetrating more than half of all households in the country. One week into the new year, it would for the first time become the highest-valued company in the world.

The countdown began, and the star was lit. But a moment later, it went dark again, and it didn't come back on for another twenty minutes—a breaker problem. The visitors drove back out past the guards, and past the enormous new buildings, including DCA1, where the lights were on and the workers were handling the holiday rush, without Bo Bodani.

Corners of Northern Virginia not yet taken over by data centers included a stretch of rolling farmland and vineyards southwest of Leesburg. And so it was there, at the Stone Tower Winery, that the data center industry retreated one sunny weekday evening in late April 2019 for the first-ever banquet to celebrate the Virginia Data Center Leadership Awards.

It felt like a celebration long in coming. For years, the tech industry of Washington and Northern Virginia had grown in semi-obscurity, expanding but hidden behind the opacity of the data center buildings and the acronyms on the glass office cubes. But now, with Amazon's decision to place its second headquarters in Arlington, at the very spot where Northern Virginia met Washington, the world had finally recognized the region as the new tech capital that it had been becoming for years. Some self-congratulation was in order.

The guests arrived in a stream of late-model cars and SUVs—several Lexuses and BMWs, at least one Jaguar—turning in off Route 15 at the sign for Hogback Mountain Paintball and winding up the dirt road. One of the Lexuses bore the eye-catching Virginia license plate number 2: one of the single-digit plates reserved for members of the state senate.

Its owner was Janet Howell, a twenty-seven-year veteran of the state senate and one of a dozen current and former state legislators who had turned out for the dinner, among them the Speaker of the House of Delegates. This strong showing by the state's elected leaders was further affirmation of the industry's regional predominance. There were now more than seventy data centers in Loudoun County with more than 14.5 million square feet of space, and an additional 4.5 million square feet were in development. In Prince William County, there were thirty-four data centers representing a total of $6.9 billion in capital investment. The buildings were starting to spread even farther south and west across the state—Amazon alone was said to operate at least twenty-nine in Virginia and to be planning another eleven. Microsoft paid $73 million for 332 acres in Loudoun for a massive new cluster.

The guests descended a staircase to a large room with a long bar for the welcome reception, which was sponsored by Amazon and Microsoft: the two companies that were still in the running for the giant Pentagon contract, and that would continue to battle out the contract in court after the Pentagon finally awarded it to Microsoft. (Amazon would contend that the contract award had been influenced by President Trump's personal animosity toward the owner of the "Amazon Washington Post.") Wineglasses in hand, they drifted onto a wide terrace, beyond which the sun was starting to fall over the rows of grapes that spread downslope to the west.

The attendees were almost entirely men, and almost entirely white. It was hard to believe this was the industry's first such event: it had the air of a recurring get-together, a buzz of inside jokes and office dope.

As dusk fell, the guests were called into the dining room adjacent to the terrace. Each table was designated for a sponsor, with rank signaled by distance from the stage: AWS and Microsoft were in the first row, with Google and Dominion, the power company, next in prime center spots.

Rank was also signaled by the placement of the politicians in attendance: the AWS table played host to the most senior legislator in the room, Janet Howell, who had done so much to boost the industry over the years that her own website boasted that she was sometimes called the "Technology

Senator." A Democrat from Fairfax County, she sat on five of the most powerful committees in Richmond, including the Finance Committee (with purview over taxes and tax breaks). Tonight, she sat between Peter Hirschboeck, who worked in energy projects for AWS, and Laurie Tyson, who was AWS's lead lobbyist for the entire Southeast.

After dinner, Howell came onstage with several of the other legislators in attendance for a "public sector" panel—an update on activities in Richmond that could affect the data center industry, including an irksome state review of all the various tax incentives. The panel's moderator reminded the audience that Virginia had been the first state to dangle a tax incentive for data centers—an exemption from the state's sales and use tax that was saving the industry $65 million per year. During introductions, the three former legislators in attendance had been singled out for praise for their role in getting the tax break into law.

Now Howell downplayed the coming review and assured the audience that she and the other legislators onstage would guard their interests. "You have up here three, four, data-center lovers," she said. "And the three of us in the General Assembly represent different regions of the state and different parties, but we're all really committed to make this industry successful in Virginia and to make sure that you grow and multiply."

Howell concluded with praise for data centers' role as giant energy consumers, suggesting they were goading the state toward renewable sources of power. An environmental report had recently concluded otherwise, that the vast majority of the energy for Virginia's data centers was still coming from nonrenewable sources, much of it from coal. Amazon's data centers were getting only 12 percent of their ever-growing energy consumption from renewables, trailing Microsoft and Facebook, but ahead of Google. Nationwide, every $1 billion spent on data centers was leading to $7 billion in electricity consumed over two decades. Globally, spending on data centers had surpassed $100 billion a year.

On the topic of energy consumption, Jeff Bezos was quite blasé—it was why we needed to go to the moon. "We will run out of energy on Earth," he would say a few weeks later. "This is just arithmetic, it's going to happen."

A few years earlier, the company had considered offering consumers a "green" option for purchasing—allowing more time for deliveries in order to reduce carbon emissions—but nixed it, fearing it might lead to fewer purchases overall. After vigorous protests from his own headquarters employees, 8,700 of whom signed a petition demanding the company address climate change, Bezos would in early 2020 pledge $10 billion of his own money to the cause, to be spent on programs to be determined later. The company also operated ninety-one solar and wind projects globally, enough to power 680,000 homes, and was investing $100 million in global reforestation.

Howell made no mention of the environmental report on the data centers' reliance on coal, or of their rising energy demands.

"The data centers are forcing Virginia into a renewable energy future," she said. "I'm really very grateful to you all, because you've given us the impetus to do what we needed to do, and it's been the business community that has forced us in that direction, and our children will appreciate that."

The demolitions were now clustered on the far east side, places such as the devastated blocks of Montford Avenue north of the Amtrak line and south of North Avenue, close to where that major east-west artery dead-ended into Baltimore Cemetery. Crews had recently knocked down more than fifteen rowhouses in the 1500, 1600, and 1700 blocks of Montford. Some, but not all, had been deconstructed for salvage.

On the 1500 block, an elderly woman sat on her stoop looking at the space where the row opposite used to be. She had lived there for sixty-five years, after arriving in the city from Wrightsville, Georgia. "It don't worry me what they do," she said of the demolitions. "The good Lord will take care of me."

On the 1600 block, a younger woman emerged from the badly deteriorated home adjacent to a long row that had recently been demolished, leaving a lot that was empty but for a few small tree saplings, a trash container, and a couch cushion. The home she was leaving, built in 1920, bore marks of abandonment: boarded-up lower windows, broken upper ones.

But it was not vacant. Teresa's father had lived in it for eight years, and Teresa, thirty-four, who mostly lived elsewhere with her boyfriend, had stopped by for a change of clothes. Her hands were full: an open can of malt liquor in a brown paper bag, a plastic carryout bag, a pack of cigarettes. She was wearing a plastic boot, which she'd had since breaking her ankle five months earlier while "trying to kick my ex up the ass." She meant that literally, she said.

She had gone to Patterson High, same as Bill Bodani, Jr., then tried to get certified as a pharmacy tech at a for-profit career school. She hadn't worked for five years, since stocking shelves at Walmart; she had an application in for disability benefits. "I have my boyfriends taking care of me," she said.

Her father had recently gotten ninety days' notice to leave the house, which would soon be knocked down as well. He didn't mind leaving, she said. "He really wants to get out of the neighborhood for real," she said. "He's OK."

She was sorry to see so many houses wiped away, but only so much so. "They need to go," she said. "They've been up a long time. They're old. It's about time. It's historical Baltimore, so it's a little sad, but some things need to come to an end. Some things got to go."

At the other end of the newly vacant lot, David Johnson, Sr., was shoring up the masonry on an adjacent home to the north, which was not slated for demolition. He was using eight-inch stucco blocks and trying to make it look as much like the original brickwork as possible.

Johnson had picked up bricklaying from his father. He was conflicted about his post-demolition work. He was proud of his skill as a senior mason, but felt complicit, too. "Forty years ago, every house was inhabited," he said. "You feel like you're contributing to the blight and devastation."

"It's an iffy situation," he continued. "When you come into a neighborhood of people, people feel devalued that their community is marked for demolition. That's why you need to put love and care into the brickwork, so they feel you're contributing to the community. I try to follow every detail so that it looks like the neighborhood had. When you go around, different neighborhoods have different details, you try to put it back the best you can."

On the 1700 block, a construction crew with dump trucks was working to fill in the gaping hole in the ground left by the demolition of about nine homes stretching all the way from Montford to Port Street along Lafayette Avenue. The excavator used to knock down the homes still stood on the site. Right across Montford Street, at the southwest corner of Montford and Lafayette, four young men were selling drugs with casual disregard for the construction crew doing its own work only twenty feet away. Every five minutes or so, a car or truck pulled up and handed money to one of the young men and drove on.

Around the corner, at Lafayette and Port, George Jackson was watching the trucks in the big pit from the little bench of his walker while his dog, Jack, wandered up and down the street. "They was a long time getting to it," he said. "There wasn't nobody living in them. They were nothing but a rat home."

He wore a fedora and a tank top, and his trouser buttons were unfastened. He had been born in South Carolina eighty-eight years earlier. He had lived in his home, on the next block of Lafayette, for fifty-two years. He had raised five children. He had worked at the Beth Steel shipyard—not the one at Sparrows Point, but the repair yard on the other side of the harbor. When the shipyard closed in 1982, he was making $12 an hour—about $32 in today's dollars.

A white man passed by with the shuffle of an opioid addict. A broken syringe cap lay on the ground near Jackson's walker. The row on the other side of Lafayette bore a spray-paint homage: RIP LIL WILL. This neighborhood, Broadway East, would experience the city's biggest increase in homicides in 2019, tripling from four to twelve. "People lived all around here," Jackson said. "All the homes were full up. Now all of them are gone."

The wood being salvaged by Brick + Board went to its new headquarters in the center of the city, where it was cleaned and stacked. The bricks went to the other side of the city, to a secluded old stone warehouse in West Baltimore that the organization rented from a company that handled much of the city's recycling waste on the same property. The bricks were dumped in towering heaps in the lot, twenty feet high in spots. From there, they were loaded onto a conveyor belt that carried them into a small sealed space in the warehouse, where one of the half dozen workers on hand would determine if they were salvageable.

Those that were salvageable went on to other workers who attacked them with the most rudimentary of tools: a brush and a pick hammer. Those that were not went right back out of the warehouse on the belt and into a hopper, where they were crushed for fill that would be trucked back to demo sites to level the ground. The workers, many of whom had come to Humanim with prison records, started at $11.57 per hour; veterans made close to $20.

Once cleaned of dirt, the bricks were loaded onto pallets, 540 in each, and wrapped in plastic. And then it became Max Pollock's job to sell them.

On July 16, 2019, the United States House Judiciary Committee's Subcommittee on Antitrust, Commercial, and Administrative Law convened a hearing on Capitol Hill to address "online platforms and market power." It was a remarkable moment: after years of watching as a small handful of companies grew to dominate life and commerce online, members of Congress in both parties were all of a sudden showing concern about the extent of that dominance.

Their concern did not come out of nowhere. It had been stoked by a small but effective cadre of thinkers and activists who had for several years been articulating the nature and costs of the companies' dominance. These included Stacy Mitchell with the Institute for Local Self-Reliance, who documented the companies' effect on smaller businesses, local communities, and democracy in general: "These companies," she wrote, "have created a form of private government—autocratic regimes that are tightening their control over our main arteries of commerce and information." And they included Lina Khan, who while still in law school had written a groundbreaking paper showing how antitrust enforcement had failed to address the threat of the new aspiring monopolies, Amazon in particular. Regulators had erred, she argued, in focusing only on the question of whether companies were raising prices for consumers, not whether they were causing broader distortions in the marketplace and society in general. Amazon, she argued, was stifling competition through predatory pricing and the structural advantages that came with being a dominant online platform, in ways that would over time leave consumers with lower-quality products and less choice and innovation, even if they seemed to be benefiting from lower prices today. By example, she noted Amazon's 2010 takeover of Quidsi, the owner of the rival site Diapers.com, after driving it to desperation by pricing Amazon's own diapers far below cost. Losing tens of millions of dollars, it seemed, was worth it to eliminate a competitor.

Her arguments were being wielded by a new coalition, dubbed Athena, that included dozens of unions and activist groups, such as the Warehouse Worker Resource Center, which had for years been fighting on behalf of the thousands of Amazon workers in the San Bernardino Valley. Even some of Amazon's founding employees had started to have grave misgivings. "I think that the characterization of Amazon as being a ruthless competitor is true," said Shel Kaphan, the programmer who had toured Santa Cruz with Bezos way back at the time of the company's founding. "And under the flag of customer obsession they can do a lot of things, which might not be good for people who aren't their customers." The Federal Trade Commission, the Department of Justice, several state governments, and the European Commission had all launched investigations into the company's practices.

Now executives from four giants—Amazon, Google, Facebook, and Apple—had been called to testify on the basic question: Had they gotten too big for the country's good? "The meteoric growth of our open and competitive Internet revolutionized our lives, our work, our businesses, and our entire world. Millions of new good-paying jobs were created, greater access to information promised a renewal of our democracy and social progress," said the subcommittee's chairman, David Cicilline, a Rhode Island Democrat. "Each of these American companies have contributed immense technological breakthroughs and economic value to our country. They were started on shoestring budgets, in dorm rooms and garages, and are a testament to our core values as a country. But in an effort to promote and continue this new economy, Congress and antitrust enforcers allow these firms to regulate themselves with little oversight. As a result, the Internet has become increasingly concentrated, less open, and growing really hostile to innovation and entrepreneurship."

He noted that Amazon controlled nearly half of all online commerce in the United States, that half of American families now had an Amazon Prime account, that Amazon's closest competitor, eBay, controlled less than 6 percent of the market for online commerce. He quoted Stacy Mitchell: "Powerful online gatekeepers not only control market access, but also directly compete with the businesses that depend on them." He noted that in the two decades since the Justice Department brought a landmark monopolization case against Microsoft, not a single complaint had been filed alleging anticompetitive conduct in the online market, even as signs grew of innovation and competition declining in the digital realm. "This hearing isn't just about the companies before us today," he said. "It's about ensuring that we have the conditions for the next Google, the next Amazon, the next Facebook, and the next Apple to grow and prosper."

When it came his time to speak, Nate Sutton, Amazon's "associate general counsel of competition," disputed outright the notion that the company was all that dominant. The company, he said, controlled only 1 percent of the total global retail market and 4 percent of the total U.S. retail market. "Amazon's mission is to be earth's most customer-centric company. Our core philosophy is firmly rooted in working backwards from what customers want. And we seek continually to innovate to provide customers the best experience," he said. "Amazon operates a diverse range of businesses from retail and entertainment to consumer electronics and technology services. In each of these areas we face intense competition from well-established competitors. For example, retail, which remains by far our largest business, is as old as human commercial experience. It has long been and continues to be characterized by intense competition at every level."

The committee members were skeptical. They asked whether third-party sellers really had any viable alternatives for selling their goods online other than Amazon. They asked about the rising fees that Amazon was charging them to sell on the site—an average of 27 cents on each dollar of sales, a 42 percent increase over five years—which functioned as a kind of tax on online commerce, collected by Amazon. They asked about the company's punishment of sellers that violate its terms by suspending their accounts and shutting down their product pages, freezing them out of the marketplace.

And they zeroed in on the inherent conflict between Amazon both controlling the platform on which nearly half of all online sales were made and selling its own products on that platform. They asked whether the company privileged its own products by promoting them higher on the page or pricing them well below cost to drive competitors out of business, and whether it used sales data to come up with its own versions of hot-selling items. "When people sell products on your site, do you track which products are most successful, and then do you sometimes create a product to compete with that product? Because essentially you have this massive trove of data, right?" asked Pramila Jayapal, a Democrat from Seattle who, despite representing Amazon's hometown, was not shy about criticizing the company. "Do you track that and then do you create products that directly compete with those most popular brands that are out there?"

"We do not use any of that specific seller data in creating our own private brand products," said Sutton.

Cicilline, skeptical, followed up a moment later. "You are selling your own products on a platform that you control, and they're competing with products in the marketplace from retail—from other sellers, right?" he asked.

"That practice, I think, has been common in the retail industry for decades," Sutton said. "Most retailers offer their own products in their store as well as third-party products and—"

"But—but, Mr. Sutton, the difference is Amazon is a trillion-dollar company that runs an online platform with real-time data, and millions of purchases, and billions in commerce, and can manipulate algorithms on its platform and to favor its own product," Cicilline said. "That is not the same as the local retailer who might have a CVS brand and a national brand. I mean, it's quite different. You said, we do not use seller data to compete with other sellers online. You do collect enormous data about what products are popular, what's selling, where they're selling. You're saying you don't use that in any way to promote Amazon products?"

"Let me answer it—thank you," Sutton said.

"And I remind you, sir, you're under oath," Cicilline said.

"We—we use data to serve our customers," Sutton said. "We don't use individuals' seller data to directly compete with them."

Ten months later, reporting by *The Wall Street Journal* would directly contradict Sutton's testimony: Amazon employees, the paper found, had repeatedly accessed documents and data about specific popular products before Amazon introduced almost identical products, from car-trunk organizers to office-chair seat cushions. It was just the sort of practice that advocates like Stacy Mitchell and Mike Tucker, the office-supply association director, had been warning small businesses about. Members of Congress, angry about the contradiction, would demand that Jeff Bezos himself testify before the subcommittee. When he did so, in July 2020, it would emerge from records obtained by the subcommittee that Amazon had in fact referred to third-party sellers on the site as "internal competitors," rather than as the "partners" it publicly proclaimed them to be. And Bezos would acknowledge in testimony that the company steered shoppers to sellers who paid for Amazon's shipping services, helping drive its large gains against other delivery companies but undercutting the company's claim to being a neutral marketplace.

Three months later, in October 2020, the Democratic staff of the House subcommittee released a 449-page report on its investigation into the tech giants' dominance, calling on Congress to take action to break up the companies. "To put it simply, companies that once were scrappy, underdog startups that challenged the status quo have become the kinds of monopolies we last saw in the era of oil barons and railroad tycoons," the report stated. "These firms have too much power, and that power must be reined in and subject to appropriate oversight and enforcement. Our economy and democracy are at stake."

One day, Max Pollock drove down to Washington to visit some of his customers. There was a big house in the wealthy Maryland suburb of

Potomac. There was a "specialty doughnut" cafe where varieties included pumpkin-spice latte crème brûlée, salted dulce de leche, and caramel apple streusel. This was at the Wharf, the $2.5 billion redevelopment of D.C.'s Southwest waterfront—four hotels, 1,375 luxury apartments, restaurants that didn't accept cash, and nearly a million square feet of offices—where visitors could arrive by jitney motorboats or yachts, and where a firepit called the Torch sent flames leaping twelve feet in the air.

And there was Chapman Stables. This was a large new condominium complex in the Truxton Circle neighborhood, near the intersection of New York Avenue and North Capitol Street. A couple decades ago, this part of town was heavily Black and working class. Just to the south was Sursum Corda, a public housing project that was being torn down and redeveloped by Toll Brothers, who had promised to set aside 136 units for displaced Sursum Corda residents. The nearby Temple Courts housing project had been demolished in 2008 and replaced with a parking lot. They weren't supposed to knock down Temple Courts until they'd finished a new apartment building nearby, which was called 2M, so that the residents displaced from the former could move right into the latter. But in the end there had been a ten-year gap between demolition and completion, and the people who'd lost their Temple Courts homes were long gone. Luxury apartment buildings were sprouting across the area, including one, the Belgard, that was particularly unapologetic in its pretensions: LIFE IN HIGH REGARD read the large sign on its western face.

Chapman Stables had once, in fact, been home to stables and a coal yard, and its developers had done all they could to capitalize on this hint of archaic authenticity in their marketing. Very little of the historic structure could be retained in a high-end condo building, but the developers had an easy solution for this problem: Brick + Board. They had bought no fewer than 60,000 bricks from Baltimore, one of Max Pollock's biggest sales. Now he was visiting the complex, which was nearing completion, to take some pictures.

He saw his bricks in the big interior wall as you entered the building. He saw them in the wall overlooking the courtyard. He saw them in the units, in big walls that were forty bricks high, seventeen bricks wide. One model unit had been outfitted with deluxe Bosch appliances and odd aspirational touches, such as a booklet of random pages torn from books and tied artfully together with string.

The units cost $500,000 for a 700-square-foot apartment, and up to $1 million for larger ones. "Can you imagine, $500,000?" Max Pollock said. "It's cheap for D.C., but it's half a million dollars for a studio. It's a dorm room." He couldn't imagine what sort of young person could afford such an apartment.

Many could not afford it, which was why Washington, D.C., was now in the grips of a housing crisis. The city was having the same debates they were having in New York and Boston and Seattle and San Francisco, over whether it was best to impose limits on rents or build a lot more supply. Oddly absent from these debates was the broader context, that these cities had become so expensive because so much of the country's growth and prosperity had been clustered in so few places—that people in these successful cities, too, would be better off if more of that wealth and dynamism had spread to other cities and towns.

People were struggling to afford small half-million-dollar apartments decorated with bricks from demolished homes forty miles away that could have been bought for ten or twenty thousand dollars. A less concentrated economy might have created buyers for those vacant homes in Baltimore, eager to bring life to unloved buildings and underpopulated neighborhoods. Instead, the great paradox galloped onward: the spread of blight and abandonment in one city, the spread of congestion and exclusion in another only an hour away. One city rushing to demolish three-story rowhouses that would cost $1 million in the other down the road.

These had come to be seen as completely different worlds, but they were connected, and perhaps one solution applied to both. To break up the giants that had concentrated wealth not only in themselves, but in the places in which they had chosen to reside. To disperse prosperity more broadly across a great big country, its many cities and towns—not evenly, by any means, but enough to restore some balance, to deter resentment and despair in one set of places and complacency and anxiety in the other.

Max Pollock was well aware that most of those living in Chapman Stables would have no idea where the bricks came from. They would probably assume they were original to the building—it was "historic," after all.

This bothered him a little. Before he left, he paused in a main hallway on the ground level that had a particularly rich sampling in a long floor-to-ceiling wall. There were some D.C. bricks here and there—they were easy to spot because they were crumbly, inferior. But most of these were Baltimore bricks.

He could even tell which streets they had come from.

The orange ones were from Chase Street.

The oldest-looking ones were from Federal Street.

The ones with the vertical lines were from Fenwick Avenue. Those homes had been built later, around 1915, when the ovens were able to fire bricks at a higher temperature. They'd stack the bricks in such a way that part of them was more exposed to the high heat, and those were the lines you saw on the Fenwick bricks.

He had his pictures. It was time to go. It was always a relief to leave this city, back to the one he now called home.

Overtime: May Day

On the Saturday before Easter 2020, I set off on a drive from Baltimore, where I live, to Pittsfield, Massachusetts, where I grew up. There were stay-at-home orders in effect in Maryland, but I decided that a visit to my parents, whom I had not seen in several months, qualified as essential. I would stay elsewhere for the night, to keep a safe distance; we would go for an Easter Sunday walk.

I departed Baltimore in the early evening. Interstate 95, the perpetually clogged corridor of the Eastern Seaboard, was emptier than I had ever seen it. Digital highway signs overhead declared SAVE LIVES NOW. STAY HOME. I had never been in the vicinity of a war zone, but it occurred to me that it might feel somewhat like this—only the most essential or foolhardy travelers on the roads, the rest of the world hunkered down.

Except there were no troop carriers or munitions haulers in this war zone. Instead, there were trucks. The majority of the few vehicles on the road were tractor trailers, and the vast plurality of those were Amazon trucks. I counted two dozen of them on the hundred-mile stretch between Baltimore and southern New Jersey, where it got too dark to see logos. I had seen many, many Amazon trucks on my travels around the country over the past few years. I had never seen a concentration anywhere close to this.

If we were in a war against the novel coronavirus, then Amazon was our troop carrier. In this war, mobilizing to attack the enemy meant universal withdrawal and self-isolation, and Amazon was supplying that mobilization by bringing us everything at home, allowing us to stay there. All at once, it had become our civic duty, our cause larger than ourselves, to fulfill our needs online. An act of convenience that had once been tinged—at least for some—with misgivings was now infused with righteousness. By placing a one-click order, one was flattening the curve.

The boxes came, in great numbers. Often, they sat on porches or in garages for a day or two in case they'd been tainted with viral particles by their delivery handler. When this quarantine passed, the boxes were allowed into the home.

The boxes came in such quantity, the orders were placed in such quantity, that the company famed for its peerless logistics operation was for once having trouble keeping up. It announced it was hiring 100,000 more workers at its warehouses, then a few weeks later announced it was hiring 75,000 more. It told buyers and third-party sellers that it was deprioritizing orders deemed less than essential. In the most startling move of all, it briefly removed some of the web features intended to get shoppers to buy more from the site— Amazon was for once *discouraging* people from spending more money. The company had seen into the future, when it would truly be the Everything Store, the Be-All, End-All Store, but it wasn't ready to carry it off. Not yet.

Such emergency measures were temporary. The usual buying goads returned, as did the nonessential items. It emerged that the company's algorithms were in fact finding new ways to drive product makers to sell goods only on the site, rather than through other retailers. And as the peak of the spring 2020 national crisis passed, certain consequences became unmistakable. The pandemic had taken a series of related developments in American life and accelerated them to hyper-speed, like a film reel gone haywire.

The news organizations that had already lost the majority of their advertising revenue to Silicon Valley were now losing what little remained as a result of the halt in commerce—to try to survive, many furloughed their entire newsrooms, on rotating shifts, leaving them understaffed to cover first one huge story, the pandemic, and then another, the protests over George Floyd's death at the hands of a police officer in Minneapolis. By August, things had grown so dire that one chain of papers, Tribune, announced it was shuttering its physical newsrooms for good at, among others, *The New York Daily News*, *Orlando Sentinel*, and *Allentown Morning Call*, the newspaper that had broken the 2011 story about workers passing out from heat exhaustion at the local Amazon warehouse. In December, Tribune closed the offices of the *Hartford Courant*, the largest newspaper in Connecticut and the oldest continuously published paper in the United States.

The legacy retail companies that had survived the upheaval of the prior two decades were now careening toward extinction. JCPenney, Neiman Marcus, and J.Crew filed for bankruptcy. Macy's temporarily shuttered all 775 of its stores and furloughed nearly all of its 125,000 workers; after its stock fell by 75 percent in two months, it was dropped from the S&P 500. Amazon's Seattle neighbor, Nordstrom, announced it was laying off thousands. The toll was no less widespread among the country's small independent businesses. All told, 25,000 retail stores were expected to go out of business by the end of 2020, a figure that nearly tripled the mass closure figures of recent years.

Meanwhile, the companies that had for several decades been capitalizing on the trends reshaping the economy were growing larger and more successful in what seemed like the exact inverse of the economic hemorrhage underway all across the country. By late May, the five biggest tech companies—Apple, Facebook, Microsoft, Amazon, and Google's Alphabet—had added a stunning $1.7 trillion to their combined market cap in just two months, a rise of 43 percent. The combined value of only these five companies was now a fifth of the S&P 500. And they were only going to grow larger: the five were sitting on a combined $557 billion in cash. They used it to finance new acquisitions and to raise their spending on research and development to nearly $30 billion—more than NASA's entire budget—even as their smaller rivals were retrenching. "What is unusual at this moment is the extreme divergence in the health of different types of companies," wrote the economist Austan Goolsbee, a former adviser to Barack Obama. "Many of the biggest are flush with money, while smaller competitors have never been in more precarious shape."

The biggest winner of all was Amazon. Its first-quarter sales were up by more than a quarter over those the year prior—this, at a time when overall retail sales were plunging. Its stock surged so much in mid-April—up by more than 30 percent on the year, as the pandemic was nearing its deadliest period—that Jeff Bezos's net worth increased by $24 billion in the span of only two months. In late July, Amazon announced that its profit had doubled in the second quarter, with sales up by a stunning 40 percent from those a year earlier. On the news, its share price surged yet higher—by early September, it was up by 84 percent on the year, more than double the rise of other tech giants. "Simply put, Covid-19, in our view, has injected Amazon with a growth hormone," wrote one industry analyst in a note to investors.

To handle the surge in business, the company had, between January and October, added more than 425,000 employees worldwide, bringing its total number of nonseasonal employees in the United States to 800,000 and its global total to more than 1.2 million, up by half from a year earlier and now behind only Walmart and China National Petroleum (and that tally didn't even include the 500,000 drivers who were delivering its packages). To house these workers, the company went on a building and leasing spree, opening 100 builldings in September, on its way to occupying nearly 100 million additional square feet of warehouse space by the end of 2020, a roughly 50 percent increase. Its warehouses weren't the only part of the company in high demand: its data centers were ramping up capacity for customers like Zoom, as hundreds of millions of daily human interactions shifted online.

The midsummer announcement of Amazon's massive pandemic profits had come on the same day that the Commerce Department reported that the U.S. economy had shrunk by nearly 10 percent, the largest quarterly drop on record. In other words, Amazon was flourishing more than ever before at one of the lowest moments for the country as a whole: the fates of the company and the nation had diverged entirely.

———

Such profound imbalance in fortunes had contributed greatly to the political convulsions of the era. And, as the dread year of 2020 neared its close, it was plain that one of the first orders of business facing the newly elected president, Joe Biden, and his incoming administration would be deciding how to address the divergence. The nation could hardly afford for it to grow any wider.

E ven as the pandemic accelerated the concentration of wealth and power within some of the most dominant companies, it was possible to imagine ways that it *might* disperse prosperity and dynamism more broadly across the country. Some of the many New Yorkers who had fled the city— there were upscale apartment buildings in Manhattan left almost entirely vacant—were considering permanent relocation. There was talk that the pandemic might spell the end of the office, that we would, at long last, be free to work from anywhere. If there was no more need to report to work in a downtown tower, why stick around the big city, at exorbitant cost? Why *not* head for a quiet hamlet upstate, or even to Syracuse or Erie or Akron?

It was a romantic notion, tinged with the aura of a simpler time—a time when Samuel Grumbacher sent his sons and sons-in-law off to make the family name in small cities across Pennsylvania. But the notion was up against all manner of brute economic reality. The digital economy had produced winner-take-all companies and cities, and it was hard to imagine that the great leap forward in digitalization brought on by the pandemic lockdowns would not simply intensify that winner-take-all effect as the tech giants and their associated cities consolidated their market power yet further. It was not so surprising, then, that Facebook would seize the moment to lease all 730,000 square feet of converted office space in the monumental former post office building across from Penn Station in New York, or that Amazon would announce that it was adding at least 2,000 white-collar employees at the former Lord & Taylor flagship on Fifth Avenue in Manhattan, which it had bought for $1 billion. In Seattle, where there were now more than 50,000 Amazon employees, the company announced plans to accommodate 25,000 more across Lake Washington in Bellevue by 2025—just like that, the Seattle metro area would be absorbing the equivalent of the entire HQ2 complex in Northern Virginia, further entrenching its long-term prosperity. And while rents and condo prices started to retreat from their stratospheric highs in the wealthiest cities, the rising demand for suburban New York office parks and bedroom communities, Western ski-resort real estate, and Hamptons school districts suggested that the benefits of any dispersal would remain well within the bounds of the winner-take-all metropolis and its satellites, and would not trickle out to smaller cities farther afield.

Meanwhile, those same smaller cities were poised to suffer deep cuts as the federal pandemic rescue package targeted municipal aid only to cities with populations over 500,000. There were already signs that restaurant and bar closures would particularly harm places such as St. Louis and Detroit, whose glimmers of belated revival had been fueled in part by the sprouting of new nightlife options. By August, American Airlines was announcing it was ending flights to fifteen small and midsize cities, making it more likely that their isolation and decline would only accelerate.

That is to say, the pandemic's toll was going to fall hardest on the places that had the least cushion to fall back on. And the same was true of the impact on individuals. In Las Vegas, officials painted rectangles on the asphalt of a parking lot to try to keep the homeless people sleeping there six feet apart. On the Jersey Shore, a food bank called Fulfill saw a 40 percent increase in demand and served more than 364,000 extra meals. Nationwide, people who earned more than $28 per hour had seen their employment levels return to pre-pandemic levels by the fall of 2020, while those who made less than $16 per hour had seen more than a quarter of their jobs wiped out.

In Dayton, Todd Swallows had lost his cardboard job after another car breakdown had kept him from getting to work. By the start of the pandemic, he was working at a Popeyes not far from where he and Sara and the kids were living, half an hour south of Dayton. But when the pandemic hit, his hours were cut as the restaurant switched to drive-through only, while Sara struggled to homeschool the children in their small unit. The stress had its predictable result: they split up again in May, agreeing to share custody of the kids. Todd, frustrated at Popeyes' refusal to give him a promised raise over his $11-per-hour wage, had by October found a job back in logistics—at a tire warehouse adjacent to one of the smaller Amazon distribution hubs that were popping up everywhere. The pay was $13 per hour, almost what he had once been making in cardboard.

One hundred fifty miles to the east, in Nelsonville, Taylor Sappington had his hours cut so much at Texas Roadhouse that he decided to get a new job as a checkout clerk at Kroger, the only grocery store in Nelsonville. The job paid a third less than the old one did. He had a new position in town, too: he had won election to be city auditor, a paid part-time position. Someone else might have found it awkward to scan groceries for the same constituents whose tax dollars he was overseeing, but Taylor thought nothing of it. There were other things to worry about, including the fact that someone had been tearing up some of the star brick from sidewalks to sell on the black market, leaving sad bare patches around town, and that one business after another was closing in the county, including the Ruby Tuesday where Jared had died. It now sat empty on the Athens strip.

The crisis had hit hard, too, for Sandy Grodin in El Paso. His office-supply sales dropped by 65 percent in April, and he sent almost everyone home, for their safety. But he got a federal small-business loan, and in May, one of the local school districts made a large order of school supplies to send to all the kids doing remote classwork. He won the contract partly because his business, unlike Amazon, was able to organize all the supplies by grade level and classroom, to make it easier for the district to distribute them. Across town, the Gandaras were also in scary straits at the outset of the crisis. "Everything just dropped out," said Teresa. "We fell into a pit." But then they adapted: Pencil Cup saw an unmet demand and started delivering janitorial and sanitation supplies to all the businesses and families encountering empty shelves in stores and price-gouging online.

In Seattle, Katie Wilson and the other members of the Transit Riders Union were taking part in some of the city's protests over George Floyd's death, which eventually led to the creation of an "autonomous zone," decreed to be free of police officers, in the heart of Capitol Hill, the hipster neighborhood near downtown. The protests stirred Katie's activist spirit, but she had suffered too much disappointment at the hands of powerful opponents to get her hopes up. "It's cool," she said, "but it's not the revolution."

In Washington, D.C., the huge protests around the city drew, among others, Amazon's Jay Carney, the head of the public relations operation. He tweeted a selfie of himself near the White House, wearing sunglasses, a face mask, and a Black Lives Matter T-shirt.

In Baltimore, a twenty-six-year-old woman named Shayla Melton was trying to decide whether to go back to work at Amazon. She had been working as a picker at the Broening Highway warehouse, where the GM plant used to be, until she had her baby, her second child, just as the pandemic was arriving. Her husband also worked as a picker, but at the other Amazon warehouse, at Sparrows Point, and he, too, had taken time off from the job, because there had been a lot of coronavirus cases there.

The company's initial reaction to the pandemic was to announce that it was seeding a charitable fund for its temp workers and contract delivery drivers who lacked health coverage and to encourage the public to donate to it. This met with some derision. It also promised two weeks of paid leave to anyone with a COVID-19 diagnosis and offered unpaid time off, without risk of being penalized for missing shifts, to anyone who wanted to stay home as a precaution. It offered a temporary $2 bump in hourly pay to those who kept working. It set up temperature checks and COVID-19 testing stations for arriving workers. It issued masks and provided hand sanitizer and disinfectant.

Hector Torrez watched the measures go into effect at the warehouse in Thornton, Colorado. A small army of cleaners came in one day, wearing what looked like suits from *Ghostbusters*. The usual group stretching routine at shift start was canceled, which made the physical work only riskier, as did the fact that jobs like loading boxes into trucks now had to be done solo, without a partner. What most upset Hector was the contrast with the company's headquarters employees, who were being allowed—encouraged—to work from home. So superficial did the warehouse precautions seem that he decided to keep living in the basement, well into the summer. He had not so much as hugged his wife and kids for months; his companions were the family's dogs and cats. "We don't sit together, we don't do anything together," he said. "My assumption is that I'm being exposed to something every day."

Meanwhile, the new hires kept arriving. Several had backgrounds as elevated as his own: a former industrial engineer, a former litigator, a former owner of a real estate firm. "What I see around me is a lot of people who don't have much choice," he said. "We're economic refugees." Many other workers were quite young, and Hector would strike up conversations with them and urge them to move on as quickly as they could. "Time passes," he told them. "Get out when you still have time, and can still make a decision."

At the company's warehouses in France, union demands over safety measures had forced a weeks-long shutdown and an eventual deal that included a reduction of shifts by 15 minutes, without a reduction to pay, to allow for more social distancing at crowded shift changes. In the absence of unions at the U.S. warehouses, discontent took other forms. WELCOME TO HELL read the graffiti inside truck trailers, out of sight of warehouse cameras. FUCK BEZOS. Workers began sharing their disquiet in online back channels, and at some warehouses, they organized protests, signaling that the pandemic just might set in motion a new era of workplace activism.

The company moved to head off any such swell. It fired a worker who organized a walkout at the huge warehouse in Staten Island, saying he violated safety protocol by coming to the warehouse while under self-quarantine for having had contact with an infected worker. It also fired two headquarters employees in Seattle who had spoken up for the protesting warehouse workers.

More than worker activism alone would be necessary to provide a check on so vast and powerful a company, as well as its fellow industry giants. It would require federal action. Joe Biden's election victory showed a continuation of the political trends of the era: Democrats strengthened their hold on wealthy suburbs, while making up scant ground in the struggling rural areas and small towns that had elected Donald Trump. Ominously for Democrats, there were signs that, as they transformed into the party of highly educated urban professionals, their erosion of support in white working-class communities was spreading to Hispanic voters and Black men.

It would be up to Biden, his new administration, and Democrats in Congress to decide whether to address that erosion, and the great class and regional imbalances that lay behind it, by challenging their party's longtime natural allies in the tech industry. The Democratic Party was, in a sense, becoming the party of upper-middle-class consumers and the people who packed and delivered things to them. Holding together such a coalition posed a challenge.

By late April, several months into the pandemic, the allowance of unpaid time off was about to expire, which meant Shayla Melton's husband was going to have to go back if he wanted to keep the job. Her decision was coming due, too. She had recently started driving for Uber and was considering sticking with that instead of Amazon. It seemed easier to control her exposure to the coronavirus there, with the windows open and constant sanitizing of her car, than in the high-pressure whirlwind of the warehouse. "I'm not sure I want to go back," she said. "At least with Uber, I feel a little more at ease."

Melton and her family lived just outside Baltimore, in another of the many housing complexes in the area owned by Jared Kushner's family real estate company, only a mile and a half from the one where the delivery van had killed the seven-year-old girl. A young woman who lived a few doors down from Melton had recently stopped working for Amazon because the exertion had gotten too hard on her back. Increasingly, it seemed as if a significant fraction of people living in the complexes were or had been working at Amazon, as if the complexes had become the new company town, replacing the lettered streets at Sparrows Point with their loops and cul-de-sacs with names like Skipjack Court and Tidewater Lane.

On May Day, there were rumors circulating of large walkouts by workers at Amazon warehouses around the country. But there was no sign of any unrest outside the fulfillment center at Broening Highway, where the vast parking lot appeared fuller than ever before, or at the adjacent sortation center, where the collapsed wall had been rebuilt and where half the building was now given over to packing Prime Now deliveries of groceries and household items, which were in high demand.

Nor was there any sign of May Day ferment outside the warehouse at Sparrows Point. The day before, the company had announced that it would soon open a second warehouse on the Point, with 500 more workers, to pack and ship large items such as sports equipment and furniture. It would be in an even longer building, over where the rod-and-wire mill had once stood. Those new workers would be some of the 4,400 the company was adding in Maryland on top of the 17,500 it already employed in the state, bringing it ever closer to Beth Steel's numbers at the Point's midcentury peak.

The street sign leading into the parking lot of the existing warehouse still read TIN MILL ROAD. It evoked another era when the country had been at war, truly at war, and had managed in a short period of time to build in this very place more than one hundred ships—navy fleet oilers, attack transports, ore carriers—and produce the armor plate and gun forgings for countless more. Now, seven decades later, the country was struggling to rebuild its supply chains to muster enough protective equipment for its health workers.

A man was standing outside the hiring office run by Integrity, the human-resources contractor, waiting for his Lyft ride home after coming to file a job application. He was thirty-three years old, and he was applying for the first regular job of his life. He had spent most of his adulthood making a good livelihood from selling heroin and fentanyl near Lexington Market on the west side of Baltimore's downtown, but that had gotten harder during the pandemic: with stores closed, his usual customers couldn't steal things to sell to support their habit. "You can't steal, you can't do nothing," he said. "It's definitely tough out here. Ain't no money out here."

So here he was, accepting the path that everyone, it seemed, was now taking. "My other homeboy was talking about driving for Amazon. Everyone trying to come to Amazon."

He wasn't sure how he was going to get by on warehouse wages, but he didn't really have a choice. "It's definitely tough out here. It definitely ain't the same," he said.

"I got to change up how I'm doing everything."

Notes

Introduction: The Basement

3   *Hector Torrez was living in the basement*: Hector Torrez is a pseudonym, as is the name, Laura, given for his wife. These pseudonyms are intended to protect this worker from retaliation by Amazon, where he was still employed at the time of publication. No other pseudonyms are used in this book.

4   *Its general manager, Clint Autry*: Joe Rubino, "Amazon's Gamble on Finding 1,500 Workers for Robotic Warehouse in Thornton May Not Have Been a Gamble After All," *The Denver Post*, March 20, 2019.

6   *the Bronx . . . twice as likely to be fatal*: Ese Olumhense and Ann Choi, "Bronx Residents Twice as Likely to Die from COVID-19 in NYC," *The City*, April 3, 2020.

6   *money for his mother's cremation*: Joshua Chaffin, "Elmhurst: Neighborhood at Center of New York's COVID-19 Crisis," *Financial Times*, April 10, 2020.

6   *in the small city of Albany, Georgia*: Ellen Barry, "Days After Funeral in a Georgia Town, Coronavirus 'Hit Like a Bomb,'" *The New York Times*, March 30, 2020.

7   *starting in 1980, this convergence reversed*: Robert Manduca, "Antitrust Enforcement as Federal Policy to Reduce Regional Economic Disparities," *The Annals of the American Academy of Political and Social Science* 685, no. 1 (September 2019): 156–171.

8   *they were now off the charts*: Robert Manduca, "The Contribution of National Income Inequality to Regional Economic Divergence," *Social Forces* 98, no. 2 (December 2019): 622–648.

8   *Job growth was almost twice as fast*: Eduardo Porter, "Why Big Cities Thrive, and Smaller Ones Are Being Left Behind," *The New York Times*, October 10, 2017.

8   *twenty-five cities with the highest median income*: Phillip Longman, "Bloom and Bust," *Washington Monthly*, November/December 2015.

Notes

8 *Wages in the very largest cities in the country*: Greg Ip, "Bloomberg Puts Geographic Inequality on the 2020 Agenda," *The Wall Street Journal*, January 8, 2020.

8 *venture capital was flowing to just three states*: Justin Fox, "Venture Capital Keeps Flowing to the Same Places," *Bloomberg Opinion*, January 8, 2019.

8 *"A handful of metro areas have seen"*: Manduca, "Antitrust Enforcement," 156.

9 *one-bedroom apartments renting for $3,600*: "Democrats Clamor Again for Rent Control," *The Economist*, September 9, 2019.

9 *Moody's issued a warning*: E. J. Dionne, "The Hidden Costs of the GOP's Deficit Two-Step," *The Washington Post*, October 21, 2018.

10 *upper-income households living in wealthy neighborhoods*: Carol Morello, "Study: Rich, Poor Americans Increasingly Likely to Live in Separate Neighborhoods," *The Washington Post*, August 1, 2012.

10 *three-quarters of all U.S. industries, by one estimate*: Gustavo Grullon, Yelena Larkin, and Roni Michaely, "Are US Industries Becoming More Concentrated?" *Review of Finance* 23, no. 4 (July 2019): 697–743.

10 *Mergers in sectors like banking and insurance*: Brian S. Feldman, "The Real Reason Middle America Should Be Angry," *Washington Monthly*, March/April/May 2016.

1. Community

15 *"a raw settlement in a new territory"*: Jonathan Raban, *Hunting Mister Heartbreak* (New York: Vintage, 1998), 254.

16 *"become a vast pawnshop"*: "City of Despair," *The Economist*, May 22, 1971.

16 *"The Seattle of that time"*: Charles D'Ambrosio, "Seattle, 1974," in *Loitering: New and Collected Essays* (Tin House Books, 2013), 31.

17 *from Jim Crow Texas into the Ambiguous West*: For an evocative account of the Great Migration route from Louisiana, Texas, and Oklahoma to the West Coast, see Isabel Wilkerson's *Warmth of Other Suns* (New York: Vintage, 2011).

17 *"The small numbers of blacks in the city"*: Quintard Taylor, *The Forging of a Black Community: Seattle's Central District from 1870 Through the Civil Rights Era* (Seattle: University of Washington Press, 1994), 14.

18 *gravitated to two places*: Taylor, 35.

18 *just four census tracts*: Taylor, 194.

19 *jazz clubs had sprouted*: Quin'Nita Cobbins, Paul de Barros, et al., *Seattle on the Spot: The Photographs of Al Smith* (Seattle: Museum of History and Industry, 2017).

21 *ticketed twice by the same airplane*: Paul Allen, *Idea Man: A Memoir by the Cofounder of Microsoft* (New York: Penguin, 2011), 117; and James Wallace and Jim Erickson, *Hard Drive: Bill Gates and the Making of the Microsoft Empire* (New York: Harper Business, 1993), 138.

21 *"The rainy days were a plus"*: Allen, 116.

21 *Gates was less committed to Seattle*: Wallace and Erickson, *Hard Drive*, 133.

22 *The company's phone number ended in 8080*: Wallace and Erickson, 136.

22 *Seattle proved an easier sell*: Allen, *Idea Man*, 146–147.

22 *"chest slides on the balustrade"*: Allen, 147.

24 *"the court rules for the right"*: Taylor, *The Forging*, 203.

24 *A letter protesting the proposed ordinance*: Taylor, 204.

24 *The ordinance was defeated*: Taylor, 205.

25 *"social climbers who were trying to get away"*: Taylor, 206.

25 *no longer home to a majority*: Taylor, 209.

25 *"once they learned it, they were unbeatable"*: Tyron Beason, "Total Experience Gospel Choir's Last Days," *The Seattle Times*, October 1, 2018.

26 *"If the music is too loud, that's too bad"*: Peter Blecha, "Total Experience Gospel Choir (Seattle)," HistoryLink.org, June 4, 2013, https://historylink.org/file/10391.

26 We represent God. We're going to sing: *Patrinell: The Total Experience*, directed by Tia Young and Andrew Elizaga (Seattle: Baby Seal Films, 2019), documentary film.

27 *"Most successful entrepreneurs start a company"*: Richard L. Brandt, *One Click: Jeff Bezos and the Rise of Amazon.com* (New York: Portfolio, 2012), 46.

27 *He came to Santa Cruz*: Brandt, 55.

27 *merchants needed to collect sales tax*: Brad Stone, *The Everything Store: Jeff Bezos and the Age of Amazon* (New York: Little, Brown, 2013), 28.

28 *He said half-jokingly years later*: Jim Brunner, "States Fight Back Against Amazon.com's Tax Deals," *The Seattle Times*, April 9, 2012.

28 *Hanauer . . . made a strong case for it*: Brandt, *One Click*, 57; and Stone, *The Everything Store*, 31.

28 *"bracing smell of possibility"*: Raban, *Hunting Mister Heartbreak*, 254.

28 *It was "the recruiting pool"*: "Jeff Bezos at the Economic Club of Washington (9/13/18)," CNBC livestream, https://youtu.be/xv_vkA0jsyo.

29 *"Cities are effectively machines"*: Geoffrey West, *Scale: The Universal Laws of Growth, Innovation, Sustainability, and the Pace of Life in Organisms, Cities, Economies, and Companies* (New York: Penguin, 2017), 323.

29 *"Economic value depends on talent"*: Enrico Moretti, *The New Geography of Jobs* (New York: Mariner Books, 2013), 66.

30 *deliberately choosing one that had a garage*: Brandt, *One Click*, 60.

30 *"This is not only the largest river"*: Stone, *The Everything Store*, 55.

30 *"For me the city is still inarticulate"*: D'Ambrosio, "Seattle, 1974," 33.

31 *The average income for the top 20 percent*: Gene Balk, "Seattle Hits Record High for Income Inequality, Now Rivals San Francisco," *The Seattle Times*, November 17, 2017.

31 *the median cost of buying a home*: Mike Rosenberg, "Seattle Home Prices Have Surpassed Los Angeles, New York and San Diego in the Last Four Years," *The Seattle Times*, August 29, 2018.

31 *the scarcity of children*: Mike Maciag, "The Most and Least Kid-Filled Cities," *Governing*, November 13, 2015.

31 *software developers moving to the city*: Gene Balk, "50 Software Developers a Week: Here's Who's Moving to Seattle," *The Seattle Times*, June 11, 2018.

31 *cranes rising across downtown*: Harrison Jacobs, "A Walk Through Seattle's 'Amazonia' Neighborhood," *Business Insider*, February 14, 2019.

31 *Gucci store selling slippers*: Tyrone Beason, "Will Seattle Figure Out How to Deal with Its New Wealth?," *The Seattle Times*, July 6, 2017.

31 *rooftop bar with . . . a $200 martini*: Tan Vinh, "The $200 Martini: Seattle's Frolik Launches 'Millionaires Menu,'" *The Seattle Times*, April 11, 2018.

32 *"wizard pub" in the trendy Ballard neighborhood*: Meghan Walker, "Wizard Pub and

Wand Shop Coming to Old Ballard," My Ballard, August 24, 2018, https://myballard .com/2018/08/24/wizard-pub-and-wand-shop-coming-to-old-ballard/.

32 *They earned $150,000 in average compensation*: Robert McCartney and Patricia Sullivan, "Amazon Says It Will Avoid a Housing Crunch with HQ2 by Planning Better Than It Did in Seattle," *The Washington Post*, May 3, 2019.

32 *The company accounted for 30 percent of all jobs added in Seattle*: Mike Rosenberg, "Will Amazon's HQ2 Sink Seattle's Housing Market?," *The Seattle Times*, November 12, 2018.

32 *a swath of land . . . called South Lake Union*: Noah Buhayar and Dina Bass, "How Big Tech Swallowed Seattle," *Bloomberg Businessweek*, August 30, 2018.

33 *"high-tech ghetto"*: Keith Harris, "Making Room for the Extraeconomic," *City* 23, no. 6 (November 2019): 751–773.

34 *"Alexa . . . Open the Spheres"*: Jena McGregor, "Why Amazon Built Its Workers a Mini Rain Forest Inside Three Domes in Downtown Seattle," *The Washington Post*, January 29, 2018.

2. Cardboard

38 *Ritty came up with the mechanical cash register*: Mark Bernstein, *Grand Eccentrics: Turning the Century—Dayton and the Inventing of America* (Wilmington, OH: Orange Frazer, 1996), 23.

38 *Patterson took the innovation national*: Bernstein, 27.

38 *Above all there was . . . Kettering*: Bernstein, 8–9.

39 *did their business at bronze check desks*: Curt Dalton, *Dayton Through Time* (n.p.: Arcadia, 2015), 42.

40 *kids were scolded by the cops*: Author interview with a retired schoolteacher who grew up in West Dayton, Ohio, January 2018.

42 *"Trade adjustment is a slow-moving process"*: David H. Autor, David Dorn, and Gordon H. Hanson, "China Shock: Learning from Labor Market Adjustment to Large Changes in Trade," National Bureau of Economic Research Working Paper 21906, January 2016, https://nber.org/papers/w21906.pdf.

43 *would not deign to move to Dayton*: Dan Barry, "In a Company's Hometown, the Emptiness Echoes," *The New York Times*, January 24, 2010.

43 *Ohio's industrial electricity consumption would fall*: Steve Bennish, "Industrial Power Use Plummets," *Dayton Daily News*, September 25, 2011.

43 *Montgomery County would suffer the steepest drop*: Steve Bennish, *Scrappers: Dayton, Ohio, and America Turn to Scrap* (self-published, 2015), 7.

48 *rate of adults . . . ever been married*: Janet Adamy and Paul Overberg, "Affluent Americans Still Say 'I Do.' More in the Middle Class Don't," *The Wall Street Journal*, March 8, 2020.

52 *bulwark of Republican sobriety*: Alec MacGillis, "The Great Republican Crack-Up," *ProPublica*, July 15, 2016.

54 *"intimate partner violence"*: Leigh Goodmark, "Stop Treating Domestic Violence Differently from Other Crimes," *The New York Times*, July 23, 2019.

57 *Dayton was spiraling as never before*: Chris Stewart, "Coroner Investigates 145 Suspected Overdose Deaths in Month," *Dayton Daily News*, January 31, 2017.

59 *double its next nine rivals*: Annie Gasparro and Laura Stevens, "Brands Invent New Lines for Only Amazon to Sell" (graph accompanying article), *The Wall Street Journal*,

January 25, 2019; and Scott Galloway, *The Four: The Hidden DNA of Amazon, Apple, Facebook, and Google* (New York: Random House, 2017), 27.

60 *costing states hundreds of millions*: Ben Casselman, "As Amazon Steps Up Tax Collection, Some Cities Are Left Out," *The New York Times*, March 25, 2018.

60 *soon handing out $3 billion per year*: Louis Story, "As Companies Seek Tax Deals, Governments Pay High Price," *The New York Times*, December 1, 2012.

61 *without a single "no" vote*: Joe Vardon, "Tax-Credit Requests to State Panel on Long Winning Streak," *The Columbus Dispatch*, August 21, 2013.

61 *"Enjoy the holidays"*: From emails obtained by a public information request from the Ohio Development Services Agency in June 2019.

62 *assured Amazon's lawyer in August 2017*: From emails obtained by a public information request from the City of Monroe, Ohio, in April 2019.

63 *The agreement called for a . . . tax credit*: Kara Driscoll, "'Project Big Daddy': How Monroe Landed Amazon's Next Fulfillment Center," *Dayton Daily News*, October 5, 2017.

65 *40 billion square feet of material*: Jo Craven McGinty, "A Nation Awash in Cardboard, but for How Long?," *The Wall Street Journal*, August 8, 2019.

66 *A third of all U.S. jobs*: Heather Long, "This Doesn't Look Like the Best Economy Ever," *The Washington Post*, July 5, 2019.

3. Security

68 *healthy cut off the top*: Alec MacGillis, "Much of Stimulus Funding Going to Washington Area Contractors," *The Washington Post*, December 3, 2009.

68 *seven of the ten richest counties*: Carol Morello and Ted Mellnik, "Seven of Nation's 10 Most Affluent Counties Are in Washington Region," *The Washington Post*, September 20, 2012.

69 *Gucci flip-flops and Air Jordans*: "Private School Confidential," *Washingtonian*, October 2018.

70 *"He wanted to be rich"*: Robert G. Kaiser, *So Much Damn Money: The Triumph of Lobbying and the Corrosion of American Government* (New York: Vintage, 2010), 43.

71 *omitted the l-word*: Kaiser, 62.

71 *there was demand for lobbying*: Kaiser, 67.

71 *The pair's real breakthrough*: Kaiser, 71.

72 *"We perfected a technique"*: Author interview with Kenneth Schlossberg, April 20, 2020.

72 *"a new kind of business"*: Kaiser, *So Much Damn Money*, 98.

73 *"The danger had suddenly escalated"*: Jacob S. Hacker and Paul Pierson, *Winner-Take-All Politics: How Washington Made the Rich Richer—and Turned Its Back on the Middle Class* (New York: Simon & Schuster, 2011), 117.

73 *Big business heeded the call*: Hacker and Pierson, 116–119.

74 *quadrupled to $343 million*: Kaiser, *So Much Damn Money*, 115.

74 *each taking home about $500,000 annually*: Kaiser, 140.

74 *"Ever since I was a kid"*: Author interview with Schlossberg.

74 *"It was a lot of fun"*: Author interview with Schlossberg.

75 *"he was very, very quiet"*: Alec MacGillis, "The Billionaires' Loophole," *The New Yorker*, March 7, 2016.

75 *"didn't have charisma"*: David Montgomery, "David Rubenstein, Co-Founder of Carlyle Group and Washington Philanthropist," *The Washington Post*, May 14, 2012.

Notes

75   *"I tried to help my country"*: Montgomery.

75   *"I had a pretty good I.Q."*: Michael Lewis, "The Access Capitalists," *The New Republic*, October 18, 1993.

76   *"His vision was to combine capital"*: MacGillis, "The Billionaires' Loophole."

77   *"I just view myself as an American"*: Olivia Oran, " 'Obama Not Anti-Business': Carlyle's Rubenstein," Reuters, October 11, 2013.

77   *Thirty-three federal building complexes*: Dana Priest and William Arkin, "Top Secret America," *The Washington Post*, July 19, 2010.

79   *the government's spending on contractors*: Priest and Arkin.

79   *they mumbled, "With the military"*: Priest and Arkin.

79   *high-net-worth households*: Annie Gowen, "Region's Rising Wealth Brings New Luxury Brands and Wealth Managers," *The Washington Post*, December 17, 2012.

80   *The Cuvee No. 25*: Alina Dizik, "High-End Dining for the High-Chair Set," *The Wall Street Journal*, April 3, 2018.

80   *mansion modeled on Versailles*: Justin Jouvenal, "Planned Palace Upset Some Neighbors in Tony D.C. Suburb," *The Washington Post*, April 23, 2012.

81   *subscription rates as high as $8,000*: John Heltman, "Confessions of a Paywall Journalist," *Washington Monthly*, November/December 2015.

82   *"comfortable around people in power"*: Jeremy Peters, "Tests for a New White House Spokesman," *The New York Times*, March 16, 2011.

82   *one website had tallied*: Philip Bump and Jaime Fuller, "The Greatest Hits of Jay Carney," *The Washington Post*, May 30, 2014.

85   *In 1970, only 3 percent of members of Congress became lobbyists*: Daniel Markovits, *The Meritocracy Trap* (New York: Penguin, 2019), 57.

85   *industry had leaned liberal*: Margaret O'Mara, "How Silicon Valley Went from Conservative, to Anti-Establishment, to Liberal," Big Think, August 14, 2019, https://bigthink.com /videos/how-silicon-valley-went-from-conservative-to-anti-establishment-to-liberal.

86   *"It was a blast"*: Benjamin Wofford, "Inside Jeff Bezos's DC Life," *Washingtonian*, April 22, 2018.

86   *largest lobbying office of any tech firm*: Luke Mullins, "The Real Story of How Virginia Won Amazon's HQ2," *Washingtonian*, June 6, 2019.

87   *The company lobbied more federal agencies*: Charles Duhigg, "Is Amazon Unstoppable?," *The New Yorker*, October 10, 2019.

87   *"undertaking of pharaonic proportions"*: Wofford, "Inside Jeff Bezos's DC Life."

88   *"It's a very big house"*: Nick Wingfield and Nellie Bowles, "Jeff Bezos, Mr. Amazon, Steps Out," *The New York Times*, January 12, 2018.

89   *"I have a question, Tom"*: Alex Leary, "How Florida Lobbyist Brian Ballard Is Turning Close Ties to Trump into Big Business," *Tampa Bay Times*, June 9, 2017.

89   *buy himself a silver BMW*: Paul Anderson and Mark Silva, "Aide, 26, Key to Fresh Start for Governor," *The Miami Herald*, January 10, 1988.

89   *suspenders with toy soldiers*: Charles Fishman, "Apprentice to Power," *Florida Magazine*, August 5, 1990.

89   *"I reached back out to him"*: Leary, "How Florida Lobbyist Brian Ballard."

89   *"If you're good at this"*: Brent Kallestad, "Day in the Life of a Lobbyist," Associated Press, April 24, 2004.

90   *"an incredibly fine human being"*: Leary, "How Florida Lobbyist Brian Ballard."

90   *the firm had pulled in more than $13 million in fees*: Theodoric Meyer, "The Most Powerful Lobbyist in Trump's Washington," *Politico*, April 2, 2018.

4. Dignity

101   *named for Thomas Sparrow*: Mark Reutter, *Sparrows Point: Making Steel: The Rise and Ruin of American Industrial Might* (New York: Summit Books, 1988), 30.

101   *scouting trip to Cuba in 1882*: Reutter, 24–27.

102   *30,000 bricks per day*: Reutter, 30–32.

102   *the works were ready for their grand opening*: Reutter, 17–20.

103   *bottleneck-free production line*: Deborah Rudacille, *Roots of Steel: Boom and Bust in an American Mill Town* (New York: Pantheon Books, 2010), 33.

103   *300 tons of steel per day*: Reutter, *Sparrows Point*, 45.

103   *3,000 people were working*: C. B. Niederling, "Slow Death of a Company Town," *Baltimore*, August 1973.

103   *enough tonnage . . . to lay double tracks*: Reutter, *Sparrows Point*, 81.

103   *workers on a brutal schedule*: Reutter, 41–42.

103   *$1.10 per day in 1895*: Reutter, 45.

103   *only two holidays all year*: Reutter, 182.

103   *The settlement designed by Rufus Wood*: Rudacille, *Roots of Steel*, 25–29; Reutter, *Sparrows Point*, 59–63.

104   *His vast preference . . . was Black men*: Reutter, *Sparrows Point*, 63–64.

104   *They were too headstrong*: Rudacille, *Roots of Steel*, 45.

104   *"the race problem . . . has practically [been] solved"*: Reutter, *Sparrows Point*, 71.

104   *large complex with a Smokers Hall*: Elmer J. Hall, *A Mill on the Point: 125 Years of Steel Making at Sparrows Point, Maryland* (self-published, 2013). The book contains a wide array of maps and photos of the company town at various stages in its development, plus a glossary of buildings.

104   *the main goods store*: George L. Moore "The Old 'Company Store' at Sparrows Point," *The Baltimore Sun Magazine*, January 4, 1959.

105   *houseboats in the creek selling sweets*: Margaret Lunger, "Growing Up in the 'Little Kingdom' of Sparrows Point," *The Baltimore Sun*, December 1, 1968.

105   *first kindergarten south of the Mason-Dixon Line*: Mary Sue Fielding, "Sparrows Point Was Once a Community of Handsome Farms," *The Union News*, September 10, 1937.

105   *the state's first home-ec courses*: *Real Stories from Baltimore County History* (Hatboro, PA: Tradition Press, 1967), 209–210.

105   *many saloons that sprang up*: Rudacille, *Roots of Steel*, 34.

105   *the extent of the peril*: Rudacille, 36–37.

105   *"accident expense account"*: Reutter, *Sparrows Point*, 53.

105   *It was called Dolores*: Reutter, 188.

105   *"only work in a union-free atmosphere"*: Reutter, 46–49.

106   *by supplying the war machine*: Reutter, 115–123.

106   *Sparrows Point expanded rapidly*: Reutter, 127–131.

106   *Bethlehem seized on new markets*: Reutter, 155–158.

Notes

106 *the so-called tin floppers*: Reutter, 360–378.

107 *a whole new town sprang up to the north*: *Roots of Steel* includes many evocations of Dundalk, where Rudacille grew up.

107 *the average worker was making $2,000 per year*: Reutter, *Sparrows Point*, 142.

107 *"our own labor unions"*: Reutter, 149.

107 *"be a glutton for work"*: Charles Schwab, *Succeeding with What You Have* (Mechanicsburg, PA: Executive Books, 2005) 16–17.

107 *"Always More Production"*: Reutter, *Sparrows Point*, 146.

107–108 *Schwab earned $21 million*: Reutter, 135.

108 *This fortune made its way*: Robert Hessen, *Steel Titan: The Life of Charles M. Schwab* (Pittsburgh: University of Pittsburgh Press, 1990), 250.

108 *by the late 1920s, home to more than 4,000 people*: Michael Hill, "Sparrows Point Has Reunion Week," *The Baltimore Evening Sun*, May 24, 1973.

108 *"going over the creek"*: Louis S. Diggs, *From the Meadows to the Point: The Histories of the African American Community in Sparrows Point* (self-published, 2003), 214.

108 *The crash devastated steelmaking*: Reutter, *Sparrows Point*, 209–214.

108 *it swung heavily Democratic*: Reutter, 222.

108 *Secretary of Labor Frances Perkins*: Reutter, 233–236.

109 *John L. Lewis . . . made it his mission*: Reutter, 247–250.

109 *signing a contract with U.S. Steel*: Reutter, 253–254.

109 *Beth Steel . . . would prove a tougher target*: Reutter, 257–265.

110 *They held secret meetings*: Rudacille, *Roots of Steel*, 74.

110 *the plant's Black workers*: Rudacille, 82–83; Reutter, *Sparrows Point*, 292–294.

110 *the coming war that did it*: Rudacille, *Roots of Steel*, 82–84; Reutter, *Sparrows Point*, 296–299.

110 *the extraordinary benefits of this wartime expansion*: Reutter, 303–309.

110 *more than five hundred ships*: "Decline in Shipbuilding Hits Labor and Industry," *The Baltimore Evening Sun*, March 5, 1947.

110 *the war was giving new purpose*: Reutter, *Sparrows Point*, 311.

111 *an "artistry" to steelmaking*: John Strohmeyer, *Crisis in Bethlehem: Big Steel's Struggle to Survive* (Pittsburgh: University of Pittsburgh Press, 1994), 37.

111 *some of the astonishing metrics*: Reutter, *Sparrows Point*, 321.

111 *"he invited the rain of metal"*: *The Baltimore Sun*, September 10, 1944.

112 *honorary citizen of the city*: *Baltimore*, May 1941.

112 *Detroit's demand for flat-rolled steel*: Reutter, *Sparrows Point*, 329.

112 *the General Motors plant . . . on Broening Highway*: Reutter, 160.

112 *Bethlehem Steel company heaped capital into the peninsula*: "Bethlehem Steel Plans $30,000,000 Expansion of Sparrows Point Plant," *The Baltimore Sun*, January 27, 1950.

112 *as far as Chile and Venezuela*: Carrol E. Williams, "Local Steel Plant to Import Venezuelan Iron Ore in 1948," *The Baltimore Sun*, February 28, 1947.

112 *larger than that of . . . Germany*: Reutter, *Sparrows Point*, 382.

112 *When Arthur Vogel arrived*: "Life at the Point," *The Baltimore Sun Magazine*, September 5, 1982.

112 *boost in hourly wages*: Reutter, *Sparrows Point*, 329.

112 *first private-sector pension*: Reutter, 359.

112 *strike in 1959*: Strohmeyer, *Crisis in Bethlehem*, 64.

113 *something less tangible*: Reutter, *Sparrows Point*, 346.

113 *"the greatest show on earth"*: Reutter, 397.

113 *it presented a veritable skyline*: Hall's *A Mill on the Point* contains many photos from this era.

113 *uric whiff of its origins*: Reutter, *Sparrows Point*, 338.

113 *the Point's pistol range*: John Ahlers, "Plant Soot Called 'Gold Dust,' It Means People Are Working," *The Baltimore Evening Sun*, November 12, 1951.

113 *$2 million per year . . . in local taxes*: "Bethlehem Pays $2 Million in County Taxes," *The Baltimore Evening Sun*, January 31, 1956.

113 *high school commencements*: Rudacille, *Roots of Steel*, 102.

114 *The North Side had its own commercial cluster*: Diggs, *From the Meadows*, 228.

114 *shop on the south side*: Diggs, 214.

114 *the Black school on the Point*: Niederling, "Slow Death."

114 *Racist taunts sometimes arose*: Diggs, *From the Meadows*, 209.

114 *nostalgia for the togetherness*: Diggs, 211.

115 *"this ashen red pall"*: Mark Bowden, "Inside Sparrows Point," *Baltimore News-American*, May 1979.

115 *Locals called it "gold dust"*: Ahlers, "Plant Soot."

115 *the town was . . . shrinking to make room*: Spencer Davidson, "'Point' to Raze Homes of 187 Families," *The Baltimore Evening Sun*, November 21, 1951.

116 *Edmondson Village*: Antero Pietila, *Not in My Neighborhood: How Bigotry Shaped a Great American City* (Chicago: Ivan R. Dee, 2010) 159–165.

116 *Gwynns Falls Elementary*: Pietila, 122.

117 *The bathrooms were still segregated*: Rudacille, *Roots of Steel*, 19, 29.

117 *Work was segregated, too*: Rudacille, 43–44.

117 *Black employees now worked as crane operators*: Diggs, *From the Meadows*, 207.

117 *only one Black electrician*: Rudacille, *Roots of Steel*, 153.

117 *refusal to promote Charlie Parrish*: Reutter, *Sparrows Point*, 346–352.

117 *two workers marched into . . . the Congress of Racial Equality*: Rudacille, *Roots of Steel*, 148–151.

118 *The pressure worked, to a degree*: Rudacille, 152–154.

118 *The U.S. Department of Justice settled discrimination suits*: Rudacille, 155–157.

118 *still plenty of resistance*: Rudacille, 163.

118 *"There was no welfare"*: Diggs, *From the Meadows*, 217.

119 *"They finally got the message"*: Author interview with James Drayton, January 2019.

119 *There had been precious few innovations*: Reutter, *Sparrows Point*, 266–275.

119 *men with "good physique"*: Carol Loomis, "The Sinking of Bethlehem Steel," *Fortune*, April 5, 2004.

120 *The board would sit in silence*: Loomis.

120 *"hallways were lined with gold"*: Strohmeyer, *Crisis in Bethlehem*, 29–32.

120 *a tempting target for upstart rivals*: Strohmeyer, 101.

120 *U.S. imports of steel surged*: Rudacille, *Roots of Steel*, 186.

121 *the costs of the pollution*: Reutter, *Sparrows Point*, 400.

121 *forbidden even to dip her toe*: Rudacille, *Roots of Steel*, 128.

121 *The last vestiges had been cleared*: "Company Town Is Being Leveled," *The Baltimore Sun*, March 22, 1974.

Notes

124 *there were twelve fatal accidents*: Bowden, "Inside Sparrows Point."

124 *membership at Local 2610*: Rudacille, *Roots of Steel*, 196.

124 *The cutbacks had started for real*: Lorraine Branham, "1,020 Are Laid Off at Bethlehem," *The Baltimore Sun*, March 29, 1982.

124 *major wage concessions in 1983 and 1986*: Branham, "Workers Here Angry, Resigned," *The Baltimore Sun*, March 21, 1983.

124 *15 percent of the global total*: Reutter, *Sparrows Point*, 12.

124 *thirteen weeks off every five years*: "What Would You Do with 13 Weeks of Paid Vacation?," *Baltimore News-American*, March 27, 1966.

124 *"past practices" clause in their contract*: Strohmeyer, *Crisis in Bethlehem*, 65, 192, 232.

125 *bureaucratic bloat and empire-building*: Strohmeyer, 142.

125 *global tour in the corporate jet*: Reutter, *Sparrows Point*, 433.

125 *$1 million severance packages*: Rudacille, *Roots of Steel*, 192.

125 *vacation retreat in upstate New York*: Strohmeyer, *Crisis in Bethlehem*, 33.

125 *"It was a screwed-up culture*: Author interview with Len Shindel, January 15, 2019.

125 *Drug and alcohol use*: Rudacille, *Roots of Steel*, 200.

125 *workers were turning to harder stuff*: Author interviews with Len Shindel in January 2019 and with Baltimore resident Derrick Chase, who was raised in a Beth Steel family, in October 2018.

127 *"The ultimate shock was that no one would want that mill"*: Author interview with Shindel.

128 *an elegy for the Point*: Chris MacLarion, "Ode to Sparrows Point," reprinted in Hall's *A Mill on the Point*, 335. There is video footage online of MacLarion reading the elegy in the Mill Stories oral histories assembled by the University of Maryland, Baltimore County.

129 *"This was a city on the hill"*: Pamela Wood, "Sign of the Times: Sparrows Point Blast Furnace Demolished," *The Baltimore Sun*, January 28, 2015.

130 *The GM jobs on Broening Highway*: Stacy Hirsh, "Broening GM Plant to Close May 13," *The Baltimore Sun*, February 9, 2005.

130 *showering the company with incentives*: Natalie Sherman, "Amazon Hiring Outpaces Projects," *The Baltimore Sun*, July 30, 2015.

130 *The leaders rose one by one*: Audio of event recorded by author.

131 *the Advils that Amazon provided in vending machines*: Heather Long, "Amazon's $15 Minimum Wage Doesn't End Debate over Whether It's Creating Good Jobs," *The Washington Post*, October 5, 2018.

131 *making their own existence more robotic*: Noam Scheiber, "Inside an Amazon Warehouse, Robots' Ways Rub Off on Humans," *The New York Times*, July 3, 2019.

131 *two patents for a wristband*: Ceyland Yeginsu, "If Workers Slack Off, a Wristband Will Know. (And Amazon Has a Patent For It.)," *The New York Times*, February 1, 2018.

131 *on the verge of building a new rail transit line*: Alec MacGillis, "The Third Rail," *Places Journal*, March 2016.

132 *fired by an algorithm*: Colin Lecher, "How Amazon Automatically Tracks and Fires Warehouse Workers for 'Productivity,'" The Verge, April 25, 2019, https://theverge.com/2019/4/25/18516004/amazon-warehouse-fulfillment-centers-productivity-firing-terminations.

133 *somewhat higher-skilled jobs*: "What Amazon Does to Wages," *The Economist*, January 20, 2018.

133 *the CamperForce of retirees*: Jessica Bruder, *Nomadland: Surviving America in the Twenty-First Century* (New York: W. W. Norton, 2017).

134 *almost designed to isolate employees*: Emily Guendelsberger, *On the Clock: What Low-Wage Work Did to Me and How It Drives America Insane* (New York: Little, Brown, 2019), 52.

134 *the company deployed tried-and-true defenses*: See discussion of failed 2014 unionizing effort by Amazon equipment maintenance and repair technicians in Delaware in Duhigg, "Is Amazon Unstoppable?"

134 *remaking it as a hub for logistics*: Tom Maloney and Heater Perlberg, "Businesses Flock to Baltimore Wasteland in Epic Turnaround Tale," *Bloomberg Businessweek*, August 8, 2019.

134 *largest of the . . . cleanup sites*: Rona Kobell, "New Ownership All Fired Up to Raise Sparrows Point from the Ashes," *Bay Journal*, December 2014.

135 *"Because our customers count on us"*: The author entered into the application process for one of the jobs but did not accept the offer of employment.

138 *"There is little public opinion with regard to the perils of a steel mill"*: Reutter, *Sparrows Point*, 54.

5. Service

150 *desire to serve in Washington*: Charles S. Clark, "GSA Acquisition Officer Bound for White House Role," *Government Executive*, May 9, 2014.

151 *paper jams in a mail-inserting machine*: Jan Murphy, "Welfare Renewals Take a Wrong Turn," *Patriot News*, August 26, 2008.

152 *"Don't break the rules"*: Clark, "White House Procurement Chief Wants Acquisition SWAT Team," *Government Executive*, April 24, 2015.

152 *"I'm personally proud of this work"*: Anne Rung, "Transforming the Federal Marketplace, Two Years In," States News Service, September 30, 2016.

157 *the cooperative . . . didn't even bother to bid*: Stacy Mitchell and Olive LaVecchia, "Amazon's Next Frontier: Your City's Purchasing," Institute for Local Self-Reliance, July 10, 2018.

158 *"Are you looking for just the platform"*: Mitchell and LaVecchia.

158 *Amazon set about approaching school districts*: Mitchell and LaVecchia.

158 *"With this strategy . . . Amazon is following an approach"*: Mitchell and LeVecchia.

160 *The amendment also enabled government-wide use*: David Dayen, "The 'Amazon Amendment' Would Effectively Hand Government Purchasing Power Over to Amazon," *The Intercept*, November 2, 2017, https://theintercept.com/2017/11/02/amazon-amendment-online-marketplaces/.

160 *Rung had arranged a meeting in Seattle*: Stephanie Kirchgaessner, "Top Amazon Boss Privately Advised US Government on Web Portal Worth Billions to Tech Firm," *The Guardian*, December 26, 2018.

160 *the company's famous "flywheel" of success*: For an in-depth treatment of the flywheel concept, see Brian Dumaine's *Bezonomics: How Amazon Is Changing Our Lives and What the World's Best Companies Are Learning from It* (New York: Simon & Schuster, 2020).

161 *Sellers are blocked from building relationships*: Jason Del Rey, "An Amazon Revolt Could Be Brewing as the Tech Giant Exerts More Control over Brands," Vox,

November 29, 2018, https://vox.com/2018/11/29/18023132/amazon-brand-policy-changes -marketplace-control-one-vendor.

161   *more than 30 cents of every dollar spent*: Jay Greene, "Amazon Sellers Say Online Retail Giant Is Trying to Help Itself, Not Consumers," *The Washington Post*, October 1, 2019.

161   *It was making a 20 percent margin*: Dan Gallagher, "Why Amazon Needs Others to Keep Selling," *The Wall Street Journal*, April 11, 2019.

161   *the number of third-party vendors . . . jumped by two-thirds*: Karen Weise, "Prime Power: How Amazon Squeezes the Businesses Behind Its Store," *The New York Times*, December 19, 2019.

161   *Amazon's cut of third-party sales*: Shira Ovide, "How Amazon's Bottomless Appetite Became Corporate America's Nightmare," *Bloomberg Businessweek*, March 14, 2018.

162   *a quarter of all retail shopping now took place in independent stores*: James Kwak, "The End of Small Business," *The Washington Post*, July 9, 2020.

163   *emailed Collins and other city officials*: Correspondence obtained by a public information request from the City of El Paso in January 2019.

167   *Not anyone could attend*: The author attended the session as a registered guest, under his own name.

171   *600 million items for sale*: Franklin Foer, "Jeff Bezos's Master Plan," *The Atlantic*, November 2019.

171   *Amazon was allowing its third-party sellers . . . to sell countless counterfeit goods*: Justin Scheck, Jon Emont, and Alexandra Berzon, "Amazon Sells Clothes from Factories Other Retailers Blacklist," *The Wall Street Journal*, October 23, 2019.

6. Power

174   *among those to make a purchase was one Livinia Blackburn Johnson*: Antonio Olivo, "As Data Centers Bloom, a Century-Old African American Enclave Is Threatened," *The Washington Post*, July 2, 2017.

176   *we were creating 2.5 quintillion bytes of data every day*: Bernard Marr, "How Much Data Do We Create Every Day? The Mind-Blowing Stats Everyone Should Read," *Forbes*, May 21, 2018.

177   *a group of internet providers met*: Andrew Blum, *Tubes: A Journey to the Center of the Internet* (New York: Ecco, 2013), 59–60.

178   *"We don't comment on any project"*: Amy Joyce, "DataPort Plans Virginia 'Super-Hub'; Firm Close to Deal for 200-Acre Prince William Campus," *The Washington Post*, July 15, 2000.

178   *spared the cost . . . running their own servers*: Stephen Orban, *Ahead in the Cloud: Best Practices for Navigating the Future of Enterprise IT* (North Charleston, SC: CreateSpace, 2018), 3.

179   *while bringing in more than $17 billion in revenue*: Jordan Novet, "Amazon Cloud Revenue Jumps 45 Percent in Fourth Quarter," CNBC, February 1, 2018, https://cnbc.com /2018/02/01/aws-earnings-q4-2017.html.

179   *"one of the most feature-full and disruptive technology platforms"*: Orban, *Ahead in the Cloud*, xxv.

179   *"I see parallels in Amazon's behavior"*: Rana Foroohar, "Amazon's Pricing Tactic Is a Trap for Buyers and Sellers Alike," *Financial Times*, September 2, 2018.

179   *reminiscent of the railroad giants*: For more, see Ida Tarbell's classic *History of the Standard Oil Company* (New York: McClure, Phillips and Co., 1904).

180   *more than 9 million square feet*: Jonathan O'Connell, "Loudoun Rivals Silicon Valley for Data Centers," *The Washington Post*, October 28, 2013.

180   *projecting a 40 percent increase*: D. J. O'Brien, "Region Likely to See Continued Growth in Data Center Industry," *The Washington Post*, September 6, 2013.

180   *as much energy as 5,000 homes*: Lori Aratani, "Greenpeace Report: Amazon Is Wavering on Its Commitment to Renewable Energy," *The Washington Post*, February 14, 2019.

180   *not a single square foot of traditional office space*: O'Connell, "Data Centers Boom in Loudoun County, but Jobs Aren't Following," *The Washington Post*, January 17, 2014.

180   *more than $1 million per acre*: "The Godfather of Data Center Alley," *InterGlobix* 1, no. 1, 2019.

180   *"I'm not overstating things"*: "The Godfather of Data Center Alley."

181   *no zoning rules for data centers*: Olivo, "As Data Centers Bloom."

181   *two trips to Seattle*: Travel receipts produced by public information requests by Inside NoVa.com in April 2016 and obtained by the author in April 2019.

182   *completely detached its fate*: "From Akron to Zanesville: How Are Ohio's Small and Mid-Sized Cities Faring?," Greater Ohio Policy Center, June 2016.

182   *when Amazon chose Ohio*: Mark Williams, "Amazon's Central Ohio Data Centers Now Open," *The Columbus Dispatch*, October 18, 2016.

182   *"I love that they don't come"*: Orban, *Ahead in the Cloud*, 7.

183   *created out of the soybean fields*: Emily Steel, Steve Eder, Sapna Maheshwari, and Matthew Goldstein, "How Jeffrey Epstein Used the Billionaire Behind Victoria's Secret for Wealth and Women," *The New York Times*, July 25, 2019.

183   *Amazon laid down its terms*: All subsequent correspondence between the three towns and Amazon obtained by public information requests to the towns by the author in April 2019.

183   *sales tax exemption . . . worth $77 million*: Mya Frazier, "Amazon Isn't Paying Its Electric Bills. You Might Be," *Bloomberg Businessweek*, August 20, 2018.

184   *"the mirror of our identities"*: Blum, *Tubes*, 229.

184   *who was behind the 500,000-square-foot data center*: O'Connell, "Data Centers Boom."

185   *"The fight was not about a transmission line"*: Author interview with Elena Schlossberg, April 8, 2019.

186   *Dominion had enormous sway*: Jacob Geiger, "Dominion Wields Influence with Political Contributions, Charitable Donations," *Richmond Times-Dispatch*, February 14, 2015.

189   *monthly fee on all ratepayers*: Frazier, "Amazon Isn't Paying."

189   *Amazon filed a seventy-eight-page application*: Frazier.

190   *"Bezos . . . adamantly refuses to consider slowing"*: Duhigg, "Is Amazon Unstoppable?"

190   *A survey done in June and July of 2018*: Kaitlyn Tiffany, "In Amazon We Trust—but Why?," Vox, October 25, 2018, https://vox.com/the-goods/2018/10/25/18022956 /amazon-trust-survey-american-institutions-ranked-georgetown.

191   *its spending on TV ads would swell*: Suzanne Vranica, "Amazon Seizes TV's Biggest Stage, After Shunning Mass-Market Ads," *The Wall Street Journal*, January 30, 2019.

191   *"an act of corporate citizenship"*: Ross Douthat, "Meet Me in St. Louis, Bezos," *The New York Times*, September 16, 2017.

Notes

192 *"I'm starting to see a bifurcation"*: Nan Whaley remarks at the National Press Club, January 22, 2019.

192 *"Nowhere did Amazon say"*: Scott Shane, "Prime Mover: How Amazon Wove Itself into the Life of an American City," *The New York Times*, November 30, 2019.

193 *"Right a social wrong?"*: Author interview with Nick Hanauer, June 14, 2018.

196 *capital spending by Amazon, Microsoft, Google, and Facebook*: Dan Gallagher, "Hey, Big Spender: Tech Cash Will Keep Flowing," *The Wall Street Journal*, February 11, 2019.

196 *data-center scrap recycling*: Riahnnon Hoyle, "Cloud Computing Is Here. Cloud Recycling Is Next," *The Wall Street Journal*, July 29, 2019.

198 *the suitor had ordered contenders to keep negotiations confidential*: Julie Creswell, "Cities' Offers for Amazon Base Are Secrets Even to Many City Leaders," *The New York Times*, August 5, 2018.

198 *visits to inspect the sites*: Laura Stevens, Shibani Mahtani, and Shayndi Raice, "Rules of Engagement: How Cities Are Courting Amazon's New Headquarters," *The Wall Street Journal*, April 2, 2018.

198 *bidders grasped at any clues*: Karen Weise, "The Mystery of Amazon HQ2 Has Finalists Seeing Clues Everywhere," *The New York Times*, September 7, 2018.

7. Shelter

207 *The poorest households in the state*: Gene Balk, "Seattle Taxes Ranked Most Unfair in Washington—a State Among the Harshest on the Poor Nationwide," *The Seattle Times*, April 13, 2018.

209 *"an extreme idea of the right to make money"*: Anand Giridharadas, *Winners Take All: The Elite Charade of Changing the World* (New York: Knopf, 2018), 163.

209 *Among the signatories of the Giving Pledge was David Rubenstein*: This and the remainder of this section from MacGillis, "The Billionaires' Loophole," *The New Yorker*, March 7, 2016.

211 *The housing market . . . was "straight-up crazy"*: Mike Rosenberg, "Seattle's Median Home Price Hits Record: $700,000, Double 5 Years Ago," *The Seattle Times*, April 6, 2017.

211 *the $1 million threshold for a median home sale*: Mike Rosenberg, "No Escape for Priced-Out Seattleites: Home Prices Set Record for an Hour's Drive in Every Direction," *The Seattle Times*, June 6, 2017.

212 *third-largest homeless population*: Vernal Coleman, "King County Homeless Population Third-Largest in U.S.," *The Seattle Times*, December 7, 2017.

212 *The number of homeless kids*: Zachary DeWolf, "For Seattle's Homeless Students, a Lack of Housing Is Just the Beginning," *The Seattle Times*, May 25, 2018.

212 *more homeless people had died*: Coleman, "Deaths Among King County's Homeless Reach New High amid Growing Crisis," *The Seattle Times*, December 30, 2017.

213 *first income tax passed*: Daniel Beekman, "Seattle City Council Approves Income Tax on the Rich, but Quick Legal Challenge Likely," *The Seattle Times*, July 10, 2017.

213 *"It's not punitive"*: Author interview with Teresa Mosqueda, August 1, 2019.

215 *Mike McGinn . . . had not met Bezos once*: Author interview with Mike McGinn, August 2, 2019.

215 *urging its engineers to teach computer science classes*: Nick Wingfield, "Fostering Tech Talents in Schools," *The New York Times*, September 30, 2012.

215   *a tenth of a percent of his net worth*: Robert Frank, "At Last, Jeff Bezos Offers a Hint of His Philanthropic Plans," *The New York Times*, June 15, 2017.

216   *an "overriding corporate obsession"*: Franklin Foer, *World Without Mind* (New York: Penguin, 2017), 196.

216   *misleading business cards*: Brad Stone, *The Everything Store: Jeff Bezos and the Age of Amazon* (New York: Little, Brown, 2013), 290–291.

216   *close its only warehouse in Texas*: Karen Weise, Manny Fernandez, and John Eligon, "Amazon's Hard Bargain Extends Far Beyond New York," *The New York Times*, March 13, 2019.

216   *the company had even created a secret internal goal*: Shayndi Raice and Dana Mattioli, "Amazon Sought $1 Billion in Incentives on Top of Lures for HQ2," *The Wall Street Journal*, January 16, 2020.

216   *zero corporate income taxes*: Christopher Ingraham, "Amazon Paid No Federal Taxes on $11.2 Billion in Profits Last Year," *The Washington Post*, February 16, 2019.

217   *an effective tax rate of 3 percent*: Ingraham.

217   *It noted in its defense*: From Amazon's written response to questions submitted by the author, July 13, 2020.

218   *"I don't agree with them"*: Beekman, "Tech Giant's Seattle Campus a Backdrop for 'Tax Amazon' Rally," *The Seattle Times*, April 11, 2018.

220   *"We remain very apprehensive"*: Nick Wingfield, "Seattle Scales Back Tax in Face of Amazon's Revolt, but Tensions Linger," *The Seattle Times*, May 14, 2018.

220   *"Not that we needed their buyoff"*: Author interview with Mosqueda.

220   *"They said yes on Mother's Day"*: Author interview with Mosqueda.

221   *a $350,000 operation . . . requisite 17,632 petition signatures*: Beekman, "Amazon, Starbucks Pledge $25,000 Each to Campaign for Referendum on Seattle Head Tax," *The Seattle Times*, May 23, 2018.

221   *Recordings caught signature gatherers*: Alana Samuels, "How Amazon Helped Kill a Seattle Tax on Business," *The Atlantic*, June 13, 2018.

221   *"The city does not have a revenue problem"*: Wingfield, "Seattle Scales Back Tax."

222   *"That did not feel like Seattle"*: Vianna Davila, "Fury, Frustration Erupt over Seattle's Proposed Head Tax for Homelessness Services," *The Seattle Times*, May 4, 2018.

222   *"people are losing their minds"*: Author interview with Nick Hanauer, June 14, 2018.

223   *Michael Schutzler . . . sat in his office*: Author interview with Michael Schutzler, June 13, 2018.

227   *San Francisco, where 5,000 homeless lived on the streets*: "How to Cut Homelessness in the World's Priciest Cities," *The Economist*, December 18, 2019.

229   *Katie Wilson . . . composed a ten-page essay*: An edited version of this essay appeared in *The Cost of Free Shipping: Amazon in the Global Economy*, edited by Jake Alimahomed-Wilson and Ellen Reese (London: Pluto Press, 2020).

230   *"Seattle has a lot of folks"*: Author interview with Sara Rankin, July 31, 2019.

231   *ruling by the state court of appeals*: Beekman, "State Court of Appeals Rules Seattle's Wealth Tax Is Unconstitutional, but Gives Cities New Leeway," *The Seattle Times*, July 16, 2019.

233   *"It made the election . . . about Amazon"*: Beekman, "Egan Orion Concedes to Kshama Sawant in Seattle City Council Race, Cites Amazon Spending," *The Seattle Times*, November 12, 2019.

Notes

233 *"It looks like our movement"*: Beekman.

234 *demographers were predicting it would be below 10 percent*: Balk, "Historically Black Central District Could Be Less Than 10% Black in a Decade," *The Seattle Times*, May 26, 2015.

234 *Amazon's professional, salaried workforce*: Jay Greene, "Amazon Far More Diverse at Warehouses Than in Professional Ranks," *The Seattle Times*, August 14, 2015.

234 *more than one-quarter Black* and *not a single member of . . . "S-Team"*: Karen Weise, "Amazon Workers Urge Bezos to Match His Words on Race with Actions," *The New York Times*, June 24, 2020.

234 *ninth-lowest median income for Black households* and *rate of Black homeownership*: Gene Balk, "As Seattle Gets Richer, the City's Black Households Get Poorer," *The Seattle Times*, November 12, 2014.

235 *"In tight housing markets"*: Janna L. Matlack and Jacob L. Vigdor, "Do Rising Tides Lift All Prices? Income Inequality and Housing Affordability," National Bureau of Economic Research Working Paper 12331, June 2006, https://nber.org/papers/w12331.pdf.

235 *what two British researchers found in 2019*: Richard Florida, "The Benefits of High-Tech Job Growth Don't Trickle Down," *Bloomberg CityLab*, August 8, 2019.

235 *"Racial toleration is meaningless"*: Quintard Taylor, *The Forging of a Black Community: Seattle's Central District from 1870 Through the Civil Rights Era* (Seattle: University of Washington Press, 1994), 239.

237 *"Welcome to what we now call sacred ground"*: Ann Dornfield, "A Bold Plan to Keep Black Residents in Seattle's Central District," KUOW, July 14, 2017, https://kuow.org/stories/a-bold-plan-to-keep-black-residents-in-seattle-s-central-district.

237 *"We basically filled a void"*: Author interview with Wyking Garrett, August 26, 2019.

238 *"I don't go to Union and Twenty-Third anymore"*: Author interview with Ronica Hairston, August 3, 2019.

239 *"Music is my life"*: Author interview with James Edward Jones, August 3, 2019.

8. Isolation

244 *Bill Brooks had sold it in 1958*: John Case, "Sole Survivor," *Inc.*, June 1, 1994.

244 *John's son Mike had entered the shoe industry, too*: Case.

246 *double what Rocky's workers were making in Puerto Rico*: Rita Price, "It All Changes," *The Columbus Dispatch*, April 29, 2002.

246 *Brooks called a meeting*: Nick Claussen, "Boot Factory to Leave Nelsonville for Puerto Rico, Lay Off 67," *Athens News*, September 20, 2001.

247 *about 160 jobs total*: Claussen, "County Hit Hard by Recent Closings, Layoffs," *Athens News*, October 11, 2001.

247 *The last pair of boots*: Rita Price, "Rocky Clocks Out," *Columbus Dispatch*, April 28, 2002.

247 *were made elsewhere, mostly in China*: Nelson D. Schwartz and Sapna Maheshwari, "'Catastrophic,' 'Cataclysmic': Trump's Tariff Threat Has Retailers Sounding Alarm," *The New York Times*, June 16, 2019.

248 *Rural areas and towns with populations under 50,000*: Clara Hendrickson, Mark Muro, and William A. Galston, "Countering the Geography of Discontent: Strategies for Left-Behind Places," Brookings Institution, November 2018, https://brookings.edu/research/countering-the-geography-of-discontent-strategies-for-left-behind-places/.

248 *Max Grumbacher sent a letter . . . to his father*: For this and much of the following history of the Bon-Ton, see Nancy Elizabeth Cohen, *Doing a Good Business: 100 Years at the Bon-Ton* (Lyme, CT: Greenwich Publishing Group, 1998).

249 *a shopper once called Robert Lazarus*: Bob Greene, "When Retailing Was Very Personal," *The Wall Street Journal*, December 17, 2018.

249 *the average visit . . . lasted two hours*: Suzanne Kapner, "Bon-Ton Scion's Fix for Ailing Department Stores: Blow Up the Model," *The Wall Street Journal*, June 1, 2018.

253 *the book he read on Bobby Kennedy*: Thurston Clarke, *The Last Campaign: Robert F. Kennedy and 82 Days That Inspired America* (New York: Henry Holt, 2008).

255 *"People weren't coming downtown anymore"*: Author interview with Tim Grumbacher and Debbie Simon, May 1, 2019.

255 *"Dad started talking to me again"*: Author interview with Grumbacher and Simon.

257 *"Yes, it's tough to donate your resources"*: Cohen, *Doing a Good Business*, 88.

257 *"you used to have regional everything"*: Author interview with Nick Hanauer, June 14, 2018.

257 *Elder-Beerman had grown from its grand store*: "Elder-Beerman Agrees to Be Bought by Bon-Ton," *Toledo Blade*, September 17, 2003.

260 *large cities like San Francisco, Boston, and New York*: Hendrickson, Muro, and Galston, "Left-Behind Places."

260 *just twenty counties accounted for half*: William A. Galston, "Why Cities Boom While Towns Struggle," *The Wall Street Journal*, March 13, 2018.

260 *More than 44 percent of all digital-services jobs*: Jack Nicas and Karen Weise, "Chase for Talent Pushes Tech Giants Far Beyond West Coast," *The New York Times*, December 13, 2018.

260 *a mere 1 percent of the country's job and population growth*: Monica Potts, "In the Land of Self-Defeat," *The New York Times*, October 4, 2019.

260 *A report by McKinsey Global Institute*: "The Future of Work in America: People and Places, Today and Tomorrow," McKinsey Global Institute, July 11, 2019, https://mckinsey.com/featured-insights/future-of-work/the-future-of-work-in-america-people-and-places-today-and-tomorrow#.

261 *Trump won eighteen of the twenty poorest states in the country*: Jeffrey Goldberg interview with Tara Westover, "The Places Where the Recession Never Ended," *The Atlantic*, December 2019.

261 *Trump won 61 percent of rural voters*: Eduardo Porter, "Why Big Cities Thrive, and Smaller Ones Are Being Left Behind," *The New York Times*, October 10, 2017.

262 *"Maybe . . . they'll keep voting against their own interests"*: Frank Rich, "No Sympathy for the Hillbilly," *New York*, March 2017.

264 *fewer than 10 percent of Americans moved that year*: Sabrina Tavernise, "Frozen in Place: Americans Are Moving at the Lowest Rate on Record," *The New York Times*, November 20, 2019.

267 *The calls ran the gamut*: Mya Frazier, "Amazon Is Getting a Good Deal in Ohio. Maybe Too Good," *Bloomberg Businessweek*, October 26, 2017.

267 *Some were more serious*: From injury reports obtained by a public information request from the Occupational Safety and Health Administration (OSHA), August 2019.

267 *the forklift was being driven by someone who was legally blind*: From injury reports obtained by a public information request from OSHA, August 2019.

Notes

267   *The basic social compact*: Frazier, "Amazon Is Getting a Good Deal."

268   *Twinsburg added a . . . tax exemption*: Michelle Jarboe, "Amazon.com Project in Twinsburg Gets Approval for State Job-Creation Tax Credit," *Cleveland Plain Dealer*, May 23, 2016.

268   *mall vacancies would reach their highest level*: Esther Fung, "Shopping-Mall Vacancies Are Highest in Seven Years After Big-Box Closings," *The Wall Street Journal*, October 3, 2018.

268   *the market valuation of Amazon*: Scott Galloway, "Silicon Valley's Tax-Avoiding, Job-Killing, Soul-Sucking Machine," *Esquire*, February 8, 2018.

269   *more major malls died in Ohio*: Esther Fung, "The Internet Isn't Killing Shopping Malls—Other Malls Are," *The Wall Street Journal*, April 18, 2017.

269   *"It's not stores that are dying"*: Scott Galloway, *The Four: The Hidden DNA of Amazon, Apple, Facebook, and Google* (New York: Random House, 2017), 41.

270   *the astonishing rise in mortality*: Gina Kolata and Sabrina Tavernise, "It's Not Just Poor White People Driving a Decline in Life Expectancy," *The New York Times*, November 26, 2019.

270   *death rates for white people*: Betsy McKay, "Death Rates Rising for Young, Middle-Aged U.S. Adults," *The Wall Street Journal*, July 23, 2019.

270   *His friend from high school who had fallen into opioid addiction*: Alec MacGillis, "The Last Shot," *ProPublica*, June 27, 2017.

273   *a major annual survey of five thousand shoppers by UPS*: Laura Stevens, "Survey Shows Rapid Growth in Online Shopping," *The Wall Street Journal*, June 8, 2016.

273   *online sales would rise . . . more than thirtyfold*: Austan Goolsbee, "Never Mind the Internet. Here's What's Killing Malls," *The New York Times*, February 13, 2020.

273   *The Bon-Ton was hardly blind to this trend*: Author interview with Grumbacher and Simon.

274   *Some workers . . . would take a job at the Bon-Ton*: Author interview with Grumbacher and Simon.

275   *Nearly all the unions had . . . sided with Edwards*: Alec MacGillis, "Why the Perfect Red-State Democrat Lost," *The New York Times*, November 16, 2018.

278   *in January 2019, the Ohio Tax Credit Authority met*: Author attended this meeting.

278   *no other occupation had shrunk more*: Andrew Van Dam, "If That Was a Retail Apocalypse, Then Where Are the Refugees?," *The Washington Post*, November 22, 2019.

278   *about 76,000 per year*: Galloway, *The Four*, 50.

278   *In Ohio alone, it was up to 8,500 employees*: From Amazon's written response to questions submitted by the author, July 13, 2020.

278   *about half of all retail openings . . . were dollar stores and discount grocers*: Alec MacGillis, "The True Cost of Dollar Stores," *The New Yorker*, June 29, 2020.

279   *more than 500,000 loads on many days*: Paul Page, "Truck Orders Soaring on Growing Freight Demand," *The Wall Street Journal*, June 5, 2018.

279   *one of the most dangerous positions*: Heather Long, "America's Severe Trucker Shortage Could Undermine the Prosperous Economy," *The Washington Post*, June 28, 2018.

9. Delivery

283   *The April 2014 article in* The Sun: Natalie Sherman, "City Hopes Reclaimed Brick Will Pave Way to Jobs, Sustainability," *The Baltimore Sun*, April 24, 2014.

283 *cost . . . more per house than a regular demo*: Scott Calvert, "Brick by Brick, Baltimore's Blighted Houses Get a New Life," *The Wall Street Journal*, April 5, 2019.

284 *a sixty-nine-year-old man . . . had been crushed*: Tim Prudente, "When Vacant House Fell in West Baltimore, a Retiree Was Crushed in His Prized Cadillac," *The Baltimore Sun*, March 30, 2016.

285 *Rondell Street . . . shot to death*: Prudente, "Two Men, One Heart: Transplant Links Baltimore Homicide Victim to Western Maryland Retiree," *The Baltimore Sun*, December 28, 2018.

285 *Amazon's Ring doorbell cameras*: Kevin Rector, "'Virtual Neighborhood Watch': Baltimore Faith Group Building Surveillance Network with Help from Amazon Ring," *The Baltimore Sun*, August 21, 2019.

286 *Baltimore had put in its own bid*: Ian Duncan, "Baltimore Unveils Failed Bid to Lure Amazon Headquarters," *The Baltimore Sun*, February 14, 2018.

286 *median incomes had risen by nearly 10 percent*: Tara Bahrampour, "Household Incomes in the District Rise Dramatically in 2017," *The Washington Post*, September 13, 2018.

287 *in Arlington, Virginia, the rate was even higher*: Justin Fox, "Where the Educated Millennials Congregate," *Bloomberg Opinion*, May 22, 2019.

287 *a Hot Wheels collection worth $1.5 million*: *Washingtonian*, April 2019.

287 *condo units in former suburban office parks*: Katherine Shaver, "Looking for 'City' Living in the Suburbs? Some Are Finding It in Aging Office Parks," *The Washington Post*, August 5, 2017.

288 *"It's just become New York South"*: Author interview with Kenneth Schlossberg, April 20, 2020.

288 *three times that for Black households*: Andre Giambrone, "Census: In D.C., Black Median Income Is Now Less Than a Third of White Median Income," *Washington City Paper*, September 15, 2017.

288 *one of the worst levels of racial disparity*: Gillian B. White, "In D.C., White Families Are on Average 81 Times Richer Than Black Ones," *The Atlantic*, November 26, 2016.

288 *The unemployment rate was six times higher for Black residents*: Marissa J. Lang, "The District's Economy Is Booming, but Many Black Washingtonians Have Been Left Out, Study Finds," *The Washington Post*, February 11, 2020.

288 *a youth boxing club*: Alan Neuhauser, "This D.C. Corridor Has Flourished. A Boxing Gym for Its Youth Is Battling for Its Life," *The Washington Post*, January 28, 2019.

288 *tensions at Howard University*: Tara Bahrampour, "Students Say Dog Walkers on Howard Campus Are Desecrating Hallowed Ground," *The Washington Post*, April 19, 2019.

289 *20,000 Black residents had been displaced*: Katherine Shaver, "D.C. Has the Highest 'Intensity' of Gentrification of Any U.S. City, Study Says," *The Washington Post*, March 19, 2019.

289 *in fact delivering packages for Amazon*: Author interview with NaTasha Newman's family, April 6, 2020.

290 *Amazon could avoid liability*: Patricia Callahan, "The Deadly Race," *ProPublica*, September 5, 2019.

290 *"I'm not allowed to talk about it"*: Author interview with Newman's family.

291 *Israel Espana Argote*: Christina Tkacik, "Israel Espana, Killed When Tornado Strikes Baltimore Amazon Facility, Remembered as Loyal Friend and Father," *The Baltimore*

Sun, November 5, 2018; and Alexa Ashwell, "Tornado Victim Husband, Father of 3," WBFF, November 4, 2018, https://foxbaltimore.com/news/local/tornado-victim -husband-father-of-3.

292 *an employee filed a complaint with state regulators*: Records obtained by a public information request from the Maryland Occupational Safety and Health division in April 2019.

292 *he told her he felt "blessed"*: Author interview with Lorraine, September 2019.

293 *"I didn't know he was a contractor"*: Author interview with Lorraine.

293 *"Let's think he's not there"*: Ashwell, "Tornado Victim."

293 *"It still hasn't really sunk in that my brother is gone"*: Facebook post by Angel Lindsey, November 2018.

295 *the same proportion of their employer's stock as Sears workers*: Robert B. Reich, "When Bosses Shared Their Profits," *The New York Times*, June 25, 2020.

295 *"Aren't you excited?"*: Abha Bhattarai, "Amazon Is Doling Out Raises of as Little as 25 Cents an Hour in What Employees Call 'Damage Control,'" *The Washington Post*, September 24, 2018.

296 *among those deemed out of bounds*: The author participated in one tour with one of his sons on July 23, 2019.

296 *video-game contests*: Greg Bensinger, "'MissionRacer': How Amazon Turned the Tedium of Warehouse Work into a Game," *The Washington Post*, May 21, 2019.

296–97 *In Kentucky, an employee at an Amazon call center*: Benjamin Romano, "Fired Amazon Employee with Crohn's Disease Files Lawsuit over Lack of Bathroom Access," *The Seattle Times*, February 2, 2019.

297 *"Associates are allowed to use the toilet whenever needed"*: From Amazon's written response to questions submitted by the author, July 13, 2020.

297 *a group of Somali American workers*: Jessica Bruder, "Meet the Immigrants Who Took On Amazon," *Wired*, November 12, 2019.

297 *a study of twenty-three Amazon warehouses by the Center for Investigative Reporting*: Will Evans, "Behind the Smiles," Reveal, November 25, 2019, https://revealnews.org /article/behind-the-smiles/.

297 *another in-depth report*: "Packaging Pain: Workplace Injuries Inside Amazon's Empire," Amazon Packaging Pain, https://amazonpackagingpain.org/the-report.

297 *Amazon said in response that it was simply more responsible*: From Amazon's written response to questions submitted by the author, July 13, 2020.

298 *a heart attack in Joliet, Illinois*: Alicia Fabbre, "Amazon Employee Dies After Company Delays 9-1-1 Call," *The Chicago Tribune*, January 26, 2019.

298 *a heart attack . . . in Murfreesboro, Tennessee*: Lindsay Bramson, "Safety Changes Made at Amazon Facility After News4 I-Team Investigation," WSMV, December 27, 2018, https://wsmv.com/news/safety-changes-made-at-amazon-facility-after-news4-i-team -investigation/article_6b20ed28-0a2d-11e9-ac15-ffd1e20911d0.html.

298 *crushed to death . . . in Plainfield, Indiana*: Will Evans, "Indiana Manipulated Report on Amazon Worker's Death to Lure HQ2, Investigation Says," *The Indianapolis Star*, November 25, 2019.

299 *to prevent a building from going up next to them*: J. David Goodman, "How Much Is a View Worth in Manhattan? Try $11 Million," *The New York Times*, July 22, 2019.

300 *suing to block a bike lane*: James Barron, "The People of Central Park West Want Their Parking Spaces (Sorry, Cyclists)," *The New York Times*, August 18, 2019.

300   *e-commerce deliveries to households*: Matthew Haag and Winnie Hu, "1.5 Million Packages a Day: The Internet Brings Chaos to New York Streets," *The New York Times*, October 27, 2019.

300   *The number of tech jobs overall in the city*: Haag, "Silicon Valley's Newest Rival: The Banks of the Hudson," *The New York Times*, January 5, 2020.

301   *house cleaner . . . stuck in the home's elevator*: Ben Yakas, "Woman Trapped in Upper East Side Townhouse Elevator for Three Days Doesn't Plan to Sue Billionaire Boss," *Gothamist*, January 29, 2019.

301   *it began keeping a secret log*: Jimmy Vielkind and Katie Honan, "The Missing Piece of Amazon's New York Debacle: It Kept a Burn Book," *The Wall Street Journal*, August 28, 2019.

301   *"That type of bad behavior"*: Author interview with Teresa Mosqueda, August 1, 2019.

302   *"Amazon's HQ2 could be a launching pad"*: "Amazon's HQ2 Could Be a Launching Pad for a Bright Future for the D.C. Region," *The Washington Post*, November 13, 2018.

302   *emails showing the lengths to which Arlington officials had gone*: Joanne S. Lawton, "Partnership or Pandering?," *Washington Business Journal*, May 2, 2019.

303   *"We can be a resource"*: *Frontline*, season 2020, episode 12, "Amazon Empire: The Rise and Reign of Jeff Bezos," aired February 18, 2020, on PBS, https://pbs.org/wgbh/frontline/film/amazon-empire/.

302   *it had created a map for Amazon*: Luke Mullins, "The Real Story of How Virginia Won Amazon's HQ2," *Washingtonian*, June 16, 2019.

304   *The company later denied that any such suspensions had occurred*: From Amazon's written response to questions submitted by author, July 13, 2020.

305   *There were entire zip codes in Arlington and Alexandria*: Taylor Telford, Patricia Sullivan, Hannah Denham, and John D. Harden, "Amazon's HQ2 Prompts Housing Price Spikes in Northern Virginia, *Washington Post* Analysis Shows," *The Washington Post*, June 13, 2019.

305   *someone called her in five minutes begging*: Patricia Sullivan, "Area Residents, Not Amazon Newcomers, Are Fueling Northern Virginia Real Estate Frenzy, Agents Say," *The Washington Post*, August 26, 2019.

306   *Once the jobs arrived*: Steven Pearlstein, "Washington Won Its Piece of Amazon's HQ2. Now Comes the Hard Part," *The Washington Post*, November 12, 2018.

306   *"We want to be part of the solution"*: Robert McCartney and Patricia Sullivan, "Amazon Says It Will Avoid a Housing Crunch with HQ2 by Planning Better Than It Did in Seattle," *The Washington Post*, May 3, 2019.

314   *at least twenty-nine in Virginia*: Mya Frazier, "Amazon Is Getting a Good Deal in Ohio. Maybe Too Good," *Bloomberg Businessweek*, October 26, 2017.

315   *An environmental report had recently concluded*: Cassady Craighill, "Greenpeace Finds Amazon Breaking Commitment to Power Cloud with 100% Renewable Energy," Greenpeace, February 13, 2019, https://greenpeace.org/usa/news/greenpeace-finds-amazon-breaking-commitment-to-power-cloud-with-100-renewable-energy/.

315   *every $1 billion spent on data centers*: Mark P. Mills, "The 'New Energy Economy': An Exercise in Magical Thinking," Manhattan Institute, March 26, 2019, https://manhattan-institute.org/green-energy-revolution-near-impossible.

Notes

315 *"We will run out of energy on Earth"*: Kenneth Chang, "Jeff Bezos Unveils Blue Origin's Vision for Space, and a Moon Lander," *The New York Times*, May 9, 2019.

316 *a "green" option for purchasing*: Matt Day, "Amazon Nixed 'Green' Shipping Proposal to Avoid Alienating Shoppers," *Bloomberg News*, March 5, 2020.

319 *"have created a form of private government"*: Stacy Mitchell, "Amazon Is a Private Government. Congress Needs to Step Up," *The Atlantic*, August 10, 2020.

319 *a groundbreaking paper*: Lina M. Khan, "Amazon's Antitrust Paradox," *Yale Law Journal*, January 2017.

320 *"the characterization of Amazon as being a ruthless competitor"*: *Frontline*, "Amazon Empire."

321 *an average of 27 cents on each dollar*: Karen Weise, "Prime Power: How Amazon Squeezes the Businesses Behind Its Store," *The New York Times*, December 12, 2019.

323 *reporting . . . would directly contradict Sutton's testimony*: Dana Mattioli, "Amazon Scooped Up Data from Its Own Sellers to Launch Competing Products," *The Wall Street Journal*, April 23, 2020.

324 *the people who'd lost their Temple Courts homes*: Robert Samuels, "In District, Affordable Housing Plan Hasn't Delivered," *The Washington Post*, July 7, 2013.

Overtime: May Day

328 *discouraging people from spending more money*: Dana Mattioli, "Amazon Retools with Unusual Goal: Get Shoppers to Buy Less Amid Coronavirus Pandemic," *The Wall Street Journal*, April 16, 2020.

328 *algorithms were . . . finding new ways to drive product makers*: Renee Dudley, "The Amazon Lockdown: How an Unforgiving Algorithm Drives Suppliers to Favor the E-Commerce Giant Over Other Retailers," *ProPublica*, April 26, 2020.

329 *25,000 retail stores were expected to go out of business*: Kim Bhasin, "As Many as 25,000 U.S. Stores May Close in 2020, Mostly in Malls," *Bloomberg*, June 9, 2020.

329 *sitting on a combined $557 billion in cash*: Mike Isaac, "The Economy Is Reeling. The Tech Giants Spy Opportunity," *The New York Times*, June 13, 2020.

329 *more than NASA's entire budget*: Christopher Mims, "Not Even a Pandemic Can Slow Down the Biggest Tech Giants," *The Wall Street Journal*, May 23, 2020.

330 *"the extreme divergence in the health of different types of companies"*: Austan Goolsbee, "Big Companies Are Starting to Swallow the World," *The New York Times*, September 30, 2020.

330 *"Covid-19 . . . has injected Amazon with a growth hormone"*: Daisuke Wakabayashi, Karen Weise, Jack Nicas, and Mike Isaac, "Lean Times, but Fat City for the Big 4 of High Tech," *The New York Times*, July 31, 2020.

330 *the company has . . . added more than 425,000 employees worldwide*: Karen Weise, "Pushed by Pandemic, Amazon Goes on a Hiring Spree Without Equal," *The New York Times*, November 27, 2020.

332 *places such as St. Louis and Detroit*: Jennifer Steinhauer and Pete Wells, "As Restaurants Remain Shuttered, American Cities Fear the Future," *The New York Times*, May 7, 2020.

332 *people who earned more than $28 per hour*: Eric Morath, Theo Francis, and Justin Baer, "Covid Economy Carves Deep Divide Between Haves and Have-Nots," *The Wall Street Journal*, October 6, 2020.

Acknowledgments

My original notion for this book traces back more than a decade, but it was my conversations in 2017 and 2018 with my agent, Lauren Sharp, and my editor, Alex Star, that helped me decide on its focus and structure. Without their encouragement and judgment, the book might never have taken shape. Also providing a crucial early nudge was Lynette Clemetson, whose invitation to give a lecture at the Knight-Wallace Fellowships at the University of Michigan in 2017 prompted me to start giving form to the arguments at play here.

I could not have researched a book in so many places around the country without the assistance of many people along the way. In Seattle, I benefited from the hospitality of Gene and Rainee Johnson; from the introductions to community members in the Central District provided by Kameko Thomas, Felix Ngoussou, and Tia Young; and from the insights of Margaret O'Mara, Mike Rosenberg, Ethan Goodman, Laura Loe, Nick Licata, Cary Moon, and Mike McGinn. In Dayton, Ohio, my explorations were aided by my fellow collaborators on a 2018 PBS *Frontline* documentary set in that city: Nancy Guerin, Van Royko, Shimon Dotan, and Frank Koughan. In Baltimore, I relied on Sparrows Point context and introductions from

Acknowledgments

J. M. Giordano, Bill Barry, Derrick Chase, Len Shindel, and Mark Reutter; on the helpful staff of the Enoch Pratt Free Library; and on reporting by Valerie Hsu, who covered an event while I was traveling out of state for the book. In Washington, D.C., I received valuable guidance from Mark Muro, Clara Hendrickson, Greg LeRoy, Matt Stoller, Ben Zipperer, and Marshall Steinbaum.

Along the way, I benefited from the support of the McCoy Family Center for Ethics in Society at Stanford University, which held a workshop critique organized by Joan Berry and attended by Rob Reich, Alison McQueen, Leif Wenar, Michelle Wilde Anderson, Sarah Frisch, Barbara Kiviat, Michael Kahan, Marietje Schaake, Aaron Foley, Garance Burke, Collin Anthony, and Diana Aguilera. Also offering reviews of drafts were Franklin Foer, Mark Vanhoenacker, Stacy Mitchell, Nathan Pippenger, Adam Plunkett, Simon van Zuylen-Wood, Mya Frazier, Perry Bacon, Jr., Avi Zenilman, B. J. Bethel, Seth Sawyers, and, with an especially close read, Rachel Morris.

In addition to the guiding hand of my editor, Alex Star, the book benefited in the latter stages from conscientious fact-checking by Hilary McClellen, copyediting by Susan VanHecke, and production editorial assistance by Ian Van Wye and Carrie Hsieh. In recent years, I received deft editing on several articles that served as partial foundations for the book from, among others, Larry Roberts, Nick Varchaver, Charles Homans, Rachel Dry, Willing Davidson, and Ann Hulbert.

I am grateful to Stephen Engelberg and Robin Fields at *ProPublica*, who provided me with the encouragement and time to work on the book. I am grateful to my mother, Ingrid MacGillis, and sister, Lucy MacGillis, for helping instill the attachment to place that motivated this book from the start. I am grateful to the home crew in Baltimore who were my understanding companions throughout this undertaking: my sons, Harry and John, and my wife, Rachel Brash. Finally, I would not have been able to take on this book without the lifelong example provided by my father, the journalist Donald MacGillis, who provided a final read of the manuscript shortly before his untimely death.

Index

Index

Index

Index

A Note About the Author

Alec MacGillis is a senior reporter for *ProPublica* and the recipient of a George Polk Award, the Toner Prize for Excellence in Political Reporting, and other honors. He worked previously at *The Washington Post*, *The Baltimore Sun*, and *The New Republic*, and his journalism has appeared in *The New York Times Magazine*, *The New Yorker*, *The Atlantic*, and other publications. His *ProPublica* reporting on Dayton, Ohio, was the basis of a PBS *Frontline* documentary about the city. He is the author of *The Cynic*, a 2014 biography of Mitch McConnell. He is a native of Pittsfield, Massachusetts, and lives in Baltimore.